KB132479

고등학교 영어

평가문제집

최인철 | 박리리 | 장민경 | 채지선 | 김근영 | 최수하
김주혜 | 손지해 | 전예지 | Ksan Rubadeau

금성출판사

HIGH SCHOOL ENGLISH

CONTENTS

이 책의 구성과 특징

Key Concept

1st Step

출제 가능한 교과서 자료의 완벽한 정리와 언어 기능별 집중대비 문제를 통해 기초적인 이해를 다집니다.

2nd Step

대화 자료와 읽기 자료를 중심으로 반드시 파악해 두어야 할 핵심 평가 포인트를 파악하기 위한 문제를 통해 기초 적응력을 다집니다.

3rd Step

수준별 문제와 서술형 문제를 포함한 다양한 내신 유형의 문제를 통해 각 단원의 평가에 대비한 실전 적응력을 기릅니다.

1st Step 교과서 핵심정리

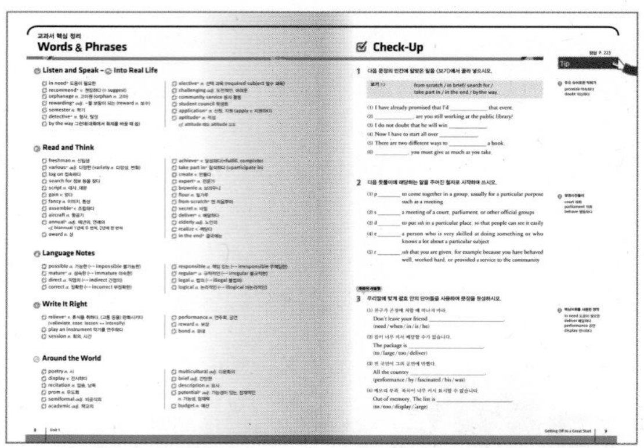

Words & Phrases

각 차시별 주요숙어와 어휘를 확인하고 핵심유형별로 문제를 풀어보며 익힙니다.

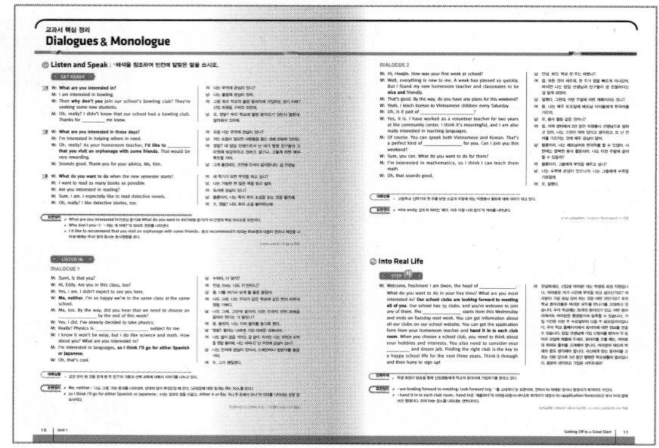

Dialogues & Monologue

주요 녹음 대본의 해석과 상황 및 핵심표현을 정리합니다.

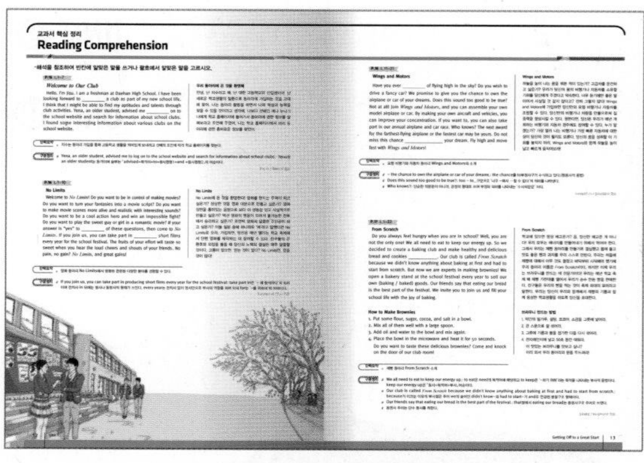

Reading Comprehension

본문의 해석과 요약, 구문을 정리하고 핵심구문을 문제를 통해 익힙니다.

2nd Step 언어기능별 집중대비

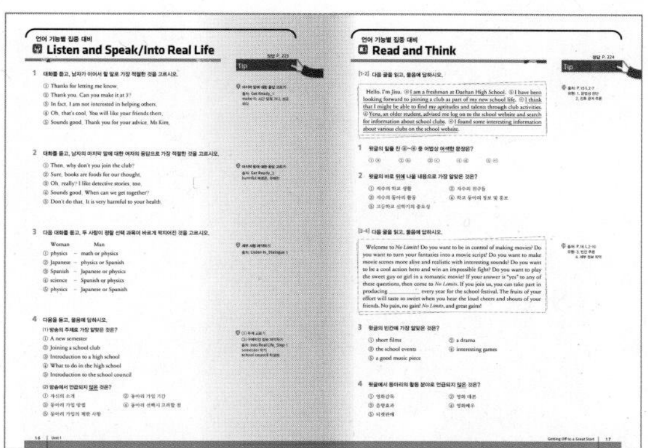

Listen and Speak/Into Real Life

교과서의 대본을 수능형 문제로 익힙니다.

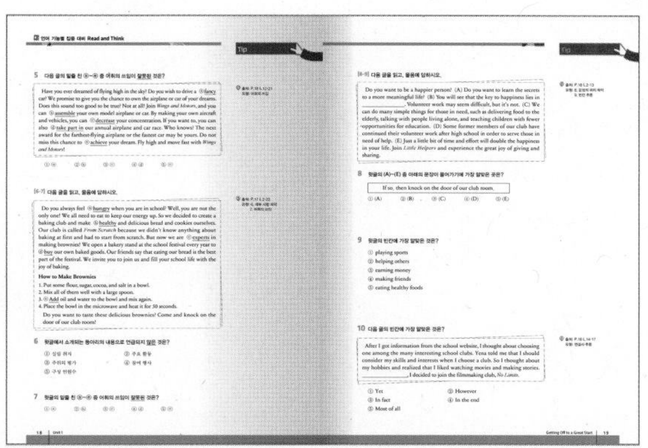

Read and Think

본문 읽기 자료를 수능형 문제로 익힙니다.

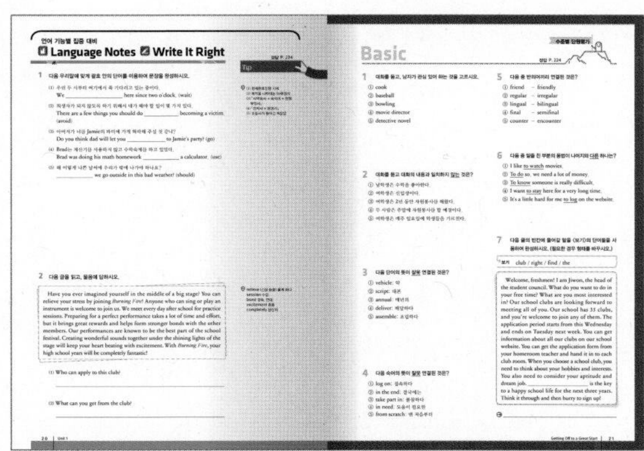

Language Notes/Write It Right

어휘, 표현, 문법과 쓰기 활동자료를 주관식 서술형 문제로 익힙니다.

3rd Step 단원평가

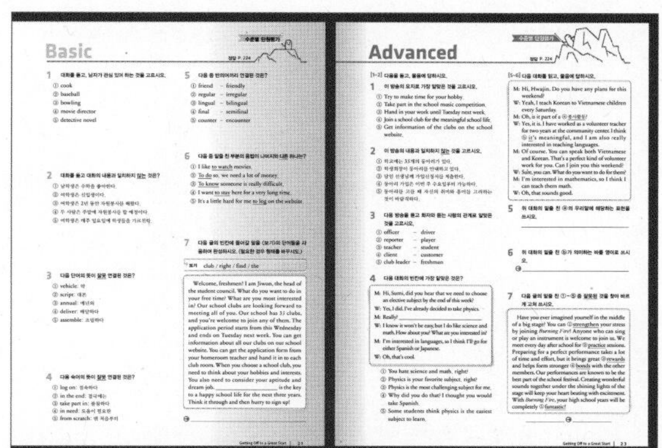

Basic/Advanced

지식과 이해문제를 위주로 한 기초수준의 문제와 적용, 추론적 이해, 서술형을 포함한 상위수준 문제를 차례로 풀어봅니다.

중간 · 기말고사 대비문제

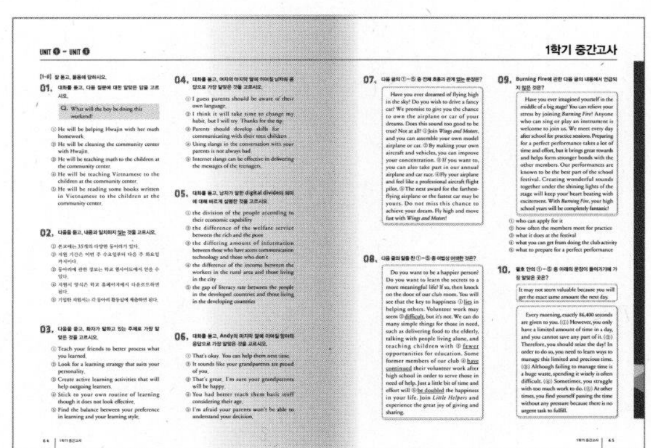

1 · 2학기 중간 · 기말고사

주관식 서술형, 논술형이 포함된 내신 시험 예상 문제를 풀어 보며 최종 실전 대비를 합니다.

UNIT

1

Getting Off to a Great Start

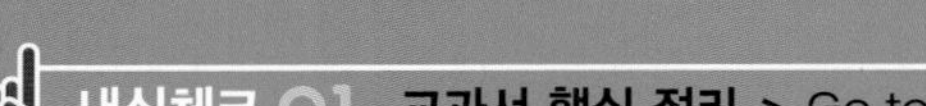

내신체크 01 교과서 핵심 정리 > Go to p. 8

- **어휘 총정리**
- **대본 정리**
  신학기 생활에 관한 대화와 학생회장의 학교 동아리 가입에 대한 방송
- **본문 정리**
  지수가 학교 동아리 가입을 위해 학교 홈페이지에서 확인하는 동아리 정보

내신체크 02 언어 기능별 집중 대비 > Go to p. 16

- **듣기와 말하기** 대본별 필수 출제 유형
- **읽기** 각 단락별 필수 점검 유형
- **언어 재료 및 쓰기** 어휘 및 구문, 주관식 서술형 대비 문제

내신체크 03 수준별 단원 평가 > Go to p. 21

- **Basic** 지식, 사실적 이해 대비 문제
- **Advanced** 추론적 이해 및 감상, 주관식 서술형 대비 문제

교과서 핵심 정리

Words & Phrases

Listen and Speak ~ Into Real Life

- ☐ in need* 도움이 필요한
- ☐ recommend* *v.* 권장하다 (= suggest)
- ☐ orphanage *n.* 고아원 (orphan *n.* 고아)
- ☐ rewarding* *adj.* ~할 보람이 되는 (reward *n.* 보수)
- ☐ semester *n.* 학기
- ☐ detective* *n.* 형사, 탐정
- ☐ by the way 그런데(대화에서 화제를 바꿀 때 씀)
- ☐ elective* *n.* 선택 과목 (required subject 필수 과목)
- ☐ challenging *adj.* 도전적인, 어려운
- ☐ community service 봉사 활동
- ☐ student council 학생회
- ☐ application* *n.* 신청, 지원 (apply *v.* 지원하다)
- ☐ aptitude* *n.* 적성
  cf. attitude 태도 altitude 고도

Read and Think

- ☐ freshman *n.* 신입생
- ☐ various* *adj.* 다양한 (variety *n.* 다양성, 변화)
- ☐ log on 접속하다
- ☐ search for 정보 등을 찾다
- ☐ script *n.* 대사 ,대본
- ☐ gain *v.* 얻다
- ☐ fancy *n.* 이미지, 환상
- ☐ assemble**v.* 조립하다
- ☐ aircraft *n.* 항공기
- ☐ annual* *adj.* 매년의, 연례의
  cf. biannual 1년에 두 번씩, 2년에 한 번씩
- ☐ award *n.* 상
- ☐ achieve* *v.* 달성하다(=fulfill, complete)
- ☐ take part in* 참석하다 (=participate in)
- ☐ create *v.* 만들다
- ☐ expert* *n.* 전문가
- ☐ brownie *n.* 브라우니
- ☐ flour *n.* 밀가루
- ☐ from scratch* 맨 처음부터
- ☐ secret *n.* 비밀
- ☐ deliver* *v.* 배달하다
- ☐ elderly *adj.* 노인의
- ☐ realize *v.* 깨닫다
- ☐ in the end* 결국에는

Language Notes

- ☐ possible *a.* 가능한 (↔ impossible 불가능한)
- ☐ mature* *a.* 성숙한 (↔ immature 미숙한)
- ☐ direct *a.* 직업의 (↔ indirect 간접의)
- ☐ correct *a.* 정확한 (↔ incorrect 부정확한)
- ☐ responsible *a.* 책임 있는 (↔ irresponsible 무책임한)
- ☐ regular* *a.* 규칙적인 (↔ irregular 불규칙한)
- ☐ legal *a.* 법의 (↔ illegal 불법의)
- ☐ logical *a.* 논리적인 (↔ illogical 비논리적인)

Write It Right

- ☐ relieve* *v.* 휴식을 취하다, (고통 등을) 완화시키다
  (=alleviate, ease, lessen ↔ intensify)
- ☐ play an instrument 악기를 연주하다
- ☐ session *n.* 회의, 시간
- ☐ performance *n.* 연주회, 공연
- ☐ reward *n.* 보상
- ☐ bond *n.* 유대

Around the World

- ☐ poetry *n.* 시
- ☐ display *v.* 전시하다
- ☐ recitation *n.* 암송, 낭독
- ☐ prom *n.* 무도회
- ☐ semiformal *adj.* 비공식의
- ☐ academic *adj.* 학교의
- ☐ multicultural *adj.* 다문화의
- ☐ brief *adj.* 간단한
- ☐ description *n.* 묘사
- ☐ potential* *adj.* 가능성이 있는, 잠재적인
  n. 가능성, 잠재력
- ☐ budget *n.* 예산

Check-Up

정답 P. 223

1 다음 문장의 빈칸에 알맞은 말을 〈보기〉에서 골라 넣으시오.

보기 >> from scratch / in brief/ search for / take part in / in the end / by the way

(1) I have already promised that I'd ____________ that event.
(2) ____________, are you still working at the public library?
(3) I do not doubt that he will win ____________.
(4) Now I have to start all over ____________.
(5) There are two different ways to ____________ a book.
(6) ____________, you must give as much as you take.

2 다음 뜻풀이에 해당하는 말을 주어진 철자로 시작하여 쓰시오.

(1) p________ to come together in a group, usually for a particular purpose such as a meeting
(2) s ________ a meeting of a court, parliament, or other official groups
(3) d________ to put *sth* in a particular place, so that people can see it easily
(4) e________ a person who is very skilled at doing something or who knows a lot about a particular subject
(5) r ________ *sth* that you are given, for example because you have behaved well, worked hard, or provided a service to the community

주관식 서술형

3 우리말에 맞게 괄호 안의 단어들을 사용하여 문장을 완성하시오.

(1) 친구가 곤경에 처할 때 떠나지 마라.
Don't leave your friend ______________________.
(need / when / in / is / he)

(2) 짐이 너무 커서 배달할 수가 없습니다.
The package is ______________________.
(to / large / too / deliver)

(3) 전 국민이 그의 공연에 반했다.
All the country ______________________.
(performance / by / fascinated / his / was)

(4) 메모리 부족. 목록이 너무 커서 표시할 수 없습니다.
Out of memory. The list is ______________________.
(to / too / display / large)

Tip

❶ 주요 숙어표현 익히기
promise 약속하다
doubt 의심하다

❷ 영영사전풀이
court 의회
parliament 의회
behave 행동하다

❸ 핵심어휘를 사용한 영작
in need 도움이 필요한
deliver 배달하다
performance 공연
display 전시하다

교과서 핵심 정리

Dialogues & Monologue

Listen and Speak | *해석을 참조하여 빈칸에 알맞은 말을 쓰시오.

GET READY

1 W: **What are you interested in?**
M: I am interested in bowling.
W: Then **why don't you** join our school's bowling club? They're seeking some new students.
M: Oh, really? I didn't know that our school had a bowling club. Thanks for __________ me know.

여: 너는 무엇에 관심이 있니?
남: 나는 볼링에 관심이 있어.
여: 그럼 우리 학교의 볼링 동아리에 가입하는 것이 어때? 신입 회원을 구하고 있던데.
남: 오, 정말? 우리 학교에 볼링 동아리가 있는지 몰랐네. 알려줘서 고마워.

2 W: **What are you interested in these days?**
M: I'm interested in helping others in need.
W: Oh, really? As your homeroom teacher, **I'd like to __________ that you visit an orphanage with some friends.** That would be very rewarding.
M: Sounds good. Thank you for your advice, Ms. Kim.

여: 요즘 너는 무엇에 관심이 있니?
남: 저는 도움이 필요한 사람들을 돕는 것에 관심이 있어요.
여: 정말? 네 담임 선생으로서 난 네가 몇몇 친구들과 고아원에 방문하라고 권하고 싶구나. 그렇게 하면 매우 뿌듯할 거야.
남: 그게 좋겠네요. 조언해 주셔서 감사합니다. 김 선생님.

3 W: **What do you want to do** when the new semester starts?
M: I want to read as many books as possible.
W: Are you interested in reading?
M: Sure, I am. I especially like to read detective novels.
W: Oh, really? I like detective stories, too.

여: 새 학기가 되면 무엇을 하고 싶니?
남: 나는 가능한 한 많은 책을 읽고 싶어.
여: 독서에 관심이 있니?
남: 물론이지. 나는 특히 추리 소설을 읽는 것을 좋아해.
여: 오, 정말? 나도 추리 소설 좋아하는데.

표현정리
- What are you interested in?(관심 묻기)와 What do you want to do?(바람 묻기)가 이 단원의 핵심 의사소통 표현이다.
- Why don't you~?: '~하는 게 어때?'의 의미로 권유를 나타낸다.
- I'd like to recommend that you visit an orphanage with some friends.: 동사 recommend가 이끄는 that절의 내용이 권유나 제안을 나타낼 때에는 that 절의 동사는 동사원형을 쓴다.

정답 letting / recommend

LISTEN IN

DIALOGUE 1

M: Sumi, is that you?
W: Hi, Eddy. Are you in this class, too?
M: Yes, I am. I didn't expect to see you here.
W: **Me, neither.** I'm so happy we're in the same class at the same school.
M: Me, too. By the way, did you hear that we need to choose an ______________ by the end of this week?
W: Yes, I did. I've already decided to take physics.
M: Really? Physics is ____________________ subject for me.
W: I know it won't be easy, but I do like science and math. How about you? What are you interested in?
M: I'm interested in languages, **so I think I'll go for either Spanish or Japanese.**
W: Oh, that's cool.

남: 수미야, 너 맞지?
여: 안녕, Eddy. 너도 이 반이니?
남: 응. 너를 여기서 보게 될 줄은 몰랐어.
여: 나도 그래. 나는 우리가 같은 학교에 같은 반이 되어서 정말 기쁘다.
남: 나도 그래. 그런데 말이야, 이번 주까지 선택 과목을 골라야 한다는 거 들었니?
여: 응, 들었어. 나는 이미 물리를 듣기로 했어.
남: 정말? 물리는 나에게 가장 어려운 과목이야.
여: 나도 쉽지 않을 거라는 걸 알아, 하지만 나는 과학과 수학을 정말 좋아해. 너는 어떠니? 넌 무엇에 관심이 있니?
남: 나는 언어에 관심이 있어서, 스페인어나 일본어를 들을 거야.
여: 오, 그거 괜찮겠다.

대화상황
- 같은 반이 된 것을 알게 된 두 친구의 기쁨과 선택 과목에 대해서 이야기를 나누고 있다.

표현정리
- Me, neither.: '나도 그래.'라는 동의를 나타내며, 상대의 말이 부정문일 때 쓴다. (긍정문에 대한 동의는 Me, too.를 쓴다.)
- so I think I'll go for either Spanish or Japanese.: so는 결과의 절을 이끌고, either A or B는 'A나 B 중에서 하나'의 의미를 나타내는 상관 접속사이다.

정답 elective subject / the most challenging

DIALOGUE 2

M: Hi, Hwajin. How was your first week at school?

W: Well, everything is new to me. A week has passed so quickly. But I found my new homeroom teacher and classmates to be **nice and** friendly.

M: That's good. By the way, do you have any plans for this weekend?

W: Yeah, I teach Korean to Vietnamese children every Saturday.

M: Oh, is it part of ____________________?

W: Yes, it is. I have worked as a volunteer teacher for two years at the community center. I think it's meaningful, and I am also really interested in teaching languages.

M: Of course. You can speak both Vietnamese and Korean. That's a perfect kind of ______________ for you. Can I join you this weekend?

W: Sure, you can. What do you want to do for them?

M: I'm interested in mathematics, so I think I can teach them math.

W: Oh, that sounds good.

남: 안녕, 화진. 학교 첫 주는 어땠니?

여: 음, 모든 것이 새로워. 한 주가 정말 빠르게 지나갔어. 하지만 나는 담임 선생님과 친구들이 참 친절하다는 걸 알게 되었어.

남: 잘됐다. 그런데, 이번 주말에 어떤 계획이라도 있니?

여: 응, 나는 매주 토요일에 베트남 아이들에게 한국어를 가르쳐.

남: 오, 봉사 활동 같은 것이니?

여: 응. 지역 센터에서 2년 동안 자원봉사 선생님으로 일하고 있어. 나는 그것이 의미 있다고 생각하고, 또 난 언어를 가르치는 것에 매우 관심이 많아.

남: 물론이지. 너는 베트남어와 한국어를 할 수 있잖아. 너한테는 완벽한 봉사 활동이야. 나도 이번 주말에 같이 할 수 있을까?

여: 물론이지. 그들에게 무엇을 해주고 싶니?

남: 나는 수학에 관심이 있으니까, 나는 그들에게 수학을 가르칠래.

여: 오, 잘됐다.

대화상황 • 고등학교 신학기의 첫 주를 보낸 소감과 주말에 하는 자원봉사 활동에 대해 이야기 하고 있다.

표현정리 • nice and는 강조의 의미인 '매우, 아주 더할 나위 없이'의 의미를 나타낸다.

정답 a community service / volunteer work

Into Real Life

W: Welcome, freshmen! I am Jiwon, the head of ______________. What do you want to do in your free time? What are you most interested in? **Our school clubs are looking forward to meeting all of you**. Our school has 35 clubs, and you're welcome to join any of them. The ______________ starts from this Wednesday and ends on Tuesday next week. You can get information about all our clubs on our school website. You can get the application form from your homeroom teacher and **hand it in to each club room**. When you choose a school club, you need to think about your hobbies and interests. You also need to consider your ________ and dream job. Finding the right club is the key to a happy school life for the next three years. Think it through and then hurry to sign up!

여: 안녕하세요, 신입생 여러분! 저는 학생회 회장 지원입니다. 여러분은 여가 시간에 무엇을 하고 싶으신가요? 여러분이 가장 관심 있어 하는 것은 어떤 것인가요? 우리 학교 동아리들은 여러분 모두를 만나기를 고대하고 있습니다. 우리 학교에는 35개의 동아리가 있고, 어떤 동아리에서도 여러분은 환영받으며 등록할 수 있습니다. 가입 기간은 이번 주 수요일부터 다음 주 화요일까지입니다. 우리 학교 홈페이지에서 동아리에 대한 정보를 얻을 수 있습니다. 담임 선생님께 가입 신청서를 받아서 각 동아리 교실에 제출해 주세요. 동아리를 고를 때는, 여러분의 취미와 흥미를 고려해야 합니다. 여러분의 태도와 미래의 꿈도 생각해야 합니다. 자신에게 맞는 동아리를 고르는 것은 앞으로 3년 동안 행복한 학교생활의 열쇠입니다. 충분히 생각하고 가입은 서두르세요!

담화주제 • 학생 회장이 방송을 통해 신입생들에게 학교의 동아리에 가입하기를 권하고 있다.

표현정리
- ~are looking forward to meeting: look forward to는 '~를 고대하다'는 표현이며, 전치사 to 뒤에는 명사나 동명사가 목적어로 쓰인다.
- ~hand it in to each club room.: hand in은 '제출하다'의 이어동사(동사+부사)로 목적어가 대명사 it(=application form)이므로 부사 in의 앞에 쓰인 형태이다. 뒤의 to는 장소를 나타내는 전치사이다.

정답 the student council / application period / aptitude

교과서 핵심 정리

Reading Comprehension

*해석을 참조하여 빈칸에 알맞은 말을 쓰거나 괄호에서 알맞은 말을 고르시오.

P.15 L.1~7

Welcome to Our Club

Hello. I'm Jisu. I am a freshman at Daehan High School. I have been looking forward to __________ a club as part of my new school life. I think that I might be able to find my aptitudes and talents through club activities. Yena, an older student, advised me __________ on to the school website and search for information about school clubs. I found some interesting information about various clubs on the school website.

우리 동아리에 온 것을 환영해

안녕, 난 지수라고 해. 난 대한 고등학교의 신입생이야. 난 새로운 학교생활의 일환으로 동아리에 가입하는 것을 고대해 왔어. 나는 동아리 활동을 하면서 나의 적성과 능력을 찾을 수 있을 것이라고 생각해. 나보다 선배인 예나 누나가 나에게 학교 홈페이지에 들어가서 동아리에 관한 정보를 살펴보라고 조언해 주었어. 나는 학교 홈페이지에서 여러 동아리에 관한 흥미로운 정보를 찾았어.

단락요약
• 지수는 동아리 가입을 통해 고등학교 생활을 의미있게 보내려고 선배의 조언에 따라 학교 홈페이지를 찾는다.

구문정리
• Yena, an older student, advised me to log on to the school website and search for information about school clubs.: Yena와 an older student는 동격이며 술부는 「advised+목적어+to+동사원형1+and +동사원형2」의 어순이다.

정답 joining / to log

P.16 L.1~10

No Limits

Welcome to *No Limits*! Do you want to be in control of making movies? Do you want to turn your fantasies into a movie script? Do you want to make movie scenes more alive and realistic with interesting sounds? Do you want to be a cool action hero and win an impossible fight? Do you want to play the sweet guy or girl in a romantic movie? If your answer is "yes" to __________ of these questions, then come to *No Limits*. If you join us, you can take part in __________ short films every year for the school festival. The fruits of your effort will taste so sweet when you hear the loud cheers and shouts of your friends. No pain, no gain? *No Limits*, and great gains!

No Limits

No Limits에 온 것을 환영한다! 영화를 만드는 주역이 되고 싶은가? 상상한 것을 영화 대본으로 만들고 싶은가? 영화 장면을 흥미있는 음향으로 보다 더 생동감 있고 사실적으로 만들고 싶은가? 액션 영화의 영웅이 되어서 불가능한 전투에서 승리하고 싶은가? 로맨틱 영화의 달콤한 주인공이 되고 싶은가? 이들 질문 중에 하나라도 '예'라고 답했다면 No Limits로 오라. 가입하면, 당신은 매년 열리는 학교 축제에서 단편 영화를 제작하는 데 참여할 수 있다. 친구들의 큰 환호와 외침을 들을 때 당신의 노력의 결실은 매우 달콤할 것이다. 고통이 없으면, 얻는 것이 없다? No Limits면, 얻을 것이 많다!

단락요약
• 영화 동아리 No Limits에서 영화와 관련된 다양한 분야를 경험할 수 있다.

구문정리
• If you join us, you can take part in producing short films every year for the school festival: take part in은 '~ 에 참석하다'의 의미이며 전치사 in 뒤에는 명사나 동명사의 형태가 쓰인다. every year는 전치사 없이 명사만으로 부사의 역할을 하며 뒤의 for는 '~를 위하여'의 의미이다.

정답 any / producing

P.16 L.11~21

Wings and Motors

Have you ever __________ of flying high in the sky? Do you wish to drive a fancy car? We promise to give you the chance to own the airplane or car of your dreams. Does this sound too good to be true? Not at all! Join *Wings and Motors*, and you can assemble your own model airplane or car. By making your own aircraft and vehicles, you can improve your concentration. If you want to, you can also take part in our annual airplane and car race. Who knows? The next award for the farthest-flying airplane or the fastest car may be yours. Do not miss this chance ______________ your dream. Fly high and move fast with *Wings and Motors*!

Wings and Motors

하늘을 높이 나는 꿈을 꿔본 적이 있는가? 고급차를 운전하고 싶은가? 우리가 당신의 꿈의 비행기나 자동차를 소유할 기회를 당신에게 주겠다고 약속한다. 너무 듣기에만 좋은 말이어서 사실일 것 같지 않다고? 전혀 그렇지 않다! Wings and Motors에 가입하면 당신만의 모형 비행기나 자동차를 조립할 수 있다. 당신만의 비행기나 차량을 만듦으로써 집중력을 향상시킬 수 있다. 원한다면, 당신은 우리가 매년 개최하는 비행기와 자동차 경주에도 참여할 수 있다. 누가 알겠는가? 가장 멀리 나는 비행기나 가장 빠른 자동차에 대한 상이 당신의 것이 될지도 모른다. 당신의 꿈을 성취할 이 기회를 놓치지 마라. Wings and Motors와 함께 하늘을 높이 날고 빠르게 움직여보라!

단락요약
- 모형 비행기와 자동차 동아리 Wings and Motors의 소개

구문정리
- ~ the chance to own the airplane or car of your dreams.: the chance를 to부정사구가 수식하고 있다.(형용사적 용법)
- Does this sound too good to be true?: too ~ to...구문으로 '너무 ~해서 …할 수 없다'의 의미를 나타낸다.
- Who knows?: 단순한 의문문이 아니라, 긍정의 형태로 쓰여 부정의 의미를 나타내는 '수사의문문' 이다.

정답 dreamed / to achieve

P.17 L.1~22

From Scratch

Do you always feel hungry when you are in school? Well, you are not the only one! We all need to eat to keep our energy up. So we decided to create a baking club and make healthy and delicious bread and cookies ____________. Our club is called *From Scratch* because we didn't know anything about baking at first and had to start from scratch. But now we are experts in making brownies! We open a bakery stand at the school festival every year to sell our own (baking / baked) goods. Our friends say that eating our bread is the best part of the festival. We invite you to join us and fill your school life with the joy of baking.

How to Make Brownies

1. Put some flour, sugar, cocoa, and salt in a bowl.
2. Mix all of them well with a large spoon.
3. Add oil and water to the bowl and mix again.
4. Place the bowl in the microwave and heat it for 50 seconds.

Do you want to taste these delicious brownies? Come and knock on the door of our club room!

From Scratch

학교에 있으면 항상 배고픈가? 음, 당신만 배고픈 게 아니다! 우리 모두는 에너지를 만들어내기 위해서 먹어야 한다. 그래서 우리는 제빵 동아리를 만들기로 결심했고 몸에 좋고 맛도 좋은 빵과 과자를 우리 스스로 만든다. 우리는 처음에 제빵에 대해서 아무 것도 몰랐고 바닥부터 시작해야 했기에 우리 동아리 이름은 From Scratch이다. 하지만 이제 우리는 브라우니를 만드는 데 전문가이다! 우리는 매년 학교 축제 때 제빵 가판대를 열어서 우리가 손수 만든 빵을 판매한다. 친구들은 우리의 빵을 먹는 것이 축제 최대의 묘미라고 말한다. 우리는 당신이 우리와 함께해서 제빵의 기쁨과 함께 풍성한 학교생활을 하도록 당신을 초대한다.

브라우니 만드는 방법

1. 약간의 밀가루, 설탕, 코코아, 소금을 그릇에 넣어라.
2. 큰 스푼으로 잘 섞어라.
3. 그릇에 기름과 물을 첨가한 다음 다시 섞어라.
4. 전자레인지에 넣고 50초 동안 데워라.

이 맛있는 브라우니를 맛보고 싶니?
이리 와서 우리 동아리의 문을 두드려라!

단락요약
- 제빵 동아리 From Scratch 소개

구문정리
- We all need to eat to keep our energy up.: to eat은 need의 목적어에 해당하고 to keep은 '~하기 위해'라는 목적을 나타내는 부사적 용법이다. keep our energy up은 「동사+목적어+부사」 어순이다.
- Our club is called *From Scratch* because we didn't know anything about baking at first and had to start from scratch.: because가 이끄는 이유의 부사절은 주어 we의 술어인 didn't know~와 had to start~가 and로 연결된 병렬구조 형태이다.
- Our friends say that eating our bread is the best part of the festival.: that절에서 eating our bread는 동명사구로 주어로 쓰였다.
- 동명사 주어는 단수 동사를 취한다.

정답 ourselves / baked

P.18 L.1~13

Little Helpers

Do you want to be a happier person? Do you want to learn the secrets to a more meaningful life? If so, then knock on the door of our club room. You will see that the key to happiness (lies / lays) in helping others. Volunteer work may seem difficult, but it's not. We can do many simple things for those in need, such as delivering food to the elderly, talking with people living alone, and teaching children with fewer opportunities for education. Some former members of our club have continued their volunteer work after high school in order to serve ____________ in need of help. Just a little bit of time and effort will double the happiness in your life. Join *Little Helpers* and experience the great joy of giving and sharing.

Hi, my name is Jihyeong. I am a former member of *Little Helpers*. Since high school, some other former members and I have been working as volunteers in order to serve those in need of help. We feel closer to each other than we used to when we were in high school. If you join this club, you'll surely have the best high school experience!

Little Helpers

더 행복한 사람이 되고 싶은가? 더욱 의미 있는 삶의 비밀을 배우고 싶은가? 그렇다면, 우리 동아리의 문을 두드려라. 당신은 행복의 열쇠가 남을 돕는 것에 있다는 것을 알게 될 것이다. 자원봉사는 어려워 보이지만 그렇지 않다. 노인에게 식사를 가져다주거나, 혼자 사는 사람들에게 말벗이 되어주거나, 교육을 받을 기회가 적은 아이들을 가르쳐 주는 것처럼 도움을 필요로 하는 사람들에게 많은 단순한 것들을 해줄 수 있다. 우리 동아리 출신의 몇몇 이전 회원들은 졸업 후에도 도움이 필요한 사람들을 위해서 자원봉사를 계속 하고 있다. 약간의 시간과 노력은 당신 삶의 행복을 두 배로 만들어 줄 것이다. Little Helpers에 가입해서 기부와 나눔의 큰 기쁨을 경험해라.

안녕, 내 이름은 지형이야. 난 Little Helpers의 이전 회원이야. 고등학교 때부터, 몇몇 이전 회원들과 나는 도움을 필요로 하는 사람들을 위해서 자원봉사를 하고 있어. 우리는 학생 때보다 더욱 서로 가까워졌다고 느끼고 있어. 이 동아리에 가입하면, 넌 분명 고등학교에서 최고의 경험을 하게 될 거야!

단락요약
- 자원봉사 동아리 Little Helpers 소개

구문정리
- If so, then knock on the door of our club room.: so는 앞의 두 문장을 받는 지시대명사이다.
- You will see that the key to happiness lies in helping others.: the key to ~에서 to는 전치사이며 뒤에는 명사 상당어구가 온다.
- We can do many simple things for those in need, such as delivering food to the elderly, talking with people living alone, and teaching children with fewer opportunities for education: such as 뒤에 delivering ~, talking ~, teaching ~이 and로 연결된 병렬구조이다.
- We feel closer to each other than we used to when we were in high school.:used to는 뒤에 feel close가 생략된 조동사이며 when 이하의 과거의 어느 한 때의 동작이 한동안 지속되었는데, 지금은 달라졌음을 내포한다.

정답 lies / those

P.18 L.14~17

After I got information from the school website, I thought about choosing one among the many interesting school clubs. Yena told me that I should consider my skills and interests when I choose a club. So I thought about my hobbies and realized that I liked watching movies and making stories. ______________________ I decided to join the filmmaking club, *No Limits*.

학교 홈페이지에서 정보를 얻은 뒤, 나는 많은 흥미로운 학교 동아리들 사이에서 하나를 고르는 것에 대해 생각했다. 예나 누나는 나에게 동아리를 고를 때는 재주와 흥미를 고려해야 한다고 말했다. 그래서 나는 내 취미를 생각한 후 내가 영화 보는 것과 이야기 집필을 좋아한다는 것을 깨닫게 되었다. 결국에는, 난 영화 동아리인 No Limits에 가입하기로 결심했다.

단락요약
- 동아리 정보를 살펴본 지수는 자신의 취미를 고려하여 동아리를 선택한다.

구문정리
- So I thought about my hobbies and realized that I liked watching movies and making stories.: 주절의 동사는 thought와 realized이고 that절의 동사 liked의 목적어는 동명사 watching~과 making~ 인데 모두 병렬구조의 형태이다.

정답 In the end

Focus on Structure

P. 15 L.2 I **have been looking** forward to | joining a club | as part of my new school life.
S *V* *O* 수식어구

⊖ 과거의 시점부터 현재까지 진행 중인 동작을 강조할 때 현재완료진행시제「have been + -ing」를 쓴다.

cf. 현재완료 진행은 대체로 기간이 비교적 짧거나 일시적인 행위 또는 상황에 쓴다. 장기간 지속되거나 영구적인 상황에서는 현재완료를 쓴다.

ex I've been living in Sam's flat for the last month. 나는 지난 한달 동안 Sam의 아파트에서 지냈다.
My uncle has lived in New York all his lives. 나의 삼촌은 평생 뉴욕에서 사셨다.
상태를 나타내는 동사는 진행시제로 쓰이면 어색해진다.
기간을 나타내는 부사는「for+시간/ since+과거의 시점」을 쓴다.

P. 16 L.13 We promise | **to give** you the chance | **to own** the airplane or car of your dreams.
S *V* *O* 형용사적 용법 (명사 수식) 전치사구 후치 수식

⊖ to부정사는 문장에서 명사구, 형용사구, 부사구 등의 다양한 역할을 한다. to부정사구의 구성 형태인「to부정사+목적어(구)+수식어구」의 범위를 파악해야 문장에서 어떤 성분으로 쓰이는지 알 수 있다.

구분	용법
명사적 용법	주로 동사의 목적어, 또는 보어로 쓰이며, 주어로 쓰일 때는 가주어 It을 사용한다.
형용사적 용법	명사를 뒤에서 수식하거나, 문장의 보어로 쓰인다.
부사적 용법	목적이나 감정의 원인 등을 나타내는 부사로 쓰인다.

P. 17 L.8 Our club is called *From Scratch* | because we didn't know anything about baking at first
수동태 이유의 부사절 *S* *V1*

and had to start from scratch.
등위접속사 *V2*

⊖ 등위접속사(and, or, but, so)에 의해 연결되는 명사, 동사, 부정사구, 동명사구, 절 등은 병렬구조를 이루어야 한다.

cf. 세 개 이상이 연결될 때, 접속사는 마지막 연결대상 앞에 쓴다.
The dog ran across the yard, jumped over the fence, **and** sprinted down the alley. (동사로 연결된 병렬 구조)
그 개는 마당을 가로질러 달리고 담장을 뛰어넘어 골목길을 따라 전력 질주하였다.

Check-Up

정답 P. 223

1 다음 괄호 안의 단어들을 순서대로 바르게 배열 하시오.

(1) My sister has no (her / help / to / friend).
(2) My brother (sleeping / been / since / has) he returned.

2 다음 문장의 밑줄 친 부분을 바르게 고쳐 쓰시오.

(1) The last person left the office must turn off the light.
(2) My brother has been worked for a bank since he graduated from university.
(3) I tried to find out what my problem was and corrected it, but I failed.

Tip

❶ (1) to부정사의 형용사적 용법
(2) 현재완료진행형

❷ (1) to부정사의 형용사적 용법
(2) 현재완료진행형
(3) 병렬구조
turn off the light:불을 끄다
correct: 수정하다

언어 기능별 집중 대비

Listen and Speak/Into Real Life

정답 P. 223

1 대화를 듣고, 남자가 이어서 할 말로 가장 적절한 것을 고르시오.

① Thanks for letting me know.
② Thank you. Can you make it at 3?
③ In fact, I am not interested in helping others.
④ Oh, that's cool. You will like your friends there.
⑤ Sounds good. Thank you for your advice, Ms Kim.

2 대화를 듣고, 남자의 마지막 말에 대한 여자의 응답으로 가장 적절한 것을 고르시오.

① Then, why don't you join the club?
② Sure, books are foods for our thought.
③ Oh, really? I like detective stories, too.
④ Sounds good. When can we get together?
⑤ Don't do that. It is very harmful to your health.

3 다음 대화를 듣고, 두 사람이 정할 선택 과목이 바르게 짝지어진 것을 고르시오.

	Woman		Man
①	physics	–	math or physics
②	Japanese	–	physics or Spanish
③	Spanish	–	Japanese or physics
④	science	–	Spanish or physics
⑤	physics	–	Japanese or Spanish

4 다음을 듣고, 물음에 답하시오.

(1) 방송의 주제로 가장 알맞은 것은?

① A new semester
② Joining a school club
③ Introduction to a high school
④ What to do in the high school
⑤ Introduction to the school council

(2) 방송에서 언급되지 않은 것은?

① 자신의 소개　　② 동아리 가입 기간
③ 동아리 가입 방법　　④ 동아리 선택시 고려할 점
⑤ 동아리 가입의 제한 사항

Tip

1. 마지막 말에 대한 응답 고르기
출처: Get Ready_1
make it: 시간 맞춰 가다, 성공하다

2. 마지막 말에 대한 응답 고르기
출처: Get Ready_3
harmful 해로운, 유해한

3. 세부 사항 파악하기
출처: Listen In_Dialogue 1

4. (1) 주제 고르기
(2) 구체적인 정보 파악하기
출처: Into Real Life_Step 1
semester 학기
school council 학생회

언어 기능별 집중 대비

Read and Think

정답 P. 224

Tip

[1-2] 다음 글을 읽고, 물음에 답하시오.

Hello. I'm Jisu. ⓐ I am a freshman at Daehan High School. ⓑ I have been looking forward to joining a club as part of my new school life. ⓒ I think that I might be able to find my aptitudes and talents through club activities. ⓓ Yena, an older student, advised me log on to the school website and search for information about school clubs. ⓔ I found some interesting information about various clubs on the school website.

1-2 출처: P.15 L.2-7
유형: 1. 문법성 판단
2. 전후 관계 추론

1 윗글의 밑줄 친 ⓐ~ⓔ 중 어법상 어색한 문장은?

① ⓐ ② ⓑ ③ ⓒ ④ ⓓ ⑤ ⓔ

2 윗글의 바로 뒤에 나올 내용으로 가장 알맞은 것은?

① 지수의 학교 생활
② 지수의 친구들
③ 지수의 동아리 활동
④ 학교 동아리 정보 및 홍보
⑤ 고등학교 신학기의 중요성

[3-4] 다음 글을 읽고, 물음에 답하시오.

Welcome to *No Limits*! Do you want to be in control of making movies? Do you want to turn your fantasies into a movie script? Do you want to make movie scenes more alive and realistic with interesting sounds? Do you want to be a cool action hero and win an impossible fight? Do you want to play the sweet guy or girl in a romantic movie? If your answer is "yes" to any of these questions, then come to *No Limits*. If you join us, you can take part in producing ___________ every year for the school festival. The fruits of your effort will taste so sweet when you hear the loud cheers and shouts of your friends. No pain, no gain? *No Limits*, and great gains!

3-4 출처: P.16 L.2-10
유형: 3. 빈칸 추론
4. 세부 정보 파악

3 윗글의 빈칸에 가장 알맞은 것은?

① short films
② a drama
③ the school events
④ interesting games
⑤ a good music piece

4 윗글에서 동아리의 활동 분야로 언급되지 않은 것은?

① 영화감독
② 영화 대본
③ 음향효과
④ 영화배우
⑤ 티켓판매

Tip

5 다음 글의 밑줄 친 ⓐ~ⓔ 중 어휘의 쓰임이 잘못된 것은?

Have you ever dreamed of flying high in the sky? Do you wish to drive a ⓐ fancy car? We promise to give you the chance to own the airplane or car of your dreams. Does this sound too good to be true? Not at all! Join *Wings and Motors*, and you can ⓑ assemble your own model airplane or car. By making your own aircraft and vehicles, you can ⓒ decrease your concentration. If you want to, you can also ⓓ take part in our annual airplane and car race. Who knows? The next award for the farthest-flying airplane or the fastest car may be yours. Do not miss this chance to ⓔ achieve your dream. Fly high and move fast with *Wings and Motors*!

① ⓐ ② ⓑ ③ ⓒ ④ ⓓ ⑤ ⓔ

❺ 출처: P.16 L.12-21
유형: 어휘의 쓰임

[6-7] 다음 글을 읽고, 물음에 답하시오.

6-7 출처: P.17 L.2-22
유형: 6. 세부 사항 파악
7. 어휘의 쓰임

Do you always feel ⓐ hungry when you are in school? Well, you are not the only one! We all need to eat to keep our energy up. So we decided to create a baking club and make ⓑ healthy and delicious bread and cookies ourselves. Our club is called *From Scratch* because we didn't know anything about baking at first and had to start from scratch. But now we are ⓒ experts in making brownies! We open a bakery stand at the school festival every year to ⓓ buy our own baked goods. Our friends say that eating our bread is the best part of the festival. We invite you to join us and fill your school life with the joy of baking.

How to Make Brownies

1. Put some flour, sugar, cocoa, and salt in a bowl.
2. Mix all of them well with a large spoon.
3. ⓔ Add oil and water to the bowl and mix again.
4. Place the bowl in the microwave and heat it for 50 seconds.

Do you want to taste these delicious brownies? Come and knock on the door of our club room!

6 윗글에서 소개되는 동아리의 내용으로 언급되지 않은 것은?

① 설립 취지
② 주요 활동
③ 주위의 평가
④ 참여 행사
⑤ 구성 인원수

7 윗글의 밑줄 친 ⓐ~ⓔ 중 어휘의 쓰임이 잘못된 것은?

① ⓐ ② ⓑ ③ ⓒ ④ ⓓ ⑤ ⓔ

Tip

[8-9] 다음 글을 읽고, 물음에 답하시오.

Do you want to be a happier person? (A) Do you want to learn the secrets to a more meaningful life? (B) You will see that the key to happiness lies in ______________. Volunteer work may seem difficult, but it's not. (C) We can do many simple things for those in need, such as delivering food to the elderly, talking with people living alone, and teaching children with fewer opportunities for education. (D) Some former members of our club have continued their volunteer work after high school in order to serve those in need of help. (E) Just a little bit of time and effort will double the happiness in your life. Join *Little Helpers* and experience the great joy of giving and sharing.

8-9 출처: P.18 L.2-13
유형: 8. 문장의 위치 파악
9. 빈칸 추론

8 윗글의 (A)~(E) 중 아래의 문장이 들어가기에 가장 알맞은 곳은?

If so, then knock on the door of our club room.

① (A) ② (B) ③ (C) ④ (D) ⑤ (E)

9 윗글의 빈칸에 가장 알맞은 것은?

① playing sports
② helping others
③ earning money
④ making friends
⑤ eating healthy foods

10 다음 글의 빈칸에 가장 알맞은 것은?

After I got information from the school website, I thought about choosing one among the many interesting school clubs. Yena told me that I should consider my skills and interests when I choose a club. So I thought about my hobbies and realized that I liked watching movies and making stories. ______________, I decided to join the filmmaking club, *No Limits*.

10 출처: P.18 L.14-17
유형: 연결사 추론

① Yet ② However
③ In fact ④ In the end
⑤ Most of all

언어 기능별 집중 대비

Language Notes Write It Right

정답 P. 224

1 다음 우리말에 맞게 괄호 안의 단어를 이용하여 문장을 완성하시오.

(1) 우린 두 시부터 여기에서 쭉 기다리고 있는 중이다.
We ____________ here since two o'clock. (wait)

(2) 희생자가 되지 않도록 하기 위해서 네가 해야 할 일이 몇 가지 있다.
There are a few things you should do ____________ becoming a victim. (avoid)

(3) 아버지가 너를 Jamie의 파티에 가게 허락해 주실 것 같니?
Do you think dad will let you ____________ to Jamie's party? (go)

(4) Brad는 계산기를 사용하지 않고 수학숙제를 하고 있었다.
Brad was doing his math homework ____________ a calculator. (use)

(5) 왜 이렇게 나쁜 날씨에 우리가 밖에 나가야 하나요?
____________ we go outside in this bad weather? (should)

Tip

❶ (1) 현재완료진행 시제
(2) 목적을 나타내는 to부정사
(3) 「사역동사 + 목적어 + 원형부정사」
(4) 「전치사 + 동명사」
(5) 조동사가 들어간 의문문

2 다음 글을 읽고, 물음에 답하시오.

Have you ever imagined yourself in the middle of a big stage? You can relieve your stress by joining *Burning Fire*! Anyone who can sing or play an instrument is welcome to join us. We meet every day after school for practice sessions. Preparing for a perfect performance takes a lot of time and effort, but it brings great rewards and helps form stronger bonds with the other members. Our performances are known to be the best part of the school festival. Creating wonderful sounds together under the shining lights of the stage will keep your heart beating with excitement. With *Burning Fire*, your high school years will be completely fantastic!

❷ relieve (긴장 등을) 풀게 하다
session 수업
bond 결속, 연대
excitement 흥분
completely 완전히

(1) Who can apply to this club?

____

(2) What can you get from the club?

____

Basic

정답 P. 224

1 대화를 듣고, 남자가 관심 있어 하는 것을 고르시오.

① cook
② baseball
③ bowling
④ movie director
⑤ detective novel

2 대화를 듣고 대화의 내용과 일치하지 않는 것은?

① 남학생은 수학을 좋아한다.
② 여학생은 신입생이다.
③ 여학생은 2년 동안 자원봉사를 해왔다.
④ 두 사람은 주말에 자원봉사를 할 예정이다.
⑤ 여학생은 매주 일요일에 학생들을 가르친다.

3 다음 단어의 뜻이 잘못 연결된 것은?

① vehicle: 약
② script: 대본
③ annual: 매년의
④ deliver: 배달하다
⑤ assemble: 조립하다

4 다음 숙어의 뜻이 잘못 연결된 것은?

① log on: 접속하다
② in the end: 결국에는
③ take part in: 불참하다
④ in need: 도움이 필요한
⑤ from scratch: 맨 처음부터

5 다음 중 반의어끼리 연결된 것은?

① friend – friendly
② regular – irregular
③ lingual – bilingual
④ final – semifinal
⑤ counter – encounter

6 다음 중 밑줄 친 부분의 용법이 나머지와 다른 하나는?

① I like to watch movies.
② To do so, we need a lot of money.
③ To know someone is really difficult.
④ I want to stay here for a very long time.
⑤ It's a little hard for me to log on the website.

7 다음 글의 빈칸에 들어갈 말을 〈보기〉의 단어들을 사용하여 완성하시오. (필요한 경우 형태를 바꾸시오.)

보기 club / right / find / the

Welcome, freshmen! I am Jiwon, the head of the student council. What do you want to do in your free time? What are you most interested in? Our school clubs are looking forward to meeting all of you. Our school has 35 clubs, and you're welcome to join any of them. The application period starts from this Wednesday and ends on Tuesday next week. You can get information about all our clubs on our school website. You can get the application form from your homeroom teacher and hand it in to each club room. When you choose a school club, you need to think about your hobbies and interests. You also need to consider your aptitude and dream job. ____________ is the key to a happy school life for the next three years. Think it through and then hurry to sign up!

→ ______________________

8 다음 〈보기〉의 우리말과 같도록 할 때, 빈칸에 알맞은 것은?

> **보기** 나는 내년에 파리에 계신 이모님 집을 방문하고 싶어.
> I ______________ my aunt in Paris next year.

① have to ask
② wish to plan
③ want to visit
④ hang out with
⑤ like going abroad

9 다음 글의 내용과 일치하지 않는 것을 모두 고르시오.

> Freshmen, your attention, please. I am Lee Sia, the head of the school orchestra. What do you want to do for extracurricular activities? If you are interested in playing any musical instrument, why don't you try out for the school orchestra? Tomorrow we are going to have auditions for new members of the orchestra in the auditorium after school at 5 p.m. There will be a brief introduction to our club and some great performances by senior students. Each individual audition will last about 10 minutes. Don't forget to bring the musical instrument you want to play. For more information, please visit our club room. We hope to see you at the auditions. Thank you for your attention.

① This is an announcement.
② Lee Sia is the head of the school orchestra.
③ The audition will be held in the auditorium at 5 p.m.
④ Applicants don't need to bring musical instruments.
⑤ There will be an introduction to the club and great performances by graduated students.

10 다음 중 어법상 어색한 문장은?

① Paul hasn't arrived yet.
② I have been watching you.
③ Jina has been playing badminton.
④ How long have you been studying math?
⑤ I've been cycling from midday until five o'clock.

11 다음 중 〈보기〉와 비슷한 의미의 표현이 아닌 것은?

> **보기** What are you interested in?

① What do you like?
② What is your hobby?
③ What interests do you have?
④ Do you know what my hobby is?
⑤ What do you usually do when you are free?

[12~13] 다음 〈보기〉의 우리말과 같도록 괄호 안의 단어를 이용하여 빈칸에 알맞은 말을 쓰시오.

12

> **보기** 그 여자가 그 회사를 관리하고 있습니다.
> (control / in / of)

→ She is ______________________ the company.

13

> **보기** 자원봉사 동아리들에 대한 정보를 찾아라.
> (the / volunteering / clubs / for / search)

→ __________ information about __________.

Advanced

정답 P. 224

[1~2] 다음을 듣고, 물음에 답하시오.

1 이 방송의 요지로 가장 알맞은 것을 고르시오.

① Try to make time for your hobby.
② Take part in the school music competition.
③ Hand in your work until Tuesday next week.
④ Join a school club for the meaningful school life.
⑤ Get information of the clubs on the school website.

2 이 방송의 내용과 일치하지 않는 것을 고르시오.

① 학교에는 35개의 동아리가 있다.
② 학생회장이 동아리를 안내하고 있다.
③ 담임 선생님께 가입신청서를 제출한다.
④ 동아리 가입은 이번 주 수요일부터 가능하다.
⑤ 동아리를 고를 때 자신의 취미와 흥미를 고려하는 것이 바람직하다.

3 다음 방송을 듣고 화자와 듣는 사람의 관계로 알맞은 것을 고르시오.

① officer – driver
② reporter – player
③ teacher – student
④ client – customer
⑤ club leader – freshman

4 다음 대화의 빈칸에 가장 알맞은 것은?

M: Hi, Sumi, did you hear that we need to choose an elective subject by the end of this week?
W: Yes, I did. I've already decided to take physics.
M: Really? ____________________
W: I know it won't be easy, but I do like science and math. How about you? What are you interested in?
M: I'm interested in languages, so I think I'll go for either Spanish or Japanese.
W: Oh, that's cool.

① You hate science and math, right?
② Physics is your favorite subject, right?
③ Physics is the most challenging subject for me.
④ Why did you do that? I thought you would take Spanish.
⑤ Some students think physics is the easiest subject to learn.

[5~6] 다음 대화를 읽고, 물음에 답하시오.

M: Hi, Hwajin. Do you have any plans for this weekend?
W: Yeah, I teach Korean to Vietnamese children every Saturday.
M: Oh, is it part of a ⓐ 봉사활동?
W: Yes, it is. I have worked as a volunteer teacher for two years at the community center. I think ⓑ it's meaningful, and I am also really interested in teaching languages.
M: Of course. You can speak both Vietnamese and Korean. That's a perfect kind of volunteer work for you. Can I join you this weekend?
W: Sure, you can. What do you want to do for them?
M: I'm interested in mathematics, so I think I can teach them math.
W: Oh, that sounds good.

5 위 대화의 밑줄 친 ⓐ의 우리말에 해당하는 표현을 쓰시오.

____

6 위 대화의 밑줄 친 ⓑ가 의미하는 바를 영어로 쓰시오.

→ ____________________

7 다음 글의 밑줄 친 ①~⑤ 중 잘못된 것을 찾아 바르게 고쳐 쓰시오.

Have you ever imagined yourself in the middle of a big stage? You can ① strengthen your stress by joining *Burning Fire*! Anyone who can sing or play an instrument is welcome to join us. We meet every day after school for ② practice sessions. Preparing for a perfect performance takes a lot of time and effort, but it brings great ③ rewards and helps form stronger ④ bonds with the other members. Our performances are known to be the best part of the school festival. Creating wonderful sounds together under the shining lights of the stage will keep your heart beating with excitement. With *Burning Fire*, your high school years will be completely ⑤ fantastic!

__________ → __________

[8~9] 다음 글을 읽고, 물음에 답하시오.

(A) Welcome to *No Limits!* Do you want to be in control of making movies? Do you want to turn your fantasies into a movie script? Do you want to make movie scenes more alive and realistic with interesting sounds? Do you want to be a cool action hero and win an impossible fight? Do you want to play the sweet guy or girl in a romantic movie? If your answer is "yes" to any of these questions, then come to *No Limits*. If you join us, you can take part in producing short films every year for the school festival. The fruits of your effort will taste so sweet when you hear the loud cheers and shouts of your friends. No pain, no gain? *No Limits*, and great gains!

(B) Have you ever dreamed of flying high in the sky? Do you wish to drive a fancy car? We promise to give you the chance to own the airplane or car of your dreams. Does this sound too good to be true? Not at all! Join *Wings and Motors*, and you can assemble your own model airplane or car. ________________ aircraft and vehicles, you can improve your concentration. If you want to, you can also take part in ⓑ our annual airplane and car race.

Who knows? The next award for the farthest-flying airplane or the fastest car may be yours. Do not miss this chance to achieve your dream. Fly high and move fast with *Wings and Motors*!

8 다음 <보기>의 단어들을 이용하여 빈칸 ⓐ에 알맞은 말을 쓰시오. (필요하면 형태를 고치시오.)

보기 your / own / make / by

⊝ ________________________________

9 윗글의 밑줄 친 ⓑ의 어구에 대응하는 것을 (A)에서 찾아 쓰시오.

⊝ ________________________________

[10~11] 다음 글을 읽고, 물음에 답하시오.

Do you want to be a happier person? Do you want to learn the secrets to a more meaningful life? If so, then knock on the door of our club room. You will see that the key to happiness lies in helping others. Volunteer work may seem difficult, but it's not. We can do many simple things for those in need, such as delivering food to the elderly, talking with people living alone, and teaching children with fewer opportunities for education. Some former members of our club have continued their volunteer work after high school in order to serve those in need of help. Just a little bit of time and effort will double the ________ in your life. Join *Little Helpers* and experience the great joy of giving and sharing.

10 윗글의 빈칸에 들어갈 말을 쓰시오.

⊝ ________________

11 윗글의 내용과 일치하지 않는 것은?

① 행복하고 의미 있는 삶을 배우고 싶으면 Little Helpers에 가입해라.
② Little Helpers에 가입하면 행복의 열쇠가 남을 돕는 것에 있다는 것을 알게 된다.
③ 자원봉사는 어려워 보이지만 실은 그렇지 않다.
④ Little Helpers 출신들은 모두가 졸업 후에도 봉사 활동을 계속 하고 있다
⑤ 글쓴이는 Little Helpers라는 동아리를 소개하고 있다.

주관식 서술형 대비

12 다음 글을 참조하여 자신만의 요리 방법을 소개하는 글을 쓰시오.

How to Make Brownies

1. Put some flour, sugar, cocoa, and salt in a bowl.
2. Mix all of them well with a large spoon.
3. Add oil and water to the bowl and mix again.
4. Place the bowl in the microwave and heat it for 50 seconds.

____
____
____
____
____

UNIT 2

Living Life to the Fullest

교과서 핵심 정리

Words & Phrases

Listen and Speak ~ Into Real Life

- ☐ make it* 시간 맞춰 가다, (어려운 일을) 해내다
- ☐ catch up with* ~을 따라 잡다
- ☐ article *n.* 기사, 사설, 항목
- ☐ on average 평균적으로
- ☐ disappointing *adj.* 실망스러운
- ☐ be about to* 막 ~하려던 참이다
- ☐ take one's time (서두르지 않고) 천천히 하다
- ☐ struggle *v.* 투쟁하다, 분투하다 *n.* 투쟁, 분투
- ☐ associate* *v.* 연계하다 (association *n.* 연계, 협회)
- ☐ investigate *v.* 조사하다, 수사하다
- ☐ reflective *adj.* 사색적인, 반영하는 (reflect *v.* 반영하다)
- ☐ stick to ~를 (바꾸지 않고) 고수하다
- ☐ consult* *v.* 상의하다, 상담하다 (consultation *n.*협의, 상담)

Read and Think

- ☐ seize *v.* 붙잡다, 장악하다
- ☐ account *n.* 계좌 *cf.* bank account 은행 계좌
- ☐ valuable *adj.* 가치 있는 (value *n.* 가치)
- ☐ precious* *adj.* 귀중한, 값비싼
- ☐ huge *adj.* 거대한, 엄청난
- ☐ urgent *adj.* 긴급한 (urgency *n.* 긴급, 급박함)
- ☐ get the most out of* ~를 최대한 활용하다
- ☐ lead a life 생활하다
- ☐ responsibility *n.* 책임 (responsible *adj.* 책임 있는)
- ☐ organize *v.* 조직하다 (organization *n.* 조직, 기구)
- ☐ accomplish* *v.* 성취하다 (accomplishment *n.* 업적)
- ☐ figure out* *v.* (생각한 끝에) 이해하다, 알아내다
- ☐ be caught up with* ~에 발목 잡히다
- ☐ in advance 미리, 사전에
- ☐ hang out (사람과) 어울리다, 함께 시간을 보내다
- ☐ prevent *A* from -ing* A가 ~하지 못하게 막다
- ☐ spare *adj.* (쓰지 않아서) 남는, 여분의
- ☐ actually *adj.* 사실상
- ☐ assignment *n.* 과제, 숙제, 임무 (assign *v.* 부과하다)
- ☐ productive* *adj.* 생산적인 (productivity *n.* 생산성)
- ☐ concentrate *v.* 집중하다
- ☐ at one's best 가장 좋은 상태에 있는
- ☐ a night person 야간형 생활자 (=a night owl)

Language Notes

- ☐ particular *adj.* 특정한
- ☐ occasion *n.* (어떤 일이 일어나는) 경우, (특별한) 행사
  cf. occasional *adj.* 가끔의
- ☐ daily *adj.* 매일의
  cf. weekly 매주의 monthly 매달의 yearly 매년의
- ☐ freeze* *v.* 얼다, 얼리다 (freeze – froze – frozen)
- ☐ marble *n.* 대리석, (아이들이 갖고 노는) 구슬
- ☐ represent* *v.* 나타내다, 상징하다 (=stand for)
- ☐ time-taking *adj.* 시간이 (오래) 걸리는 (=time-consuming)
- ☐ extent* *n.* 정도
  cf. to a ~extent :~ (만큼의) 정도로

Write It Right

- ☐ recall* *v.* 기억하다, 상기하다 (=recollect ↔ forget)
- ☐ look back on ~를 회상하다, 돌이켜보다 (=reflect on) *cf.* reminiscence *n.* 회고, 회상
- ☐ in terms of* ~와 관련해서
- ☐ regret *v.* 후회하다 *n.* 후회
- ☐ primary* *adj.* 주요한, 기본적인
- ☐ midterm exam *n.* 중간고사
- ☐ resolution *n.* 결심, (국회 등의) 결의안

Around the World

- ☐ management *n.* 경영
- ☐ invest *v.* 투자하다
- ☐ philosopher *n.* 철학자
- ☐ deliberately *ad.* 의도적으로, 신중하게
- ☐ nap *n.* 낮잠
- ☐ chief* *adj.* 주요한 *n.* 우두머리, 장
- ☐ self-improvement *n.* 자기 개선, 자기 계발
- ☐ thoughtful *adj.* 사려 깊은
- ☐ routine* *n.* 일과 *adj.* 일상적인
- ☐ workout *n.* (건강이나 몸매 유지를 위해 하는) 운동 *v.* 운동하다

☑ Check-Up

정답 P. 225

1 다음 문장의 빈칸에 알맞은 말을 〈보기〉에서 골라 쓰시오.

> **보기 >>** on average / in terms of / at her best
> get the most out of / hang out / to some extent

(1) I've solved this problem ________________.

(2) He tried to ________________ his employees.

(3) Is this where you guys ________________ all the time?

(4) She was speaking ________________ improving students' grades.

(5) The singer was ________________ when she performed ballads.

(6) Families are throwing away $700 worth of food a year ________________.

Tip

❶ 주요 숙어표현 익히기
employee 피고용인, 직원
worth 가치

2 다음 뜻풀이에 해당하는 말을 주어진 철자로 시작하여 쓰시오.

(1) a ____________: to achieve or conclude successfully; complete

(2) p ____________: producing or doing a lot for the amount of resources used

(3) r ____________: thinking deeply about something that he or she has done

(4) s ____________: to take hold of something quickly, firmly, and forcefully

(5) u ____________: requiring speedy action or attention; necessary to be dealt with as soon as possible

❷ 영영사전풀이
resource 자원
firmly 굳건히
require 요구하다, 필요로 하다

주관식 서술형

3 우리말에 맞게 괄호 안의 단어들을 사용하여 문장을 완성하시오.

(1) 경찰은 대통령의 방문 전에 건물을 확인했다.
The police ________________________________.
(the president's / visit / in / advance / of / checked / the building)

(2) 그녀는 마감 기한을 맞추기 위해 고군분투했다.
She ________________.
(hard / meet / to / struggled / the / deadline)

(3) Bill은 일에 발이 묶여 있어서 가족을 위한 시간이 거의 없다.
Bill has little time for his family because he is ________________.
(the work / caught / up / with)

(4) 경찰은 그들이 무기를 가지고 다니지 못하도록 막기 위해 노력했다.
The police tried to ________________.
(prevent / from / carrying / weapons / them)

❸ 핵심어휘를 사용한 영작
check 확인하다
meet the deadline
마감 기한을 맞추다
catch-caught-caught
prevent *A* from -ing
A가 ~하지 않도록 막다

교과서 핵심 정리

Dialogues & Monologue

Listen and Speak | *해석을 참조하여 빈칸에 알맞은 말을 쓰시오.

GET READY

1 M: What time do you think is best to watch *The Lion King* this Saturday?
W: **Can you make it at** 3? I think we could watch the 3:30 show.
M: That sounds perfect.
W: Great. I'll mark it on my calendar.
M: I can't wait for the show!

남: 이번 주 토요일에 Lion King을 보려면 몇 시가 가장 좋을까?
여: 3시에 올 수 있어? 난 3시 30분 공연을 볼 수 있을 것 같아.
남: 그거 괜찮겠다.
여: 좋아. 내가 달력에 표시해 놓을게.
남: 정말 기다려지는데.

2 M: I'm so __________ in my science class. **It's so hard to catch up with the new lessons.**
W: Really? I'm actually quite enjoying it.
M: How do you do that? **Can I get your advice on effective ways to study science?**
W: Of course. I'd love to help you.
M: Thank you so much! It means a lot to me.

남: 과학 수업이 뭐가 뭔지 모르겠어. 새 단원을 따라가기가 너무 힘들어.
여: 정말? 사실 난 무척 재미있는데.
남: 어떻게 그래? 과학 공부에 효과적인 방법들에 대해 조언 좀 해 줄 수 있겠어?
여: 물론이지. 내가 너에게 도움을 줄 수 있으면 좋겠다.
남: 정말 고마워. 그게 나에겐 큰 힘이 돼.

3 W: This cookie is amazing! Did you bake it?
M: Yes, I did. Glad you like it!
W: I love it! How did you bake it? Can you teach me?
M: Sure. I can give you the recipe.
W: It'd be even __________ if I could learn as we bake it together.
M: That works for me, too. Come over to my place tomorrow. Can you make it at 3?

여: 이 과자 정말 놀라워! 네가 구운 거야?
남: 응. 내가 구웠어. 네가 좋아하니까 기뻐.
여: 정말 맛있어. 어떻게 구운 거야? 나에게 가르쳐줄래?
남: 물론이지. 요리법을 줄 수도 있어.
여: 우리가 같이 구우면서 배울 수 있으면 더 좋겠어.
남: 나도 그게 좋겠어. 내일 우리 집으로 와. 3시에 올 수 있어?

표현정리
- Can you make it at ~? (가능성 묻기)와 Can I get your advice on~? (충고 구하기)이 단원의 핵심 의사소통 표현이다.
- It's so hard to catch up with the new lessons.: 가주어 It이 가리키는 것은 진주어 to catch up with the new lessons이다.

정답 lost / better

LISTEN IN

DIALOGUE 1

W: Hey, I found a very interesting article.
M: What is it about?
W: It's about how many days or years we ______________ certain activities in our whole life.
M: Sounds interesting. What do we spend most of our life on?
W: This might make you sad. The article says it is working. We spend 26 years working when we consider people live for 80 years on average.
M: Really? I'm surprised it's not sleep. **What do we spend the least time on,** then?
W: It says it's __________. We only spend about 88 days doing this.
M: That is very disappointing. I think **we'd better smile more,** even when there is nothing to smile about.
W: I think so, too.
M: Can I get your advice on ways to ______________ positive and smile more? I noticed you smile more than most people do.
W: I'm glad you think so. I'm happy to help you.

여: 야, 나 정말 재미있는 기사를 발견했어.
남: 뭐에 관한 건데?
여: 우리가 살면서 어떤 특정 활동에 얼마나 많은 시간을 보내는지에 관한 거야.
남: 재미있겠는데. 우리가 제일 시간을 많이 보내는 활동이 뭐야?
여: 좀 슬프게 들릴 수도 있어. 그 기사에 따르면 우린 일하는 것에 가장 많은 시간을 보낸대. 우리가 평균 80년을 산다고 가정했을 때 26년을 일하는 데 쓴대.
남: 정말? 잠자는 것에 쓰는 게 아니어서 좀 놀랍네. 그럼 가장 적은 시간을 보내는 건 뭐야?
여: 기사에 따르면 웃는 거래. 웃는 것에는 고작 88일을 쓴대.
남: 정말 아쉽네. 앞으론 웃을 일이 없어도 더 많이 웃어야겠어.
여: 나도 같은 생각이야.
남: 좀 더 긍정적이고 좀 더 많이 웃으려면 어떻게 해야 할지 조언 좀 해 줄 수 있어? 넌 대부분의 사람들보다 더 많이 웃는 것 같아.
여: 그렇게 생각해 줘서 기뻐. 기꺼이 도와줄게.

대화상황 • 살면서 무엇을 하는 데 어느 정도의 시간을 보내는지에 관한 흥미로운 기사를 읽고 대화하는 상황

표현정리
- What do we spend the least time on?은 On what do we spend the least time?으로 물을 수도 있다.
- we'd better smile more : we'd는 we had의 축약형이며, had better 는 '~하는 게 좋겠다'의 뜻으로, 제안이나 충고를 나타내는 표현이다.

정답 spend on / smiling / stay more

DIALOGUE 2

(Phone rings)
M: Hello?
W: Hi, Jinho. It's Jin. I'm so sorry, but I'm running a little late....
M: You're late again? How come you always come late?
W: I really tried not to be late, but my mom asked for help when I was about ______________.
M: Is everything okay?
W: Actually, she is very sick. She needed me to stay until my brother came back home.
M: Oh, no. Sorry to hear that. Well, now I'm worried.
W: Sorry I couldn't let you know earlier.
M: It's okay. I can wait. **What time should I expect you?** Can you make it at 4?
W: Yes, I think I can make it by then. I'll run.
M: ______________________.

남: 여보세요?
여: 여보세요, 진호야. 나 진이야. 정말 미안한데 나 좀 늦을 것 같아....
남: 또 늦는다고? 넌 어떻게 항상 늦을 수가 있어?
여: 안 늦으려고 정말 노력했는데, 내가 막 출발하려고 할 때 엄마가 도움을 요청하셔서 말이야.
남: 무슨 일 있는 건 아니고?
여: 사실은, 엄마가 많이 아프셔. 오빠가 집에 올 때까지는 내가 있어드려야 했어.
남: 이런, 그 말 들으니 유감이네. 걱정이다.
여: 미리 알려주지 못해 미안해.
남: 괜찮아. 기다릴게. 몇 시면 올 수 있겠어? 4시까지 올 수 있어?
여: 응, 그 때까지는 갈 수 있을 거야. 뛰어 갈게.
남: 천천히 와.

대화상황 • 약속 시간에 늦은 친구가 전화로 사과하며 늦는 이유를 설명하는 상황

표현정리
- What time should I expect you?는 What time can you make it?과 비슷한 표현으로 '도착 예정 시간'을 물어보는 말이다.

정답 to leave / Take your time

Into Real Life

STEP 1

M: Everyone struggles to learn something new. However, if you know your ______________ and the associated ______________, your learning will be assisted **to a great extent**. For example, if you are outgoing, having a discussion on the topic will help you investigate the topic further. Even teaching your friends will help you process the content better. If you are not so outgoing and rather shy, making ______________ could assist your learning. If you are reflective, ask yourself questions about the concept you are learning **so that you can process** it step by step. You might already have your own learning style that you developed, but I advise you not to stick to your own routine. It might not suit your personality type. What you are used to is not always the best! For further information, consult my blog. Good luck with your studies!

남: 모든 사람은 새로운 것을 배우려고 애씁니다. 하지만, 여러분이 자신의 성격 유형과 그와 연관된 학습 전략을 알게 된다면 학습에 엄청난 도움을 받을 겁니다. 예를 들어, 만약 당신이 외향적이라면 주제에 관해 토론하는 것이 그 주제를 심화하여 탐구하도록 도울 겁니다. 심지어 친구를 가르치는 것도 그 내용을 좀 더 잘 학습하는 데 도움을 줄 겁니다. 만약 당신이 그다지 외향적이지 않고 오히려 수줍음이 많다면, 마인드맵을 작성하는 것이 학습에 도움이 될 겁니다. 생각이 깊은 성격이라면 내용을 이해하는 과정을 프로세스 할 수 있도록 당신이 배우고 있는 개념에 대해 스스로에게 질문을 던져보세요. 어쩌면 여러분은 이미 자신의 학습 스타일 가지고 있을 겁니다. 하지만 저는 여러분에게 자신의 일상적인 것만 고수하지는 말라고 충고합니다. 그게 당신의 성격 유형에 적합하지 않은 것일 수도 있습니다. 익숙한 것이 항상 최고는 아닙니다! 더 많은 정보를 얻으려면, 제 블로그를 참조하세요. 여러분의 공부에 행운이 있기를 바랍니다.

담화주제
- 성격 유형에 맞는 학습 스타일을 찾아 공부하는 것이 효과적임을 알려주고 있음.

표현정리
- to a great extent는 '엄청나게'라는 뜻으로 정도의 크기가 큼을 말한다.
- ~ so that you can process it: 「so that + 주어 + can/could +동사원형」은 '~가 … 할 수 있도록'이라는 뜻이다.

정답 personality type / learning strategies / mind maps

Check Your Progress

M: Wow, Kristin, it looks like you already finished your math project.

W: Hey, Tyler! Yes, **I got it done** yesterday.

M: How do you do that? I always finish everything at the last minute.

W: **I used to be like that,** too, but I'm trying to treat my time ______________ these days.

M: Can I get your advice on how to manage my time?

W: Well, it takes some time to fully explain it. Let's meet up some time and talk about it.

M: Why don't we do it tomorrow? Can you ______________ at 4 tomorrow to the school library after school?

W: I don't think I can make it by then. Can we ______________ by 30 minutes?

M: Yes, that's fine too. Thanks a lot, Kristin!

남: 와, Kristin, 너 벌써 수학 프로젝트 끝낸 것 같이 보인다.

여: 어, Tyler! 그래 맞아. 나 그거 어제 끝냈어.

남: 넌 어떻게 그렇게 하니? 난 항상 모든 걸 마지막에야 끝내는데.

여: 나도 그랬었어. 하지만 난 요즘 시간을 돈처럼 취급하려고 노력하는 중이야.

남: 시간을 관리하는 법에 대해 조언 좀 해 줄 수 있어?

여: 음, 완벽히 설명하려면 좀 시간이 걸려. 다음에 만나서 얘기하자.

남: 내일 만나면 어때? 내일 방과 후 4시에 학교 도서관에서 만날 수 있어?

여: 그때까지는 못 갈 거 같아. 30분 정도 미룰 수 있을까?

남: 그래, 괜찮아. 고마워, Kristin!

대화상황
- 주어진 기일 내에 과제를 수행하는 습관을 가진 친구에게 시간 관리법에 대한 조언을 구하는 상황

표현정리
- I got it done.: 「get + 목적어 + 과거분사」의 구문은 '~를 … 된 상태로 만들다'라는 의미이다.
- I used to be like that.: 「used to + 동사원형」은 '(과거에) ~하곤 했다'라는 뜻으로 과거의 습관이나 상태를 나타낸다.

정답 like money / make it /push it back

교과서 핵심 정리

Reading Comprehension

*해석을 참조하여 빈칸에 알맞은 말을 쓰거나 괄호에서 알맞은 말을 고르시오.

P.35 L.1~6

Seize the Day!

Imagine that you have a bank account. And let's say that this is the only bank account that you have. Every morning, exactly 86,400 won goes into it, and every night, all of the money __________. You cannot __________ the money for the next day. If this is the case, you would want to try very hard to spend your money ____________ and get the most out of it during the day.

오늘을 즐겨라!

당신에게 은행 계좌가 있다고 상상해 보라. 그리고 이것은 당신이 가진 유일한 계좌라고 해 보자. 아침마다, 정확히 86,400원이 그 통장으로 들어가고, 매일 밤, 모든 돈은 사라진다. 다음 날을 위해 그 돈을 저축해 놓을 수도 없다. 만약 이런 경우라면, 당신은 하루 동안 당신의 돈을 현명하게 쓰기 위해 열심히 노력할 것이고 그 돈을 최대한 활용하고 싶어 할 것이다.

단락요약 • 아침마다 일정한 액수의 돈이 주어지고 하루 동안 그것을 모두 써야만 하는 상황이라면 사람들은 낮 동안 그 돈을 최대한 현명하게 쓰려고 노력할 것이다.

구문정리 • ~ get the most out of it에서 it은 하루에 주어진 86,400원이라는 액수의 돈을 가리킨다.

정답 disappears / save / wisely

P.35 L.7~18

Time works just the same way. Every morning, exactly 86,400 seconds are given to you. It may not seem valuable because you will get the exact __________ amount the next day. However, you only have a limited amount of time in a day, and you cannot save any part of it. Therefore, you should seize the day! In order to do so, you need to learn ways to manage this limited and precious time. Although failing to manage time is a huge waste, (spend/spending) it wisely is often difficult. Sometimes, you struggle with too much work to do. At other times, you find yourself passing the time without any pressure because there is no urgent task to fulfill. So what is the best way to lead our daily lives with these 86,400 seconds?

시간은 바로 그와 같은 방식으로 작동한다. 매일 아침, 정확히 86,400초가 당신에게 주어진다. 다음 날 정확히 같은 금액을 받기 때문에 가치 있게 보이지 않을 수도 있다. 하지만, 여러분은 하루에 제한된 양의 시간만을 가지는 것이고, 그것의 일부를 저축해 둘 수도 없다. 그러므로, 오늘을 즐겨야 한다! 그렇게 하려면, 당신은 이 제한된 귀한 시간을 관리하는 법을 배울 필요가 있다. 비록 시간을 관리하지 못하는 것이 엄청난 낭비이긴 하지만, 그것을 현명하게 보내는 것은 종종 어렵다. 가끔, 당신은 해야 할 많은 양의 일 때문에 쩔쩔 맨다. 어떤 때는 완수해야 할 긴급한 일이 없어서 아무런 부담 없이 시간을 보내는 자신을 보게 될 수도 있다. 그래서 이 86,400초를 가지고 우리의 하루의 삶을 이끌어 갈 최상의 방법은 무엇인가?

단락요약 • 돈과 마찬가지로 하루라는 시간도 제한된 양만 주어지고, 나중을 위해 저축해 놓을 수도 없는 것이므로 시간 관리를 현명하게 할 필요가 있다.

구문정리 • ~ you find yourself passing ~에서 「find oneself -ing」(~ 하고 있는 자신을 발견하다)에서 -ing는 진행의 의미를 가진 현재분사이다.

정답 same / spending

P.36 L.1~10

Here are some tips that will help you manage your time more effectively.

1. Plan Ahead

Figure out the amount of time you need for your activities and make a weekly plan. This way, you'll be able to take greater _______ of your time and perform your responsibilities in a timely fashion. Without __________, you may find yourself easily caught up with more than one task and end up finishing none of them. You see some people keeping a calendar or making a daily to-do list. These are also good ways to organize your schedule in advance. Don't forget that for every minute you spend (to organize/organizing), an hour is earned.

여기 여러분으로 하여금 시간을 좀 더 효과적으로 관리하게 해 줄 팁이 있다.

1. 미리 계획하라.

활동을 위해 필요한 시간의 양을 파악해서 주간 계획을 만들어라. 이렇게 하면, 당신은 시간에 대해 더 큰 통제권을 쥘 수가 있고 해야 할 일들을 시간에 맞춰 수행할 수 있다. 계획이 없으면 여러분은 아마 틀림없이 한 개 이상의 일에 쫓겨 어떤 것도 끝마치지 못하게 될 것이다. 여러분은 어떤 사람들이 달력에 기록하거나 매일 해야 할 일을 목록으로 작성하는 것을 볼 것이다. 이런 것도 스케줄을 미리 조직하는 좋은 방법들이다. 당신이 계획하는 데 보내는 일 분이 한 시간을 벌어줄 수도 있다는 것을 잊지 말라.

단락요약 • 시간 관리법의 첫 번째 요소인 '미리 계획하기의 장점과 중요성'에 대해 말하고 있다.

구문정리
- Figure out the amount of time (that) you need for your activities ~ : time을 수식하는 관계대명사 that이 생략된 형태이다.
- ~ end up finishing ~ : 「end up -ing」(결국 ~이 되다'–다소 부정적이거나 실망스러운 결과를 말할 때 사용)에서 -ing는 동명사이다.

정답 control / planning / organizing

P.36 L.11~20

2. Put Your Responsibilities in the Order of ________

Divide your activities into four categories: (1) important and urgent, (2) important but not urgent, (3) unimportant but urgent, and (4) unimportant and not urgent. Those that fall under the first category are your top responsibilities. Make sure that all of these are met before you move on to those that are less important or urgent. For example, let's say there will be an exam next week. You might want to study (important and urgent) first before you hang out with your friends (important but not urgent). It is easy to do the things you want to do first. However, categorizing will prevent you from (lost/losing) focus and will help you accomplish the things that actually matter.

2. 너의 임무를 중요도의 순서로 배열하라.

여러분의 활동을 네 개의 범주, 즉 (1) 중요하고 급박한 일, (2) 중요하지만 급박하지 않은 일, (3) 중요하지 않으나 급박한 일, (4) 중요하지도 않고 급박하지도 않은 일로 나뉘어보라. 첫 번째 범주에 속하는 일들은 여러분이 가장 먼저 해야 할 일들이다. 이 일들을 다 한 후에야 덜 중요하거나 덜 급박한 일로 옮겨갈 수 있다는 걸 명심하라. 예를 들어, 다음 주에 시험이 있다고 하자. 당신은 친구들과 어울려 놀기(중요하지만 급박하지는 않은 일) 전에 먼저 공부(중요하고 긴박한) 하기를 원할 것이다. 하고 싶은 일을 먼저 하는 것은 쉽다. 하지만, 이렇게 범주화하는 것은 초점을 잃지 않게 해 주고, 진짜로 중요한 것들을 성취하도록 도와줄 것이다.

단락요약
- 해야 할 일들을 중요도의 순서에 따라 4개의 범주로 분류하는 방법을 말하고 있다

구문정리
- Those that fall under the first category are your top responsibilities. : Those는 your activities를 대신해서 쓰인 대명사이고, that으로 시작하는 관계대명사절의 수식을 받는 선행사로서 '~ 한 것들'이라고 해석을 하면 된다. 주어 Those가 복수이므로 동사 are가 쓰였다.
  cf. Those who ~ : ~ 한 사람들
- Categorizing will prevent you from losing focus and ~ : 「prevent *A* from -ing」는 'A가 ~하지 않도록 막다'라는 의미로 전치사 from 때문에 동명사형인 losing이 쓰였다.
- ~ and will help you accomplish the things that actually matter.: that은 여기서 주격 관계대명사로 쓰였고, 동사 matter는 '중요하다'라는 의미로 the things that matter는 '중요한 것들'이라고 해석을 하면 된다.

정답 importance/losing

P.37 L.1~14

3. Make Every Second Count

Use your spare time wisely. Sometimes you may find yourself having only ten minutes before the next activity. You may think that nothing much can be (doing/done) during this short time. However, you can actually do many things in just ten minutes, like writing a paragraph for an assignment or solving about five math problems. You can even do some reading on the subway.

3. 매 순간을 소중한 순간으로 만들라.

남는 시간을 지혜롭게 사용하라. 가끔 여러분은 다음 할 일을 시작하기 전에 10분 정도 있다는 것을 알게 된다. 여러분은 이렇게 짧은 시간 동안에는 할 수 있는 것이 별로 없다고 생각할지도 모른다. 하지만, 이 10분 동안 실제로 과제를 위해 한 단락 글쓰기나 약 5개의 수학 문제 풀이 같은 여러 가지 일을 할 수 있다. 심지어 지하철에서 독서도 할 수 있다.

4. Find Your Most Productive Time

You'll be able to concentrate better and work more ________ when you are at your best. When do you feel you can do your best work? If you think you can handle writing papers better in the morning, don't wait until late at night to do it. If you think you are a night person, then schedule your study time for late hours because that's when you can be most productive.

4. 가장 생산적인 시간을 찾아라.

여러분은 상태가 가장 좋을 때 더 잘 집중하고 더 효율적으로 일할 수 있다. 당신은 언제 가장 일을 잘 할 수 있다고 느끼는가? 만일 아침에 논문 쓰는 것을 잘 할 수 있다고 생각한다면 그것을 하기 위해 밤까지 기다릴 필요가 없다. 만약 당신이 야간에 활동적인 사람이라면 그 때가 당신이 가장 생산적일 수 있는 시간이므로 공부 시간을 늦은 시간으로 계획하라.

단락요약
- 자투리 시간도 소중한 시간으로 활용해야 하고, 일의 효율성을 위해 자신이 가장 생산적이 될 수 있는 시간을 찾아 그때 중요한 일을 하는 것이 좋다.

구문정리
- Make Every Second Count.: 「사역동사 make + 목적어 + 동사원형」의 구문으로 '~를 …하도록 만들다'라는 의미이다. 여기서 count는 '중요하다'라는 의미의 자동사로 쓰였다.
- You may think (that) nothing much can be done in just ten minutes.: '-thing'으로 끝나는 명사는 수식하는 형용사가 뒤에 오는데 여기서는 much가 nothing을 수식하여 '많은 아무 것(도 ~하지 않다)'라는 뜻이다. *cf.* something good 좋은 (어떤) 것
- ~ because that's when you can be most productive.: 'that's when ~'은 '그때가 ~할 때이다'라는 의미이다.

정답 done/efficiently

P.38 L.1~19

Jinu's Diary

What a productive day!

April 10

I used my time in a very productive way today! It was all thanks to an article I read the other day. It had a lot of useful tips on effective time management. After reading it, I decided to put my responsibilities in the order of importance and plan ahead. I was really stressed out because I had assignments in both History and English. So, I first wrote down the activities I had to do and then put them into four different categories based on their __________ and __________. I figured out that doing research for my history paper was my top responsibility. My English assignment was the second most important thing. After that, I made a schedule for the day by assigning more time to my top responsibilities.

It was a great success! First, I was able to finish my research for the history assignment. All I have to do now is arrange the information in an organized fashion and make it readable. Also, I finished some reading for my English class. After finishing these important activities, I spent some quality time with my family. I learned that good __________ works wonders.

진우의 일기

참 생산적인 하루였어!

4월 10일

난 오늘 하루를 아주 생산적인 방식으로 시간을 썼다. 그건 모두 며칠 전 읽은 기사 덕분이다. 그 기사는 효과적인 시간 관리에 대한 유용한 조언들로 가득했다. 그것을 읽고 나서 나는 내 할 일들을 중요도의 순서대로 배열하고 미리 계획을 짜기로 결심했다. 난 역사와 영어 과목에 숙제가 있어서 정말 스트레스를 받고 있었다. 그래서 난 내가 해야 할 일들을 적은 후 긴급성과 중요도에 기초하여 네 가지의 다른 항목에 집어넣었다. 난 역사 보고서를 쓰기 위해 조사하는 일이 가장 급선무임을 알게 되었다. 영어 숙제는 두 번째로 중요한 일이었다. 그 다음에 나는 제일 먼저 할 일에 더 많은 시간을 할애하여 하루 동안의 계획을 짰다. 그것은 대성공이었다. 우선, 난 역사 숙제를 위한 조사를 마칠 수 있었다. 이제 내가 해야 하는 것은 조사한 정보를 조직적인 형태로 배열하여 그것을 읽을 수 있게 만드는 것이다. 또한 나는 영어 수업을 위한 약간의 독서를 끝냈다. 이 중요한 일들을 마치고 난 후, 난 가족과 소중한 시간을 가졌다. 난 훌륭한 계획이 놀라운 일을 만들어낸다는 것을 배웠다.

단락요약

- 효율적인 시간 관리 방법에 대한 기사를 읽고 자신의 하루 생활에 성공적으로 적용한 후 느낀 점에 대해 쓴 일기문이다.

구문정리

- ~ by assigning more time to my top responsibilities : 'by -ing'는 '~함으로써'라는 의미로 방법을 표현한다.
- ~ good planning works wonders : 'work'은 여기에서 '작동하게 하다'라는 의미로 'work wonders'는 '놀라운 일이 일어나도록 하다'라는 뜻이다.

정답 urgency / importance / planning

P.38 L.20~24

We all have a limited amount of time in a day. We cannot repeat a single second from yesterday. Also, we cannot use tomorrow's time in advance. At the end of the day, the things we did or didn't do cannot be changed. Therefore, we need to do our best with the time we have each day. Time does not wait for us. If there is no today, there is no tomorrow. We need to be thankful for today. That is __________ we call the present the "present."

우리는 모두 하루에 한정된 시간을 갖는다. 우리는 어제로부터 한 순간도 반복할 수 없다. 또한, 우리는 내일의 시간을 미리 사용할 수도 없다. 하루가 끝날 때, 우리가 한 일과 하지 않은 일은 바뀔 수 없다. 그러므로, 우리는 우리가 매일 가지는 시간에 최선을 다해야 한다. 시간은 우리를 기다려주지 않는다. 오늘이 없으면 내일도 없다. 우리는 오늘이 있는 것에 감사할 필요가 있다. 그것이 우리가 현재를 '선물'이라고 부르는 것이다.

단락요약

- 한정된 시간을 효율적으로 관리하려면 늘 현재에 최선을 다해야 한다.

구문정리

- ~ the things (that) we did or didn't do cannot be changed. : the things를 수식하는 관계대명사 that이 생략된 상태로 쓰였고, cannot be changed의 주어는 the things이다.
- That is why we call the present the "present." : 「That is why +주어 +동사」의 구문은 '그래서 ~가 …한 것이다'라는 의미이고 이때 관계부사 why는 the reason으로 바꿔 쓸 수 있다. 또한 「call+*A*+*B*」는 'A를 B라고 부르다'는 뜻이다.

정답 why

Focus on Structure

P. 35 L.2 Let's say | that this is the only bank account | **that** you have.
접속사 / 선행사 / 관계대명사(목적격) 주어 동사

➔ 선행사를 뒤에서 수식하는 관계대명사절에서 관계대명사는 선행사와의 관계에 따라 주격, 목적격, 소유격으로 구분하여 쓴다. 이 중 목적격 관계대명사는 생략할 수 있다. 목적격 관계대명사 뒤에는 주어와 동사가 이어진다.

ex. Here are some tips **that** will help you manage your time effectively. : 주격 관계대명사 + 동사 (생략 불가)

They are searching a man **whose** first name is Jake. : 소유격 관계대명사 + 명사 (생략 불가)

P.35 L.13 At other times, you **find** yourself | **passing** the time | without any pressure.
find / 목적어 / 목적격보어(현재분사) / 전치사구

➔ 동사 find 역시 지각동사와 비슷하게 목적어의 행동을 나타낼 때 목적격보어를 현재분사(-ing) 형태로 사용하고, 특징이나 상태를 나타낼 때는 형용사를 사용한다. 특히 「find oneself -ing」는 '~하고 있는 자신을 발견하다'라는 뜻으로 주어에 따라 oneself의 형태가 바뀐다.

ex. The professor **found** the students using their cell phones during the lecture.

그 교수는 학생들이 강의 중에 휴대 전화를 사용하는 것을 알게 되었다.

The judge **found** the young lawyer very arrogant.

그 판사는 그 젊은 변호사가 매우 거만하다는 것을 알게 되었다.

*arrogant 오만한, 거만한

P.36 L.7 You **see** | some people | **keeping** a calendar | or **making** a daily to-do list.
지각동사 목적어 / 현재분사① / 접속사 현재분사②

➔ see, watch, hear, listen to, feel 등의 지각동사는 목적어의 행동을 나타내는 목적격보어를 현재분사(-ing)나 동사원형의 형태로 쓴다. 하지만 목적어의 상태나 이미 완료된 일을 나타낼 경우는 목적격보어를 과거분사의 형태로 쓴다.

ex. She **felt** something moving slowly in the box. 그녀는 상자 안에서 뭔가가 천천히 움직이는 걸 느꼈다.
지각동사 / 목적어 / 현재분사

The girl **saw** her ice cream melted completely. 그 소녀는 자기 아이스크림이 다 녹아버린 것을 보았다.
지각동사 / 목적어 / 과거분사

☑ Check-Up

정답 P. 225

1 다음 괄호 안의 단어들을 순서대로 바르게 배열하시오.

(1) She put (her grandma / sent / that / the plant) on the dining table.
(2) They are building (that / teach / robots / social / skills) to children.

2 다음 밑줄 친 부분을 바르게 고쳐 쓰시오.

(1) Did you hear him to speak in Indian-English accent?
(2) People saw the car abandoning at the corner of the street.
(3) I found the article very bored.

Tip

❶ (1) 목적격 관계대명사의 쓰임
(2) 주격 관계대명사의 쓰임

❷ (1) 지각동사+목적어+현재분사
(2) 지각동사+목적어+과거분사
(3) find +목적어+분사/형용사
accent 억양
abandon 버리다, 유기하다
article 기사문

언어 기능별 집중 대비

Listen and Speak/Into Real Life

정답 P. 226

1 대화를 듣고, 여자의 마지막 말에 대한 남자의 응답으로 가장 알맞은 것을 고르시오.

① Take your time.
② That'll work for me.
③ I can't wait for the show!
④ I really enjoyed doing it.
⑤ I'm afraid I can't make it by then.

2 대화를 듣고, 남자가 여자에게 구하는 조언의 내용으로 가장 알맞은 것을 고르시오.

① How to lead a healthy life
② How to read articles critically
③ How to stay positive and smile more
④ How to deal with daily stress effectively
⑤ How to solve the sleep deprivation problem

3 대화를 듣고, 여자의 어조로 가장 알맞은 것을 고르시오.

① upset　② relaxed
③ frustrated　④ disappointed
⑤ apologetic

4 다음을 듣고, 물음에 답하시오.

(1) 강의의 주제로 가장 알맞은 것은?
① Reflect on your learning style.
② Help shy people to be more outgoing.
③ Use mind maps to improve your long-term memory.
④ Find more about how to get rid of your bad habits.
⑤ Match your learning strategies with your personality type.

(2) 외향적인 성격의 사람에게 추천하고 있는 학습 방법을 모두 고르시오.
① 마인드맵 만들기
② 친구들 가르치기
③ 주제에 관해 토론하기
④ 원래의 일상적인 공부법을 고수하기
⑤ 배운 개념에 대해 스스로 질문해 보기

Tip

❶ 마지막 말에 대한 응답 고르기
출처: Get Ready_1

❷ 대화의 내용 파악하기
출처: Listen In_Dialogue 1
critically 비판적으로
sleep deprivation 수면 부족

❸ 화자의 어조 파악하기
출처: Listen In_Dialogue 2
frustrated 좌절한, 분노한
relaxed 편안한, 느긋한
apologetic 사과하는, 미안해하는

❹ (1) 주제 고르기
(2) 구체적인 정보 파악하기
출처: Into Real Life_Step 1
reflect on ~에 대해 성찰하다, 돌이켜 생각해 보다
long-term memory 장기 기억
get rid of ~을 없애다, 제거하다

언어 기능별 집중 대비

Read and Think

정답 P. 226

Tip

⑫ 출처: P.35 L.2-10
유형: 1. 문장의 위치 파악
2. 연결사 추론
consequently 결과적으로
likewise 또한, 비슷하게

[1-2] 다음 글을 읽고, 물음에 답하시오.

Imagine that you have a bank account. And let's say that this is the only bank account that you have. (A) Every morning, exactly 86,400 won goes into it, and every night, all of the money disappears. (B) You cannot save the money for the next day. (C)If this is the case, you would want to try very hard to spend your money wisely and get the most out of it during the day. (D) Every morning, exactly 86,400 seconds are given to you. (E) It may not seem valuable because you will get the exact same amount the next day. ___ⓐ___, you only have a limited amount of time in a day, and you cannot save any part of it. ___ⓑ___, you should seize the day!

1 윗글의 (A) ~ (E) 중 아래의 문장이 들어가기에 가장 알맞은 곳은?

Time works just the same way.

① (A) ② (B) ③ (C) ④ (D) ⑤ (E)

2 윗글의 빈칸 ⓐ와 ⓑ에 알맞은 말이 차례대로 연결된 것은?

① However – Therefore
② Consequently – Finally
③ Therefore – However
④ Likewise – However
⑤ Likewise – Finally

㉞ 출처: P.36 L.3-10
유형: 3. 빈칸 추론
4. 글의 제목 구하기

[3-4] 다음 글을 읽고, 물음에 답하시오.

Figure out the amount of time you need for your activities and make a weekly plan. This way, you'll be able to take greater control of your time and perform your responsibilities in a timely fashion. Without planning, you may find yourself easily ⓐ (catching / caught) up with more than one task and end up finishing none of them. You see some people ⓑ (keeping / to keep) a calendar or making a daily to-do list. These are also good ways to organize your schedule in advance. Don't forget that for every minute you spend organizing, an hour is ⓒ (earned / earning).

3 윗글의 괄호 안의 ⓐ ~ ⓒ에 알맞은 말이 차례대로 연결된 것은?

① caught – to keep – earning
② caught – to keep – earned
③ caught – keeping – earned
④ catching – to keep – earning
⑤ catching – keeping – earned

4 윗글의 제목으로 가장 알맞은 것은?

① Plan Ahead
② Keep Things Organized
③ Focus on the Present
④ Make Every Second Count
⑤ Track How Long Tasks Take

Tip

5 다음 글의 밑줄 친 ①~⑤ 중 어휘의 쓰임이 잘못된 것은?

Divide your activities into four categories: (1) important and urgent, (2) important but not urgent, (3) unimportant but urgent, and (4) unimportant and not urgent. Those that fall under the first category are your ① top responsibilities. Make sure that all of these are met before you move on to those that are ② more important or urgent. For example, let's say there will be an exam next week. You might want to study (important and urgent) first ③ before you hang out with your friends (important but not urgent). It is ④ easy to do the things you want to do first. However, categorizing will prevent you from ⑤ losing focus and will help you accomplish the things that actually matter.

① ② ③ ④ ⑤

5 출처: P.36 L.12-20
유형: 어휘의 쓰임
urgent 긴급한

6 다음 글의 밑줄 친 부분 중 어법상 어색한 것은?

Use your spare time ① wisely. Sometimes you may find yourself ② having only ten minutes before the next activity. You may think that ③ nothing much can be done during this short time. However, you can actually do many things in just ten minutes, like writing a paragraph for an assignment or ④ solve about five math problems. You can ⑤ even do some reading on the subway.

① ② ③ ④ ⑤

6 출처: P.37 L.2-7
유형: 문법성 판단

7 다음 글을 아래와 같이 요약할 때 문장의 빈칸에 가장 알맞은 것은?

You'll be able to concentrate better and work more efficiently when you are at your best. When do you feel you can do your best work? If you think you can handle writing papers better in the morning, don't wait until late at night to do it. If you think you are a night person, then schedule your study time for late hours because that's when you can be most productive.

→ Understand ____________________ in which you feel most productive, and plan your tasks accordingly.

① the periods of the day
② the place in the office
③ types of work you like
④ your moods in the morning
⑤ the way you deal with problems

7 출처: P.37 L.9-14
유형: 요약문 완성
accordingly 그에 맞게, 그것에 따라

Tip

8 다음 글의 빈칸에 가장 알맞은 것은?

Jinu's Diary

April 10

I used my time in a very productive way today! It was all thanks to an article I read the other day. It had a lot of useful tips on ________________. After reading it, I decided to put my responsibilities in the order of importance and plan ahead. I was really stressed out because I had assignments in both History and English. So, I first wrote down the activities I had to do and then put them into four different categories based on their urgency and importance. I figured out that doing research for my history paper was my top responsibility. My English assignment was the second most important thing. After that, I made a schedule for the day by assigning more time to my top responsibilities.

① managing stress
② assignment research
③ effective time management
④ improving academic skills
⑤ how to write an academic paper

⑧ 출처: P.38 L.1-12
유형: 빈칸 추론

9 다음 글의 내용과 가장 관련이 깊은 속담은?

We all have a limited amount of time in a day. We cannot repeat a single second from yesterday. Also, we cannot use tomorrow's time in advance. At the end of the day, the things we did or didn't do cannot be changed. Therefore, we need to do our best with the time we have each day. If there is no today, there is no tomorrow. We need to be thankful for today. That is why we call the present the "present."

① Better late than never.
② Time and tide wait for no man.
③ The early bird catches the worm.
④ Don't put all your eggs in one basket.
⑤ Hope for the best, prepare for the worst.

⑨ 출처: P.38 L.20-24
유형: 관련 속담 찾기

언어 기능별 집중 대비

Language Notes Write It Right

정답 P.227

1 다음 우리말에 맞게 괄호 안의 단어를 이용하여 문장을 완성하시오.

(1) Paul은 자신이 혼잣말 하고 있는 것을 발견했다.
Paul found ____________________ to himself. (talk)

(2) 그는 그것들이 다른 방향으로 날아가는 것을 보았다.
He saw ____________________ in the other direction. (fly)

(3) 내가 좋아하는 그 고양이는 Maggie 이모네 고양이다.
The cat ____________________ belongs to Aunt Maggie. (fond of)

(4) 자동 주행하는 자동차는 교통량을 최소화 할 수 있다.
Cars ____________________ themselves can minimize traffic. (drive)

(5) 내가 최근에 읽은 책 중 하나는 '오만과 편견'이다.
One of the books ____________________ is 'Pride and Prejudice.' (read)

Tip

❶ (1) find +목적어+ 현재분사
(2) 지각동사+목적어+현재분사
(3) 전치사의 목적격 관계대명사+주어+동사
(4) 주격 관계대명사+동사
(5) 목적격 관계대명사+주어+동사
talk to oneself 혼잣말하다
be fond of ~를 좋아하다
minimize 최소화하다, 줄이다
prejudice 편견, 선입견

2 다음 글을 읽고, 물음에 답하시오.

Imagine you have a big empty pickle jar that you have to fill up by using golf balls, marbles, sand, and water. You have to use as much of all four of these items as you can. Drop in as many golf balls as you can. After that, drop in some marbles and shake the jar so that the marbles can drop into the gaps that are left by the golf balls. Next, take some sand. Pour it into the even smaller spaces that are left. Finally, finish it off with water. This way, you have a full pickle jar without wasting any space.

The pickle jar itself represents your time. The golf balls are the things that are most important to you. The marbles mean the things you need to do but don't have to. The sand stands for all the small, time-taking tasks that are easy to do but not as important. The water is for anything that takes time but that doesn't really add anything, such as the hours you waste online. What will you fill your jar with for the rest of today?

(1) Among golf balls, marbles, sand, and water, which one represents the top responsibility?

____

(2) What does it mean 'to pour water into the jar last'?

____

❷ marble 대리석, 구슬
pour 붓다
represent 나타내다, 상징하다
stand for 상징하다
time-taking 시간이 걸리는

Basic

1 대화를 듣고, 여자의 마지막 말에 이어질 남자의 말로 가장 알맞은 것을 고르시오.

① That works for me, too.
② Don't worry. Take your time.
③ That's fine. I'll take care of it.
④ Thank you so much! It means a lot to me.
⑤ I cannot agree with you more. Thank you.

2 대화를 듣고, 대화의 내용과 일치하지 않는 것을 고르시오.

① 여자가 약속 시간에 늦고 있다.
② 여자는 남자에게 사과하고 있다.
③ 여자의 오빠가 아파서 집에 누워있다.
④ 여자는 늦는 것에 대해 미리 얘기를 하지 않았었다.
⑤ 여자가 4시까지는 올 수 있다고 말하고 있다.

3 다음 단어의 뜻이 잘못 연결된 것은?

① seize : 붙잡다
② urgent : 느긋한
③ concentrate : 집중하다
④ struggle : 분투하다, 애쓰다
⑤ responsibility : 책임, 의무

4 다음 숙어의 뜻이 잘못 연결된 것은?

① thanks to : ~덕분에
② in advance : 미리, 사전에
③ figure out : 이해하다, 알아내다
④ hang out : 어울려 놀다, 시간을 보내다
⑤ get the most out of : ~를 최대한 늦추다

5 다음 중 반의어끼리 바르게 연결된 것은?

① wise – smart
② success – failure
③ limited – finite
④ huge – gigantic
⑤ assignment – homework

6 다음 글의 괄호 안의 단어들을 사용하여 빈칸을 완성하시오.

Figure out the amount of time you need for your activities and make a weekly plan. This way, you'll be able to take greater control of your time and perform your responsibilities in a timely fashion. Without planning, you may find yourself easily caught up with more than one task and ________________ (finishing/end/up/them/none/of).

7 다음 글의 빈칸에 가장 알맞은 것은?

Divide your activities into four categories: (1) important and urgent, (2) important but not urgent, (3) unimportant but urgent, and (4) unimportant and not urgent. ________________ are your top responsibilities. Make sure that all of these are met before you move on to those that are less important or urgent.

① Those that fall under the first category
② Those that belong to the fourth category
③ Those that are neither urgent nor important
④ Those that are very important but not urgent
⑤ Those that are less urgent than other things

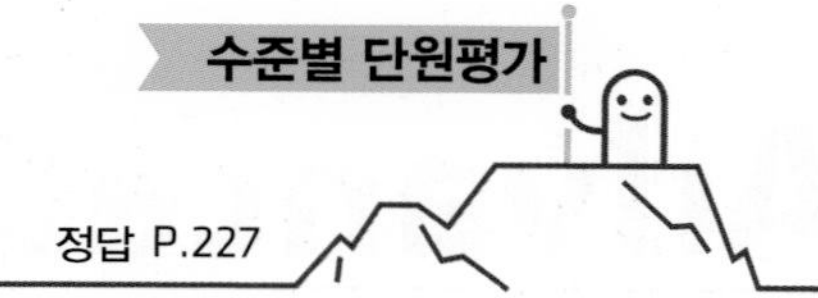

정답 P.227

8 다음 중 어법상 어색한 문장은?

① Nobody saw her enter the room.
② I heard him singing an old pop song.
③ Peter heard someone to call his name.
④ She felt something moving in her pocket.
⑤ He watched them playing soccer on the field.

9 다음 밑줄 친 부분 중 생략할 수 없는 것은?

① Let's stay in the hotel that Mike recommended.
② I bought a plant that grows well in dry places.
③ The mirror that you broke was an expensive one.
④ Let me show you the book that my uncle wrote.
⑤ This is the camera that my mom bought for me.

10 다음 글의 밑줄 친 ⓐ와 ⓑ두 단어의 뜻을 각각 우리말로 쓰시오.

We all have a limited amount of time in a day. We cannot repeat a single second from yesterday. Also, we cannot use tomorrow's time in advance. At the end of the day, the things we did or didn't do cannot be changed. Therefore, we need to do our best with the time we have each day. Time does not wait for us. If there is no today, there is no tomorrow. We need to be thankful for today. That is why we call ⓐ the present ⓑ the "present".

ⓐ the present : ____________________
ⓑ the "present": ____________________

[11~12] 다음 글을 읽고 물음에 답하시오.

Jinu's Diary

I used my time in a very productive way today! It was all thanks to an article I read the other day. It had a lot of useful tips on effective time management. After reading it, I decided to put my responsibilities in the order of importance and plan ahead. I was really stressed out because I had assignments in both History and English. (A) So, I first wrote down the activities I had to do and then put them into four different categories based on their urgency and importance. (B) I figured out that doing research for my history paper was my top responsibility. (C) My English assignment was the second most important thing. (D) After that, I made a schedule for the day by assigning more time to my top responsibilities. (E) First, I was able to finish my research for the history assignment. All I have to do now is arrange the information in an organized fashion and make it readable. Also, I finished some reading for my English class. After finishing these important activities, I spent some quality time with my family. I learned that good planning works wonders.

11 윗글의 (A) ~ (E) 중 아래의 문장이 들어가기에 가장 알맞은 곳은?

It was a great success!

① (A) ② (B) ③ (C) ④ (D) ⑤ (E)

12 윗글의 내용과 일치하지 않는 것은?

① Jinu read an article on effective time management.
② Jinu wrote down a to-do list before he scheduled for the day.
③ Jinu categorized what he had to do before he started doing his homework.
④ Jinu assigned more time to his top responsibilities.
⑤ Jinu spent some quality time with his family before he finished his History assignment.

Advanced

[1~2] 다음을 듣고, 물음에 답하시오.

1 남자가 한 말의 요지로 가장 알맞은 것을 고르시오.

① Teach your friends how to concentrate better.
② Find out what learning style best suits an outgoing person.
③ Ask yourself questions about the concept you learned today.
④ Make mind maps whenever you process the learning content.
⑤ Develop your own learning style that suits your personality type.

2 남자가 한 말의 내용과 일치하지 않는 것을 고르시오.

① 외향적인 학습자에게는 토론 학습이 적절하다.
② 외향적인 학습자에게는 남을 가르치는 학습방법이 좋다.
③ 내성적인 학습자는 마인드맵 활용 학습이 도움이 된다.
④ 사색적인 학습자는 배운 개념을 남에게 설명해가면서 학습하는 게 좋다.
⑤ 자신에게 익숙한 학습 방법이 늘 최상의 학습 방법은 아닐 수 있다.

3 대화를 듣고, 대화의 내용과 일치하는 것을 고르시오.

① Kristin hasn't finished her math project yet.
② Tyler usually finishes things long before the deadlines.
③ Kristin is going to give some tips to Tyler on time management tomorrow.
④ Kristin and Tyler are going to meet at 4:00 tomorrow.
⑤ Kristin wants to meet Tyler 30 minutes earlier than suggested.

4 다음 대화의 빈칸에 가장 알맞은 것은?

A: ____________________

B: This might make you sad, but the article says it is working. We spend 26 years working when we consider people live for 80 years on average.

A: Really? I'm surprised it's not sleep. What do we spend the least time on, then?

B: It says it's smiling. We only spend about 88 days doing this.

A: That is very disappointing.

① What do we spend most of our time on?
② What is the most interesting thing to do?
③ How long is the working hours on average?
④ How many hours do we spend working a day?
⑤ How often do people think about quitting jobs?

5 다음 글의 빈칸에 가장 알맞은 것은?

Figure out the amount of time you need for your activities and make a weekly plan. This way, you'll be able to take greater control of your time and perform your responsibilities ____________________. Without planning, you may find yourself easily caught up with more than one task and end up finishing none of them.

① in a great hurry
② in a timely fashion
③ without any difficulty
④ regardless of time limit
⑤ with less effort than before

[6~8] 다음 글을 읽고, 물음에 답하시오.

Imagine that you have a bank account. And let's say that this is ⓐ the only bank account that you have. Every morning, exactly ⓑ 86,400 won goes into it, and every night, ⓒ all of the money disappears. You cannot save the money for the next day. If this is the case, you would want to try very hard to spend your money wisely and get the most out of it during the day.

Time works just the same way. Every morning, exactly 86,400 seconds are given to you. It may not seem valuable because you will get the exact same amount the next day. However, you only have a limited amount of time in a day, and you cannot save any part of it. Therefore, you should seize the day! In order to do so, you need to learn ways to manage this limited and precious time. Although failing to manage time is a huge waste, ⓓ spend it wisely is often difficult. Sometimes, you struggle with too much work to do. At other times, you find yourself passing the time without any pressure because there is no urgent task to fulfill. So what is the best way to lead our daily lives with these 86,400 seconds?

6 윗글의 밑줄 친 ⓐ~ⓒ가 상징하는 것이 무엇인지 각각 쓰시오.

ⓐ ______________

ⓑ ______________

ⓒ ______________

7 윗글의 밑줄 친 ⓓ를 바르게 고쳐 쓰시오.

______________ → ______________

8 윗글에서 다음 영영풀이에 해당하는 한 단어를 찾아 쓰시오.

- an arrangement with a bank to keep your money there
- a description of something that happened

→ ______________

[9~11] 다음 글을 읽고, 물음에 답하시오.

Divide your activities into four categories: (1) important and urgent, (2) important but not urgent, (3) unimportant but urgent, and (4) unimportant and not urgent. ______ ⓐ ______ are your top responsibilities. Make sure that all of these are met before you move on to those that are less important or urgent. ___ⓑ___, let's say there will be an exam next week. You might want to study (important and urgent) first before you hang out with your friends (important but not urgent). It is easy to do the things you want to do first. ___ⓒ___, categorizing will prevent you from losing focus and will help you accomplish the things that actually matter.

9 윗글의 빈칸 ⓐ에 알맞은 말을 아래 주어진 단어들을 배열하여 쓰시오.

the / first / that / those / fall / under / category

→ ______________________________

10 윗글의 빈칸 ⓑ와 ⓒ에 들어갈 말이 차례대로 연결된 것은?

① For example – However
② In addition – Therefore
③ However – For instance
④ Therefore – Nevertheless
⑤ For instance – On the contrary

11 윗글의 제목을 아래와 같이 쓸 때 괄호 안의 단어들을 사용하여 빈칸에 알맞은 말을 쓰시오.

Put Your ______________________________

(of / Order / in / Responsibilities / the / Importance)

12 다음 〈보기〉의 밑줄 친 단어와 같은 의미로 쓰인 것은?

> **보기** The meeting was run in quite a casual <u>fashion</u>.

① His hair is cut in the latest <u>fashion</u>.
② The army behaved in a brutal <u>fashion</u>.
③ Short skirts have come back into <u>fashion</u>.
④ Jewelry and clothing <u>fashions</u> vary with the season.
⑤ Those tight jeans went out of <u>fashion</u> years ago.

[13~14] 다음 글을 읽고, 물음에 답하시오.

> Most of us start a day knowing the things we have to do that day: go to school, hang out with friends, finish our homework, and so on. To manage our time better, we list them, decide the importance of each activity and make a schedule based on ⓐ<u>it</u>. However, a lot of us don't think enough about the time we spend with our family. Even when you are caught up with a long to-do list, you should never miss out on the quality time you share with family, especially when you are busy. Therefore, when you are making a daily or weekly schedule, don't forget to include family time on the list of duties. Make sure _____ⓑ_____.

13 윗글의 밑줄 친 ⓐ가 가리키는 것을 본문에서 찾아 쓰시오.

⊖ ________________________________

14 윗글의 빈칸 ⓑ에 가장 알맞은 것은?

① you need to take some rest even when you are busy
② family time should be on the top of the to□do list
③ you finish all your work before having family time
④ you share the quality time with your close friends
⑤ family time ranks just as high as other important tasks

15 다음 〈보기〉의 우리말과 같도록 괄호 안의 단어들을 활용하여 빈칸에 알맞은 말을 쓰시오.

(1)

> **보기** 그는 자신이 하루 종일 그녀에 대해 생각하고 있음을 발견했다. (find / think)

⊖ He ______________ about her all day long.

(2)

> **보기** 여러분의 시간을 더 효과적으로 관리할 수 있게 도와줄 몇 가지 조언이 여기 있습니다. (help / some / manage / time / effectively)

⊖ Here are ________________________.

16 다음 글의 빈칸 ⓐ ~ ⓓ에 알맞은 말을 차례대로 쓰시오.

> Imagine you have a big empty pickle jar that you have to fill up by using golf balls, marbles, sand, and water. You have to use as much of all four of these items as you can. Drop in as many _____ⓐ_____ as you can. After that, drop in some _____ⓑ_____ and shake the jar so that the marbles can drop into the gaps that are left by the golf balls. Next, take some _____ⓒ_____. Pour it into the even smaller spaces that are left. Finally, finish it off with _____ⓓ_____. This way, you have a full pickle jar without wasting any space.

ⓐ ____________ ⓑ ____________
ⓒ ____________ ⓓ ____________

주관식 서술형 대비

17 시간 관리와 관련하여 자신의 어제 일과를 되돌아보고, 이를 바탕으로 3문장 이상의 글을 쓰시오.

> Things I did well: ________________________
> Things I didn't do well: ____________________
> What and how to change: ___________________

UNIT 3

Together We Make a Family

내신체크 01 교과서 핵심 정리 > Go to p. 46

어휘 총정리

대본 정리
디지털 기기에 관한 대화와 디지털 격차의 개념에 관한 저자의 책 소개

본문 정리
조부모님과의 세대 차이를 디지털 기기를 통해 완화 함

내신체크 02 언어 기능별 집중 대비 > Go to p. 55

듣기와 말하기 대본별 필수 출제 유형

읽기 각 단락별 필수 점검 유형

언어 재료 및 쓰기 어휘 및 구문, 주관식 서술형 대비 문제

내신체크 03 수준별 단원 평가 > Go to p. 60

Basic 지식, 사실적 이해 대비 문제

Advanced 추론적 이해 및 감상, 주관식 서술형 대비 문제

교과서 핵심 정리

Words & Phrases

Listen and Speak ~ Into Real Life

- ☐ complicated* *adj.* 복잡한
- ☐ slang *n.* 속어, 은어
- ☐ watch one's words 말조심하다
- ☐ generation gap* *n.* 세대 차이
- ☐ cancel *v.* 취소하다 (cancellation *n.* 취소)
- ☐ digital divide *n.* 정보 격차, 디지털 격차
- ☐ device *n.* 장치, 기구
- ☐ access* *n.* 입장, 접촉 기회, 접속
- ☐ term *n.* 용어, 말, 학기, 기간
- ☐ rural *a.* 시골의, 지방의 (↔ urban 도시의)
- ☐ briefly *ad.* 짧게, 간략하게
- ☐ bridge the gap* ~사이의 간극을 메우다
- ☐ recently *ad.* 최근에

Read and Think

- ☐ digital *adj.* 디지털 방식을 쓰는 *cf.* analogue 아날로그
- ☐ worsen *v.* 악화하다, 악화시키다
- ☐ generation *n.* 세대
- ☐ attitude* *n.* 태도
- ☐ narrow *a.* 좁은 (↔ wide 넓은)
- ☐ have no choice but to* ~하는 수밖에 없다
- ☐ totally *ad.* 전적으로, 완전히
- ☐ online *adj.* 온라인의
- ☐ mobile *adj.* 이동식의 *n.* 이동식 장비 (휴대전화)
- ☐ invisible *adj.* 보이지 않는 (↔ visible 보이는)
- ☐ separate *v.* 분리시키다 *adj.* 분리된, 떨어진
- ☐ pleased *adj.* 기쁜
- ☐ strengthen *v.* 강화하다 (*n.* strength 힘)
- ☐ gap *n.* 간극, 틈, 구멍, 간격
- ☐ poverty* *n.* 가난 (poor *adj.* 가난한)
- ☐ hometown *n.* 고향
- ☐ laborer *n.* 노동자, 노무자
- ☐ throughout* *prep.* 도처에
- ☐ break out* 발발하다, 일어나다
- ☐ put up with* ~를 참아내다 (= endure)
- ☐ share *v.* 공유하다
- ☐ chapter *n.* (책의) 장
- ☐ select *v.* 선택하다 (*n.* selection 선택)

Language Notes

- ☐ deepen *v.* 깊어지다, 깊게 하다 (deep *adj.* 깊은)
- ☐ arise *v.* (상황이) 생기다, 발생하다
- ☐ endure* *v.* 견디다, 참다 (endurance *n.* 인내, 참을성)
- ☐ construction site 건설 현장, 공사장
- ☐ negative *adj.* 부정적인 (↔ positive 긍정적인)
- ☐ suffer *v.* 시달리다, 고통 받다, 겪다
- ☐ bean *n.* 콩
- ☐ darken *v.* 어둡게 하다, 어두워지다 (↔ brighten 밝게 하다)

Write It Right

- ☐ instruction *n.*(사용 시 필요한) 설명, 지시
- ☐ manual *n.*설명서 *adj.* 손으로 하는
- ☐ download* *v.* (정보를) 내려 받다 (↔ upload)
- ☐ app(application의 줄임말) *n.* 앱, 응용 소프트웨어
- ☐ tap *v.* 가볍게 두드리다, 톡 치다
- ☐ install *v.* 설치하다

Around the World

- ☐ sadness *n.* 슬픔 (= sorrow)
- ☐ adopt* *v.* 입양하다, 채택하다 (adoption *n.* 입양) *cf.* adapt *v.* 맞추다, 적응하다 (adaptation *n.* 적용)
- ☐ rescue* *v.* 구조하다
- ☐ reunite *v.* 재회하다, 재결합하게 하다
- ☐ review *n.* 논평, 비평 *cf.* book review 독후감
- ☐ director *n.* (영화, 연극의) 감독, 지휘자
- ☐ genre *n.* 장르, 부문
- ☐ except *prep.* ~를 제외하고
- ☐ passion *n.* 열정 (passionate *adj.* 열정적인)
- ☐ troubled *adj.* 불안한, 문제가 많은
- ☐ curve *n.* 곡선, (야구에서의) 휘는 공

Check-Up

정답 P. 228

1 다음 문장의 빈칸에 알맞은 말을 〈보기〉에서 골라 넣으시오.

보기 >> bridge the gap / have any choice but / break out / watch your words / suffer from

(1) This fund will be used to ____________ between students' needs and their incomes.

(2) Those who ____________ depression may feel hopeless, overwhelmed, or angry.

(3) When did the Vietnam War ____________ ?

(4) I don't think I ____________ to change my mind.

(5) ____________ and be aware of what you are saying.

2 다음 뜻풀이에 해당하는 말을 주어진 철자로 시작하여 쓰시오.

(1) s ____________ : very informal language that is usually used especially by particular groups of people

(2) p ____________ : the condition of being extremely poor

(3) s ____________ : to experience physical or mental pain

(4) e ____________ : to suffer something difficult, unpleasant or painful and not giving up

(5) a ____________ : to legally take another person's child into your own family and take care of him or her as your own child

주관식 서술형

3 우리말에 맞게 괄호 안의 단어들을 사용하여 문장을 완성하시오.

(1) 그녀는 세대 차이를 해소하기 위해 노력하는 젊은 정치인이다.
She is a young politician who ________________________________.
(bridge / the / generation / gap / tries / to)

(2) 나는 더 이상 너의 못된 행동을 참아주지 않을 거야.
I will not ________________________________.
(up / put / with / bad / your / any / longer / behavior)

(3) 디지털 격차는 교육 받은 사람들과 교육 받지 못한 사람들 사이에 있을 수 있다.
The digital divide can exist ________________________________.
(between / the / and / educated / uneducated)

(4) 나는 이 상황이 마음에 들지 않아요.
I am not ________________________________.
(situation / this / satisfied / with)

Tip

❶ 주요 숙어표현 익히기
needs 필요
depression 우울증
overwhelmed 압도된, 짓눌린
aware 의식하는, 인식하는

❷ 영영사전풀이
informal 격식 없는
extremely 극도로
unpleasant 불쾌한

❸ 핵심어휘를 사용한 영작

교과서 핵심 정리

Dialogues & Monologue

Listen and Speak | *해석을 참조하여 빈칸에 알맞은 말을 쓰시오.

GET READY

1 W: Honey, what's wrong? Is it not working again?
M: It's working, but **I'm not happy with** this tablet. It's too __________.
W: It's really easy. **Let me show you how to use it.**
M: Okay, thanks.

여: 여보, 뭐가 잘못되었어요? 또 작동이 안 되나요?
남: 작동은 되는데 이 태블릿이 마음에 안 들어요. 너무 복잡해요.
여: 그거 정말 쉬워요. 내가 사용법을 보여줄게요.
남: 좋아요, 고마워요.

2 M: Did you watch the movie *My Life* last night on TV? It was wonderful!
W: I did, but I couldn't __________ on the movie.
M: Really? Why not?
W: It was because of my old TV. **I'm not satisfied with** my TV's bad speakers.

남: 어젯밤에 TV에서 한 '나의 인생' 영화 봤니? 정말 좋았어.
여: 봤어. 그런데 영화에 집중할 수가 없었어.
남: 정말? 왜 못했는데?
여: 우리 집 오래된 TV 때문이야. TV 스피커가 안 좋아서 맘에 안 들어.

3 W: Oh, no. I'm not really satisfied with this old cell phone.
M: What's the matter?
W: It's not working again.
M: Again? **I think you should** fix it.

여: 이런. 나 정말 이 낡은 휴대폰이 맘에 들지 않아.
남: 왜 그러는데?
여: 또 작동이 안 돼.
남: 또? 너 그거 고쳐야겠다.

표현정리
- I'm not satisfied/happy with~ (불만족 표현하기)와 I think you should ~(충고하기)가 이 단원의 핵심 의사소통 표현이다.
- Let me show you how to use it. :「Let me +동사원형」은 '내가 ~할게'라는 뜻으로 'I will'과 비슷한 의미이다.

정답 complicated / focus

LISTEN IN

DIALOGUE 1

W: Welcome back. This is your DJ Jennifer on FM *Forever Teen*. Here is our second caller. Hello?
M: Hi, Jennifer. My name is Ted, and I'm calling from Seattle.
W: Hi, Ted. **What can we help you with?**
M: **I'm having a hard time talking with my parents.** I'm not satisfied with this situation.
W: I'm sorry to hear that. Can you tell me more about it?
M: When I talk to my parents, they keep asking me so many questions because they don't understand some of the words that I use.
W: Do you use Internet __________ when you talk to them?
M: Yes, sometimes.
W: I know a lot of teens tend to use that kind of language, but we should watch our words.
M: But I like using those words because they are fun and cool.
W: **Let's suppose your parents used words that you didn't understand. How would you feel?**
M: Well... I guess I would feel pretty bad.

여: 다시 돌아온 걸 환영합니다. 저는 FM Forever Teen에서 일하는 여러분의 DJ Jennifer입니다. 두 번째 분 전화 받아 보겠습니다. 여보세요?
남: 안녕하세요, Jennifer. 저는 Ted라고 하고, 시애틀에서 전화하고 있어요.
여: 안녕하세요, Ted. 무엇을 도와드릴까요?
남: 저는 부모님과 얘기하는 게 힘들어요. 이 상황이 마음에 안 들어요.
여: 안됐군요. 어떤 상황인지 좀 더 얘기해 주실래요?
남: 부모님이랑 얘기하다 보면 제가 사용하는 단어들을 부모님이 이해하지 못하는 게 많아서 저에게 계속 질문을 하세요.
여: 부모님이랑 얘기할 때 인터넷 속어를 많이 쓰나요?
남: 네, 가끔요.
여: 제가 알기로 많은 십대들이 그런 종류의 언어를 쓰고 있는 것 같은데 말을 조심해야 할 필요성이 있어요.
남: 하지만 전 그런 말들이 재미있고 멋있어서 사용하는 게 좋아요.
여: 부모님이 당신이 이해하지 못하는 단어를 사용한다고 가정해 보세요. 기분이 어떨겠어요?
남: 글쎄요... 기분이 무척 안 좋을 것 같긴 해요.

W: How about __________ language like that when you talk with your parents?
M: I think it will take time to change my __________, but I'll try. Thanks for the tip.

여: 부모님이랑 얘기할 때는 그런 언어 사용을 피하는 게 어떨까요?
남: 제 습관을 바꾸려면 시간이 걸리겠지만 노력해 볼게요. 충고 고마워요.

대화상황
- 한 십대 청소년이 부모님과 대화할 때 인터넷 속어를 많이 사용하다 보니 부모님이 이해 못하는 말이 많아 대화가 힘들다는 사연을 라디오 프로그램에서 상담하고 있는 상황이다.

표현정리
- What can we help you with? : How can we help you?와 바꿔 쓸 수 있으며, 상대에게 어떻게/무엇을 도와줄지 묻는 말이다.
- I'm having a hard time talking with my parents.:「have a hard time + -ing」는 '~하는 게 힘들다'라는 뜻이다.
- Let's suppose your parents used words that~: 「Let's suppose (that) 주어 + 동사」는 '~라고 가정해 보자'라는 의미로 어떤 상황을 가정해서 말할 때 쓰는 표현이다.

정답 slang/ avoiding/ habit

DIALOGUE 2

M: Mina, we're going to visit your grandparents this weekend.
W: This weekend? Dad, I was planning to go to the library with Tyler.
M: Come on, it's been a while since you last saw them.
W: Well actually, when I talk to them, I get bored.
M: I think you should consider their age. It's __________ to feel a generation gap.
W: Dad, I'd love to go, but I have nothing to do at their house.
M: Hmm... Why don't you try helping your grandfather this time?
W: Help? What do you mean?
M: Your grandfather told me that he wanted to learn how to send a photo with his cell phone. Can you help him?
W: Oh, I can do that. Also, I can show him how to write an email on his phone.
M: That's great. I'm sure your grandfather will be happy. What about your plans with Tyler, then?
W: I'll __________ plans with him.

남: 미나야, 이번 주말에 우리 할아버지 댁에 갈 거야.
여: 이번 주말요? 아빠, 저 Tyler랑 도서관 가기로 계획하고 있었어요.
남: 할아버지와 할머니를 마지막으로 뵌 지 오래 되었잖아.
여: 저 사실은 할아버지, 할머니랑 얘기할 때 지루해요.
남: 두 분 나이를 고려해야지. 세대 차를 느끼는 건 당연해.
여: 아빠, 저 가고 싶긴 하지만 할아버지 댁에 가면 할 게 없어요.
남: 음... 이번에는 할아버지와 할머니를 도와드려 보는 건 어때?
여: 도와드린다고요? 무슨 말이에요?
남: 할아버지가 아빠한테 휴대폰으로 사진 전송하는 법을 배우고 싶다고 말씀하셨어. 그걸 도와줄 수 있겠니?
여: 네, 할 수 있어요. 휴대폰으로 이메일 쓰는 법도 가르쳐 드릴 수 있어요.
남: 그게 좋겠다. 할아버지가 기뻐하실 거야. 그럼 Tyler랑 계획한 건 어떻게 하지?
여: 걔랑 계획한 건 취소할게요.

대화상황
- 미나가 조부모님 댁을 방문해서 할아버지에게 휴대폰으로 사진 전송하는 법과 이메일 쓰는 법을 가르쳐 드리겠다고 말하는 상황이다.

표현정리
- It's been a while since you last saw them.: 「It's been a while since ~」는 '~한 지 오래되었다'는 뜻이다.
- Why don't you try helping your grandfather?: 「Why don't you +동사원형...?」은 '~하는 게 어때?'라는 제안의 표현이다.

정답 natural / cancel

Into Real Life

W: Today we have a special guest, David Smith. He is on the stage now.
M: Thanks for inviting me to your show, Kelly. You look great today.
W: Thanks. We are so happy to have you as a guest again. I heard you recently wrote a new book about the digital divide. Can you explain it briefly?

여: 오늘 특별한 손님, David Smith 씨를 모셨습니다. 지금 나오십니다.
남: Kelly, 당신의 쇼에 초대해 줘서 고마워요. 오늘 정말 멋져 보이네요.
여: 고마워요. 당신을 손님으로 다시 모시게 되어 정말 기뻐요. 최근 디지털 격차에 관해 책을 썼다고 들었어요. 간단히 소개해 주실래요?

M: Okay, as you know, these days it's hard to imagine our life without __________ devices such as smartphones, computers, and the Internet. However, have you thought about some of the people living in the Amazon Rainforest? Their lives may be quite different from ours. Not everyone in the world has access to communication technology. To describe this difference, we use the term "digital divide."
W: So, when was this term created?
M: Since the late 1990s, the term has been used to describe the growing _______ between those people who have Internet access and those who do not. This divide also exists between cities and rural areas.
W: Does the divide exist between generations?
M: That's a good question. The answer is yes. The gap between teens and older people is getting bigger. In my book, I cover some specific examples of the digital divide between generations and suggest how we can bridge the gap.

남: 네. 아시다시피 요즘 스마트폰이나 컴퓨터 그리고 인터넷 같은 통신 장치 없는 우리의 삶을 상상하기 힘들잖아요. 하지만 아마존 열대우림에 사는 사람들에 관해 생각해본 적 있나요? 그들의 삶은 우리의 삶과 많이 다를지도 몰라요. 이 세상 모든 사람들이 정보 기술에 접근할 수 있는 건 아니니까요. 이런 차이점을 설명하기 위해 우리는 "디지털 격차"라는 말을 쓰죠.
여: 그러면 이 용어는 언제 만들어졌죠?
남: 1990년대 후반부터 이 용어는 인터넷 접근성을 가진 사람들과 그렇지 못한 사람들과의 간극이 커지는 것을 묘사하기 위해 사용되었어요. 이 격차는 또한 도시와 시골 지역 사이에도 존재하죠.
여: 이 격차가 세대 간에도 존재하나요?
남: 좋은 질문입니다. 답은 '그렇다'입니다. 십대와 나이든 세대 사이의 간극이 점점 커져가고 있어요. 제 책에서는 이런 세대 간 디지털 격차의 구체적인 예시들을 다루고 있고 그 간극을 메우기 위한 방법도 제시하고 있어요.

대화상황
- 디지털 격차 또는 정보 격차라는 용어에 관해 전문가의 설명을 듣는 상황이다.

표현정리
- has access는 '~ 에 접근하다'라는 뜻이다.
- has been used to describe~는 '~를 묘사하기 위해 사용되었다'라는 뜻으로 현재완료 수동태 구문이다.

정답 communication / gap

Check Your Progress

W: Andy, we're going to visit your grandparents this Sunday.
M: Sunday? Mom, I was planning to play soccer with Patrick.
W: Oh, come on. They really want to see you. You can play soccer next time.
M: Well, to be honest, when I visit them I get __________. Sometimes it's not easy for me to talk with them.
W: I know what you mean, but I think you should consider their age.
M: Mom, I want something exciting to do at their house.
W: Hmm... Why don't you try helping them this time?
M: What do you mean? How can I help them?
W: Your grandparents told me that they wanted to learn how to download music with their smartphone. Can you help them?
M: Sure. I could also show them how to download useful __________ on their phone. I'll cancel my plans with Patrick.
W: That's great. I'm sure your grandparents will be happy.

여: Andy, 우리 이번 주 일요일에 할아버지 할머니 뵈러 갈 거야.
남: 일요일이요? 엄마, 나 Patrick이랑 축구할 계획하고 있었는데요.
여: 그럼 안 되지. 할아버지와 할머니께서 너를 얼마나 보고 싶어 하시는데. 축구는 다음에 할 수 있잖아.
남: 사실 솔직히 말씀드리자면, 할아버지 할머니 댁에 가면 따분해요. 어떨 땐 두 분이랑 얘기하는 게 쉽지 않아요.
여: 무슨 말인지 이해는 하겠는데, 두 분 나이를 고려해야지.
남: 엄마, 할아버지 댁에 가서 뭔가 흥미로운 걸 하고 싶어요.
여: 음... 이번에는 두 분을 도와드려보는 게 어떨까?
남: 무슨 말이에요? 제가 어떻게 할아버지 할머니를 도와드려요?
여: 할아버지와 할머니께서 스마트폰으로 음악을 내려 받는 법을 배우고 싶다고 나에게 말씀하신 적이 있어. 도와줄 수 있겠니?
남: 물론이죠. 핸드폰에 유용한 앱을 내려 받는 법도 가르쳐 드릴 수 있을 거예요. Patrick과의 계획은 취소할게요.
여: 그것 참 잘 됐다. 할아버지 할머니께서도 좋아하실 거야.

대화상황
- 처음에는 따분하다는 이유로 조부모님 댁 방문을 망설이다가 엄마의 권유로 조부모님 댁을 방문하여 스마트폰으로 음악을 내려 받는 법과 유용한 앱을 내려 받는 법을 조부모님께 가르쳐 드리기로 한 상황

표현정리
- I got it done.: 「get + 목적어 + 과거분사」의 구문은 '~를 … 된 상태로 만들다'라는 의미이다.
- I used to be like that.: 「used to + 동사원형」은 '(과거에) ~하곤 했다'라는 뜻으로 과거의 습관이나 상태를 나타낸다.

정답 bored / apps

교과서 핵심 정리

Reading Comprehension

*해석을 참조하여 빈칸에 알맞은 말을 쓰거나 괄호에서 알맞은 말을 고르시오.

P.55 L.1~8

Jina won first prize in the school singing contest. She chose a popular song from the 1980s to sing in front of all the students. Jina's best friend, Eunji, recorded the performance on her cell phone. After the contest, Jina showed the video file to her parents. Jina's father said, "Oh, your grandfather should watch this! This song is one of his (favorite/favorites)." Jina wanted to send the video file to her grandfather right away, but she realized he didn't have an email address or a smartphone. She felt __________ about this because she had no choice but to wait until she could visit her grandparents. Here is her story.

진아는 학교 노래 부르기 대회에서 일등을 했다. 그녀는 1980년대에 유행했던 노래를 골라 모든 학생들 앞에서 노래 부르기로 정했다. 진아의 가장 친한 친구 은지가 그녀의 공연을 핸드폰으로 녹화했다. 대회가 끝난 후, 진아는 그 비디오 파일을 그녀의 부모님에게 보여드렸다. 그랬더니 아버지가, "할아버지께서 이 영상을 보셔야 해! 이 노래는 할아버지께서 제일 좋아하는 노래 중 하나야."라고 하셨다. 진아는 그 비디오 파일을 할아버지께 당장 보내드리고 싶었지만 할아버지께는 이메일 주소나 스마트폰이 없다는 사실을 깨달았다. 진아는 할아버지 할머니를 만나러 갈 때까지 기다려야 하는 수 밖에 다른 방법이 없어서 아쉬웠다. 다음은 진아의 이야기이다.

단락요약
- 진아가 노래 부르기 대회에서 우승을 했고 녹화된 파일을 조부모님께 보내 드리려고 했으나 조부모님께서 파일을 받아보실 방법이 없어 아쉬워하는 내용이다.

구문정리
- Jina showed the video file to her parents.: show는 send와 같은 종류의 수여동사로서 「send/show/give/teach + 직접목적어 + to + 간접목적어」 구문을 쓴다. *cf.* 「buy/cook/make + 직접목적어 + for + 간접목적어」
- she had no choice but to wait ~: 「have no choice but to +동사원형」은 '~하는 수밖에 (다른) 선택의 여지가 없다'라는 뜻이다.

정답 favorites/ sorry

P.55 L.9~21

When I visited my grandfather, he used to (tell/telling) me about when he was my age. I have heard it hundreds of times, so I already know what (he will/will he) say after, "When I was your age, ..." One of his least favorite things (was/were) any kind of digital device. This time I thought I could change his mind because he really enjoyed watching my singing performance on my phone. I told him, "Grandpa, I really want you to have a smartphone or an email address. If you use it, we can share many things and talk more often." However, my grandfather kept saying that it would be too difficult to use a smartphone or email. He believed digital devices worsened the _____________ gap. I wondered why he held on to his (negative/positive) attitudes toward digital technologies. I found it hard to narrow the gap between us, so I said to my father, "Grandpa simply can't understand my generation."

내가 할아버지를 찾아뵈면, 할아버지는 할아버지께서 내 나이였을 적 이야기를 들려주곤 하셨다. 수백 번도 더 들어서 "내가 네 나이였을 때..."라는 말씀 뒤에 무슨 말씀을 하실지 이미 다 알고 있을 정도다. 할아버지께서 제일 싫어하시는 것 중 하나는 디지털 기기였다. 하지만 이번에 나는 할아버지께서 전화로 내 노래하는 모습을 보는 걸 너무 좋아하시기 때문에 할아버지의 마음을 바꿀 수 있다고 생각했다. 나는 할아버지께 "할아버지, 전 할아버지께서 이메일이나 스마트폰을 하셨으면 정말 좋겠어요. 할아버지께서 그런 걸 쓰시면 우리랑 많은 것을 공유할 수도 있고 이야기도 더 자주 할 수 있잖아요."라고 말씀드렸다. 하지만 할아버지께서는 스마트폰이나 이메일을 사용하는 게 너무 어렵다고 계속 말씀하셨다. 할아버지께서는 디지털 기기가 세대 차이를 더 악화시킨다고 믿고 계셨다. 난 할아버지께서 디지털 기술에 대해 왜 그렇게 부정적인 태도를 갖고 계신지 궁금했다. 난 할아버지와 나 사이의 간극을 메우는 게 어렵다는 것을 알았고 아버지께 "할아버진 정말 우리 세대를 이해 못 하세요."라고 말해버렸다.

단락요약
- 스마트폰과 같은 디지털 기기를 사용하는 것에 관한 글쓴이의 제안에 부정적인 태도로 일관하시는 할아버지를 이해할 수 없어서 속상해 하며 갈등하는 내용이다.

구문정리
- ~ he used to tell me about when he was my age.: 「used to +동사원형」은 '~하곤 했다'라는 의미로 과거의 습관적인 행동이나 상태를 표현하는 구문이다. *cf.* 「be/get used to + 동명사(-ing)」: -하는 것에 익숙하다 「be used to + 동사원형」: ~하는 데 사용되다
- I wondered why he held on to his negative attitudes ~ : why로 시작되는 절은 동사 wondered의 목적어로서 간접 의문문 「(의문사+주어+동사)」의 형태를 취하며 다음 두 문장이 결합된 것이다.
  I wondered. + Why did he hold on to his negative attitudes ~?
- I found it hard to narrow the gap between us ~: it은 가목적어, to narrow는 진목적어로서 「find it + 형용사 + to ~」는 '~ 하는 것이 …하다는 것을 알게 되다'라는 의미이다.

정답 tell / he will / was / generation / negative

P.56 L.1-10

After having dinner at my grandparents' house, I received a message with two photos from my father. He said, "Jina, what do you think about these two photos?"The first photo was in black and white, and it was (taking/taken) when my father was very young. In the picture, all the family members were eating some fruit together. As I saw their smiling faces in the picture, I could feel real happiness. On the other hand, the second photo was totally _________. My father had taken this photo before we had dinner. I was playing online games on my smartphone, and my brother was talking with his friends using a mobile messaging app (while/so) my grandfather was just watching TV.
There seemed to be an invisible wall (separated/separating) us from our grandfather.

할아버지 댁에서 저녁을 먹은 후, 난 아빠에게서 두 장의 사진이 든 메시지를 받았다. 아빠는, "진아야, 이 두 사진 보면서 어떤 생각이 드니?"라고 물으셨다. 하나는 흑백 사진이었는데 아빠가 아주 어렸을 때 찍은 거였다. 사진 속에서 가족 모두는 몇몇 과일을 함께 먹고 있었다. 그들의 웃는 얼굴을 보면서 나는 진정한 행복을 느낄 수 있었다. 한편, 두 번째 사진은 전혀 달랐다. 아빠는 그 사진을 우리가 저녁 먹기 전에 찍었다. 난 내 스마트폰으로 온라인 게임을 하고 있었고, 내 남동생은 모바일 메신저 앱을 사용해서 자기 친구랑 대화하고 있었는데 할아버지는 그저 TV만 보고 있었다.
우리랑 할아버지를 분리시키는 보이지 않는 벽이 있는 것 같았다.

단락요약

- 아빠가 두 장의 대조되는 사진을 진아에게 보내면서 가족 간의 대화가 단절된 지금의 모습에 관해 생각해 보도록 하고 있다.

구문정리

- ~ it was taken when my father was very young. : it은 the first photo를 가리키는 것으로 동사 was taken은 수동태이다.
- My father **had taken** this photo before we **had** dinner.: 'had taken'은 「had +p.p.」형태로 쓰인 과거완료로서, 과거 시제인 had dinner와 비교했을 때 그보다 앞서 일어난 일임을 나타내는 시제이다.
- ~ my brother was talking with his friends using a mobile messaging app ~ : using은 '사용하면서'라는 의미의 현재분사이고, using a mobile messaging app은 동시동작을 나타내는 분사구문이다. (=while/as/and he was using a mobile messaging app)
- ~ an invisible wall separating us from our grandfather: separating 앞에 which/that is (관계대명사+be동사)가 생략된 구문으로서 separating 이하는 선행사 wall을 수식한다.

정답 taken / different / while / separating

P.56 L.11~19

I felt sorry for my grandparents as I saw the photos. I began to understand how my grandfather felt, so I asked my father how (I could / could I) bridge the gap between my grandparents and me. He said, "Jina, I know you're very good at computers. Why don't you make a digital family album? Even better, you could _________ some songs we all love, along with your singing contest video file. Your grandfather will be very (annoyed/pleased) to be able to share his life history with you." I thought digital devices could _________ our family and strengthen the family bonds. I suggested the idea to my grandfather, and he accepted it with a big smile. Our digital family album starts with "When my grandfather was my age, ..."

사진을 보면서 난 조부모님이 안쓰러웠다. 할아버지께서 어떤 느낌이실지 이해가 되기 시작했고 그래서 난 아빠에게 조부모님과 나 사이의 간극을 어떻게 메울지 여쭈었다. 아빠께서는"진아야, 네가 컴퓨터를 아주 잘 하잖니. 디지털 가족 앨범을 만들어보면 어떻겠니? 너의 노래 부르기 대회 비디오 파일에다 우리 모두가 좋아하는 노래를 몇 개 첨가하면 훨씬 더 좋겠다. 할아버지께서는 자신의 인생 역사를 너희들이랑 나누게 되어 기뻐하실 거야."라고 하셨다. 나는 디지털 기기가 우리 가족을 서로 연결해 주고 가족의 유대감을 더 강화해 줄 수 있을 거라고 생각했다. 할아버지께 이 아이디어를 제안했더니 할아버지는 활짝 웃으시며 승낙하셨다. 우리의 디지털 가족 앨범은 "내 할아버지가 내 나이었을 때..."로 시작한다.

단락요약

- 할아버지와의 세대 차이를 연결하고 가족 간 유대감 강화를 위해 디지털 가족 앨범 만들기를 제안하여 제작을 시작한다.

구문정리

- I felt sorry for my grandparents ~ : 「feel sorry for + 명사(구)」는 '~에게/~에 대해 유감을 느끼다'라는 뜻이다.
- I asked my father how I could bridge the gap ~ : asked의 목적어인 「how I could ~」는 「의문사 + 주어 + 동사」 순서인 간접의문문의 형태를 취한다.

정답 I could / add / pleased / connect

P.57 L.1~19

When my grandfather was my age, the Korean War broke out. Things were quite different from the way we live now. He remembers how people ________ from cold, hunger, and poverty even after the war. My grandfather decided to leave his sick mother, two brothers, and three sisters because he was the only one who could earn money. Finally, he moved from his hometown to Seoul to make more money. As a laborer in the 1970s, he worked for a big construction company in Saudi Arabia and Iran for many years. When he thought of his family in Korea, he had to put up with all his __________.

A love of music (runs/walks) in the family. Music has been my grandfather's best friend throughout his life. He often listens to music when he feels sad. He told me he really liked the song that I sang at the singing contest. He also introduced me to a lot of songs I had never heard before. They were really (amazed/amazing). We chose the first song for the background music of our digital family album.

우리 할아버지께서 내 나이였을 때, 한국 전쟁이 발발했다. (그 당시) 상황은 지금 우리가 사는 방식과 많이 달랐다. 할아버지께서는 사람들이 심지어 전쟁 이후에도 얼마나 추위와 배고픔과 가난 때문에 고생했는지 기억하신다. 할아버지께서는 자신이 돈을 벌 수 있는 유일한 사람이었기 때문에 아픈 어머니와 두 남동생과 세 여동생을 남기고 떠나기로 결심했다. 결국 할아버지께서는 돈을 더 벌기 위해 고향을 떠나 서울로 가셨다. 1970년대에는 노동자로서 사우디아라비아와 이란에서 수년 간 큰 건설회사에서 일하셨다. 한국에 있는 가족들을 생각하며 할아버지께서는 모든 어려움을 참아내야 했다.

음악에 대한 사랑이 우리 가족에게 흐르고 있다. 음악은 할아버지의 인생 내내 그의 가장 친한 벗이었다. 그는 슬플 때 음악을 종종 들으신다. 할아버지께서는 내가 노래 부르기 대회에서 불렀던 노래를 무척 좋아한다고 내게 말씀하셨다. 할아버지께서는 또한 나에게 내가 전에 들어보지 못했던 많은 노래들도 소개시켜 주셨다. 그 노래들은 정말 굉장했다. 우리는 우리 디지털 가족 앨범의 배경 음악으로 첫 번째 노래를 골랐다.

단락요약

- 할아버지께서 어렸을 때부터 청장년이 될 때까지의 개인사를 요약한 것과 할아버지께서 좋아하는 음악에 관한 소개 등 디지털 가족 앨범에 올린 내용이다.

구문정리

- Things were quite different from the way we live now.: the way는 관계부사 how가 생략된 구문의 선행사로서 '~하는 방식/방법'이라고 해석한다.
- He remembers how people suffered ~ : 'how people suffered'는 remembers의 목적어가 되는 간접의문문으로 「의문사 + 주어 + 동사」의 어순이다.
- Music has been my grandfather's best friend ~ : has been은 과거부터 지금까지 지속되는 상태를 나타내는 현재완료 구문이다.

정답 suffered / difficulties / runs/ amazing

P.58 L.1~8

We found it (interested / interesting) to make our own digital family album together. My grandparents said they felt __________ to me and my brother because our family talked about the photos and the old days. I was glad to learn about their past, and they also looked happy to share their stories with me. We have finished making the first two chapters of our digital family album, and we decided (choosing / to choose) some photos of my grandmother for the next chapter. My grandmother has already __________ her favorite song for the background music.
Our digital family album will never end!

우리는 디지털 가족 앨범을 함께 만드는 게 재미있다는 것을 알게 되었다. 할아버지와 할머니께서는 사진들과 옛날 일들에 관해 얘기하면서 나랑 내 남동생과 더 가까워졌다는 것을 느낀다고 말씀하셨다. 나는 할아버지와 할머니의 과거에 관해 알게 되어 기뻤고, 두 분도 자신들의 이야기를 나와 나누게 되어 행복해 보이셨다. 우리는 디지털 가족 앨범의 첫 두 장을 끝냈고, 다음 장을 위해 할머니의 사진들을 몇 개 고르기로 했다. 할머니께서는 자신이 가장 좋아하는 노래를 배경 음악으로 하려고 골라 놓으셨다.
우리의 디지털 가족 앨범은 결코 끝나지 않을 것이다!

단락요약

- 디지털 가족 앨범을 만들면서 돈독해진 가족 관계에 관해 얘기하고 있고, 할머니에 관한 얘기가 실릴 다음 장을 기대하는 내용이다.

구문정리

- We found it interesting to make ~ .: 「find + it + 형용사 + to 부정사」는 '~하는 것이 …하다는 걸 알게 되다'라는 뜻으로 it은 가목적어이다. 진목적어는 to부정사이다.
- ~ they looked happy to share their stories ~ : 「감정형용사 + to 부정사」는 '~해서 …하다'라는 뜻이다.

정답 interesting / closer / to choose / selected

Focus on Structure

P. 55 L.17 I wondered | **why he held** on to his negative attitudes | toward digital technologies.
의문사 주어 동사 (간접의문문)

➔ 의문문이 다른 문장 안에 삽입되면서 문장의 주어나 목적어로 쓰이는 경우, 「의문사 + 주어 + 동사」의 어순으로 간접의문문의 형태를 취한다. 이 때, 직접의문문에 있었던 do/does/did는 동사의 인칭이나 시제에 반영되면서 없어지지만 조동사는 그대로 동사와 함께 쓴다. 의문사가 없는 의문문을 간접의문문으로 만들 때는 의문사 자리에 if/whether를 넣는다

ex. We wondered. + **Why did he choose** to become a priest? (직접의문문)

→ We wondered **why he chose** to become a priest. (wondered의 목적어로 간접의문문 형태를 취함)
의문사 주어 동사 (간접의문문)

P. 56 L.6 My father **had taken** this photo | before | we **had** dinner.
과거완료 (had + p.p.) 접속사 과거

➔ 두 개의 사건이 시간 차를 두고 과거에 일어났을 때, 둘 중 먼저 일어난 사건이나 상태는 「had + 과거분사」의 형태인 과거완료를 쓰고, 나중에 일어난 사건이나 상태는 단순 과거 시제를 써서 나타낸다.

ex. When the lawyer **arrived** at the railway station, the train **had** already **departed**.
과거 / 과거완료 → 기차역에 도착한(arrived) 행동보다 시간적으로 먼저 일어난 일임

P. 58 L.1 We found | **it** | interesting | **to make** our own digital family album together.
find 가목적어 진목적어

➔ 동사 find의 목적어가 길 경우 가목적어 it을 써서 「find + it + 형용사 + to부정사」 형태로 나타내며 '~하는 것이 …라는 것을 알게 되다'라고 해석한다. 이때 to부정사는 진목적어라고 부른다.

ex. I found it. + It is hard to control my appetite. (나는 알게 되었다. + 내 식욕을 조절하는 것은 어렵다.)

→ I found **it** hard **to control** my appetite. (나는 내 식욕을 조절하는 것이 어렵다는 것을 알게 되었다.)

cf. 「make + it + 형용사/명사 + to 부정사」: ~하는 것을 …하게/로 만들다

She **made it easy to find** the right home for the newly-married couple.

그녀는 그 신혼부부에게 맞는 집 찾는 것을 쉽게 해 주었다.

Check-Up

정답 P. 229

1 다음 괄호 안의 단어들을 순서대로 바르게 배열하시오.

(1) Emma found (difficult / to / it / study / much / night / at) after working all day.

(2) My mom found (it / impossible / for / to / me / get / there) on time.

2 다음 밑줄 친 부분을 바르게 고쳐 쓰시오.

(1) Before her seventh birthday, Linda has never been to the zoo.

(2) Sam told us about the film he saw the day before.

(3) When I got there, they have already started picking the tea leaves.

Tip

❶ (1) find + it + 형용사 + to부정사
(2) 「find + it + 형용사 + for + 목적격 + to 부정사」: ~하는 것이 …하다는 것을 알게 되다

❷ (1) 과거완료의 경험적 용법
(2) 영화 본 게 말한 것보다 먼저 일어난 일임
(3) 내가 도착한 것보다 사람들이 찻잎을 따기 시작한 일이 먼저 일어남

언어 기능별 집중 대비

Listen and Speak/Into Real Life

정답 P. 229

Tip

1 대화를 듣고, 여자의 심정으로 가장 알맞은 것을 고르시오.

① upset ② excited
③ satisfied ④ embarrassed
⑤ relieved

❶ 화자의 심정 파악하기
출처: Get Ready_2

2 대화를 듣고, 여자가 해주는 조언의 내용으로 가장 알맞은 것을 고르시오.

① Don't talk too much.
② Don't ask too many questions.
③ Be kind when you call a radio program.
④ Try to better understand your parents.
⑤ Don't use slang when talking to your parents.

❷ 대화의 내용 파악하기
출처: Listen In Dialogue_1
slang 속어

3 대화를 듣고, 미나가 주말에 할아버지 댁에 가서 하기로 한 일을 고르시오.

① 마당에 있는 잡초 제거
② 할아버지께 책 읽어 드리기
③ 할아버지 할머니 사진 찍어드리기
④ 화상으로 대화하는 법 알려 드리기
⑤ 휴대전화로 사진 전송하는 법과 이메일 쓰는 법 알려드리기

❸ 하려고 하는 일 파악하기
출처: Listen In Dialogue_2

4 다음을 듣고, 물음에 답하시오.

(1) Mr. Smith 씨가 쓴 책에서 구체적으로 다루고 있는 주제는?
① the digital divide between generations and solutions
② how to get an easier access to the Internet
③ generation gaps rooted in the modern society
④ how to keep the Amazon Rainforest for the next generations
⑤ drawbacks of using various communication devices in school

(2) 대화의 내용과 일치하지 않는 것을 고르시오.
① Smith 씨는 최근에 책을 한 권 출판했다.
② Smith 씨는 방송 프로그램의 특별 초대 손님이다.
③ 통신 기술에 관한 접근성의 차이가 디지털 격차를 초래했다.
④ 디지털 격차는 2000년 이후 최근에 쓰이기 시작한 용어이다.
⑤ 디지털 격차는 도시 농촌 지역 간에도 존재한다.

❹ (1) 주제 고르기
(2) 내용 파악하기
출처: Into Real Life_Step 1
access 접근(성)
rainforest 열대 우림
drawback 결점, 단점
device 장치, 기구

언어 기능별 집중 대비

Read and Think

정답 P. 229

Tip

1 출처: P.55 L.2- 8
유형: 빈칸 추론

1 다음 글의 빈칸에 들어갈 말로 가장 알맞은 것은?

Jina won first prize in the school singing contest. She chose a popular song from the 1980s to sing in front of all the students. Jina's best friend, Eunji, recorded the performance on her cell phone. After the contest, Jina showed the video file to her parents. Jina's father said, "Oh, your grandfather should watch this! This song is one of his favorites." Jina wanted to send the video file to her grandfather right away, but she realized he didn't have an email address or a smartphone. She felt sorry about this because ____________________ until she could visit her grandparents.

① she promised to keep secret
② she could not record the song
③ she had no choice but to wait
④ she did not practice singing the song
⑤ she could not listen to her grandfather sing

[2-3] 다음 글을 읽고, 물음에 답하시오.

2-3 출처: P.55 L.9-21
유형: 2. 어휘의 쓰임
3. 지칭 추론

When I visited my grandfather, he used to tell me about when he was my age. I have heard it hundreds of times, so I already know what he will say after, "When I was your age, ..." One of his ⓐ least favorite things was any kind of digital device. This time I thought I could change his mind because he really ⓑ enjoyed watching my singing performance on my phone. I told him, "Grandpa, I really want you to have a smartphone or an email address. If you use it, we can share many things and talk more often." ⓒ However, my grandfather kept saying that it would be too difficult to use a smartphone or email. He believed digital devices ⓓ narrowed the generation gap. I wondered why he held on to his ⓔ negative attitudes toward digital technologies. I found it hard to narrow ⓕ the gap between us, so I said to my father, "Grandpa simply can't understand my generation."

2 윗글의 밑줄 친 ⓐ~ⓔ 중 어휘의 쓰임이 잘못된 것은?

① ⓐ ② ⓑ ③ ⓒ ④ ⓓ ⑤ ⓔ

3 윗글의 밑줄 친 ⓕ가 가리키는 것으로 가장 알맞은 것은?

① 할아버지와의 대화 단절로 인한 가족의 갈등
② 시골 문화에 적응하지 못하는 자녀들과의 갈등
③ 지나친 스마트폰 사용으로 인한 부모님과의 갈등
④ 할아버지와 아버지 사이의 보이지 않는 정신적 갈등
⑤ 디지털 기기 사용을 거부하시는 할아버지와의 갈등

[4-5] 다음 글을 읽고, 물음에 답하시오.

After having dinner at my grandparents' house, I received a message with two photos from my father. He said, "Jina, what do you think about these two photos?" (A) The first photo was in black and white, and it was taken when my father was very young. (B) In the picture, all the family members were eating some fruit together. (C) On the other hand, the second photo was totally different. (D) My father had taken this photo before we had dinner. (E) I was playing online games on my smartphone, and my brother was talking with his friends using a mobile messaging app while my grandfather was just watching TV.

There seemed to be ⓐ an invisible wall separating us from our grandfather.

Tip

4-5 출처: P.56 L.1-10
유형: 4. 문장의 위치 파악
5. 어휘의 문맥상 의미 추론 (비유)

4 윗글의 (A)~(E) 중 아래의 문장이 들어가기에 가장 알맞은 곳은?

As I saw their smiling faces in the picture, I could feel real happiness.

① (A) ② (B) ③ (C) ④ (D) ⑤ (E)

5 윗글의 밑줄 친 ⓐ와 바꿔 쓸 수 있는 것은?

① digital game
② different ideas
③ communication breakdown
④ strong connection
⑤ information technology

6 다음 문장에 이어지는 글의 순서로 가장 알맞은 것은?

I felt sorry for my grandparents as I saw the photos.

(A) I thought digital devices could connect our family and strengthen the family bonds. I suggested the idea to my grandfather, and he accepted it with a big smile.

(B) I began to understand how my grandfather felt, so I asked my father how I could bridge the gap between my grandparents and me.

(C) He said, "Jina, I know you're very good at computers. Why don't you make a digital family album? Even better, you could add some songs we all love, along with your singing contest video file. Your grandfather will be very pleased to be able to share his life history with you."

① (A) – (C) – (B) ② (B) – (A) – (C) ③ (B) – (C) – (A)
④ (C) – (A) – (B) ⑤ (C) – (B) – (A)

6 출처: P.56 L.11-19
유형: 글의 순서 파악

Tip

7 다음 글의 밑줄 친 ①~⑤ 중 어법상 잘못된 것은?

When my grandfather was my age, the Korean War broke out. Things were quite different from ① the way we live now. He remembers ② how did people suffer from cold, hunger, and poverty even after the war. My grandfather decided to leave his sick mother, two brothers, and three sisters because he was the only one ③ who could earn money. Finally, he moved from his hometown to Seoul ④ to make more money. As a laborer in the 1970s, he worked for a big construction company in Saudi Arabia and Iran for many years. When he thought of his family in Korea, he ⑤ had to put up with all his difficulties.

❼ 출처: P.57 L.1-8
유형: 문법성 판단
suffer: 시달리다, 겪다

8 다음 글의 빈칸에 가장 알맞은 것은?

________________ Music has been my grandfather's best friend throughout his life. He often listens to music when he feels sad. He told me he really liked the song that I sang at the singing contest. He also introduced me to a lot of songs I had never heard before. They were really amazing. We chose the first song for the background music of our digital family album.

① A love of music runs in the family.
② Making a digital album was not easy.
③ Lyrics and melodies should match well.
④ Listening to music is my favorite pastime.
⑤ My family shares one hobby, which is singing.

❽ 출처: P.57 L.9-19
유형: 빈칸 추론
pastime 취미
lyrics 노래가사

9 다음 글의 괄호 안의 ⓐ~ⓒ에 알맞은 말이 차례대로 연결된 것은?

We found it ⓐ (interested / interesting) to make our own digital family album together. My grandparents said they felt closer to me and my brother because our family talked about the photos and the old days. I was glad to learn about their past, and they also looked ⓑ (happy / happily) to share their stories with me. We have finished making the first two chapters of our digital family album, and we decided to choose some photos of my grandmother for the next chapter. My grandmother ⓒ (has / was) already selected her favorite song for the background music.
Our digital family album will never end!

① interested – happy – has
② interesting – happy – was
③ interested – happily – was
④ interesting – happy – has
⑤ interested – happily – has

❾ 출처: P.58 L.1-7
유형: 문법성 판단
select 선택하다

언어 기능별 집중 대비

Language Notes Write It Right

정답 P.230

1 다음 우리말에 맞게 괄호 안의 단어를 이용하여 문장을 완성하시오.

(1) 너는 1차 세계대전이 언제 발발했는지 아니?
Do you know ________________? (break out)

(2) 나는 그녀가 왜 군인이 되고 싶어 하는지 모르겠다.
I don't know ________________. (soldier)

(3) 당신은 그 노인이 나에게 주었던 콩들을 모두 버렸어요?
Did you throw out all the beans that ________________? (give)

(4) 그 여행은 다른 문화들에 대한 나의 이해를 심화할 기회를 주었다.
The trip gave me an opportunity ________________. (deepen)

(5) 그는 공사장에서 들리는 소음을 견딜 수가 없었다.
He couldn't ________________ from the construction site. (put up with)

Tip

❶ (1) 간접의문문
(2) 간접 의문문 (의문사+주어+동사)
(3) 과거완료 (had + p.p.)
(4) to 부정사의 형용사적 용법
(5) put up with = endure
opportunity 기회
deepen (깊이를) 깊게 하다, 심화하다
construction site 공사장 건설 현장,

2 다음 두 문장을 연결하여 하나의 문장으로 바꿔 쓸 때 빈칸에 알맞은 말을 쓰시오.

(1) "How much does it cost to study in the U.K.?" She asked me.
→ She asked me ________________________.

(2) "What kind of errors did he make?" I wondered.
→ I wondered ________________________.

(3) "Did Tony sign the contract?" Kate wanted to know.
→ Kate wanted to know ________________________.

❷ 간접의문문
(1) 의문사 how much
(2) 의문사 what kind of errors
(3) 의문사가 없는 의문문은 간접의문문으로 만들 때 「whether/if (~인지 아닌지) + 주어+동사」의 형태를 써서 나타낸다.
contract 계약(서)

3 두 사건이 일어난 시간 차를 고려하여 문장의 빈칸을 완성하시오.

(1) My brother got to the airport at 7:30. The plane departed at 7:15.
→ When my brother got to the airport, ________________________.

(2) We sold the house in 2015. We owned the house for ten years from 2005 to 2015.
→ We sold the house that ________________________.

(3) I moved to Thailand last year. I did not study Thai before.
→ I ________________________ before I moved to Thailand.

(4) Sam received his mechanic's license in 2000. He repaired many cars before.
→ Sam ________________ before he received his mechanic's license.

❸ 과거시제와 과거완료 시제
(1) 공항에 도착한 것보다 비행기가 이륙한 일이 먼저 일어남
(2) 10년 동안 소유하고 있었던 집을 팜
(3) 태국으로 이사하기 전까지 태국어를 공부한 일이 없음
(4) 기술자 면허증을 받기 전에 많은 차를 수리한 경험이 있음
depart 출발하다
own 소유하다
Thai 태국의, 태국어
mechanic 기계 수리공

Basic

1 대화를 듣고, 여자의 마지막 말에 이어질 남자의 말로 가장 알맞은 것을 고르시오.

① I'm afraid so.
② Okay, thanks.
③ Take care of yourself.
④ I'd love to, but I can't.
⑤ I don't think you should.

2 대화를 듣고, 두 사람의 관계로 가장 알맞은 것을 고르시오.

① 학부모 – 교사
② 상담교사 – 학생
③ 언어치료사 – 환자
④ 텔레마케터 – 고객
⑤ 라디오 DJ – 청취자

3 다음 중 〈보기〉의 밑줄 친 말과 의미가 가장 가까운 것은?

보기 He promised to change the tax laws to <u>bridge</u> the gap between the rich and poor.

① widen ② narrow
③ deepen ④ worsen
⑤ strengthen

4 다음 중 유의어끼리 바르게 연결된 것은?

① rural – urban
② select – choose
③ divide – unify
④ totally – partially
⑤ darken – brighten

5 다음 중 빈칸에 가장 알맞은 것은?

She's been very patient, ____________ all kinds of inconvenience.

① setting up ② holding on to
③ standing out ④ giving way to
⑤ putting up with

6 다음 글의 밑줄 **the second photo**와 달리 **the first photo**에 잘 드러나 있는 것은?

<u>The first photo</u> was in black and white, and it was taken when my father was very young. In the picture, all the family members were eating some fruit together. As I saw their smiling faces in the picture, I could feel real happiness. On the other hand, <u>the second photo</u> was totally different. My father had taken this photo before we had dinner. I was playing online games on my smartphone, and my brother was talking with his friends using a mobile messaging app while my grandfather was just watching TV.

① family bonds ② family conflicts
③ generation gap ④ poor childhood
⑤ high technologies

[7~8] 다음 중 어법상 <u>어색한</u> 문장을 고르시오.

7

① I had met him before you introduced us.
② He has not studied Italian before he moved to Italy.
③ She had owned the house for forty years before she sold it.
④ When we got to the amusement park, the performance had already finished.
⑤ Did you know that he had never been to Switzerland before?

8

① Everybody knows what that traffic sign means.
② I don't remember what time the party started.
③ It doesn't matter how much money does he make.
④ Can you tell me why you are late for the meeting?
⑤ I wonder how many people will come to the concert.

정답 P. 230

[9~10] 다음 글을 읽고 물음에 답하시오.

When I visited my grandfather, ⓐ he used to tell me about when he was my age. I have heard it hundreds of times, so I already know ⓑ what he will say after, "When I was your age, …" One of his least favorite things was any kind of digital device. This time I thought I could change his mind because he really enjoyed watching my singing performance on my phone. I told him, "Grandpa, I really want you to have a smartphone or an email address. If you use it, we can share many things and talk more often." However, my grandfather kept saying that it would be ⓒ too difficult to use a smartphone or email. He believed digital devices worsened the generation gap. I wondered ⓓ why held he on to his negative attitudes toward digital technologies. I found ⓔ it hard to narrow the gap between us, so I said to my father, "Grandpa simply can't understand my generation."

9 윗글의 밑줄 친 ⓐ~ⓔ 중 어법상 어색한 것을 찾아 바르게 고쳐 쓰시오.

__________ → __________

10 윗글의 내용과 일치하지 않는 것은?

① The writer often heard her grandfather talked about the past.
② The writer wants her grandfather to have a smartphone or email address.
③ The writer found it hard to explain digital divide to her grandfather.
④ The writer felt that there existed the generation gap between her grandfather and herself.
⑤ The writer could not understand why her grandfather did not want to use a smartphone.

[11~12] 다음 글을 읽고, 물음에 답하시오.

I felt sorry for my grandparents as I saw the photos. I began to understand how my grandfather felt, so I asked my father how I could bridge the gap between my grandparents and me. He said, "Jina, I know you're very good at computers. Why don't you make a digital family album? Even better, you could add some songs we all love, along with your singing contest video file. Your grandfather will be very pleased to be able to share his life history with you." I thought digital devices could connect our family and _____ⓐ_____. I suggested ⓑ the idea to my grandfather, and he accepted it with a big smile. Our digital family album starts with "When my grandfather was my age, …"

11 윗글의 빈칸 ⓐ에 알맞은 것은?

① worsen the situations
② resolve all the conflicts
③ interfere with our privacy
④ make us behave ourselves
⑤ strengthen the family bonds

12 윗글의 밑줄 친 ⓑ가 가리키는 것을 영어로 쓰시오.

____

13 다음 〈보기〉의 우리말과 같도록 괄호 안의 단어들을 사용하여 빈칸을 완성하시오.

보기 그는 자정 이후에 깨어 있는 것이 어렵다는 것을 알게 되었다. (it / to / difficult / stay / awake)

→ He found __________ after midnight.

Advanced

[1~2] 대화를 듣고, 물음에 답하시오.

1 **Why doesn't Mina want to visit her grandparents?**

① She gets bored when she visits them.
② She doesn't feel connected to her grandparents.
③ They make her do what she does not want to.
④ They don't let her play soccer with her friends.
⑤ She does not get along with older people like them.

2 **Andy가 이번 주 일요일에 할아버지 댁에서 하려고 하는 일로 맞는 것을 고르시오.**

① helping them with some house chores
② playing soccer with his friend Patrick
③ teaching them how to download music and apps
④ going shopping for a phone with his grandfather
⑤ fixing his grandfather's broken smartphone

3 **대화를 듣고, 대화의 내용과 일치하지 않는 것을 고르시오.**

① Ted is asking for advice from DJ Jennifer.
② Ted does not like his parents using Internet slang.
③ Ted thinks Internet slang words are fun and cool.
④ DJ Jennifer advises Ted not to use Internet slang when he talks to his parents.
⑤ Ted does not think it will be easy to change his habit of using slang words.

4 **다음 글의 빈칸에 가장 알맞은 것은?**

These days it's hard to imagine our life without communication devices such as smartphones, computers, and the Internet. However, have you thought about some of the people living in the Amazon Rainforest? Their lives may be quite different from ours. Not everyone in the world has access to communication technology. To describe this difference, we use the term "digital divide." This term has been used to describe the growing gap between ________________. This divide also exists between cities and rural areas, and between generations. Unfortunately, the gap between teens and older people is getting bigger.

① those people who are educated and those who aren't
② those people who divide people and those who unite them
③ those people who are rich and those who are poor
④ those people who have Internet access and those who do not
⑤ those people who destroy the rainforest and those who protect it

5 **다음 글의 빈칸에 들어갈 알맞은 말을 괄호 안에 주어진 단어들을 배열하여 바르게 쓰시오.**

Jina won first prize in the school singing contest. She chose a popular song from the 1980s to sing in front of all the students. Jina's best friend, Eunji, recorded the performance on her cell phone. After the contest, Jina showed the video file to her parents. Jina's father said, "Oh, your grandfather should watch this! This song is one of his favorites." Jina wanted to send the video file to her grandfather right away, but she realized he didn't have an email address or a smartphone. She felt sorry about this because she ________________ (had / to / wait / no / choice / but) until she could visit her grandparents.

6 다음 문장에 이어지는 글의 순서로 가장 알맞은 것은?

When my grandfather was my age, the Korean War broke out.

(A) As a laborer in the 1970s, he worked for a big construction company in Saudi Arabia and Iran for many years. When he thought of his family in Korea, he had to put up with all his difficulties.

(B) Things were quite different from the way we live now. He remembers how people suffered from cold, hunger, and poverty even after the war.

(C) My grandfather decided to leave his sick mother, two brothers, and three sisters because he was the only one who could earn money. Finally, he moved from his hometown to Seoul to make more money.

① (A) – (C) – (B)　② (B) – (A) – (C)
③ (B) – (C) – (A)　④ (C) – (A) – (B)
⑤ (C) – (B) – (A)

7 다음 글의 빈칸에 알맞은 말을 주어진 철자로 시작하여 쓰시오.

A love of music runs in the family. Music has been my grandfather's best friend throughout his life. He often listens to music when he feels sad. He told me he really liked the song that I sang at the singing contest. He also introduced me to a lot of songs I had never heard before. They were really amazing. We chose the first song for the background music of our d________ family album.

→ d________

8 다음 〈보기〉의 우리말과 같도록 괄호 안의 단어들을 사용하여 빈칸을 완성하시오.

보기　그 면접관은 나에게 내가 어떻게 특정 상황들을 처리할 것인지 물었다.
(I / certain / situations / how / would / handle)

→ The interviewer asked me ________________
________________.

[9~10] 다음 글을 읽고, 물음에 답하시오.

(A) We found it ① interested to make our own digital family album together. (B) My grandparents said they ② felt closer to me and my brother because our family talked about the photos and the old days. (C) We have finished ③ making the first two chapters of our digital family album, and we decided ④ to choosed some photos of my grandmother for the next chapter. (D) My grandmother has already ⑤ selected her favorite song (E) for the background music.
Our digital family album will never end!

9 윗글의 (A)~(E) 중 아래 문장이 들어가기에 가장 알맞은 곳은?

I was glad to learn about their past, and they also looked happy to share their stories with me.

① (A)　② (B)　③ (C)　④ (D)　⑤ (E)

10 윗글의 밑줄 친 ①~⑤ 중 어법상 어색한 것을 찾아 바르게 고쳐 쓰시오.

________________ → ________________

주관식 서술형 대비

11 지역 사회의 노인들을 위한 Computer Learning Center에서 자신이 할 수 있는 자원봉사 내용을 두 가지 쓰시오. (반드시 full sentence로 쓰시오.)

I think I'll be able to help the elderly people in the computer learning center by doing two things.
First, ________________
Second, ________________

[1~6] 잘 듣고, 물음에 답하시오.

01. 대화를 듣고, 다음 질문에 대한 알맞은 답을 고르시오.

Q. What will the boy be doing this weekend?

① He will be helping Hwajin with her math homework.
② He will be cleaning the community center with Hwajin.
③ He will be teaching math to the children at the community center.
④ He will be teaching Vietnamese to the children at the community center.
⑤ He will be reading some books written in Vietnamese to the children at the community center.

02. 다음을 듣고, 내용과 일치하지 않는 것을 고르시오.

① 본교에는 35개의 다양한 동아리가 있다.
② 지원 기간은 이번 주 수요일부터 다음 주 화요일까지이다.
③ 동아리에 관한 정보는 학교 웹사이트에서 얻을 수 있다.
④ 지원서 양식은 학교 홈페이지에서 다운로드하면 된다.
⑤ 기입한 지원서는 각 동아리 활동실에 제출하면 된다.

03. 다음을 듣고, 화자가 말하고 있는 주제로 가장 알맞은 것을 고르시오.

① Teach your friends to better process what you learned.
② Look for a learning strategy that suits your personality.
③ Create active learning activities that will help outgoing learners.
④ Stick to your own routine of learning though it does not look effective.
⑤ Find the balance between your preference in learning and your learning style.

04. 대화를 듣고, 여자의 마지막 말에 이어질 남자의 응답으로 가장 알맞은 것을 고르시오.

① I guess parents should be aware of their own language.
② I think it will take time to change my habit, but I will try. Thanks for the tip.
③ Parents should develop skills for communicating with their teen children.
④ Using slangs in the conversation with your parents is not always bad.
⑤ Internet slangs can be effective in delivering the messages of the teenagers.

05. 대화를 듣고, 남자가 말한 **digital divide**의 의미에 대해 바르게 설명한 것을 고르시오.

① the division of the people according to their economic capability
② the difference of the welfare service between the rich and the poor
③ the differing amount of information between those who have access communication technology and those who don't
④ the difference of the income between the workers in the rural area and those living in the city
⑤ the gap of literacy rate between the people in the developed countries and those living in the developing countries

06. 대화를 듣고, **Andy**의 마지막 말에 이어질 엄마의 응답으로 가장 알맞은 것을 고르시오.

① That's okay. You can help them next time.
② It sounds like your grandparents are proud of you.
③ That's great. I'm sure your grandparents will be happy.
④ You had better teach them basic stuff considering their age.
⑤ I'm afraid your parents won't be able to understand your decision.

07. 다음 글의 ①~⑤ 중 전체 흐름과 관계 없는 문장은?

Have you ever dreamed of flying high in the sky? Do you wish to drive a fancy car? We promise to give you the chance to own the airplane or car of your dreams. Does this sound too good to be true? Not at all! ① Join *Wings and Motors*, and you can assemble your own model airplane or car. ② By making your own aircraft and vehicles, you can improve your concentration. ③ If you want to, you can also take part in our annual airplane and car race. ④ Fly your airplane and feel like a professional aircraft flight pilot. ⑤ The next award for the farthest-flying airplane or the fastest car may be yours. Do not miss this chance to achieve your dream. Fly high and move fast with *Wings and Motors*!

08. 다음 글의 밑줄 친 ①~⑤ 중 어법상 어색한 것은?

Do you want to be a happier person? Do you want to learn the secrets to a more meaningful life? If so, then knock on the door of our club room. You will see that the key to happiness ① lies in helping others. Volunteer work may seem ② difficult, but it's not. We can do many simple things for those in need, such as delivering food to the elderly, talking with people living alone, and teaching children with ③ fewer opportunities for education. Some former members of our club ④ have continued their volunteer work after high school in order to serve those in need of help. Just a little bit of time and effort will ⑤ be doubled the happiness in your life. Join *Little Helpers* and experience the great joy of giving and sharing.

09. Burning Fire에 관한 다음 글의 내용에서 언급되지 않은 것은?

Have you ever imagined yourself in the middle of a big stage? You can relieve your stress by joining *Burning Fire*! Anyone who can sing or play an instrument is welcome to join us. We meet every day after school for practice sessions. Preparing for a perfect performance takes a lot of time and effort, but it brings great rewards and helps form stronger bonds with the other members. Our performances are known to be the best part of the school festival. Creating wonderful sounds together under the shining lights of the stage will keep your heart beating with excitement. With *Burning Fire*, your high school years will be completely fantastic!

① who can apply for it
② how often the members meet for practice
③ what it does at the festival
④ what you can get from doing the club activity
⑤ what to prepare for a perfect performance

10. 괄호 안의 ①~⑤ 중 아래의 문장이 들어가기에 가장 알맞은 곳은?

It may not seem valuable because you will get the exact same amount the next day.

Every morning, exactly 86,400 seconds are given to you. (①) However, you only have a limited amount of time in a day, and you cannot save any part of it. (②) Therefore, you should seize the day! In order to do so, you need to learn ways to manage this limited and precious time. (③) Although failing to manage time is a huge waste, spending it wisely is often difficult. (④) Sometimes, you struggle with too much work to do. (⑤) At other times, you find yourself passing the time without any pressure because there is no urgent task to fulfill.

11. 다음 글의 빈칸에 가장 알맞은 것은?

> Divide your activities into four categories: (1) important and urgent, (2) important but not urgent, (3) unimportant but urgent, and (4) unimportant and not urgent. Those that fall under the first category are your top responsibilities. Make sure that all of these are met before you move on to those that are less important or urgent. For example, let's say there will be an exam next week. You might want to study (important and urgent) first before you hang out with your friends (important but not urgent). It is easy to do the things you want to do first. However, categorizing will prevent you from losing focus and will ______ ______________________.

① do the things less urgent or not taken care of
② lead you to achieve your life-long goals with ease
③ help you accomplish the things that actually matter
④ constantly keep you motivated to do the things by yourself
⑤ enhance your performance skills on more urgent responsibilities

12. 다음 글의 ①~⑤ 중 전체 흐름과 관계 없는 문장은?

> Use your spare time wisely. ① Sometimes you may find yourself having only ten minutes before the next activity. ② You may think that nothing much can be done during this short time. ③ However, you can actually do many things in just ten minutes, like writing a paragraph for an assignment or solving about five math problems. ④ You can even do some reading on the subway. ⑤ Don't forget that for every minute you spend organizing, an hour is earned.

[13-14] 다음 글을 읽고, 물음에 답하시오.

> (A) I used my time in a very productive way today! It was all thanks to an article I read the other day. It had a lot of useful tips on ______________________. After reading it, I decided to put my responsibilities in the order of importance and plan ahead.
>
> (B) First, I was able to finish my research for the history assignment. All I have to do now is arrange the information in an organized fashion and make it readable. Also, I finished some reading for my English class. After finishing these important activities, I spent some quality time with my family.
>
> (C) I figured out that doing research for my history paper was my top responsibility. My English assignment was the second most important thing. After that, I made a schedule for the day by assigning more time to my top responsibilities. It was a great success!
>
> (D) I was really stressed out because I had assignments in both History and English. So, I first wrote down the activities I had to do and then put them into four different categories based on their urgency and importance.

13. 윗글의 (A)에 이어질 내용을 순서에 맞게 바르게 배열한 것은?

① (B) – (D) – (C)
② (C) – (B) – (D)
③ (C) – (D) – (B)
④ (D) – (B) – (C)
⑤ (D) – (C) – (B)

14. 윗글의 빈칸에 가장 알맞은 것은?

① being efficient at work
② effective time management
③ managing negative feelings
④ successful assignment writing
⑤ how to manage stress for students

15. 다음 글의 밑줄 친 ①~⑤ 중 어법상 어색한 것은?

When I visited my grandfather, he used ①to tell me about when he was my age. I have heard it hundreds of times, so I already know what he will say after, "When I was your age, ..." One of his ②least favorite things was any kind of digital device. This time I thought I ③could change his mind because he really enjoyed watching my singing performance on my phone. However, my grandfather kept saying that it would be too difficult ④to use a smartphone or email. He believed digital devices worsened the generation gap. I wondered why he held on to his negative attitudes toward digital technologies. I found it ⑤hardly to narrow the gap between us, so I said to my father, "Grandpa simply can't understand my generation.

[16-17] 다음 글을 읽고, 물음에 답하시오.

I felt sorry for my grandparents as I saw the photos. I began to understand how my grandfather felt, so I asked my father how I could bridge the gap between my grandparents and me. He said, "Jina, I know you're very good at computers. Why don't you make a digital family album? Even better, you could add some songs we all love, along with your singing contest video file. Your grandfather will be very pleased to be able to share his life history with you." I thought digital devices could ____________________. I suggested the idea to my grandfather, and he accepted it with a big smile. Our digital family album starts with "When my grandfather was my age, ..."

We found it interesting to make our own digital family album together. My grandparents said they felt closer to me and my brother because our family talked about the photos and the old days. I was glad to learn about their past, and they also looked happy to share their stories with me. We have finished making the first two chapters of our digital family album, and we decided to choose some photos of my grandmother for the next chapter. My grandmother has already selected her favorite song for the background music. Our digital family album will never end!

16. 윗글의 빈칸에 가장 알맞은 것은?

① cause more problems in communications
② change our attitude toward our grandparents
③ contribute to the development of digital albums
④ connect our family and strengthen the family bonds
⑤ worsen the relationship between parents and children

17. 윗글의 내용과 일치하지 않는 것은?

① Jina began to understand her grandfather after looking at the photos.
② Jina asked her father for advice on how to be closer to her grandparents.
③ Jina's grandfather liked the idea of making a digital family album.
④ Jina is going to put her grandmother's photos in the third chapter of the digital family album.
⑤ Jina's grandmother sang her favorite song and put it at the end of the digital family album.

18. 다음 글의 밑줄 친 ①~⑤ 중 어법상 어색한 것은?

Things were quite different from ①the way we live now. He remembers ②how suffered people from cold, hunger, and poverty even after the war. My grandfather ③decided to leave his sick mother, two brothers, and three sisters because he was the only one who could earn money. Finally, he moved from his hometown to Seoul ④to make more money. When he thought of his family, he ⑤had to put up with all his difficulties.

서술형

19. 다음 글의 밑줄 친 부분이 의미하는 것을 주어진 표현으로 시작하여 빈칸을 완성하시오.

Welcome to *No Limits*! Do you want to be in control of making movies? Do you want to turn your fantasies into a movie script? Do you want to make movie scenes more alive and realistic with interesting sounds? Do you want to be a cool action hero and win an impossible fight? Do you want to play the sweet guy or girl in a romantic movie? If your answer is "yes" to any of these questions, then come to *No Limits*. If you join us, you can take part in producing short films every year for the school festival. The fruits of your effort will taste so sweet when you hear the loud cheers and shouts of your friends. No pain, no gain? *No Limits*, and great gains!

⊖ You will be very proud ______________________
______________________________.

서술형

[20-21] 다음 문장의 괄호 안의 단어를 올바른 형태로 쓰시오.

20.

Our club is called *From Scratch* because we didn't know anything about (bake) at first and had to start from scratch.

⊖ ______________________________

21.

Without planning, you may find yourself easily (catch) up with more than one task and end up finishing none of them.

⊖ ______________________________

서술형

[22-23] 다음 〈보기〉의 우리말과 같도록 괄호 안의 단어들을 사용하여 빈칸에 알맞은 말을 쓰시오.

22.

보기 여러분은 어떤 사람들이 달력에 기록하거나 매일의 해야 할일을 목록으로 작성하는 것을 본다.
(a / to-do list / a / keeping / making / calendar / daily)

⊖ You see some people ______________________
______________________________.

23.

보기 우리와 할아버지를 분리시키는 보이지 않는 벽이 있는 것 같았다.
(wall / invisible / us / our / an / grandfather / separating / from))

⊖ There seemed to be ______________________.

서술형

24. Write one advantage and one disadvantage of using digital devices. Answer in full sentences.

① advantage: ______________________
____
② disadvantage: ______________________
____

논술형

25. Introduce your school club in 3-4 full sentences. You should include the name of the club, why you joined the club, and what you do in the club.

____
____
____
____

UNIT 4

Let's Make Every Day Earth Day

교과서 핵심 정리

Words & Phrases

Listen and Speak ~ Into Real Life

- ☐ trash *n.* 쓰레기 *cf.* garbage (주로 음식물) 쓰레기
- ☐ marine *adj.* 바다의, 해양의
- ☐ make sure* 반드시 ~하도록 하다, 확인하다
- ☐ keep in mind* ~를 명심하다
- ☐ forum *n.* 포럼, 학술회의
- ☐ earthquake *n.* 지진
- ☐ disaster* *n.* 재난, 재해 (natural disaster 자연 재해)
- ☐ notice *n.* 통지, 알림 (notice board 게시판)
- ☐ turn in 제출하다 (=submit)
- ☐ duty *n.* 의무 (=responsibility)
- ☐ confused* *adj.* 혼란스러운, 헛갈리는
- ☐ triangular *adj.* 삼각형의 (triangle *n.* 삼각형)

Read and Think

- ☐ storm *n.* 태풍, 폭풍 (stormy *adj.* 폭풍우 치는)
- ☐ claim *v.* (목숨을) 앗아가다, 주장하다, 요구하다
- ☐ southeast *n.* 남동 (또는 동남)
- ☐ injury *n.* 부상 (injured *adj.* 부상당한)
- ☐ exceed* *v.* (특정한 수나 양을) 넘어서다,
- ☐ severely *ad.* 심하게, 혹독하게 (severe *adj.* 심한)
- ☐ damage *n.* 손상 *v.* 손상을 입히다
- ☐ climate* *n.* 기후 *cf.* weather (하루의) 날씨
- ☐ dramatic *adj.* 극적인, 감격적인
- ☐ temperature *n.* 온도
- ☐ intensity *n.* 강도, 강렬함 (intense *adj.* 강렬한)
- ☐ micro dust* *n.* 미세 먼지
- ☐ significant *adj.* 중요한 (significance *n.* 중요성)
- ☐ shortage* *n.* 부족 (short *adj.* 부족한)
- ☐ classify *v.* 분류하다 (classification *n.* 분류)
- ☐ drought *n.* 가뭄 (↔ flood 홍수)
- ☐ transform* *v.* 변형시키다 (transformation *n.* 변형)
- ☐ reduce **v.* 줄이다, 축소하다 (reduction *n.* 감소)
- ☐ at long last 오랜 시간이 흐른 후에, 마침내
- ☐ root out* ~를 뿌리 뽑다, 근절하다
- ☐ official *adj.* 공식적인
- ☐ arctic* *adj.* 북극의, 북극지방의 *cf.* antarctic 남극의
- ☐ melt *v.* 녹다 *cf.* freeze 얼리다
- ☐ carbon dioxide* *n.* 이산화탄소 *cf.* oxygen 산소
- ☐ emission* *n.* 배출 (emit *v.* 배출하다, 내뿜다)
- ☐ greenhouse gas* *n.* 온실가스
- ☐ sink *v.* 가라앉다 *cf.* float (물 위에) 뜨다
- ☐ result in (어떤 결과를) 초래하다
- ☐ alternative *n.* 대안, 어느 하나를 택할 여지
- ☐ fossil fuel* *n.* 화석 연료
- ☐ boost *v.* 밀어 올리다, 부양하다
- ☐ renewable *adj.* 재생 가능한
- ☐ resource *n.* 자원, 물자
- ☐ long-lasting *adj.* 오래 지속되는
- ☐ hydrogen *n.* 수소
- ☐ awareness* *n.* 의식, 인식 (aware *adj.* 인식하는)
- ☐ auditorium *n.* 강당, 방청석, 큰 강의실
- ☐ make up for* ~를 벌충하다, 만회하다

Language Notes

- ☐ eliminate *v.* 제거하다, 없애다 (elimination *n.* 제거)
- ☐ illegal* *adj.* 불법적인 (↔ legal 합법적인)

Write It Right

- ☐ consumption* *n.* 소비, 소진 (consume *v.* 소비하다)
- ☐ ecology *n.* 생태학, 생태 환경 *cf.* ecosystem 생태계
- ☐ agriculture* *n.* 농업, 농경 (agricultural *adj.* 농업의)

Around the World

- ☐ be supposed to* ~하도록 되어 있다, ~해야 한다
- ☐ eco-friendly* *adj.* 친환경적인
- ☐ leftover *n.* (먹다) 남은 것, 잔존물
- ☐ ban *v.* 막다, 금지하다

☑ Check-Up

정답 P. 233

1 다음 문장의 빈칸에 알맞은 말을 〈보기〉에서 골라 넣으시오.

> **보기 >>** turn in / root out / make up for
> result in / at long last / keep in mind

(1) They tried hard to ________________ police corruption.
(2) Don't forget to ________________ your paper after class.
(3) You should ________________ that repair work is expensive.
(4) No amount of money can ________________ the death of a child.
(5) Regular exercise can ________________ the reduction of stress levels.
(6) ________________ the government is starting to listen to our problems.

Tip

❶ 주요 숙어표현 익히기
corruption 부패
repair 수리

2 다음 뜻풀이에 해당하는 말을 주어진 철자로 시작하여 쓰시오.

(1) o ____________: announced publicly with authority
(2) d ____________: a long period when there is little or no rain
(3) s ____________: a situation in which there is not enough of something
(4) a ____________: one that you can use if you do not want to use another one
(5) l ____________: the part that has not been used or eaten when the other parts have been

❷ 영영사전풀이
authority 권위
publicly 공식적으로, 공개적으로

주관식 서술형

3 우리말에 맞게 괄호 안의 단어들을 사용하여 문장을 완성하시오.

(1) 해수면의 상승이 몰디브가 가라앉는 결과를 가져왔다.
The rising sea level ______________________________ of the Maldives.
(sinking / in / has / resulted / the)

(2) 그는 우리가 왜 재생 에너지를 사용해야 하는지에 관해 말했다.
He talked about ______________________________________.
(use / renewable / we / energy / why / should)

(3) 반드시 그 지시를 주의 깊게 따르도록 하세요.
______________________________________ the instructions carefully.
(sure/ follow/ that/ make/ you)

(4) 그들은 친환경적인 방식을 써서 성공적으로 해수를 담수로 바꿔 놓았다.
They successfully ______________________________________
in an environmentally friendly way.
(fresh water / sea water / transformed / into)

❸ 핵심어휘를 사용한 영작
instruction 지시, 가르침
environmentally friendly 친환경적인

교과서 핵심 정리

Dialogues & Monologue

Listen and Speak | *해석을 참조하여 빈칸에 알맞은 말을 쓰시오.

GET READY

1 W: Hey, look at the trash on the beach.
M: Oh, no. That's terrible.
W: **You know what?** It can be dangerous for __________ life.
M: Let's clean it up.
W: Yeah, **let's make sure we keep our environment clean.**

여: 야, 해변에 쓰레기 좀 봐.
남: 이런. 끔찍하네.
여: 너 그거 알아? 이런 게 해양 생물에게 위험할 수 있어.
남: 함께 치우자.
여: 그래, 우리라도 꼭 환경을 깨끗이 지키도록 하자.

2 M: Oh, Seonmi. You didn't ________________ the light again!
W: Sorry, Dad. **I'll be returning to my room soon.**
M: But you're watching TV in the living room now. **Make sure you turn the light off** when you're not using it.
W: Okay, sorry. I'll keep that in mind.

남: 아, 선미야. 너 또 불을 끄지 않았구나.
여: 죄송해요, 아빠. 곧 방으로 다시 들어갈 거예요.
남: 하지만 넌 지금 거실에서 TV를 보고 있잖니. 사용하지 않고 있을 때는 불을 꼭 꺼야지.
여: 알았어요. 죄송해요. 명심 할게요.

3 W: Ladies and gentlemen! May I have your attention, please? Please make sure that you turn your phones __________ before the forum begins. Today we have a special guest. She is the author of the book, *Seven Ways to Save Mother Earth*. Let's welcome Michelle Kim.

여: 신사 숙녀 여러분! 주목해 주시겠어요? 포럼이 시작되기 전에 반드시 휴대폰 전원을 꺼 주시기 바랍니다. 오늘 저희가 특별한 분을 모셨어요. 그녀는 '지구를 구하는 일곱 가지 방법'의 저자이십니다. Michelle Kim을 환영해 주세요.

표현정리
- You know what? : '너 그거 알아?'라는 뜻의 표현으로, 주의 환기 또는 어떤 말을 하기에 앞서 관용적으로 사용한다.
- let's make sure (that) we keep ~: make sure는 '꼭 ~하다'라는 뜻으로 반드시 해야 할 것에 관한 표현이다.
- I'll be returning to my room soon. : '곧 방에 다시 들어갈 거예요.'라는 뜻으로 진행형이라기보다는 가까운 미래시제이다.
- Make sure you turn the light off ~: 「Make sure + that 절 / to 부정사」의 형태는 상대방에게 강한 어조로 당부하는 말이다.

정답 marine / turn off / off

LISTEN IN

DIALOGUE 1

M: Have you heard about the earthquakes in Oklahoma?
W: No, I haven't. Why do you ask?
M: I heard that they were __________ caused by human activities.
W: Really? **How so?**
M: Some scientists found out the earthquakes were caused by the oil and gas business.
W: Are you sure? I thought they could cause environmental pollution.
M: Well, **it seems the process can actually cause** earthquakes.
W: That's terrible. Then should we stop using gas?
M: It's not easy to stop using gas.
W: Then what should we do?
M: We have to make sure we don't __________ our energy from now on.

남: 오클라호마에서 난 지진에 관해 들었어?
여: 아니. 왜 물어?
남: 내가 듣기로는 그게 인간의 활동 때문에 야기된 재난이라고 해서.
여: 정말? 어떻게 그렇지?
남: 어떤 과학자들이 그 지진들은 석유와 가스 (채굴) 사업 때문에 야기된 거라는 걸 알아냈어.
여: 정말이야? 나는 그런 일들이 환경오염을 일으킬 수 있다고 생각했어.
남: 그 과정에서 실제로 지진을 야기할 수 있나봐.
여: 끔찍하다. 그럼 우리 가스를 그만 사용해야 하는 건가?
남: 가스 사용을 중단하는 것은 쉽지 않아.
여: 그럼 우리 어떻게 해야 해?
남: 이제부터 우리는 에너지를 낭비하는 일이 절대 없도록 해야지.

대화상황
- 석유 가스 채굴 과정이 지진을 초래한 사건에 관해 이야기하고 있다.

표현정리
- How so? : '어떻게 그런 일이 생겼지?'라는 의미로, 어떤 일이 발생하게 된 과정을 묻고 있다.
- it seems (that) the process can actually cause ~: 「it seems + that 절」은 '~인 것 같다'는 의미이다.

정답 disasters / waste

DIALOGUE 2

W: **You know what?** Our school is holding a poster contest to celebrate World Environment Day.
M: Oh, yeah? What kind of poster contest is it?
W: I took a picture of the notice on the board. Let me show it to you.
M: Sounds interesting. We're good at art. Can we make posters as a team?
W: Yeah, the rules say we can.
M: Are there any special rules about the design and size of posters?
W: **It says posters should be** 30cm × 45cm. Also, we can use any __________ we want.
M: Should we write a slogan for the posters?
W: Good question. The rules say, "**Make sure** you don't copy any famous slogans. The school wants your __________ ideas."
M: When do we have to **turn** the poster **in**?
W: By next Friday. And the rules say, "Don't forget to write your name on the back of your posters."

여: 그거 알아? 우리학교에서 세계 환경의 날을 기념하기 위한 포스터 대회를 개최한대.
남: 어, 그래? 어떤 종류의 포스터 대회야?
여: 게시판에 공고 나온 것을 사진으로 찍었어. 너에게 보여줄게.
남: 재미있겠는데. 우리 미술 잘하잖아. 우리 팀으로 포스터 만들어 볼까?
여: 그래, 같이 해도 된다고 했어.
남: 포스터 디자인이나 크기에 관한 특별한 제한 규칙이 있어?
여: 포스터는 30cmX45cm 크기로 해야 한다고 되어 있어. 또한 재료는 원하는 대로 사용할 수 있어.
남: 포스터에 표어도 써야 하나?
여: 좋은 질문이야. 규칙에는 "유명한 표어를 모방하지 마세요. 학교는 창의적 아이디어를 원합니다."라고 되어 있어.
남: 언제까지 제출해야 해?
여: 다음 주 금요일까지야. 그리고 "포스터 뒷면에 이름을 쓰시는 것을 잊지 마세요."라고 적혀 있어.

대화상황
- '세계 환경의 날'기념 포스터 그리기 대회에 참가하기 위해 정해진 규칙에 관해 이야기하고 있다.

표현정리
- It says posters should be ~: 그림이나 간판에 있는 문구를 인용할 때 'It says (that) ~'을 써서 '~라고 써져 있어.'라는 뜻을 나타낸다.
- When do we have to turn the poster in? : 'turn in'은 '제출하다'라는 의미로 쓰여 제출 기한을 묻는 표현이다.

정답 materials / creative

DIALOGUE 3

W: Hi, Marco. What are you doing here?
M: I'm separating all the garbage produced in my classroom. It's my duty for this week.
W: Wait! You know what? The bottle caps do not belong with the glass.
M: Oh, you're right. I still get confused about which items go where.
W: **I know what you mean**, but I have a simple tip for you.
M: Really? What's that?
W: When you're confused, you can just check if the items have a triangular __________ and __________ inside.
M: I can see a triangle and number 1 on this item.
W: Items marked "1" and "2" mean they can be recycled.
M: **Got it**. Thanks for the tip.
W: Make sure you don't mix up what is recyclable and what is not.

여: 안녕, Marco. 여기서 뭐해?
남: 우리 교실에서 나온 쓰레기를 전부 분리하는 중이야. 그게 이번 주 내 임무거든.
여: 잠깐! 너 그거 알아? 유리병 뚜껑은 유리에 속하지 않는다고.
남: 어, 네 말이 맞아. 난 아직도 어떤 물건이 어디로 가야 하는지 혼동돼.
여: 무슨 말인지 알아. 그런데 내가 아주 간단한 팁을 줄게.
남: 정말? 그게 뭔데.
여: 혼동될 때는 그 물건에 삼각형 모양의 표시와 그 안에 숫자들이 들어있는지 확인해 봐.
남: 삼각형 표시랑 그 안에 1번이라고 쓰여 있는 게 보여.
여: 1이나 2라고 표시되어 있는 것은 재활용이 가능하다는 뜻이야.
남: 알겠어. 팁 고마워.
여: 재활용 가능한 것과 가능하지 않은 것을 섞지 않도록 명심해.

대화상황
- 교실에서 나온 쓰레기 중 재활용품과 쓰레기를 분리하는 것에 관련한 팁을 얘기하고 있다.

표현정리
- I know what you mean. : '무슨 말하는지 알아.'라는 뜻으로 상대방의 말에 대한 이해를 나타낸다.
- (I) Got it. : 대화 중 어떤 사실을 이해하거나 알게 되었을 때 쓰는 표현이다.

정답 symbol / numbers

Into Real Life

M: All across the world, people are facing serious environmental problems. It is May now, but it is already unusually hot. Today heat wave warnings were issued in Korea because the temperature was recorded at over 35 degrees Celsius. In India, the temperature reached 50 degrees Celsius for several days, and over a thousand people have died of heat-related illness so far. Beijing is covered with heavy yellow dust. Last Friday, schools were closed, and people were advised to avoid outdoor activities. Because of the heavy yellow dust, more than 300 flights were ________ at Beijing International Airport. Also, heavy rain and storms hit many cities in the United States. In Texas and Oklahoma, powerful storms killed at least nine people, and thirty people are still missing. On the other hand, California has been in a severe ________ for the past five years. The water levels of lakes are getting lower and lower. To stop suffering from these problems, it's time for us to take action for our earth.

남: 전 세계적으로 사람들은 심각한 환경 문제들을 직면하고 있습니다. 지금 5월인데 벌써 보통 때와 달리 덥습니다. 오늘 기온이 섭씨 35도 이상을 기록하면서 우리나라에 폭염 주의보가 발령되었습니다. 인도에서는 기온이 며칠 째 50도에 달하고 있고, 지금까지 천 명 이상의 사람들이 더위와 관련된 질병으로 사망했습니다. 북경은 강한 황사로 뒤덮여 있습니다. 지난 금요일 학교들은 휴교를 했고, 사람들은 외부 활동을 자제하도록 권유받았습니다. 짙은 황사 때문에 300편이 넘는 비행기가 북경 국제공항에서 결항했습니다. 또한 강한 폭풍우가 미국의 여러 도시를 강타했습니다. 텍사스와 오클라호마에서는 강한 태풍으로 최소 9명이 사망했고, 30명의 사람들이 실종 상태입니다. 한편, 캘리포니아에서는 지난 5년간 심한 가뭄이 기승을 부리고 있습니다. 호수의 수위는 점점 더 낮아지고 있습니다. 이런 문제들을 멈추기 위해서 우리가 지구를 위한 조치를 취해야 할 때입니다.

담화주제
- 기후 변화로 발생하고 있는 전 세계적인 자연 재해 및 피해 상황에 관해 보도하고 있다.

표현정리
- Today heat wave warnings were issued ~: issue는 '(경고 등을) 발표[공표]하다'라는 뜻이고 여기서는 수동태로 쓰였다.
- To stop suffering from these problems ~: 'suffer from'은 '~를 겪다'라는 뜻이다.

정답 canceled / drought

Check Your Progress

M: Jennifer, have you heard about the recent floods in Texas?
W: No, I haven't. Why do you ask, Brian?
M: I heard about it from my uncle who lives there. He said this flood was the worst.
W: Sorry to hear that. Are his family and his house safe?
M: Fortunately, they are all okay. He said they had heavy rains for seven days.
W: Oh, that's terrible.
M: Also, he said that all the schools were ________ because of the floods.
W: It seems that natural disasters happen a lot all over the world. We're suffering from severe droughts nowadays.
M: Right, I hope we can have some rain soon.
W: I think we should prepare for natural disasters.
M: I agree, but you know what? Some of them are ________ by human activities. Let's make sure to save our earth.

남: Jennifer, 최근 텍사스에서 있었던 홍수에 대해 들었어?
여: 아니. 왜 묻는데, Brian?
남: 거기 사는 우리 삼촌한테 들었는데 정말 최악의 홍수였대.
여: 유감이다. 삼촌네 가족이랑 집은 안전해?
남: 다행히도 우리 삼촌네는 괜찮아. 7일 동안이나 폭우가 내렸대.
여: 오, 정말 끔찍하다.
남: 그리고, 우리 삼촌이 그러는데 모든 학교가 홍수 때문에 휴교했대.
여: 전 지구상에서 자연 재해가 많이 일어나는 것 같아. 우리도 요즘 심한 가뭄 때문에 고생하고 있잖아.
남: 맞아. 곧 비가 좀 왔으면 좋겠어.
여: 우리도 자연 재해에 대비해야 할 것 같은 생각이 들어.
남: 그래, 맞아. 하지만 너 그거 알아? 어떤 자연 재해는 인간의 활동 때문에 일어난대. 우리 지구를 꼭 구하도록 하자.

담화주제
- 남자의 삼촌이 사는 텍사스의 홍수 사태를 비롯한 세계의 자연 재해의 심각성에 관해 대화하고 있다.

표현정리
- Sorry to hear that. : 들은 내용에 대해 유감이나 동정을 표할 때 쓰는 표현이다.

정답 closed / caused

교과서 핵심 정리

Reading Comprehension

*해석을 참조하여 빈칸에 알맞은 말을 쓰거나 괄호에서 알맞은 말을 고르시오.

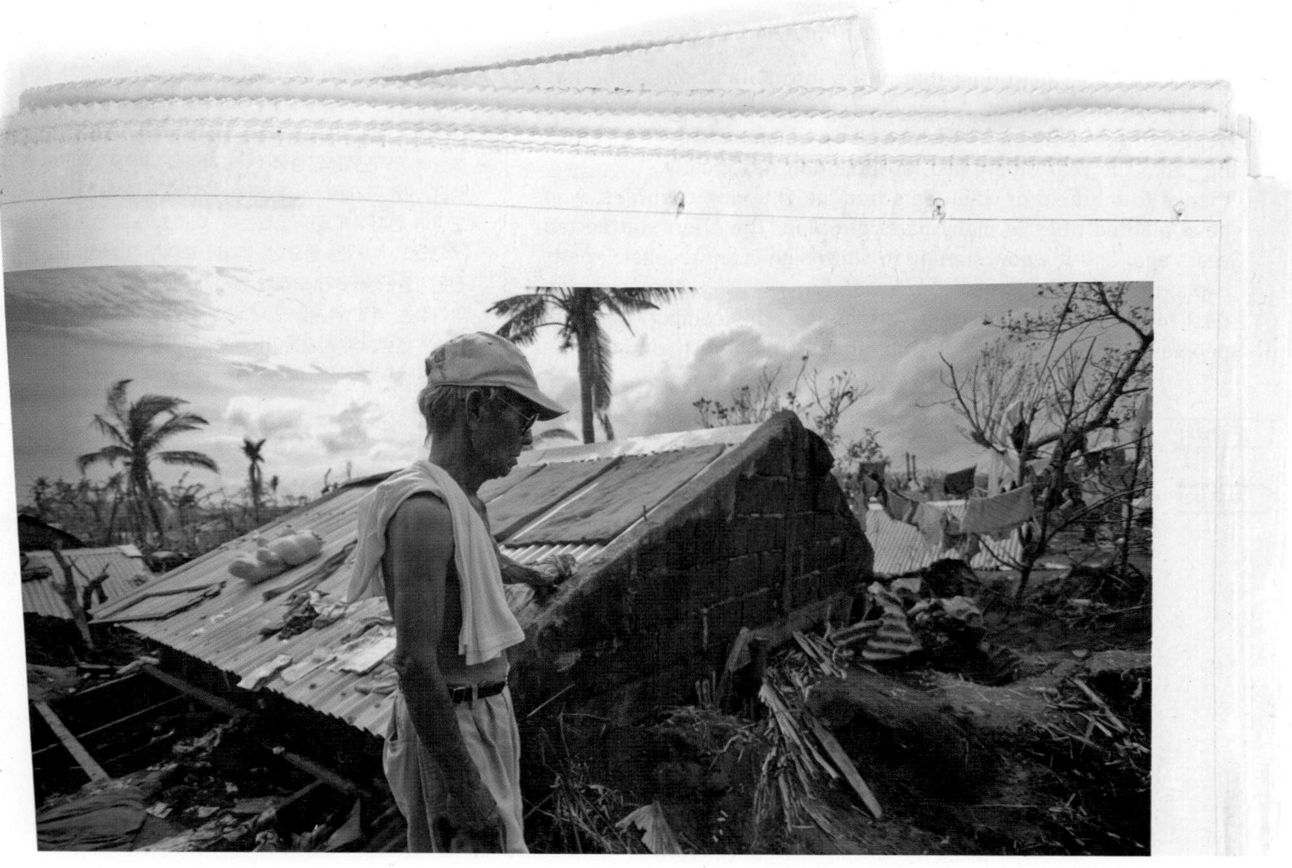

P.75 L.4~21

Weather

Super Storms Claim More than One Million Lives

Since the latest super storm hit Southeast Asia, the total number of deaths and injuries has now exceeded one million. At 3 p.m. on March 30th, 2025, an 18-hour storm severely damaged the region. On April 2nd, the number of deaths and __________ individuals stood at 514,000, with over 17,000 missing, and the numbers are expected to rise. One 65-year-old man who lost his house said, "I've never seen such strong winds in my whole life. I've lost everything." The storm left many people homeless. A __________ scientist said this super storm was obviously caused by dramatic changes in the global climate. He added, "A rise in global temperatures has increased the intensity of storms with higher wind speeds." Unfortunately, researchers predict that super storms will happen more ____________ this summer.

날씨

슈퍼 폭풍이 백만 명 이상의 목숨을 앗아가다

최근 슈퍼 폭풍이 동남아시아를 강타한 이래로, 총 사망자와 부상자 수가 현재 백만 명을 넘어섰다. 2025년 3월 30일 오후 3시, 18시간의 태풍이 그 지역에 심한 손상을 가했다. 4월 2일, 사망자와 부상자 수는 514,000명에 이르렀고 17,000명 이상이 실종되었으며, 그 수는 늘어날 것으로 보인다. 집을 잃은 한 65세 노인은 "내 평생 이렇게 강한 바람은 처음 봐요. 모든 걸 잃었어요."라고 말했다. 폭풍으로 인해 많은 사람들이 집을 잃었다. 한 기후 과학자는 이 슈퍼 폭풍이 세계 기후의 급격한 변화에 의해 야기된 게 분명하다고 말했다. 그는 "세계적 기온 상승이 더 강력해진 풍속으로 폭풍의 강도를 높였다."라고 덧붙였다. 불행히도, 연구자들은 슈퍼 폭풍이 이번 여름 더 자주 발생할 거라고 예상하고 있다.

단락요약

- 슈퍼 폭풍으로 인한 시간별 사상자 수에 대해 이야기 하면서 슈퍼 폭풍의 발생 원인에 관해 말하고 있다.

구문정리

- Since the latest ~, the total number ~ has now exceeded: 「since + 과거시점, 주어 + 동사(현재완료: have/has + p.p.)」 구문으로, 과거 시점 이래로 지금까지의 상황이나 상태를 표현한다.
- The storm left many people homeless.: 「leave + 목적어 + 형용사」는 '~를 …한 상태로 놔두다/만들다'는 뜻이다.

정답 injured / climate / frequently

P.76 L.1~26

Life Issues

Volunteers Respond to the Micro Dust Problem

For years, the micro dust that blows into Korea from China has been a serious problem. A few years ago, despite global efforts to deal with the problem, it seemed the problem was getting worse. But from the year before last, air pollution has greatly __________ thanks to the help of volunteers from neighboring countries, who have planted trees in many parts of China. The effort started ten years ago, and it's now starting to show significant results. Experts explain that the trees serve as a wall to __________ the sand and dust from crossing into Korea. At long last, this coming weekend, people of all ages are expected to breathe in the fresh air.

생활 문제

자원봉사자들이 미세먼지 문제에 답하다

몇 년간, 중국에서 한국으로 불어오는 미세먼지가 심각한 문제가 되고 있다. 몇 년 전, 이 문제를 해결하려는 세계적 노력에도 불구하고, 문제는 더 심각해지는 것으로 보였다. 그런데 재작년부터, 중국 여러 지역에 나무를 심어왔다. 그들은 이웃 국가들에서 온 자원봉사자들의 도움 덕분에 공기 오염이 현저하게 줄어들었는데, 이러한 노력은 10년 전 시작되었고, 이제는 중요한 결과를 보여주기 시작하고 있다. 전문가들은 나무가 모래와 먼지가 한국으로 이동하는 것을 막아주는 벽의 역할을 한다고 설명한다. 마침내, 이번 주말에, 전 연령층의 사람들이 신선한 공기를 마실 수 있을 것으로 기대되고 있다.

단락요약
- 미세먼지의 발원지에 자원봉사자들이 나무를 심어 우리나라로 미세먼지가 날아오는 것을 막아 준 사례를 얘기하고 있다.

구문정리
- ~ despite global efforts to deal with the problem ~: despite (=in spite of)는 '~에도 불구하고'라는 뜻의 전치사로 쓰인다.
- ~ volunteers from neighboring countries, who have planted trees ~: who는 앞에 콤마가 있으므로 관계대명사의 계속적 용법이다. 선행사 volunteers를 수식하는 관계대명사로 쓰였다.

정답 decreased / block

P.76 L.1-23

Technology

Making Up for the Water Shortage

Korea, along with many other countries in the world, is still classified as a country with a serious water __________. However, this is starting to become a thing of the past. The remarkable development of engineering and chemistry inspired Korean researchers, who have tried to solve severe drought problems. In the end, they successfully __________ sea water into fresh water in an environmentally friendly way. They also found a way to reuse water that contains high salt content. This new solution has reduced worries about the effects of this technology on marine life. Since this technology has become widely used, it has become a source of hope for the people who need __________ water. A sufficient supply of clean water using the technology is now being developed and is expected to help root out diseases that are caused by the world's lack of clean water.

기술

물 부족 현상을 보완하다

세계 여러 나라와 마찬가지로 한국도 여전히 심각한 물 부족 현상을 겪는 나라로 분류되어 있다. 하지만, 이것은 이제 과거 일이 되기 시작하고 있다. 기술과 화학의 놀라운 발전이 한국의 과학자들을 고무시켰고 이들은 심각한 가뭄의 문제를 해결하려고 노력해 왔다. 결국, 그들은 친환경적인 방법으로 해수를 담수로 성공적으로 바꾸어 놓았다. 그들은 또한 높은 소금 농도를 함유한 물을 재사용하는 방법도 찾아냈다. 이 새로운 해결책은 이 기술이 해양 생물에게 미칠 영향에 대한 걱정도 줄여주었다. 이 기술이 폭넓게 사용된 이래로, 이것은 식수가 필요한 사람들에게 희망의 원천이 되어왔다. 기술을 사용하여 깨끗한 물을 충분히 공급하는 방법이 현재 개발 중이고 깨끗한 물의 부족으로 인해 야기되는 질병을 근절하는 데 도움이 될 수 있기를 기대하고 있다.

단락요약
- 물 부족 현상 해결을 위한 과학자들의 노력으로 해수를 담수로 바꾸고 오염된 물을 깨끗한 물로 바꾸는 기술이 개발되었다.

구문정리
- Korea, ~is still classified as a country ~: 「be동사+classified as ~」는 '~로 분류되다'라는 의미의 수동태 구문이다.
- ~ inspired Korean researchers, who have tried : who는 선행사 Korean researchers를 가리키는 관계대명사이고 콤마(,)와 함께 쓰여 계속적 용법을 나타낸다.
- ~ the technology is now being developed: 「be동사(현재형) +being +p.p.」는 현재진행형 수동태로 '~되고 있는 중이다'라는 의미이다.

정답 shortage / transformed / drinkable

P.77 L.1~15

Focus

Rising Sea Levels Threaten Nations

It's now official. The Arctic ice has melted away and is now only one-fifth of what it was in 1979. Many climate scientists have said that the Arctic could have a summer entirely free of __________ by 2030 due to global warming. So what is causing the temperature to rise? The main cause is carbon dioxide emissions. Greenhouse gases are being trapped within the earth's atmosphere, which has led to rising temperatures. The rising sea level has resulted in the sinking of the Maldives, which is a famous tourist destination. According to many researchers, by 2100, New York and Shanghai will also sink, and the average global temperature is expected to be about 3.6 degrees __________ than now. Some may wonder why we should worry about a three-degree increase in warming. A one-degree global change is highly significant because it takes a vast amount of heat to warm all the earth's oceans, atmosphere, and land. In the past, just a one- to two-degree drop caused the earth to go through the Little Ice Age. World leaders have realized the __________ of climate change, so they will meet in Paris next month for a climate forum.

초점

해수면의 상승이 여러 나라를 위협하다

이제 이것은 일반적으로 알려진 사실이다. 북극의 얼음이 녹고 있고 1979년 얼음 양의 겨우 1/5 밖에 안 된다. 많은 기후학자들은 2030년이면 지구 온난화 때문에 북극이 완전히 얼음 없는 여름을 맞게 될 거라고 말해왔다. 그러면 무엇이 온도 상승을 야기하고 있는가? 주된 원인은 이산화탄소의 배출이다. 온실가스는 지구 대기 상에 갇혀 있으면서 온도의 상승을 이끈다. 해수면의 상승은 몰디브의 침몰을 초래했고, 이곳은 유명한 관광지이다. 많은 연구가들에 의하면, 2100년쯤이면 뉴욕과 상하이가 가라앉을 것이고 평균 지구의 온도는 지금보다 약 3.6도가 올라갈 것으로 예상되고 있다. 어떤 사람들은 왜 우리가 3도 정도 더워지는 것에 대해 걱정을 해야 하는지 궁금해 할 것이다. 지구 전체의 해양과 대기와 땅을 덥히기 위해서는 엄청난 양의 열이 필요하기 때문에 전체적으로 1도가 증가한다는 것은 아주 심각한 일이다. 과거에 1도 또는 2도 정도 온도의 하락이 소빙하기를 야기했었다. 세계 지도자들은 기후 변화의 심각성을 깨닫고 있으며 그래서 그들은 다음 달 기후 포럼을 위해 파리에서 만날 예정이다.

단락요약

- 지구 온난화로 인한 해수면 상승의 심각성과 지구 표면 온도의 작은 변화의 위험성을 설명하고 있다.

구문정리

- ~ only one-fifth of what it was in 1979: 「분수 + of + what it was」는 '과거 ~때의 분수'라고 해석한다. 분수 표현은 분자를 기수(one, two, three...)로, 분모를 서수(third, fourth, tenth ...)로 하여 표현하고, 분자가 2 이상일 때에는 분모에 복수형을 쓴다.

정답 ice / higher / seriousness

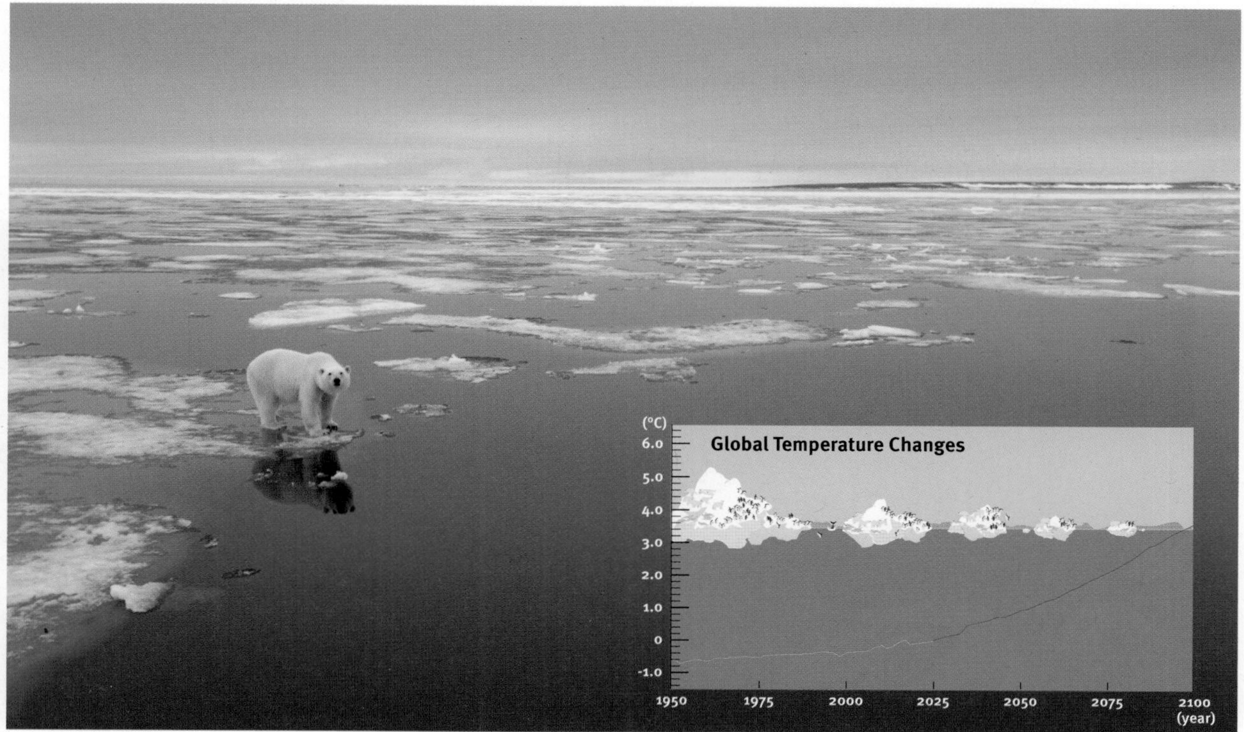

P.78 L.1~15

Energy

The Pursuit of More Efficient Alternative Energy Sources

The global ban on fossil fuels gave a boost to alternative energy. A number of companies around the world have built up more effective energy sources that can make up for the shortage of fossil fuels. Thanks to the development of _________ energy resources, they now make up more than half of the country's entire power, and this rate is set to grow even bigger. Renewable energy resources come from a wide variety of sources including the sun, the wind, and the sea. Using renewable energy produces less air or water pollution and _________ carbon dioxide emissions than using fossil fuels. The rapid development of renewable energy sources will help us meet energy demands without creating much _________.

에너지

더 효율적인 대체 에너지 자원을 찾아서

세계적인 화석연료 금지는 대체 에너지(개발)를 촉진시켰다. 세계 많은 회사들이 화석연료의 부족을 보충할만한 더 효과적인 에너지 자원을 개발해왔다. 재생에너지 자원 개발 덕분에, 우리는 국가 전체의 전력 중 절반 이상을 메울 수 있게 되었고, 이 비율은 훨씬 더 커져갈 것이다. 재생에너지 자원은 태양, 바람, 바다 등 다양한 원천에서 온다. 이러한 재생 가능 에너지는 대기 오염과 수질 오염을 덜 야기하고 화석 연료를 쓰는 것보다 이산화탄소 배출이 적다. 재생 가능 에너지 자원의 급속한 개발은 많은 오염을 야기하지 않고 에너지 수요를 충족시키는 데 도움이 될 것이다.

The Green Car Market

As the competition in the electric car market has become more intense, many companies have long been struggling to develop long-lasting electric car batteries. At the same time, hydrogen cars with satellite communications have also joined in this competition. They can eliminate polluted air produced by fossil fuel engines. Heating up the green car market fever, the launch of new hydrogen cars is expected to help reduce air pollution and eventually solve the energy crisis.

친환경 자동차 시장

전기 자동차 시장의 경쟁이 점차 치열해지면서 많은 회사가 오래 가는 전기 자동차 배터리를 개발하는 데 오랫동안 힘써오고 있다. 동시에, 위성 통신을 장착한 수소차가 이 경쟁에 뛰어들었다. 이 차들은 화석 연료 엔진으로부터 나오는 오염된 공기를 제거할 수 있다. 이 친환경 자동차 시장의 열기를 높이며, 새로운 수소차의 도입은 대기 오염을 줄이고 결국 에너지 위기를 해결하는 데 도움이 될 것으로 기대된다.

단락요약

- 대체 에너지 자원 개발의 장점과 친환경 자동차 시장의 활성화를 통한 환경문제 개선이 기대된다는 기사이다.

구문정리

- A number of companies around the world have built up ~: a number of는 numerous, many 등과 같은 의미로서 복수 명사와 같이 쓰인다. 따라서 동사는 has가 아닌 have를 사용해야 한다.
- Using renewable energy produces less ~ than using fossil fuels.: 비교구문에서 than 앞의 주어가 Using이므로 비교 대상의 동사도 같은 동명사 형태인 using을 쓴다.

정답 renewable / fewer / pollution

Focus on Structure

P.76 L.17-20 Air pollution has greatly decreased | thanks to the help of volunteers from neighboring countries, | who have planted trees in many parts of China.

(S: Air pollution / V: has greatly decreased / 선행사: volunteers / 쉼표 / who: 관계대명사(주격, 계속적 용법))

⊖ that을 제외한 관계대명사의 경우, 앞에 콤마(,)를 쓰고 선행사에 대한 추가적 정보를 제공할 수 있는데, 이를 계속적 용법이라고 한다. (제한적 용법인 경우와 달리 계속적 용법인 경우는 「and + 주어(대명사)」로 바꿔 쓸 수 있다.

cf. My sister **who** lives in London got married to a lawyer. 런던에 사는 (내) 누나는 변호사와 결혼했다.

(→ 런던 이외의 지역에 사는 또 다른 누나가 있을 수 있음)

My sister, **who** lives in London, got married to a lawyer. 내 누나는 런던에 사는데 변호사와 결혼했다.

관계대명사 which가 계속적 용법으로 쓰여, 특정한 선행사가 아니라 앞 절(문장) 전체를 가리키는 경우가 있다.

ex. Greenhouse gases are being trapped in the atmosphere, **which** has led to rising temperatures.
(온실가스는 대기에 갇혀 있는데 그것이 기온 상승의 원인이 된다.) (= and it)

P.76 L.19-21 A sufficient supply of clean water | using the technology | is now being developed.

(S: A sufficient supply of clean water / 형용사구: using the technology / V「be동사 + being + p.p.」: is now being developed)

⊖ 동사의 시제와 태를 한꺼번에 나타내는 현재진행 수동태는「be동사의 현재형 + being + p.p.」의 형태로 나타내고, '~되고 있는 중이다'는 의미이다.

cf. Harry **is measuring** the room. (Harry는 방을 측정하고 있다.: 진행형 – 능동태)

→ The room **is being measured** by Harry. (Harry에 의해 방이 측정되고 있다. : 진행형 – 수동태)

She **was putting** the pumpkins into the basket. (그녀는 호박들을 바구니에 넣고 있었다.: 과거진행 능동태)

→ The pumpkins **were being put** into the basket by her. (그녀에 의해 호박이 바구니에 담겨지고 있었다.: 과거진행 수동태)

☑ Check-Up

정답 P. 233

1 다음 문장을 수동태로 바꿔 쓰시오.

(1) The drone is delivering the mail.
→ The mail ______________________.

(2) GPS is calculating the route to your destination.
→ The route to your destination ______________.

2 다음 두 문장을 관계대명사의 계속적 용법을 이용하여 한 문장으로 만드시오.

(1) It inspired the researchers. They tried to solve the problem.
→ It ______________________.

(2) My grandfather goes swimming every day. He is 87 years old.
→ ______________ goes swimming every day.

(3) The film is released on Friday. It stars Tom Carter.
→ ______________ is released on Friday.

Tip

❶ (1) 드론에 의해 우편물이 배송되는 중이다. (현재진행 수동태)
(2) be동사의 현재형 + being + p.p. (현재진행 수동태)

❷ 관계대명사의 계속적 용법
(1) researchers는 사람이므로 관계대명사는 who를 쓴다.
(2) He가 가리키는 grandfather가 선행사이므로 주격 관계대명사를 쓴다.
(3) it이 가리키는 film이 선행사이다.
release (영화를) 개봉하다

언어 기능별 집중 대비

Listen and Speak/Into Real Life

정답 P. 233

1 다음을 듣고, 여자가 당부하고 있는 것을 고르시오.

① Do not be late for the forum.
② Ask for a permission to take a picture.
③ Do not bring the phones to the forum.
④ Do not take a picture of the special guest.
⑤ Turn off the phones before the forum starts.

2 대화를 듣고, 학교에서 개최하는 포스터 대회에 관해 맞지 않는 것을 고르시오.

① 팀으로 참가하는 것도 가능하다.
② 세계 환경의 날을 기념하는 행사이다.
③ 그림의 재료는 몇 가지로 제한되어 있다.
④ 유명한 표어나 문구를 그대로 사용해서는 안 된다.
⑤ 포스터 작품 뒷면에 작성자 이름을 써서 내야 한다.

3 대화를 듣고, 여자의 마지막 말로 가장 알맞은 것을 고르시오.

① Make sure you mark items properly.
② Make sure you don't litter in public places.
③ Make sure you perform your duty of separating items.
④ Make sure you don't mix up what is recyclable and what is not.
⑤ Make sure you don't buy any items produced in an unethical way.

4 다음을 듣고, 물음에 답하시오.

(1) 방송의 주제로 가장 알맞은 것은?
① Heavy yellow dust in large cities
② Climate change and its consequences
③ How to save energy for our environment
④ Increasing severe droughts in urban areas
⑤ Natural disasters caused by human activities

(2) 방송에서 언급되지 않은 것은?
① 이례적으로 심한 무더위
② 열사병으로 인한 환자 발생
③ 짙은 황사로 인한 임시 휴교
④ 심한 황사로 인한 항공편 결항
⑤ 오염된 식수로 인한 전염병 발생

Tip

❶ 유의사항 파악하기
출처: Get Ready_3
permission 허가, 허락

❷ 세부사항 파악하기
출처: Listen In_Dialogue 2

❸ 출처: Listen In_Dialogue 3
properly 적절히
recyclable 재활용 가능한
unethical 비윤리적인

❹ (1) 주제 고르기
(2) 구체적인 정보 파악하기
출처: Into Real Life_Step 1
drought 가뭄
urban 도시의

언어 기능별 집중 대비

Read and Think

정답 P. 234

Tip

[1-2] 다음 글을 읽고, 물음에 답하시오.

Since the latest super storm hit Southeast Asia, the total number of deaths and injuries ① <u>have</u> now exceeded one million. At 3 p.m. on March 30th, 2025, an 18-hour storm severely ② <u>damaged</u> the region. On April 2nd, the number of deaths and injured individuals stood at 514,000, with over 17,000 missing, and the numbers ③ <u>are expected</u> to rise. One 65-year-old man who lost his house said, "I've never seen such strong winds in my whole life. I've lost everything." The storm left many people homeless. A climate scientist said this super storm was obviously ④ <u>caused by</u> dramatic changes in the global climate. He added, "A rise in global temperatures ⑤ <u>has increased</u> the intensity of storms with higher wind speeds." Unfortunately, researchers predict that super storms will happen more frequently this summer.

1-2 출처: P.75 L.2-21
유형: 1. 문법성 판단
2. 제목 고르기
claim (목숨을) 빼앗다
vulnerable 취약한

1 윗글의 밑줄 친 ①~⑤ 중 어법상 <u>어색한</u> 것을 골라 바르게 고쳐 쓰시오.

2 위 기사문의 제목으로 가장 알맞은 것은?

① Dramatic Changes in the Global Climate
② Homeless People Ask for International Aids
③ Climate Scientists Warn the Super – hot Summers
④ Super Storms Claim More than One Million Lives
⑤ Southeast Asian Countries Vulnerable to Climate Change

3 다음 글의 밑줄 친 ①~⑤ 중 문맥상 <u>어색한</u> 것은?

3 출처: P.77 L.3-12
유형: . 문맥에 따른 어휘의 쓰임

It's now official. The Arctic ice has melted away and is now only one-fifth of what it was in 1979. Many climate scientists have said that the Arctic could have a summer entirely ① <u>free of</u> ice by 2030 due to global warming. So what is causing the temperature ② <u>to rise</u>? The main cause is carbon dioxide emissions. Greenhouse gases are being trapped within the earth's atmosphere, which has led to ③ <u>rising</u> temperatures. The rising sea level has resulted in the ④ <u>sinking</u> of the Maldives, which is a famous tourist destination. According to many researchers, by 2100, New York and Shanghai will also sink, and the average global temperature is expected to be about 3.6 degrees ⑤ <u>lower</u> than now. Some may wonder why we should worry about a three-degree increase in warming. A one-degree global change is highly significant because it takes a vast amount of heat to warm all the earth's oceans, atmosphere, and land. In the past, just a one- to two-degree drop caused the earth to go through the Little Ice Age.

①  ③  ⑤

Tip

4 다음 문장의 뒤에 이어질 글의 순서로 가장 알맞은 것은?

Korea, along with many other countries in the world, is still classified as a country with a serious water shortage.

(A) This new solution has reduced worries about the effects of this technology on marine life. Since this technology has become widely used, it has become a source of hope for the people who need drinkable water.

(B) However, this is starting to become a thing of the past. The remarkable development of engineering and chemistry inspired Korean researchers, who have tried to solve severe drought problems.

(C) A sufficient supply of clean water using the technology is now being developed and is expected to help root out diseases that are caused by the world's lack of clean water.

(D) In the end, they successfully transformed sea water into fresh water in an environmentally friendly way. They also found a way to reuse water that contains high salt content.

① (B) – (C) – (D) – (A)
② (B) – (D) – (A) – (C)
③ (B) – (D) – (C) – (A)
④ (C) – (B) – (D) – (A)
⑤ (C) – (D) – (A) – (B)

4 출처: P.76 L.2-24
유형: 글의 순서 파악하기

[5-6] 다음 글을 읽고, 물음에 답하시오.

For years, the micro dust that blows into Korea from China has been a serious problem. (A) A few years ago, despite global efforts to deal with the problem, it seemed the problem was getting worse. (B) But from the year before last, air pollution has greatly decreased thanks to the help of volunteers from neighboring countries, who have planted trees in many parts of China. (C) Experts explain that the trees serve as a wall to block the sand and dust from crossing into Korea. (D) ___________, this coming weekend, people of all ages are expected to breathe in the fresh air. (E)

5-6 출처: P.76 L.2-25
유형: 5. 문장의 위치 파악
6. 연결어 추론
to make things worse 설상가상으로

5 윗글의 (A)~(E) 중 아래의 문장이 들어가기에 가장 알맞은 곳은?

The effort started ten years ago, and it's now starting to show significant results.

① (A) ② (B) ③ (C) ④ (D) ⑤ (E)

6 윗글의 빈칸에 가장 알맞은 것은?

① At long last
② In addition
③ For instance
④ To make things worse
⑤ More often than not

[7-8] 다음 글을 읽고, 물음에 답하시오.

The global ban on fossil fuels ① gave a boost to alternative energy. ② A number of companies around the world have built up more effective energy sources that can ③ make up for the shortage of fossil fuels. Thanks to the development of renewable energy resources, they now ④ make up more than half of the country's entire power, and this rate is set to grow even bigger. Renewable energy resources come from ⑤ a wide variety of sources including the sun, the wind, and the sea. Using renewable energy produces less air or water pollution and fewer carbon dioxide emissions than using fossil fuels. The rapid development of renewable energy sources will help us meet energy demands ____________________.

7-8 출처: P.78 L.3-15
유형: 7. 숙어의 뜻
8. 빈칸 추론

7 윗글의 밑줄 친 ①~⑤ 중 한글 뜻풀이로 잘못된 것은?

① 기세를 떨어뜨리다　　② 많은
③ 만회하다　　④ 차지하다
⑤ 매우 다양한

8 윗글의 빈칸에 가장 알맞은 것은?

① without creating much pollution
② in spite of the high cost of development
③ regardless of the impact on our environment
④ giving us a doubt on zero emissions of carbon dioxide
⑤ keeping car companies from competing with each other

9 다음 글의 괄호 안의 (a)~(c)에 들어갈 단어의 형태가 맞는 것끼리 연결된 것은?

9 출처: P.78 L.4-15
유형: 문법성 판단

As the competition in the electric car market has become more intense, many companies have long been (a) (struggled / struggling) to develop long-lasting electric car batteries. At the same time, hydrogen cars with satellite communications (b) (has / have) also joined in this competition. They can eliminate polluted air produced by fossil fuel engines. (c) (Heated / Heating) up the green car market fever, the launch of new hydrogen cars is expected to help reduce air pollution and eventually solve the energy crisis.

① struggled — has — Heated
② struggled — has — Heating
③ struggled — have — Heating
④ struggling — have — Heated
⑤ struggling — have — Heating

언어 기능별 집중 대비

Language Notes / Write It Right

정답 P. 234

1 다음 우리말에 맞게 괄호 안의 단어를 이용하여 문장을 완성하시오.

(1) 온실가스들이 지구의 대기권 내에서 (빠져나가지 못하게) 가둬지고 있는 중이다.
Greenhouse gases ______________ within the earth's atmosphere. (trap)

(2) 깨끗한 물 공급 시스템을 위한 기술들이 개발되고 있는 중이다.
Technologies for clean water supply system ______________. (develop)

(3) 물 부족은, 가뭄과는 다른데, 수요를 충족시킬 만큼의 물이 없다는 것이다.
Water shortage, ______________, is related to a shortage of water availability to satisfy demands. (differ)

(4) 수소 자동차는, 연료 전지에 의해 동력을 얻는데, 단지 물과 열만 방출한다.
Hydrogen cars, _________ by fuel cells, emit only water and heat. (power)

(5) 그녀는 손가락을 톡톡거리고 있었는데 그것이 나를 짜증나게 했다.
She was tapping her fingers, ______________ me angry. (make)

Tip

❶ (1), (2) 현재진행 수동태
(3), (4) 관계대명사의 계속적 용법
(5) 앞 문장 전체를 선행사로 받는 관계대명사의 계속적 용법

2 다음 글을 읽고, 물음에 답하시오.

It's now official. The Arctic ice has melted away and is now only one-fifth of what it was in 1979. Many climate scientists have said that the Arctic could have a summer entirely free of ice by 2030 due to global warming. So what is causing the temperature to rise? The main cause is carbon dioxide emissions. Greenhouse gases are being trapped within the earth's atmosphere, which has led to rising temperatures. The rising sea level has resulted in the sinking of the Maldives, which is a famous tourist destination.

(1) What is the main cause for the rising temperature of the earth?

____

(2) What has happened as a result of the sea level rising?

____

❷ result in ~(의 결과를) 초래하다
result from ~에서 결과가 빚어지다

Basic

정답 P. 234

1 대화를 듣고, 남자의 마지막 말에 이어질 여자의 응답으로 알맞은 것을 고르시오.

① Thank you for your kindness.
② That's okay. Be careful next time.
③ Okay, sorry. I'll keep that in mind.
④ Never mind. Everything will be okay.
⑤ Keep in mind that we should save energy.

2 대화를 듣고, 포스터 대회에 관해 언급되지 <u>않은</u> 것을 고르시오.

① 대회 목적
② 팀별 참가 가능성
③ 포스터 사이즈
④ 표어 길이 제한
⑤ 제출 마감 기한

3 다음 중 유의어끼리 바르게 연결된 것은?

① duty – right
② classify – sort
③ severe – mild
④ drought – flood
⑤ confused – clear

4 다음 중 반의어끼리 바르게 연결된 것은?

① micro – tiny
② sink – emerge
③ boost – raise
④ transform – alter
⑤ alternative – substitute

5 다음 중 〈보기〉와 의미가 가장 가까운 것은?

> 보기 Make sure you cook the meat long enough.

① You don't have to cook the meat long enough.
② You doubt whether you cooked the meat long enough.
③ You are certain that the meat is cooked long enough.
④ You'd like to have the meat cooked long enough.
⑤ You should check whether you cook the meat long enough.

6 다음 밑줄 친 부분 중 어법상 <u>어색한</u> 것은?

① Using renewable energy <u>produces</u> less air or water pollution.
② It will help us meet energy demands without <u>creating</u> much pollution.
③ Just a two-degree drop caused the earth <u>to go</u> through the Little Ice Age.
④ A number of companies around the world <u>have built</u> up more effective energy sources.
⑤ Greenhouse gases are being trapped within the earth's atmosphere, <u>that</u> has led to rising temperatures.

7 다음 〈보기〉의 빈칸에 가장 알맞은 것은?

> 보기 Many companies have built up more effective energy sources that can ____________ the shortage of fossil fuels.

① root out
② make sure
③ take place
④ make up for
⑤ result from

8 다음 글의 빈칸에 들어갈 말을 〈보기〉의 단어들을 사용하여 완성하시오. (필요한 경우 형태를 바꾸시오.)

보기 expect / breathe / fresh / air

For years, the micro dust that blows into Korea from China has been a serious problem. A few years ago, despite global efforts to deal with the problem, it seemed the problem was getting worse. But from the year before last, air pollution has greatly decreased thanks to the help of volunteers from neighboring countries, who have planted trees in many parts of China. The effort started ten years ago, and it's now starting to show significant results. Experts explain that the trees serve as a wall to block the sand and dust from crossing into Korea. At long last, this coming weekend, people of all ages ____________________.

→ ____________________

[9~10] 다음 〈보기〉의 우리말과 같도록 괄호 안의 단어를 사용하여 빈칸에 알맞은 말을 쓰시오.

9

보기 그 기술을 사용하여 깨끗한 물을 충분히 공급하는 방법이 개발되고 있는 중이다. (develop)

→ A sufficient supply of clean water using the technology ____________________.

10

보기 난 하루 종일 걸었고 그게 내 발을 아프게 했다. (feet / sore / made / which)

→ I walked all day long, ____________________.

[11~13] 다음 글을 읽고, 물음에 답하시오.

(A) Korea, along with many other countries in the world, is still classified as a country with a serious water shortage. ___ⓐ___, this is starting to become a thing of the past. (B) The remarkable development of engineering and chemistry inspired Korean researchers, who have tried to solve severe drought problems. ___ⓑ___, they successfully transformed sea water into fresh water in an environmentally friendly way. (C) They also found a way to reuse water that contains high salt content. (D) Since this technology has become widely used, it has become a source of hope for the people who need drinkable water. (E) A sufficient supply of clean water using the technology is now being developed and is expected to help root out diseases that are caused by ______ⓒ______.

11 윗글의 (A)~(E) 중 아래의 문장이 들어가기에 가장 알맞은 곳은?

This new solution has reduced worries about the effects of this technology on marine life.

① (A) ② (B) ③ (C) ④ (D) ⑤ (E)

12 윗글의 빈칸 ⓐ와 ⓑ에 들어갈 말이 차례대로 연결된 것은?

① However — In the end
② In contrast — Eventually
③ Therefore — For example
④ However — In a similar way
⑤ Therefore — To make it worse

13 윗글의 빈칸 ⓒ에 가장 알맞은 것은?

① the world's lack of clean water
② the global warming in general
③ the malnutrition of the children
④ the enormous carbon dioxide emissions
⑤ the poor facilities in medical institutions

Advanced

정답 P. 235

[1~2] 다음을 듣고, 물음에 답하시오.

1 이 방송의 목적으로 가장 알맞은 것은?

① To persuade more people to save energy
② To provide examples of economic problems
③ To give information about natural phenomena
④ To encourage people to take action for the earth
⑤ To argue that we should build eco-friendly buildings

2 이 방송에서 언급되지 <u>않은</u> 것은?

① heat wave ② yellow dust
③ desertification ④ severe drought
⑤ powerful storms

3 대화를 듣고, 남자가 새로 알게 된 정보로 알맞은 것을 고르시오.

① Items marked "1" and "2" are hardly recycled.
② The bottle caps and the glass are not recyclable.
③ Recycling symbols have only two numbers inside.
④ Recycling plastic produces more toxic chemicals.
⑤ If an item has a triangle and number 1 or 2, it can be recycled.

4 다음 중 밑줄 친 부분을 우리말로 옮겨 쓴 것 중 <u>어색한</u> 것은?

① It <u>resulted in</u> the sinking of the island. (~결과를 초래했다)
② <u>At long last</u>, the train arrived at the station. (마침내)
③ Many hair problems <u>result from</u> what you eat. (~가 원인이다)
④ He practiced harder to <u>make up for</u> the time lost. (보상하다)
⑤ It can help <u>root out</u> diseases caused by mosquitoes. (확산 시키다)

5 다음 대화의 빈칸에 가장 알맞은 것은?

A: Some scientists found out the earthquakes in Oklahoma were caused by the oil and gas business.
B: Are you sure? I thought that they could cause environmental pollution.
A: Well, it seems the process can actually cause earthquakes.
B: That's terrible. Then should we stop using gas?
A: It's not easy to stop using gas.
B: Then what should we do?
A: ______________________________

① We have to make sure we don't waste our energy from now on.
② We need to make people stop using gas immediately.
③ We have to change our energy sources right now.
④ We'll have more earthquakes no matter what we do.
⑤ We should increase gas and oil consumption globally.

6 다음 글의 밑줄 친 부분 중 쓰임이 <u>어색한</u> 것은?

Since the latest super storm hit Southeast Asia, the total number of deaths and injuries has now ① <u>exceeded</u> one million. At 3 p.m. on March 30th, 2025, an 18-hour storm ② <u>severely</u> damaged the region. On April 2nd, the number of deaths and injured individuals stood at 514,000, with over 17,000 missing, and the numbers are expected to ③ <u>rise</u>. One 65-year-old man who lost his house said, "I've never seen such strong winds in my whole life. I've lost everything." The storm left many people ④ <u>homeless</u>. A climate scientist said this super storm was obviously caused by dramatic changes in the global climate. He added, "A rise in global temperatures has ⑤ <u>decreased</u> the intensity of storms with higher wind speeds." Unfortunately, researchers predict that super storms will happen more frequently this summer.

[7~9] 다음 글을 읽고, 물음에 답하시오.

It's now official. The Arctic ice has melted away and is now only ____________ in 1979. Many climate scientists have said that the Arctic could have a summer entirely free of ice by 2030 due to global warming. So what is causing the temperature to rise? The main cause is carbon dioxide emissions. Greenhouse gases are ⓐ being trapped within the earth's atmosphere, which has led ⓑ to rising temperatures. The rising sea level has resulted in the sinking of the Maldives, which is a famous tourist destination. According to many researchers, by 2100, New York and Shanghai will also sink, and the average global temperature is expected to be about 3.6 ⓒ degree higher than now. Some may wonder why we should worry about a three-degree increase in warming. A one-degree global change is highly significant because it takes a vast amount of heat to warm all the earth's oceans, atmosphere, and land. ⓓ In the past, just a one- to ⓔ two-degree drop caused the earth to go through the Little Ice Age. World leaders have realized the seriousness of climate change, so they will meet in Paris next month for a climate forum.

7 다음 〈보기〉의 단어들을 알맞게 배열하여 빈칸에 들어갈 말을 쓰시오.

보기 it / was / what / one-fifth / of

⊖ ____________________

8 윗글의 밑줄 친 ⓐ~ⓔ 중 어법상 어색한 것은?

① ⓐ ② ⓑ ③ ⓒ ④ ⓓ ⑤ ⓔ

9 윗글의 밑줄 친 forum에서 다루어질 주제나 내용으로 알맞은 것을 본문에서 찾아 쓰시오.

⊖ ____________________

10 다음 문장의 뒤에 이어질 글의 순서로 알맞은 것은?

As the competition in the electric car market has become more intense, many companies have long been struggling to develop long-lasting electric car batteries.

(A) They can eliminate polluted air produced by fossil fuel engines.

(B) Heating up the green car market fever, the launch of new hydrogen cars is expected to help reduce air pollution and eventually solve the energy crisis.

(C) At the same time, hydrogen cars with satellite communications have also joined in this competition.

① (A)–(B)–(C) ② (B)–(C)–(A)
③ (B)–(A)–(C) ④ (C)–(A)–(B)
⑤ (C)–(B)–(A)

주관식 서술형 대비

11 다음 글의 앞부분을 참조하여 주어진 빈칸에 재생 에너지의 개발 및 사용의 장점에 대해 두 문장으로 쓰시오.

The global ban on fossil fuels gave a boost to alternative energy. A number of companies around the world have built up more effective energy sources that can make up for the shortage of fossil fuels. Thanks to the development of renewable energy resources, they now make up more than half of the country's entire power, and this rate is set to grow even bigger. Renewable energy resources come from a wide variety of sources including the sun, the wind, and the sea.

____

____

UNIT 5

Bon Voyage

교과서 핵심 정리

Words & Phrases

Listen and Speak ~ Into Real Life

- ☐ bunch *n.* 다발, 묶음(a bunch of ~: 한 다발의)
- ☐ memorable* *adj.* 기억에 남는, 기억할만한
- ☐ by oneself 혼자서(=alone), 저절로
- ☐ professional* *adj.* 전문적인 (profession *n.* 전문성이 있는 직업)
- ☐ instructor *n.* 강사, 가르치는 사람
- ☐ reservation *n.* 예약 (reserve *v.* 예약하다, 보류하다)
- ☐ unique* *adj.* 독특한, 특이한 (uniqueness *n.* 독특함)
- ☐ rock formation 암반층, 바위
- ☐ coastal *adj.* 해안(연안)의 (coast *n.* 해안)
- ☐ cliff *n.* (바닷가) 절벽
- ☐ symbolic* *adj.* 상징적인 (symbol *n.* 상징)
- ☐ observatory *n.* 관측소, 천문대
- ☐ themed *adj.* (특정한) 주제를 가진
- ☐ depending on* ~에 따라 (뭔가가 달려있는)

Read and Think

- ☐ interaction* *n.* 상호작용 (interact *v.* 상호작용하다)
- ☐ architectural *adj.* 건축학적인(architecture *n.* 건축 architect *n.* 건축가)
- ☐ astonish* *v.* 깜짝 놀라게 하다 (astonishment *n.* 놀람)
- ☐ incredible *adj.* 놀라운, 믿기 어려운
- ☐ scenery* *n.* 풍경, 경치 *cf.* scene 장면
- ☐ emphasis *n.* 강조 (emphasize *v.* 강조하다)
- ☐ delicately ad. 우아하게, 섬세하게 (delicate *adj.* 우아한)
- ☐ pattern *n.* 패턴, 양식, 문양
- ☐ absolute* *adj.* 완전한, 완벽한, 절대적인
- ☐ a must* 필수적인 것
- ☐ border *n.* 국경(경계), 경계선
- ☐ impressed* *adj.* 감명(감동) 받은 (impression *n.* 인상)
- ☐ definitely *ad.* 분명히, 절대로
- ☐ devil *n.* 악마 *cf.* evil *adj.* 악한, *n.* 악
- ☐ throat *n.* 목구멍, 목
- ☐ waterfall *n.* 폭포
- ☐ gleam* *v.* (희미하게) 빛나다
- ☐ in person* 직접, 실제로
- ☐ entire *adj.* 전체의
- ☐ passion *n.* 열정, 정열
- ☐ awesome* *adj.* 멋진, 근사한 *cf.* awful 끔찍한, 형편없는
- ☐ legend *n.* 전설 (legendary *adj.* 전설상의)
- ☐ exhibit* *v.* 전시하다 (exhibition *n.* 전시회)
- ☐ absorb *v.* 흡수하다, 빨아들이다 *cf.* absolve (죄를)용서하다
- ☐ no wonder* 당연하다
- ☐ sweat *n.* 땀 *v.* 땀을 흘리다
- ☐ cruise *n.* 유람선 여행
- ☐ ever-changing *adj.* 늘 변화하는, 변화무쌍한
- ☐ landscape* *n.* 풍경, 경관
- ☐ jaw *n.* 턱
- ☐ aboriginal *adj.* 호주 원주민의
- ☐ preserve* *v.* 지키다, 보존하다 (preservation *n.* 보존)
- ☐ destination* *n.* 목적지
- ☐ keep someone posted about/on ~에게 …에 대해 계속 정보를 업데이트 해주다 (= keep someone updated about/on)

Language Notes

- ☐ appreciation* *n.* (작품의 진가에 대한) 감상, 감사
- ☐ fit* *v.* 딱 들어맞다 *adj.* 잘 들어맞는
- ☐ informed* *adj.* 정보에 근거한, 정보를 알고 있는
- ☐ emergency *n.* 비상사태

Write It Right

- ☐ exotic *adj.* 이국적인, 외국(풍)의
- ☐ layer *n.* 층, 겹
- ☐ length* *n.* 길이, 기간 (lengthen *v.* 늘리다, 연장하다) *cf.* breath 폭, 너비, width 너비 height 높이

Around the World

- ☐ freshwater *n.* 담수, 민물 *adj.* 민물의
- ☐ horseback riding 승마, 말 타기
- ☐ lagoon *n.* 석호, 호수
- ☐ annual* *adj.* 연간의, 매년의
- ☐ spot* *n.* 장소, 점 *v.* 발견하다

☑ Check-Up

정답 P. 235

1 다음 문장의 빈칸에 알맞은 말을 〈보기〉에서 골라 넣으시오.

보기 >> by himself / depending on / in person
no wonder / keep you posted / a must

(1) Once I have any news, I will ____________.

(2) Member states are alloted seats ____________ their population.

(3) The actor looked even shorter ____________ than he does on the screen.

(4) There are countless professions where a master's degree is ____________.

(5) He is doing it ____________ . He does not need any help from me or my husband.

(6) Kids enjoy eating fatty foods. It is ____________ that they are getting fatter and unhealthier.

2 다음 뜻풀이에 해당하는 말을 주어진 철자로 시작하여 쓰시오.

(1) d____________ : fine in texture, quality, etc.

(2) a ____________ : to suck up or drink in (a liquid)

(3) a ____________ : the character or style of building

(4) a ____________ : free from imperfection or not limited in any way; complete, utter

(5) b ____________ : the line separating political divisions or geographic regions

주관식 서술형

3 우리말에 맞게 괄호 안의 단어들을 사용하여 문장을 완성하시오.

(1) 에펠탑이 파리의 경관을 망친다고 여겨졌다.
The Eiffel Tower was ______________________________.
(Paris / spoil / the / scenery / to / considered / of)

(2) 강의 흐름의 변화는 전체적인 풍경에 영향을 미쳤다.
The change in the river's flow ______________________________.
(entire / the / affected / landscape)

(3) 자연 서식지를 보존하기 위해 많은 노력을 해야 한다.
Lots of efforts should be made ______________________________.
(preserve / natural / to / habitats)

(4) 그녀는 한라산의 풍경에 깊이 감동받았다.
She was ______________________________ of Mt. Halla.
(by / view / deeply / impressed / the)

Tip

❶ 주요 숙어표현 익히기
allot 할당하다, 배당하다
master's degree 석사학위

❷ 영영사전풀이
suck up 빨아들이다
free from ~이 없는
utter 완전한, 완벽한

❸ 핵심어휘를 사용한 영작
spoil 망치다
habitat 서식지

교과서 핵심 정리

Dialogues & Monologue

Listen and Speak | *해석을 참조하여 빈칸에 알맞은 말을 쓰시오.

GET READY

1 M: Oh my gosh. We are finally flying in the sky. There are many clouds under our plane.
W: I know. **I feel like** we are flying on a huge bunch of cotton candy.
M: This is **one of the most beautiful views** I've ever seen.
W: You can say that again.

남: 와, 이럴 수가. 우리 드디어 하늘을 날고 있는 거야. 비행기 아래로 구름이 많이 있어.
여: 나도 알아. 마치 한 뭉치의 솜사탕 위를 나는 것 같아.
남: 내가 본 가장 멋진 전망 중 하나야.
여: 정말 그래.

2 W: Excuse me, how do I get to April department store?
M: It's very close to here. Go __________ one block and turn left. It's just around the corner. You can't miss it.
W: Thank you for your help.

여: 실례지만 에이프릴 백화점에 가는 길이 어떻게 되지요?
남: 여기서 굉장히 가까워요. 한 블록 직진해서 가셔서 좌회전하세요. 바로 그 모퉁이 도는 곳에 있어요. 보이실 거예요.
여: 도와주셔서 감사합니다.

3 M: Look at this painting. This is **one of the most impressive works** I've ever seen.
W: This painting is called "The Dream."
M: It was a good decision to come to the Pablo Picasso Art Museum on this trip.
W: I totally __________. It's great to see his amazing works of art.

남: 이 그림 좀 봐. 이건 내가 지금까지 봐 온 것 중 가장 인상적인 작품들 중 하나야.
여: 이 그림은 "꿈"이라는 제목의 그림이야.
남: 이번 여행에서 Pablo Picasso의 미술 박물관에 오기로 한 결정은 참 잘한 결정이었어.
여: 정말 그래. 그의 놀라운 미술 작품들을 보는 건 정말 굉장해.

표현정리
- I feel like (that) ~: '~인 것 같다'라는 의미로 느낌이나 감정을 표현하는 말이다.
- 「one of the + 최상급 + 복수보통명사」: 가장 ~한 것 중 하나

정답 straight / agree

LISTEN IN

DIALOGUE 1

W: Mike, I've decided to go to New Zealand this summer.
M: Wow, that sounds awesome! Why New Zealand?
W: **I'm a huge fan of** the movie *The Hobbit: An Unexpected Journey*, so I've always wanted to visit the country that was the __________ for the movie. Here, this town on the North Island on this map is Hinuera, which has the Hobbiton movie set.
M: Oh, I remember this place. The Hobbiton movie set has one of the most memorable places from the movie.
W: Exactly. That town is where I want to go on the very first day of my trip.
M: Where else are you going to go to in New Zealand?
W: I'm going to go to Lake Wanaka on the South Island the next day. That place is very famous for skydiving.
M: But you don't even know how to skydive. Can you do it by yourself? That sounds really dangerous.
W: I don't need to do it by myself. They have professional instructors. They will take control as I enjoy an amazing __________ of New Zealand.
M: Lucky for you! **How long are you going to stay** in New Zealand?
W: I'll stay there for two weeks. I'm so excited!
M: I hope you have a great and safe trip.

여: Mike, 나 이번 여름에 뉴질랜드 가기로 결정했어.
남: 와, 정말 멋있다! 왜 뉴질랜드로 가?
여: 내가 그 유명한 영화 '호빗: 예상치 못한 여행'의 열렬한 팬이잖아. 그래서 그 영화의 배경이 되는 장소가 있는 나라를 방문하고 싶었어. 여기 이 지도상의 북섬에 있는 이 도시가 히누에라인데 여기 호비튼의 영화의 세트장이 있어.
남: 아, 나 이 장소 기억 나. 이 호비튼 영화의 세트장은 이 영화 중 가장 기억에 남을만한 한 장소를 가진 곳이야.
여: 맞아. 그 도시는 내 여행 첫날에 가고 싶은 곳이야.
남: 뉴질랜드에서 또 어디를 갈 예정이야?
여: 그 다음 날에는 남섬에 있는 와나카 호수에 갈 예정이야. 그곳은 스카이다이빙으로 유명한 곳이야.
남: 하지만 너는 스카이다이빙 하는 법도 모르잖아. 너 그거 혼자 할 수 있어? 그것 매우 위험해 보이던데.
여: 나 혼자 하지 않아도 되는 거야. 전문적인 강사들이 있거든. 그 강사들이 내가 뉴질랜드의 놀라운 풍광을 즐기는 동안 조종을 해 주실 거야.
남: 그것 참 다행이다. 너 뉴질랜드에서 얼마나 오래 있을 거야?
여: 2주 동안 머무를 거야. 너무 신나.
남: 멋지고 안전한 여행이 되길 바랄게.

대화상황
- 뉴질랜드에 여행가는 친구와 여행 일정과 기간 및 여행지에서의 활동에 대해 묻고 대답하는 상황이다.

표현정리
- I'm a huge fan of ~: '~를 엄청 좋아한다.'라는 의미의 표현이다.
- How long are you going to stay ~? : '얼마나 오래 머무를지'를 묻는 일반적인 표현이다.

정답 background / view

DIALOGUE 2

(Phone rings.)
W: Lion Hotel. How can I help you?
M: Excuse me. How do I get to your hotel? **I made a __________ for today.**
W: Where are you now? Tell me your location.
M: I'm near Woodlands subway station.
W: Woodlands station. Okay, you are not far from our hotel. Take line 5 toward the south, and get off at Newton station.
M: Line 5 toward the south and Newton station. I got it.
W: Then, you should go out of exit 6. After that, walk straight two blocks.
M: Exit 6, walk two blocks. Is that right?
W: You got it. After you walk two blocks, you can see the Jumbo restaurant on your right. That means you're almost here. It's just around the left __________. It's a very big hotel, so **you can't miss it.**
M: I really appreciate your help.
W: Oh, here is one more tip. If you have a cell phone, download the Singapore Subway Map app. It will make your trip easier.
M: I will. Thanks.

(전화가 울린다.)
여: 라이온 호텔입니다. 무엇을 도와드릴까요?
남: 실례지만, 그 호텔에 어떻게 가나요? 오늘 예약을 한 사람입니다.
여: 지금 어디신가요? 계신 위치를 말씀해 주세요.
남: 저는 우드랜드 지하철 역 근처에 있습니다.
여: 우드랜드 역이라고요. 네, 저희 호텔에서 멀지 않은 곳이에요. 남쪽 방향으로 가는 5호선을 타시고 뉴턴 역에서 내리세요.
남: 5호선 남쪽 방향으로 가는 것 타고 뉴턴 역에서 내리라는 거군요. 알겠습니다.
여: 그러고 나서 6번 출구로 나가세요. 그런 다음 두 블록 직진하시면 됩니다.
남: 6번 출구, 두 블록 직진. 맞나요?
여: 맞습니다. 두 블록 걸어오시면, 점보 식당이 오른쪽에 있을 거예요. 그럼 거의 다 오신 거예요. 바로 왼쪽 모퉁이 돌면 있거든요. 아주 큰 호텔이라 금방 보일 겁니다.
남: 도와주셔서 정말 감사해요.
여: 아, 한 가지 더 팁을 드릴게요. 휴대전화가 있으시면, 싱가포르 지하철 지도 앱을 다운로드 받으세요. 여행이 훨씬 쉬워질 거예요.
남: 그럴게요. 감사합니다.

대화상황 • 예약한 호텔까지 가는 법을 전화로 묻는 투숙자와 이에 대한 길 안내를 해 주는 호텔 직원 간의 대화이다.

표현정리
• I made a reservation for today. 에서 make a reservation은 '예약하다'라는 뜻이다.
• You can't miss it.: '그것을 놓치시지 않을 거예요.'라는 의미로 금방 쉽게 눈에 띈다는 표현이다.

정답 reservation / corner

Into Real Life

W: Hi everyone. This is the Daehan High School Broadcasting System. As you know, we're going on a field trip next month to have some valuable learning experiences outside the school. To make your trip more interesting, Daehan High School will provide **three field trip destinations for you to choose from.**

여: 안녕하세요, 여러분. 대한 고등학교 방송국입니다. 아시다시피, 저희가 다음 달에 교외에서의 소중한 학습 경험을 위해 체험 학습을 갈 예정입니다. 여행을 더욱 재미있게 해주기 위해 대한 고등학교에서는 여러분이 선택할 수 있도록 세 가지 현장 체험 학습 장소를 제공할 예정입니다.

1. Students who love beautiful nature are __________ to choose Ulleungdo and Dokdo. Ulleungdo is full of the beauty of nature including many unique rock formations and coastal cliffs. On the second day, you can actually visit Dokdo, a symbolic island in the hearts of Koreans. You can also do activities like sea fishing. We will take a bus and a ship to get there, and it takes about six hours in total.
2. If you love history and tradition, you can choose Andong. Andong Hahoe Folk Village is a UNESCO World Heritage site. You will stay in this village and experience the traditional ways of life in the past. You can also watch many traditional __________ like a traditional wedding performance in the village. To get there, it's a three-hour train ride.
3. If you want some __________ experiences from the trip, the Daejeon Citizen Observatory will be the perfect place for you. It's one of the largest space-themed parks in Korea. You can appreciate a beautiful night sky and the Milky Way on the mountain. In addition to this, you can take a tour of the Space Museum and do many space-related activities. We will take a bus to get there, and it only takes an hour and a half.

I hope you can choose the best place depending on your interests.

1. 아름다운 자연을 사랑하는 학생들은 울릉도와 독도를 선택하시길 권합니다. 울릉도는 많은 독특한 암석들과 해안 절벽들을 포함하여 자연의 아름다움으로 가득 차 있는 곳입니다. 이틀째 되는 날에는, 한국인들의 심장 속에 있는 상징적인 섬, 독도를 실제로 방문합니다. 바다 낚시와 같은 활동도 즐길 수 있습니다. 버스와 배로 갈 예정이며 총 6시간 정도가 소요됩니다.
2. 역사와 전통을 사랑하신다면, 안동을 선택하시면 됩니다. 안동 하회 마을은 유네스코 세계 문화유산입니다. 이 마을에 머무르면서 과거의 전통적인 생활 양식들을 체험할 수 있습니다. 또한 마을에서의 결혼식과 같은 전통 행사들을 볼 수 있습니다. 이곳에 가는 데는 기차로 3시간 정도 소요됩니다.
3. 여행에서 어느 정도의 교육적 경험을 원하신다면 대전 시민 천문대가 최적의 장소가 될 것입니다. 이곳은 한국에서 가장 큰 테마 공원들 중 하나입니다. 산에서 아름다운 밤하늘과 은하수를 감상하실 수 있습니다. 게다가, 우주 과학관 관람도 하시면서 우주와 관련된 많은 활동도 할 수 있습니다. 버스로 가게 되며, 1시간 30분 밖에 걸리지 않습니다.

여러분의 관심 분야에 따라 최상의 장소를 고르시기 바랍니다.

담화주제
- 현장체험 학습 장소 선정과 관련하여 교내 방송으로 학생들에게 후보 장소에 대한 간략한 안내를 하고 있다.

표현정리
- ~ three field trip destinations for you to choose from: you choose from three field trip destinations 구문에서 변형된 문장구조로 to부정사가 destinations를 수식하는 형용사적 용법으로 쓰였다.

정답 recommended / performances / educational

Check Your Progress

W: Hi, Cheolsu. How was your trip to India? You were really worried about your first __________ trip with your family.
M: Well, my family was really impressed by the cultures of India.
W: That sounds interesting! What was so impressive about the country?
M: First of all, the food. We had a lot of local food like Indian curries and liked everything we ate very much.
W: **That's good to hear.** Oh, did you see any __________ performances?
M: Yes! We arrived there on the last day of the Hemis Festival. **Luckily, we got to see** the last performance.
W: You were very lucky. Where else did you go?
M: We also visited lots of UNESCO World Heritage sites, like the Taj Mahal.
W: You did? I heard that the architecture is really amazing.
M: It was one of the most beautiful buildings I have ever seen. Actually, it was so wonderful that it looked unreal.
W: Wow. **Now that I have heard** your story, I want to fly to India!

여: 안녕, 철수야. 인도 여행 어땠어? 너 가족이랑 처음 가보는 외국 여행이라 걱정이 많았었잖아.
남: 우리 가족들 모두 인도의 문화에 깊은 인상을 받았어.
여: 흥미로운데! 인도의 어떤 게 그렇게 인상 깊었어?
남: 무엇보다, 음식이었어. 인도 카레를 포함한 많은 지역 음식을 먹었는데 먹은 것 모두 맘에 들었어.
여: 다행이네. 아, 전통 공연들 본 거 있어?
남: 그럼! 우리가 도착한 게 헤미스 축제 마지막 날이었는데 다행히도 마지막 공연을 볼 수 있었어.
여: 참 운이 좋았네. 또 어떤 곳에 갔어?
남: 타지마할 같은 유네스코 세계 유적지도 많이 방문했어.
여: 그랬어? 그 건축물이 정말 놀랍다는 말은 들었었어.
남: 내가 본 건축물들 중 가장 아름다운 건축물 중 하나였어. 정말이지 너무 멋있어서 실제 같지 않았다니까.
여: 와우. 네 이야기 들으니까 나도 인도로 날아가고 싶다.

담화주제
- 인도 여행을 다녀온 친구와 방문지에서의 경험과 감상에 대해 이야기 하고 있다.

표현정리
- That's good to hear. : 상대방이 한 말의 내용에 대해 '잘 됐구나,' '다행이다,' '반가운 소리다' 정도의 의미를 갖는 표현이다.
- Luckily, we got to see ~ : 「get to + 동사원형」은 '~을 해내다/기회를 갖게 되다'라는 의미의 표현이다.
- Now that I have heard ~: now that은 '이제 ~하고 나니'또는 '이제 ~이기 때문에'라는 의미의 이유를 나타내는 표현이다.

정답 overseas / traditional

교과서 핵심 정리

Reading Comprehension

*해석을 참조하여 빈칸에 알맞은 말을 쓰거나 괄호에서 알맞은 말을 고르시오.

P.95 L.3~21

Hi everyone, I'd like to share with you one of my most memorable trips, which was a trip to the city of Granada, a city in the southern part of Spain.

Granada is where a whole city was influenced by Arabic culture because of wars and interactions between Spanish and Arabic people a long time ago. I decided to visit the Alhambra palace, (what / which) is one of the greatest architectural _________ of Spain. People say this palace was left undamaged during wars because the beauty of the palace was (astonished / astonishing).

In front of the palace, there was a beautiful garden called *Generalife*. I was totally amazed by the incredible scenery. The fountains were running, and the pools reflected the beautiful flowers and trees in the garden. Later I found out that water meant life and richness to Arabic people in the Middle Ages. Their emphasis on water is expressed in the many water tunnels and fountains in the palace.

Next to the garden were the Nasrid Palaces, which I thought were the most beautiful palaces I had ever seen. The rooms are delicately decorated with colorful works of art, wooden ceilings, and various patterns. After I finished the tour, I could understand why the palace wasn't destroyed. In Spain, it is an absolute _________ to visit the Alhambra palace! I hope you will have a chance to go there.

안녕하세요, 여러분. 저는 제가 가장 기억에 남는 여행들 중 하나인 스페인 남부의 도시 그라나다의 여행담을 함께 나누고 싶어요.

그라나다는 스페인 사람들과 아랍 사람들이 오래 전부터 전쟁이나 상호 교류를 해 왔기 때문에 도시 전체가 아랍 문화의 영향을 받은 곳이에요. 저는 스페인에서 건축학적으로 가장 경이로운 곳 중의 하나인 알함브라 궁전을 방문하기로 결정했어요. 사람들은 이곳이 전쟁 중에도 손상을 입지 않은 이유가 궁전의 아름다움이 너무 뛰어나서라고 이야기 하고 있어요.

궁전 앞에는 헤네랄리페라고 불리는 아름다운 정원이 있었어요. 저는 그 믿을 수 없는 경관에 온통 놀랄 뿐이었어요. 분수가 솟구치고 있었고 물웅덩이들은 정원에 있는 아름다운 꽃과 나무들의 그림자를 비치고 있었어요. 나중에 저는 중세 아랍사람들에게는 물이 생명과 부를 의미했었다는 것을 알게 되었어요. 물에 대한 그들의 강조는 많은 수로나 궁전의 분수들에 잘 표현되어 있어요.

정원 옆에는 나스리드 궁전이 있었는데 그건 제가 여태껏 보았던 가장 아름다운 궁전이라는 생각이 들었어요. 방들은 정교하게 다양한 색깔의 미술 작품들과 원목 천장과 다양한 문양들로 장식되어 있었어요. 다 둘러보고 나서 저는 왜 그 궁전이 부서지지 않았는지 이해할 수 있게 되었어요. 스페인에서 알함브라 궁전은 꼭 가보아야 할 곳이에요. 저는 여러분이 그곳에 갈 기회를 갖게 되길 바라요.

단락요약
- 스페인을 여행했던 경험담을 얘기하면서 알함브라 궁전에 대한 자세한 기술 및 아름다움에 대한 감상을 덧붙이고 있다.

구문정리
- Granada is where a whole city was influenced ~: 선행사 the place가 생략된 관계부사 where는 뒤에 오는 절과 함께 '~한 곳'이라는 의미를 갖는다.
- Next to the garden were the Nasrid Palaces ~ : next to the garden이라는 장소 부사구가 문장 앞에 위치하게 되면서 주어(the Nasrid Palaces)와 동사(were)가 도치된 구문이다. 따라서 원래의 문장은 the Nasrid Palaces ~ were next to the garden.이 된다.

정답 which / wonders / astonishing / must

P.96 L.1~16

Chris: I'm planning to visit South America this summer vacation. Since you've been there, where do you think I should go in South America?

Grace: There are many places to see, but I recommend Iguazu Falls. They were why I decided to go to Brazil. I can't __________ their beauty in words. You have to see them in person.

Chris: I've heard of Iguazu Falls. Why do you think they are famous?

Grace: It's because they are the tallest and largest falls in the world.

Chris: Oh, I see. So, where exactly are they located?

Grace: They are located on the __________ between Argentina and Brazil. If you're on the Brazilian side, you can take a helicopter or a boat to look around the falls.

Chris: What were you most impressed with?

Grace: Definitely the Devil's Throat. It was as big and fantastic as the name sounds. The sight of large waterfalls and gleaming rainbows was incredible. Once you see this area, you will be totally (amazed / amazing) by its beauty.

Chris: 나 이번 여름방학 때 남미를 방문할 예정이야. 너 거기 다녀왔으니까 내가 남미에서 어디를 가면 좋을까?

Grace: 볼 곳은 많이 있는데 난 이구아수 폭포를 추천하고 싶어. 내가 브라질을 가기로 결정한 이유가 이구아수 폭포 때문이었어. 말로 다 표현할 수 없을 정도로 아름답거든. 너도 꼭 직접 가서 봐야 돼.

Chris: 나도 이구아수 폭포에 대해 들어보긴 했어. 왜 그곳이 그렇게 유명한 거지?

Grace: 그건 그 폭포가 세계에서 가장 높고 큰 폭포라서 그래.

Chris: 아, 그렇구나. 그럼 그게 정확히 어디에 위치하고 있어?

Grace: 아르헨티나와 브라질 국경선에 위치하고 있어. 만약 네가 브라질 쪽에 있으면 헬리콥터나 배를 타고 폭포를 둘러볼 수 있어.

Chris: 네가 가장 인상 깊었던 게 뭐야?

Grace: 그건 단연코 악마의 목구멍이라는 곳이지. 그건 이름에서 느껴지듯이 크고 환상적이야. 커다란 폭포의 풍경과 빛나는 무지개들이 황홀해. 한번 이 지역을 보면 너는 그 아름다움에 완전히 매료될 거야.

단락요약
- 남미를 여행하고 온 Grace와 여름방학 동안 남미를 여행하려고 하는 Chris가 남미의 이구아수 폭포에 대해 얘기하고 있는 상황이다.

구문정리
- They were why I decided to go to Brazil. : 여기서 관계부사 why는 앞에 선행사 the reason이 생략된 구문으로 '~한 이유'라고 해석한다.
- Why do you think they are famous?: do you think / guess / assume 등의 인지적 판단을 묻는 말이 간접의문문 안에 삽입될 때, 문장구조는 「의문사 + do you think/guess/assume + 주어 + 동사 ~?」의 형태를 취한다.

정답 describe / border / amazed

P.97 L.1-15

Chris: I can't wait to go there. Where else did you go?

Grace: Since I am a huge fan of football, São Paulo was a __________ city. It was like the entire city went on vacation during big matches. There is even a football museum in São Paulo. This shows Brazilians' great passion for football.

Chris: A football museum? That's awesome! No wonder so many internationally famous football legends, like Pele, Ronaldo, and Ronaldinho, are Brazilians.

Grace: I know. This museum __________ interesting things like some of the footballs used in the World Cup matches, pictures, and video of historical football matches. There's even a whole room (where/which) is filled with the history of Brazilian football.

Chris: It sounds like Brazil is the perfect place to absorb the beauty of nature and the passion of football fans. I'm already excited!

Grace: Yes, Brazil is a great place. I hope you enjoy yourself there.

Chris: 정말 가보고 싶어 못 기다리겠다. 또 어디를 갔었어?

Grace: 내가 워낙 축구광이어서 상파울로는 반드시 가야 할 도시였지. 커다란 경기가 있을 때는 도시 전체가 휴가 기간인 것 같았어. 심지어 상파울로에는 축구 박물관이 있을 정도야. 브라질 사람들의 축구에 대한 엄청난 열정을 보여주는 거지.

Chris: 축구 박물관? 정말 멋지다! Pele, Ronaldo, 그리고 Ronaldinho와 같은 세계적으로 유명한 축구의 전설들이 다 브라질 사람들인 게 이해가 가.

Grace: 나도 알아. 이 박물관은 월드컵 경기에 쓰였던 축구공이라든가 역사적인 축구 경기의 사진과 비디오 같은 흥미로운 것들을 전시하고 있어. 심지어 브라질 축구 역사로 전체가 가득한 방도 있어.

Chris: 브라질은 마치 자연의 아름다움과 축구팬들의 열정을 다 흡수하는 완벽한 장소인 것 같이 들려. 벌써 막 신나.

Grace: 그래. 브라질은 대단한 곳이야. 가서 재미있게 지내다 오길 바랄게.

단락요약
- 브라질 상파울로에 있는 축구 박물관을 다녀온 이야기와 브라질 사람들의 축구에 대한 열정에 대해 얘기하고 있다.

구문정리
- No wonder so many internationally famous football legends ~ are Brazilians.: 「(It is) No wonder + (that) + 주어 +동사」는 '~가 …하는 것은 놀랄 일이 아니다(당연하다/자연스럽다)'라는 뜻의 구문이다.

정답 must-visit / exhibits / which

P.98 L.1~21

My family's trip across Australia is going well. The land is very big, so we have experienced four seasons in just a week! This week, we felt very cold on snowy Blue Mountain, and I enjoyed a nice warm walk along the Sunshine Coast. And now we are sweating in Kakadu National Park, which is located in the north area of Australia. Kakadu National Park is a home to thousands of animals. We spent two days in the park.

On the first day of our trip, we took a little cruise. It was a cruise on Yellow Water, which has a variety of wild animals, dramatic scenery, and ever-changing __________. We spotted more than twenty different species of birds and wild crocodiles in the river. Until this trip, I had only seen crocodiles in the zoo, so the sight of wild crocodiles made my jaw drop.

The second day at Kakadu National Park was all about (exploring / explored) *Aboriginal rock art. The paintings of animals provide a fascinating record of Aboriginal life over thousands of years. Our guide told us that some of the oldest rock arts might be as much as 40,000 years old. We were (impressive / impressed) by the well preserved rock paintings. Also, some Aboriginals are still living in Kakadu and have kept their cultural traditions. After the trip, I learned to appreciate the beauty of nature and old traditions. Our next __________ is Canberra, the capital city of Australia. I'll keep you posted about my trip.

호주를 횡단하는 우리 가족 여행은 잘 진행되고 있어. 여기는 땅이 워낙 커서 우리는 일주일에 4개의 계절을 경험하고 있어. 이번 주에는 눈 내린 블루마운틴에서 엄청 추웠고, 선샤인 해안을 따라 따뜻하고 좋은 산책을 했어. 그리고 지금 우리는 호주의 북부에 위치한 카카두 국립공원에서 땀을 뻘뻘 흘리고 있어. 카카두 국립공원은 수천 종의 동물들이 서식하고 있는 곳인데 우리는 이 공원에서 이틀을 보냈어. 우리는 여행 첫째날에는 작은 여객선을 탔는데 그것은 옐로우 워터를 다니는 여객선이었고 그 곳은 수많은 종류의 야생 동물들과 드라마틱한 경관, 그리고 끊임없이 변하는 풍경을 가진 곳이었어. 우리는 20여 종의 서로 다른 새들과 강에 있는 야생 악어들을 보았는데, 이 여행을 오기까지 나는 동물원에 있는 악어만 보았었기 때문에 야생 악어의 모습은 내 입을 쩍 벌어지게 만들었어.

카카두 국립공원에서의 둘째 날은 온통 호주 원주민의 암석화 미술을 찾아다녔어. 동물들의 그림은 수천 년 동안의 호주 원주민들의 삶에 대한 놀라운 기록을 제공해줘. 우리 여행 안내원께서 우리에게 얘기해 주신 것에 따르면, 가장 오래된 암석화들 중 일부는 4만년 정도 된 것일 수 있다고 해. 우리는 잘 보존되어 있는 암석화에 경탄했어. 또한, 일부 원주민들은 여전히 카카두에 살고 있고 그들의 문화적 전통을 지켜오고 있어. 이 여행이 끝난 후 나는 자연과 오래된 전통을 감상하는 것을 배웠어. 우리의 다음 여행지는 호주의 수도 캔버라야. 내 여행에 대해 계속 소식 전할게.

* Aboriginal rock art_www.parksaustralia.gov.au/kakadu/people/rock-art-html

단락요약

- 호주의 여러 여행지를 다니면서 본 풍경, 야생동물, 원주민 벽화 미술 등에 관해 이야기를 해 주고 있다.

구문정리

- Until this trip, I had only seen crocodiles in the zoo. : 이 여행이 과거 시제이기 때문에 이 여행 이전까지의 일은 과거완료(had seen) 시제로 나타내고 있다.
- so the sight of wild crocodiles made my jaw drop.: 「사역동사(made) + 목적어(my jaw)+ 동사원형(drop)」의 구문으로서, make someone's jaw drop은 ~를 놀라게/경탄하게 하다'라는 뜻의 표현이다.

정답 landscapes / exploring / impressed / destination

Focus on Structure

P. 95 L.6 Granada is | **where** a whole city was influenced | by Arabic culture.
관계부사 주어 동사

Iguazu Falls were | **why** I decided to go to Brazil.
관계부사 주어 동사

⊖ where, why, when, how 등으로 시작하는 관계부사 절은 선행사를 생략한 상태로 be동사의 보어로 쓰일 수 있다. 이 경우 where는'~ 한/하는 장소,' why는 '~한/하는 이유', when은 '~한/하는 때,' 그리고 how는 '~한/하는 방법'으로 해석한다.

ex. The water was **where** he found peace. 물은 그가 평화를 찾았던 곳이다.= 물에서 그는 평화를 찾았다.
March is **when** the flowers start to grow. 3월은 꽃들이 자라나기 시작하는 때이다.
My daughter is **why** I want to become a better person. 내 딸은 내가 더 나은 사람이 되고 싶은 이유이다.
That was **how** things worked in India. 그게 인도에서 일이 진행되는 방식이었다.

cf. 구체적인 내용의 선행사는 생략하지 않는다.

ex. The meeting will be held in a conference hall **where** 300 people can easily take seats.
그 회의는 300명이 쉽게 좌석을 잡을 수 있는 회의장에서 열리게 될 것이다.

P. 96 L.13 **Where** / do you think | **I should go** in South America?
의문사 주어 동사

⊖ 「의문사 + 간접의문문」의 구조에서 의문문에 쓰인 동사가 think, believe, suppose 등일 때는 간접의문문의 의문사가 문두로 나온다.

ex. **Why** do you think **they voted** for Sam? 왜 너는 그들이 Sam을 뽑았다고 생각해?
Where do you believe **gender stereotypes come** from? 너는 성 고정관념이 어디에서 왔다고 믿니?

cf. think, believe, suppose 등의 동사가 쓰인 경우에 의문사가 없는 의문문의 간접의문문은 접속사 that을 써서 연결한다.

ex. Does he want to apply for the job? + Do you think so?
그는 그 직장에 지원하기를 원하니? 너는 그렇게 생각해?
→ Do you think **that** he wants to apply for the job? 그가 그 직장에 지원하기를 원한다고 너는 생각하니?

☑ Check-Up

정답 P. 236

1 다음 괄호 안의 단어들을 알맞은 순서대로 배열하시오.

(1) The village (you / is / a / museum / tour / where / can / take)
(2) The holiday (to / return / when / workers / is / are / expected) to their home villages.

2 다음 문장의 밑줄 친 부분을 바르게 고쳐 쓰시오.

(1) Do you think how smart you are?
(2) Why do you suppose does he want to keep losing weight?
(3) Do you believe when will he return to town?

Tip

1. (1) 선행사가 생략된 관계부사
(2) 선행사가 생략된 관계부사

2. 「의문사 + do you suppose / think / believe + 주어 + 동사」 구문
(1) 의문사 how
(2) 의문사 why
(3) 의문사 when

Listen and Speak/Into Real Life

정답 P. 236

Tip

1 대화를 듣고, 대화가 일어나는 장소로 알맞은 것을 고르시오.

① library
② airplane
③ mountain
④ candy store
⑤ amusement park

❶ 대화 장소 추론하기
출처: Get Ready_1

2 대화를 듣고, 여자에 대한 내용과 일치하지 않는 것을 고르시오.

① She is going to New Zealand this summer.
② She loves the Hobbiton movies and wants to visit the movie set.
③ She is planning to go skydiving all by herself.
④ She is going to stay in New Zealand for two weeks.
⑤ She is looking forward to going to New Zealand.

❷ 내용 일치 및 불일치 파악하기
출처: Listen In_Dialogue 1
look forward to -ing: ~를 고대하다

3 대화를 듣고, 남자가 타야 할 전철과 내릴 역 및 출구 번호로 맞는 것을 고르시오.

① Line 5 toward the south – Newton Station – Exit 6
② Line 5 toward the north – Newton Station – Exit 5
③ Line 6 toward the south – Woodlands Station – Exit 6
④ Line 6 toward the north – Woodlands Station – Exit 5
⑤ Line 5 toward the south – Woodlands Station – Exit 5

❸ 길 묻고 위치 찾기
출처: Listen In_Dialogue 2

4 다음을 듣고, 물음에 답하시오.

(1) 방송의 목적으로 알맞은 것을 고르시오.
① To persuade the students to participate in extracurricular activities
② To help the students write a report on tourist attractions in Korea
③ To help the students make a decision of which place to go for a field trip
④ To encourage the students to book public transportation for their trip
⑤ To inform the students of the advantages of making a reservation online

(2) 방송의 내용과 일치하지 않는 것을 고르시오.
① 울릉도, 독도 코스 – 해안 절벽 관람, 바다낚시 가능
② 울릉도, 독도 코스 – 가는 데 총 6시간 정도 소요
③ 안동 코스 – 하회 마을 방문, 전통 혼례식 관람 가능
④ 안동 코스 – 기차로 3시간 정도 소요
⑤ 대전 시민천문대 코스 – 천문대까지 도보로 1시간 30분 정도 소요

❹ (1) 방송의 목적 파악하기
(2) 구체적인 정보 파악하기
출처: Into Real Life_Step 1
extracurricular activities 교외 활동, 학과(수업) 외 활동

언어 기능별 집중 대비

Read and Think

정답 P. 237

Tip

1 출처: P.95 L.6-15
유형: 문법성 판단

1 다음 글의 밑줄 친 ①~⑤ 중 어법상 어색한 것을 고르시오.

Granada is ① what a whole city was influenced by Arabic culture because of wars and interactions between Spanish and Arabic people a long time ago. I decided to visit the Alhambra palace, ② which is one of the greatest architectural wonders of Spain. People say this palace was left ③ undamaged during wars because the beauty of the palace was astonishing.

In front of the palace, there was a beautiful garden called *Generalife*. I was totally amazed by the incredible scenery. The fountains were running, and the pools ④ reflected the beautiful flowers and trees in the garden. Later I found out that water meant life and richness to Arabic people in the Middle Ages. Their emphasis on water is ⑤ expressed in the many water tunnels and fountains in the palace.

[2-3] 다음 대화를 읽고, 물음에 답하시오.

2-3 출처: P.96 L.2-15
유형: 2. 문장의 위치
3. 빈칸 추론

Chris: I'm planning to visit South America this summer vacation. Since you've been there, where do you think I should go in South America?

Grace: There are many places to see, but I recommend Iguazu Falls. They were why I decided to go to Brazil. I can't describe their beauty in words. (A)

Chris: I've heard of Iguazu Falls. Why do you think they are famous?

Grace: It's because they are the tallest and largest falls in the world. (B)

Chris: Oh, I see. So, where exactly are they located?

Grace: They are located on the border between Argentina and Brazil. If you're on the Brazilian side, you can take a helicopter or a boat to look around the falls. (C)

Chris: ______________________________

Grace: Definitely the Devil's Throat. It was as big and fantastic as the name sounds. (D) The sight of large waterfalls and gleaming rainbows was incredible. (E)

2 위 대화의 (A)~(E) 중 아래의 문장이 들어가기에 가장 알맞은 곳은?

You have to see them in person.

3 위 대화의 빈칸에 가장 알맞은 것은?

① Where else should I visit?
② What was the boat riding like?
③ Why do you think it is amazing?
④ What were you most impressed with?
⑤ What was the least exciting thing to do there?

Tip

4 다음 글의 성격으로 가장 알맞은 것은?

The rooms are delicately decorated with colorful works of art, wooden ceilings, and various patterns. After I finished the tour, I could understand why the palace wasn't destroyed. In Spain, it is an absolute must to visit the Alhambra palace! I hope you will have a chance to go there.

① regret and advice
② contrast and prediction
③ comparison and persuasion
④ description and encouragement
⑤ depiction and recommendation

❹ 출처: P.95 L.17-21
유형: 글의 성격

5 다음 대화의 내용을 읽고 답할 수 없는 질문은?

Chris: Where else did you go?
Grace: Since I am a huge fan of football, São Paulo was a must-visit city. It was like the entire city went on vacation during big matches. There is even a football museum in São Paulo. This shows Brazilians' great passion for football.
Chris: A football museum? That's awesome! No wonder so many internationally famous football legends, like Pele, Ronaldo, and Ronaldinho, are Brazilians.
Grace: I know. This museum exhibits interesting things like some of the footballs used in the World Cup matches, pictures, and video of historical football matches. There's even a whole room which is filled with the history of Brazilian football.
Chris: It sounds like Brazil is the perfect place to absorb the beauty of nature and the passion of football fans. I'm already excited!

① What kind of museum is in São Paulo?
② How long is the history of Brazilian football?
③ Where are Pele, Ronaldo, and Ronaldinho from?
④ Why was São Paulo a must-visit city for Grace?
⑤ What can we see in the football museum in São Paulo?

❺ 출처: P.97 L.2-14
유형: 내용 파악

6 다음 밑줄 친 ①~⑤ 중 글의 흐름과 관련 없는 문장은?

On the first day of our trip, we took a little cruise. It was a cruise on Yellow Water, which has a variety of wild animals, dramatic scenery, and ever-changing landscapes. ① We spotted more than twenty different species of birds and wild crocodiles in the river. ② Until this trip, I had only seen crocodiles in the zoo, so the sight of wild crocodiles made my jaw drop.

The second day at Kakadu National Park was all about exploring Aboriginal rock art. ③ The paintings of animals provide a fascinating record of Aboriginal life over thousands of years. ④ Our guide told us that our next destination was Canberra, the capital city. ⑤ We were impressed by the well preserved rock paintings.

❻ 출처: P.98 L.9-18
유형: 글의 흐름 파악

Tip

7 다음 글의 빈칸에 가장 알맞은 것은?

My family's trip across Australia is going well. The land is very big, so ______________________! This week, we felt very cold on snowy Blue Mountain, and I enjoyed a nice warm walk along the Sunshine Coast. And now we are sweating in Kakadu National Park, which is located in the north area of Australia.

① it took a week to cross the country by car
② we have experienced four seasons in just a week
③ public transportations were not always available
④ it was not easy to stop by every tourist attractions
⑤ they have so many dialects we couldn't understand

7 출처: P.98 L.2-7
유형: 빈칸 추론

8 다음 글의 ①~⑤ 중 아래의 문장이 들어가기에 가장 알맞은 곳은?

It is also called the largest mirror on the planet.

I've always wanted to go to Bolivia because of its beautiful nature and exotic culture. It takes 29 hours to get there. I am planning to stay two weeks, looking around at famous places. (①) The first place I want to go to is Salar de Uyuni. (②) This place is the world's largest salt lake. (③) When it rains, you can see the sky and your reflection in the thin layer of water. (④) Then, the second place I would go to is Lake Titicaca. (⑤) Although it's a lake, it looks like the sea because of its size. I want to go fishing on this peaceful lake.

8 출처: P.102 L.2-11
유형: 문장의 위치

9 다음 괄호 안의 (a)~(c)에 알맞은 말이 차례대로 연결된 것은?

Hi Mijin,

How have you been? I am doing well here at Jang Bogo Station in Antarctica. The scientists here, including me, are really proud of working here. We especially take pride in Korea's (a)(been / being) the tenth nation to build two research stations in Antarctica. Here we have discovered many interesting things (b)(what / which) will lead to more studies about the Earth. For example, we have collected various kinds of rocks and metals that Koreans have found in Antarctica. We believe that our work will be helpful to future generations. I will keep you (c)(posted / posting) about more news about this amazing place. Please take care.

Best wishes, *Yeonghun*

① been – what – posted
② been – which – posted
③ been – which – posting
④ being – what – posting
⑤ being – which – posted

9 출처: P.107 L.3-13
유형: 문법성 판단

언어 기능별 집중 대비

Language Notes Write It Right

정답 P 237

1 다음 우리말에 맞게 괄호 안의 단어를 이용하여 문장을 완성하시오.

(1) 그의 소설은 추리 소설을 좋아하는 사람이라면 읽어야 하는 필수적인 것이다.
His novel is ______________________________. (a must)

(2) 너는 언제 우리가 무인 자동차를 사용할 수 있을 거로 생각하니?
______________________________ use driverless cars? (think)

(3) 1월은 대부분의 사람들이 새로운 결심을 하는 때이다.
January is when ______________________________. (resolution)

(4) 그들은 태풍 같은 극심한 날씨에 대해 우리에게 계속 알려주고 있다.
They ____________________ extreme weathers like storms. (posted)

(5) 뉴욕은 가장 명성 있는 극장들이 있는 곳이다.
New York is where ____________________. (prestigious theaters)

Tip

❶ (1) 필수적인 것, 필수품
(2) 「의문사 + do you think + 주어 + 동사」
(3) 선행사가 생략된 관계부사 when
(4) keep someone posted about
(5) 선행사가 생략된 관계부사 where
prestigious 명성 높은, 유수한
make a resolution 결심을 하다

2 다음 의문문에 주어진 표현을 결합하여 어순에 맞게 쓰시오.

(1) "Who are you?"
→ __________ do you think ____________________?

(2) "What does he want for his birthday present?"
→ __________ do you suppose ____________________?

(3) "Where does happiness come from?"
→ __________ do you believe ____________________?

❷ do you think/believe/suppose가 결합된 간접의문문

3 〈보기〉와 같이 문장을 바꾸어 쓰시오.

보기 Hemingway learned to be poor and happy in Paris.
→ Paris is where Hemingway learned to be poor and happy.

(1) There is a great danger for wildfires in September.
→ September ______________________________.

(2) Eastern tradition and modern influences collide in Shanghai.
→ Shanghai ______________________________.

(3) My jeans do not fit any more because of Belgian chocolate.
→ Belgian chocolate is ______________________________.

(4) Deaf and blind people learn how to communicate in this way.
→ This is ______________________________.

❸ 선행사가 생략된 관계부사
(1) in September는 시간 개념이다.
(2) in Shanghai는 장소 개념이다.
(3) because of Belgian chocolate는 이유를 나타내는 표현이다.
(4) in this way는 방법을 나타낸다.
wildfire 산불, 들불
collide 충돌하다
deaf and blind 시청각 장애를 가진

Basic

1 대화를 듣고, 남자의 마지막 말에 이어질 여자의 말로 가장 알맞은 것을 고르시오.

① So am I.
② Not at all.
③ Don't mention it.
④ You can say that again.
⑤ Take good care of yourself.

2 대화를 듣고, 두 사람이 대화하고 있는 장소를 고르시오.

① art class ② art museum
③ art book fair ④ travel agency
⑤ movie theater

3 다음 중 반의어끼리 바르게 연결된 것은?

① awesome – awful
② delicate – elegant
③ legend – legendary
④ preserve – conserve
⑤ incredible – unbelievable

4 다음 짝지어진 단어의 관계가 나머지와 다른 하나는?

① exhibit – exhibition
② absorb – absorption
③ emphasize – emphasis
④ astonish – astonishment
⑤ architect – architecture

5 다음 문장의 빈칸에 가장 알맞은 것은?

The law is a ________ in a democratic society.

① burden ② must
③ wonder ④ choice
⑤ responsibility

[6~7] 다음 중 어법상 어색한 문장을 고르시오.

6

① What do you suppose he will do next?
② When do you believe she will be back?
③ Where do you think was the treasure box buried?
④ Who do you think is responsible for the tragedy?
⑤ How much do you guess your doctor earns per year?

7

① London is which most people want to work.
② Bugs are why I'm afraid of ordering from farms.
③ March is when vitamin D levels are the lowest.
④ That's how the manager treated the employees.
⑤ Theaters are where you go see live performances like plays.

8 다음 글의 밑줄 친 부분에 대한 이유로 가장 알맞은 것은?

Next to the garden were the Nasrid Palaces, which I thought were the most beautiful palaces I had ever seen. The rooms are delicately decorated with colorful works of art, wooden ceilings, and various patterns. After I finished the tour, I could understand <u>why the palace wasn't destroyed</u>. In Spain, it is an absolute must to visit the Alhambra palace! I hope you will have a chance to go there.

① The palace was too beautiful to destroy.
② The palace was located in a remote place.
③ The palace had so many beautiful gardens.
④ The palace was skillfully built not to be seen.
⑤ The palace was guarded by so many loyal soldiers.

정답 P. 237

[9~10] 다음 대화를 읽고, 물음에 답하시오.

Chris: I'm planning to visit South America this summer vacation. Since you've been there, where do you think I should go in South America?

Grace: There are many places to see, but I recommend Iguazu Falls. ① They were what I decided to go to Brazil. I can't describe their beauty in words. You have to see them ② in person.

Chris: I've heard of Iguazu Falls. ______ⓐ______

Grace: It's because they are the tallest and largest falls in the world.

Chris: Oh, I see. So, where exactly are they located?

Grace: They are located ③ on the border between Argentina and Brazil. If you're on the Brazilian side, you can take a helicopter or a boat to look around the falls.

Chris: What were you most impressed with?

Grace: Definitely the Devil's Throat. It was as big and fantastic ④ as the name sounds. The sight of large waterfalls and gleaming rainbows was incredible. Once you see this area, you will be totally amazed by its beauty.

Chris: ⑤ I can't wait to go there.

9 위 대화의 밑줄 친 ①~⑤ 중 어법상 어색한 것은?

① ② ③ ④ ⑤

10 위 대화의 빈칸 ⓐ에 〈보기〉의 단어를 사용하여 알맞게 쓰시오.

보기 why / famous / think

→ ______________________

11 다음 글의 (A)~(E) 중 아래의 문장이 들어가기에 가장 알맞은 곳은?

Our guide told us that some of the oldest rock arts might be as much as 40,000 years old.

Kakadu National Park is a home to thousands of animals. We spent two days in the park.

On the first day of our trip, we took a little cruise. (A) It was a cruise on Yellow Water, which has a variety of wild animals, dramatic scenery, and ever-changing landscapes. (B) The second day at Kakadu National Park was all about exploring Aboriginal rock art.(C) The paintings of animals provide a fascinating record of Aboriginal life over thousands of years. (D) We were impressed by the well preserved rock paintings. (E) Also, some Aboriginals are still living in Kakadu and have kept their cultural traditions. After the trip, I learned to appreciate the beauty of nature and old traditions.

① (A) ② (B) ③ (C) ④ (D) ⑤ (E)

[12~13] 두 문장이 같은 의미가 되도록 빈칸에 알맞은 말을 쓰시오.

12

East meets West in Turkey.
= Turkey is ______________.

13

I decided to go to Africa because of the unique wildlife.
= The unique wildlife was ______________.

14 다음 〈보기〉의 우리말과 같도록 괄호 안의 단어를 이용하여 빈칸에 알맞은 말을 쓰시오. (필요하면 어형을 바꾸시오)

보기 당신은 그 성당을 건축하는 데 얼마나 오래 걸렸을 거라고 생각하세요? (how / long / take)
→ ______________ to build the cathedral?

→ ______________________

Advanced

1 대화를 듣고, 내용과 일치하지 않는 것을 고르시오.

① Cheolsu went on a trip to India with his family.
② Cheolsu had been concerned about the trip because it was his first trip abroad with his family.
③ Cheolsu and his family enjoyed the Indian local food.
④ Cheolsu's family was lucky enough to see the entire traditional performances of the Hemis festival.
⑤ Cheolsu was deeply impressed and fascinated by the Taj Mahal.

2 대화를 듣고, 여자가 계획하고 있는 일정을 고르시오.

① visiting a museum in Hinuera
② visiting a folk village in Wanaka
③ visiting the Hobbiton movie set
④ watching the movie "The Hobbit"
⑤ waterskiing on Lake Wanaka

3 다음을 듣고, 내용을 통해 알 수 없는 것을 고르시오.

① How many choices of the field trip destinations are offered?
② What kind of activities can the students enjoy in Dokdo?
③ What kind of traditional Korean food can the students taste in Andong?
④ What kind of Korean traditional ceremonies can the students watch in the Folk Village of Andong?
⑤ What kind of activities are offered to the students who choose Daejeon Citizen Observatory?

4 다음 문장의 밑줄 친 말과 의미가 가장 가까운 것은?

It would be awesome if I could see him in person.

① secretly
② as he is
③ partially
④ publicly
⑤ face to face

5 다음 글의 밑줄 친 ①~⑤ 중 어색한 부분을 찾아 바르게 고쳐 쓰시오.

Granada is where a whole city was influenced by Arabic culture ① because of wars and interactions between Spanish and Arabic people a long time ago. I decided to visit the Alhambra palace, which is one of the greatest ② architectural wonders of Spain. People say this palace was left undamaged during wars because the beauty of the palace ③ was astonishing.

In front of the palace, there was a beautiful garden called *Generalife*. I was ④ totally amazed by the incredible scenery. The fountains were running, and the pools reflected the beautiful flowers and trees in the garden. Later I found out that water meant life and richness to Arabic people in the Middle Ages. Their emphasis on water ⑤ are expressed in the many water tunnels and fountains in the palace.

__________ → __________

6 다음 글에서 아래의 문장이 들어가기에 가장 알맞은 곳은?

* When it rains, you can see the sky and your reflection in the thin layer of water.

I've always wanted to go to Bolivia because of its beautiful nature and exotic culture. It takes 29 hours to get there. (①) I am planning to stay two weeks, looking around at famous places. (②) The first place I want to go to is Salar de Uyuni. (③)This place is the world's largest salt lake. (④) It is also called the largest mirror on the planet. (⑤) Then, the second place I would go to is Lake Titicaca. Although it's a lake, it looks like the sea because of its size. I want to go fishing on this peaceful lake.

7 다음 문장의 뒤에 이어질 글의 순서로 가장 알맞은 것은?

On the first day of our trip, we took a little cruise. It was a cruise on Yellow Water, which has a variety of wild animals, dramatic scenery, and ever-changing landscapes.

(A) Also, some Aboriginals are still living in Kakadu and have kept their cultural traditions. After the trip, I learned to appreciate the beauty of nature and old traditions.

(B) The second day at Kakadu National Park was all about exploring Aboriginal rock art. The paintings of animals provide a fascinating record of Aboriginal life over thousands of years. We were impressed by the well preserved rock paintings.

(C) We spotted more than twenty different species of birds and wild crocodiles in the river. Until this trip, I had only seen crocodiles in the zoo, so the sight of wild crocodiles made my jaw drop.

① (A) – (C) – (B)　② (B) – (A) – (C)
③ (B) – (C) – (A)　④ (C) – (A) – (B)
⑤ (C) – (B) – (A)

[8~10] 다음 글을 읽고, 물음에 답하시오.

In front of the palace, there was a beautiful garden called *Generalife*. I was totally amazed by the incredible scenery. (A) The fountains ① <u>were running</u>, and the pools reflected the beautiful flowers and trees in the garden. (B) Later I found out ② <u>that</u> water meant life and richness to Arabic people in the Middle Ages. (C) Their emphasis on water is expressed in the many water tunnels and fountains in the palace.

(D) Next to the garden ③ <u>was</u> the Nasrid Palaces, ④ <u>which</u> I thought were the most beautiful palaces I had ever seen. (E) After I finished the tour, I could understand why the palace wasn't destroyed. In Spain, it is an absolute must to visit the Alhambra palace! I hope you will have a chance to ⑤ <u>go there</u>.

8 윗글의 (A) ~ (E) 중 아래 문장이 들어가기에 가장 알맞은 곳은?

The rooms are delicately decorated with colorful works of art, wooden ceilings, and various patterns.

① (A)　② (B)　③ (C)　④ (D)　⑤ (E)

9 윗글의 밑줄 친 ① ~ ⑤ 중 어법상 <u>어색한</u> 것은?

①　②　③　④　⑤

10 윗글의 내용과 일치하도록 다음 문장의 빈칸에 알맞은 말이 차례대로 연결된 것은?

Many fountains, pools, and water tunnels in the palace ______________ the belief of Arabic people in the Middle Ages that water brings life and ______________.

① distort – glory
⑤ sustain – beauty
③ reflect – wealth
④ reserve – victory
② destroy – death

[11~13] 다음 글을 읽고, 물음에 답하시오.

Hi Mijin,

How have you been? I ①am doing well here at Jang Bogo Station in Antarctica. I know many people are curious about the ②reason I had to go to Antarctica, but the scientists here, including me, are really proud of working here. We especially take pride ____________ ____________ two research stations in Antarctica. Here we ③have discovered many interesting things which ④will lead to more studies about the Earth. For example, we have collected ⑤various kind of rocks and metals that Koreans have found in Antarctica. We believe that our work will be helpful to future generations. I will keep you posted about more news about this amazing place. Please take care.

Best wishes, *Yeonghun*

11 윗글의 빈칸에 알맞은 말을 괄호 안에 주어진 단어를 이용하여 바르게 쓰시오.

(in / to / the / tenth / build / Korea's / nation / being)

⊖ ______________________________

12 윗글의 밑줄 친 ①~⑤ 중 어법상 어색한 것을 찾아 바르게 고쳐 쓰시오.

______________ → ______________

13 윗글의 내용과 일치하는 것은?

① Yeonghun wants Mijin to join him in Jang Bogo Station.
② Yeonghun believes that his work in the research station will help people living in Antarctica.
③ Yeonghun hopes that the things he and his colleagues have discovered will be helpful in the future.
④ Yeonghun asks Mijin to keep in contact with him through email.
⑤ Yeonghun had told all his friends why he made such a decision to go to Antarctica.

14 다음 중 어법상 어색한 것은?

① What do you think is the most valuable thing to do?
② How long do you guess it will take to get to the moon?
③ Which do you believe is more important, truth or compassion?
④ School should be where students are able to develop their potential.
⑤ Earth Day is for many people pledge to make changes to help improve the environment.

주관식 서술형 대비

15 자신이 여행하고 싶은 장소를 정하여 아래의 항목이 모두 포함된 짧은 여행 계획을 3~4 문장으로 쓰시오.

1. country name
2. flight time
3. the length of your trip
4. famous places to visit

____
____
____
____

1학기 기말고사

[1~6] 잘 듣고, 물음에 답하시오.

01. 대화를 듣고, 여자의 마지막 말에 이어질 남자의 응답으로 가장 알맞은 것을 고르시오.

① We have to increase the daily consumption of gas.
② We should stop using gas and start using other resources.
③ We should try to find out the causes of natural disasters.
④ We need to import more gas and maintain our energy supply.
⑤ We have to make sure we don't waste our energy from now on.

02. 대화를 듣고, 내용과 일치하지 않는 것을 고르시오.

① 대회 취지 : 세계 환경의 날 기념
② 참가 방법 : 개인별 혹은 팀별 참가
③ 포스터 크기 : 30cm X 45cm
④ 그리기 재료 : 유화나 수채화 물감
⑤ 제출 기한 : 다음 주 금요일

03. 대화를 듣고, 여자가 Marco에게 해 준 조언으로 맞는 것을 고르시오.

① Bottle caps cannot be recycled with bottles.
② Items that are not recyclable should be put outside the classroom.
③ Items that have a triangular shape and number 1 or 2 inside are recyclable.
④ Read the number on the items before you decide whether to throw them or not.
⑤ Put a label on the garbage bag so that the students can know where to put their garbage.

04. 대화를 듣고, 여자의 여행 계획과 일치하지 않는 것을 고르시오.

① 좋아하는 영화의 배경인 뉴질랜드로 갈 예정이다.
② 북섬에 있는 히누에라를 여행 첫날 방문하고 싶어 한다.
③ 여행 둘째 날에는 스카이다이빙을 할 예정이다.
④ 전문가의 도움 없이 혼자 스카이다이빙을 할 예정이다.
⑤ 뉴질랜드에서 2주 동안 머무를 예정이다.

[5~6] 다음을 듣고, 내용과 일치하도록 주어진 질문에 맞는 답을 고르시오.

05.

Q. If someone is interested in astronomy and space science, which destination would be the best choice in the school trip?

① Andong
② Dokdo
③ Daejeon
④ Ulleungdo
⑤ A UNESCO World Heritage

06.

Q. What can the students experience if they choose Andong?

① They will visit the UNESCO and have an interview with the staff working there.
② They will experience the traditional ways of living in the folk village.
③ They will watch a three-hour-long wedding performance there.
④ They will learn how people built the traditional Korean houses and villages.
⑤ They will help the foreigners visiting Andong to better understand the Korean culture.

[7~8] 다음 글의 밑줄 친 ①~⑤ 중 어법상 어색한 것을 고르시오.

07.

Since the latest super storm hit Southeast Asia, the total number of deaths and injuries ① has now exceeded one million. At 3 p.m. on March 30th, 2025, an 18-hour storm severely damaged the region. On April 2nd, the number of deaths and injured individuals stood at 514,000, with over 17,000 missing, and the numbers are expected ② to rise. The storm left many people ③ homeless. A climate scientist said this super storm was obviously ④ caused by dramatic changes in the global climate. He added, "A rise in global temperatures ⑤ have increased the intensity of storms with higher wind speeds." Unfortunately, researchers predict that super storms will happen more frequently this summer.

08.

For years, the micro dust that blows into Korea from China ① has been a serious problem. A few years ago, despite global efforts ② to dealing with the problem, it seemed the problem was getting worse. But from the year before last, air pollution has greatly decreased thanks to the help of volunteers from neighboring countries, who ③ have planted trees in many parts of China. The effort started ten years ago, and it's now starting to show significant results. Experts explain that the trees serve as a wall to block the sand and dust ④ from crossing into Korea. At long last, this coming weekend, people of all ages ⑤ are expected to breathe in the fresh air.

09. 다음 괄호 안의 (A)~(C) 에 들어갈 말이 차례대로 연결된 것은?

The remarkable development of engineering and chemistry inspired Korean researchers, who have tried to solve severe (A) (drought / flood) problems. In the end, they successfully transformed seawater into fresh water in an environmentally friendly way. They also found a way to reuse water that contains high salt content. This new solution has (B) (enhanced / reduced) worries about the effects of this technology on marine life. Since this technology has become widely used, it has become a source of hope for the people who need drinkable water. A sufficient supply of clean water using the technology is now being developed and is expected to help (C) (contaminate / eliminate) diseases that are caused by the world's lack of clean water.

① flood – reduced – eliminate
② drought – enhanced – eliminate
③ drought – reduced – eliminate
④ flood – reduced – contaminate
⑤ drought – enhanced – contaminate

10. 다음 주어진 문장이 들어가기에 가장 알맞은 곳은?

Some may wonder why we should worry about a three-degree increase in warming

(①) According to many researchers, by 2100, New York and Shanghai will also sink, and the average global temperature is expected to be about 3.6 degrees higher than now. (②) A one-degree global change is highly significant because it takes a vast amount of heat to warm all the earth's oceans, atmosphere, and land. (③) In the past, just a one- to two-degree drop caused the earth to go through the Little Ice Age. (④) World leaders have realized the seriousness of climate change, so they will meet in Paris next month for a climate forum. (⑤)

11. 다음 글의 제목으로 가장 알맞은 것은?

The global ban on fossil fuels gave a boost to alternative energy. A number of companies around the world have built up more effective energy sources that can make up for the shortage of fossil fuels. Thanks to the development of renewable energy resources, they now make up more than half of the country's entire power, and this rate is set to grow even bigger. Renewable energy resources come from a wide variety of sources including the sun, the wind, and the sea. Using renewable energy produces less air or water pollution and fewer carbon dioxide emissions than using fossil fuels. The rapid development of renewable energy sources will help us meet energy demands without creating much pollution.

① The Global Consumption of Fossil Fuels
② The Shortage of the Renewable Energy Industries
③ Worldwide Investments in Renewable Technologies
④ The Pursuit of Renewable Alternative Energy Sources
⑤ Economic Benefits of Using Renewable Energy Sources

12. 다음 글의 ①~⑤ 중 전체 흐름과 관계 <u>없는</u> 문장은?

① As the competition in the electric car market has become more intense, many companies have long been struggling to develop long-lasting electric car batteries. ② At the same time, hydrogen cars with satellite communications have also joined in this competition. ③ They can eliminate polluted air produced by fossil fuel engines. ④ Green vehicles function fully or partly on alternative energy sources other than fossil fuel or less carbon intensive than gasoline or diesel. ⑤ Heating up the green car market fever, the launch of new hydrogen cars is expected to help reduce air pollution and eventually solve the energy crisis.

13. 다음 글의 밑줄 친 ①~⑤ 중 어법상 <u>어색한</u> 것은?

Granada is ① <u>where</u> a whole city was influenced by Arabic culture because of wars and interactions between Spanish and Arabic people a long time ago. I decided to visit the Alhambra palace, ② <u>which</u> is one of the greatest architectural wonders of Spain. People say this palace was left ③ <u>undamaging</u> during wars because the beauty of the palace was astonishing. In front of the palace, there was a beautiful garden called Generalife. I was totally ④ <u>amazed</u> by the incredible scenery. The fountains were running, and the pools ⑤ <u>reflected</u> the beautiful flowers and trees in the garden.

14. 다음 괄호 안의 (A)~(C)에 가장 알맞은 것은?

In front of the Alhambra palace, there was a beautiful garden called *Generalife*. I was totally amazed by the incredible scenery. The fountains were running, and the pools reflected the beautiful flowers and trees in the garden. Later I found out that water meant life and richness to Arabic people in the Middle Ages. Their emphasis on water is (A) (expressed / expressing) in the many water tunnels and fountains in the palace.

Next to the garden were the Nasrid Palaces, which I thought (B) (was / were) the most beautiful palaces I had ever seen. The rooms are delicately decorated with colorful works of art, wooden ceilings, and various patterns. After I finished the tour, I could understand why the palace wasn't destroyed. In Spain, it is an absolute must (C) (visit / to visit) the Alhambra palace!

① expressing – were – visit
② expressed – were – visit
③ expressed – was – visit
④ expressing – was – to visit
⑤ expressed – were – to visit

[15-16] 다음 대화를 읽고, 물음에 답하시오.

Chris: I'm planning to visit South America this summer vacation. Since you've been there, ① where do you think should I go in South America?

Grace: There are many places to see, but I recommend Iguazu Falls. They were ② why I decided to go to Brazil. I can't describe their beauty in words. You have to see them in person.

Chris: I've heard of Iguazu Falls. Why do you think they are famous?

Grace: It's because they are the tallest and largest falls in the world.

Chris: Oh, I see. So, ③ where exactly are they located?

Grace: They are located on the border between Argentina and Brazil. If you're on the Brazilian side, you can take a helicopter or a boat to look around the falls.

Chris: ______________________

Grace: Definitely the Devil's Throat. It was as big and fantastic ④ as the name sounds. The sight of large waterfalls and gleaming rainbows was incredible. Once you see this area, you will be totally amazed by its beauty.

Chris: ⑤ I can't wait to go there.

15. 위 대화의 밑줄 친 ①~⑤ 중 어법상 어색한 것은?

① ② ③ ④ ⑤

16. 위 대화의 빈칸에 가장 알맞은 것은?

① What were you most impressed with?
② How loud is the sound the falls make?
③ What do they call the place you were in?
④ Which country do the falls actually belong to?
⑤ Which tourist attraction would you least likely to visit again?

[17~18] 다음 대화를 읽고, 물음에 답하시오.

Chris: Where else did you go?

Grace: Since I am a huge fan of football, São Paulo was a must-visit city. (①) It was like the entire city went on vacation during big matches. There is even a football museum in São Paulo. This shows Brazilians'great passion for football. (②)

Chris: A football museum? That's awesome! No wonder so many internationally famous football legends, like Pele, Ronaldo, and Ronaldinho, are Brazilians. (③)

Grace: I know. This museum exhibits interesting things like some of the footballs used in the World Cup matches, pictures, and video of historical football matches. (④)

Chris: It sounds like Brazil is the perfect place to absorb the beauty of nature and the passion of football fans. (⑤) I'm already excited!

Grace: Yes, Brazil is a great place. I hope you enjoy yourself there.

17. 위 대화에서 아래의 문장이 들어가기에 가장 알맞은 곳은?

> There's even a whole room which is filled with the history of Brazilian football.

18. 위 대화의 내용과 일치하지 않는 것은?

① Grace has been to São Paulo, Brazil.
② In São Paulo, everyone goes on a vacation during the big football matches.
③ It is not surprising that many world famous football players are from Brazil.
④ The football museum in São Paulo displays some footballs that were used during the World Cup matches.
⑤ The football museum in São Paulo shows the passion of Brazilians about football.

[19-20] 다음 글을 읽고, 물음에 답하시오.

On the first day of our trip, we took a little cruise. It was a cruise on Yellow Water, which has a variety of wild animals, dramatic scenery, and ever-changing landscapes. We spotted more than twenty different species of birds and wild crocodiles in the river. Until this trip, I (A) (have / had) only seen crocodiles in the zoo, so the sight of wild crocodiles made my jaw drop.

The second day at Kakadu National Park was all about exploring Aboriginal rock art. The paintings of animals provide a (B) (fascinated / fascinating) record of Aboriginal life over thousands of years. Our guide told us that some of the oldest rock arts might be as much as 40,000 years old. We were impressed by the well preserved rock paintings. Also, some Aboriginals are still living in Kakadu and have kept their cultural traditions. After the trip, I learned to appreciate the beauty of nature and old traditions. Our next destination is Canberra, the capital city of Australia. I'll keep you (C) (posted / posting) about my trip.

19. 윗글의 (A)~(C)에 들어갈 말이 차례대로 연결된 것은?

① have – fascinated – posting
② have – fascinating – posted
③ had – fascinated – posting
④ had – fascinating – posted
⑤ had – fascinating – posting

20. 윗글을 읽고 답을 할 수 없는 질문은?

① What did the writer see on Yellow Water?
② What made the writer drop his or her jaw?
③ What kind of art did Aboriginals enjoy and leave?
④ Why did the early Aboriginals draw animals on rocks?
⑤ Where is the writer going after the visit of Kakadu National Park?

서술형

21. 다음 글의 빈칸 ⓐ와 ⓑ에 알맞은 말을 쓰시오.

EU energy consumption 2015

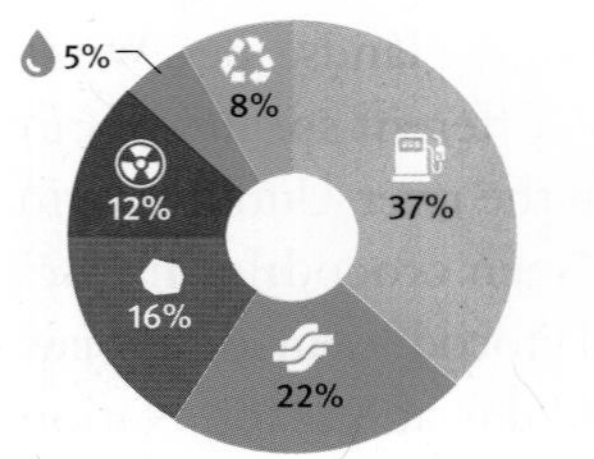

The pie chart shows the energy consumption by source in the E.U. Oil makes up ____ⓐ____ of the chart. Natural gas is the second largest part of energy consumption. On the other hand, renewable energy sources make up a very small part, which is ____ⓑ____ part. We need to try to develop more renewable energy resources in order to reduce pollution.

ⓐ ____________

ⓑ ____________

서술형

22. 괄호 안의 단어를 사용하여 다음을 영작하시오.

(1) 너는 인생에서 가장 가치 있는 것이 무엇이라고 생각하니? (valuable)

⊖ ________________________________

(2) 신청서가 처리되는 동안 잠깐 기다리세요. (application / process)

⊖ ________________________________

서술형

23. 두 문장의 의미가 같도록 관계부사를 사용하여 빈칸에 알맞은 말을 쓰시오.

(1) She chose the college because she wanted to get the scholarship.

= The scholarship was ________________________________.

(2) The old meets the new in Seoul.

= Seoul is ________________________________.

논술형

24. 다음 빈칸에 주어진 단어들을 알맞게 배열하여 문장을 완성하시오.

The main cause is carbon dioxide emissions. Greenhouse gases are being trapped within the earth's atmosphere, which has led to rising temperatures. The ________________________ of the Maldives, which is a famous tourist destination..

(sinking / rising / the / has / in / level / sea / resulted)

논술형

25. Write and share ideas on how to go green at home and at school. Write your ideas in 3 full sentences.

We can and should take actions to stop climate change. Here are my ideas.

First, ________________________________

Second, ________________________________

Finally, ________________________________

UNIT 6

Fuel Your Creativity

내신체크 01 교과서 핵심 정리 > Go to p. 116

- 어휘 총정리
- 대본 정리
  두뇌 활동과 창의적인 사고에 관한 대화 및 여섯 가지 생각 모자 전략에 관한 방담
- 본문 정리
  틀에서 벗어나는 사고 훈련을 통해 창의적인 사고의 중요성 강조

내신체크 02 언어 기능별 집중 대비 > Go to p. 126

- **듣기와 말하기** 대본별 필수 출제 유형
- **읽기** 각 단락별 필수 점검 유형
- **언어 재료 및 쓰기** 어휘 및 구문, 주관식 서술형 대비 문제

내신체크 03 수준별 단원 평가 > Go to p. 131

- **Basic** 지식, 사실적 이해 대비 문제
- **Advanced** 추론적 이해 및 감상, 주관식 서술형 대비 문제

교과서 핵심 정리

Words & Phrases

Listen and Speak ~ Into Real Life

- ☐ brilliant *adj.* 훌륭한, 멋진
- ☐ logic *n.* 논리 (logical *adj.* 논리적인)
- ☐ stain *n.* 얼룩, 더러움
- ☐ get in (good) shape* 좋은 몸(몸매) 상태를 유지하다
- ☐ disorder *n.* 장애, 엉망
- ☐ on a daily basis* 매일 *cf.* on a monthly basis 매달
- ☐ dynasty *n.* 왕조
- ☐ scholar *n.* 학자
- ☐ strategy* *n.* 전략
- ☐ psychologist *n.* 심리학자 *cf.* psychology 심리학
- ☐ critically *ad.* 비판적으로
- ☐ apply* *v.* 지원하다, 적용하다 (application *n.* 지원)

Read and Think

- ☐ incorrectly *ad.* 부정확하게, 틀리게 (incorrect *adj.* 부정확한)
- ☐ approach *n.* 접근 *v.* 접근하다
- ☐ imaginary* *adj.* 상상의, 가상의 (imagination *n.* 상상)
- ☐ creativity* *n.* 창의성 (creative *adj.* 창의적인)
- ☐ diagonally *ad.* 대각선으로, 비스듬히 (diagonal *adj.* 대각선의)
- ☐ come to mind* (생각이) 떠오르다
- ☐ tend to* ~하는 경향이 있다 (tendency *n.* 경향)
- ☐ physicist *n.* 물리학자
  cf. physics 물리학, physician (내과) 의사
- ☐ wire *n.* 철사, 전선 *cf.* wireless 무선의
- ☐ infinite* *adj.* 무한한, 끝없는
- ☐ announce *v.* 발표하다, 알리다 (announcement *n.* 발표)
- ☐ glance *n.* 곁눈질, 흘끗 보기 *v.* 흘끗 보다
- ☐ fence off* 울타리로 가로막다, 울타리를 치다
- ☐ except for* ~를 제외하고 (exception *n.* 예외,제외)
- ☐ the other way around* 그 반대로, 거꾸로
- ☐ beyond *prep.* ~를 넘어서, ~이상으로
- ☐ portrait *n.* 초상화, 인물화 (portray *v.* 묘사하다)
- ☐ switch *v.* 바꾸다, 전환하다
- ☐ step out of one's comfort zone 안주하던 영역에서 나오다
- ☐ upside down 거꾸로, 뒤집어서
- ☐ neither *A* nor *B** A도 아니고 B도 아닌 (둘 다 부정)
- ☐ include *v.* 포함하다 (↔ exclude 배제하다)
- ☐ combine *v.* 결합하다, 병행하다 (combination *n.*결합)
- ☐ five senses 오감(다섯 가지 감각기관)
- ☐ pump up 증대하다, 강화하다
- ☐ think outside the box* (고정관념에서 벗어나) 새로운 사고를 하다

Language Notes

- ☐ make fun of* ~를 비웃다
- ☐ embarrass *v.* 당황하게 하다 (embarrassment *n.*당황)
- ☐ daydream *v.* 공상에 잠기다 *n.* 공상, 백일몽
- ☐ mathematician *n.* 수학자 *cf.* mathematics 수학
- ☐ insight *n.* 통찰력
- ☐ go through* ~를 겪다, 과정을 거치다

Write It Right

- ☐ soap *n.* 비누 *cf.* soap opera (TV) 드라마 연속극
- ☐ complaint* *n.* 불만, 불평 (complain *v.*불평하다)
- ☐ assembly line (공장의) 조립 라인
- ☐ at low cost* 비용을 적게 들이고, 적은 비용으로
- ☐ current *adj.* 현재의, 지금의
- ☐ pay a fine 벌금을 물다

Around the World

- ☐ impact* *n.* 영향(력)
- ☐ unlock *v.* (잠겨 있던 것을) 열다 (↔ lock 잠그다)
- ☐ instinct* *n.* 본능, 직감 (instinctive *adj.* 본능적인)
- ☐ pioneer *n.* 개척자, 선구자

Check-Up

정답 P. 240

1 다음 문장의 빈칸에 알맞은 말을 〈보기〉에서 골라 넣으시오.

보기 >> pump up / upside down / get in shape / on a daily basis / except for

(1) If you want to ______________, try jogging or speed walking.

(2) The country is trying to ______________ exports and the economy overall.

(3) The scholarship will cover all your expenses ______________ the tuition fee.

(4) Even a small consumption of alcohol ______________ can lead to liver damage.

(5) The baby was holding the book ______________.

2 다음 뜻풀이에 해당하는 말을 주어진 철자로 시작하여 쓰시오.

(1) p________: a painting, drawing, or photograph of a person that usually includes the person's head and shoulders

(2) d________: to think pleasant thoughts about your life or future while you are awake

(3) s ________: a person who studies a subject for a long time and knows a lot about it

(4) i ________: the ability to understand people and situations in a very clear way

(5) i ________: having no limits or extremely large or great

주관식 서술형

3 우리말에 맞게 괄호 안의 단어들을 사용하여 문장을 완성하시오.

(1) 나는 쉽게 몸무게가 느는 경향이 있기 때문에 먹는 것에 주의해야 한다.
I have to be careful about what I eat ______________________________.
(gain / weight / tend / because / I / to / easily)

(2) 이 책을 읽음으로써 얻게 될 유익은 당신이 상상하는 것 이상일 겁니다.
The benefit you will gain from reading this book ________________.
(will / imagine / you / go / what / beyond)

(3) 그들은 습지를 보호하기 위해 그 땅에 울타리를 쳐야 한다고 주장했다.
They insisted that they should ______________________________.
(to / protect / the land / fence / off / the wetland)

(4) 그 컴퓨터 회사는 창의적으로 생각할 수 있는 사람들을 찾고 있다.
The computer company is looking for ________________________.
(the box / think / who / can / outside / people)

Tip

❶ 주요 숙어표현 익히기
overall 전반적으로
expense 비용, 지출 경비
tuition fee 수업료
consumption 소비, 소모
liver 간

❷ 영영사전풀이
pleasant 기분 좋은, 유쾌한
limit 제한, 한계

❸ 핵심어휘를 사용한 영작
gain weight 몸무게가 늘다
benefit 유익, 혜택
wetland 습지

교과서 핵심 정리

Dialogues & Monologue

Listen and Speak | *해석을 참조하여 빈칸에 알맞은 말을 쓰시오.

GET READY

1 M: How old is your father?
W: He is 17 years old.
M: What? How is that possible?
W: He became a father only when I was born.
M: What a brilliant answer! I like your __________ logic.

남: 너의 아버지 연세가 어떻게 되시니?
여: 17세이셔.
남: 뭐라고? 어떻게 그게 가능해?
여: 내가 태어났을 때 아빠가 되셨으니까.
남: 기막힌 대답인걸! 너의 창의적인 논리가 마음에 들어.

2 W: We're lost. I don't know which way to go. To the west? Or to the east?
M: Let's look at our location on the map.
W: Oh, yes! What a great idea! **Do you know how to read** signs and symbols on a map?

여: 우리는 길을 잃었어. 어느 쪽으로 가야할지 모르겠어. 서쪽 아님 동쪽?
남: 지도에서 우리가 있는 위치를 보자.
여: 아, 맞다. 좋은 생각이야. 지도에서 표시랑 부호들 읽는 법 알아?

3 M: Ugh, I hate food stains on clothes. **Do you know how to remove** food stains?
W: Yes, you can use a spoonful of salt.
M: A spoon of salt? Can you __________ how it works?
W: Sure. All you have to do is mix it with warm water and wash your clothes.
M: Wow, **what a brilliant idea!**

남: 이런, 옷에 음식 자국이 묻는 거 싫은데. 음식 자국 제거하는 법 아니?
여: 응. 한 숟가락의 소금을 사용하면 돼.
남: 한 숟가락의 소금이라고? 어떻게 효과가 있는지 설명해 줄래?
여: 물론이지. 그냥 소금을 따뜻한 물에 섞어서 그 물에 옷을 빨면 돼.
남: 와, 정말 기발한 생각이다.

표현정리
- What a brilliant answer! : 감탄문으로서 상대방의 답변이 예상치 못할 만큼 놀라울 때 쓰는 표현이다.
- Do you know how to read signs ~? : 「do you know how to + 동사원형」은 '~하는 법을 아니?'라는 의미의 표현이다.

정답 creative / explain

LISTEN IN

MONOLOGUE

M: Do you know how to get in good shape? Perhaps you're thinking about a __________. But when was the last time you thought about a brain workout? **Training your brain is just as important as maintaining a healthy body**. Studies show that with one hour of brain training a week, you not only improve the thinking skills you use every day but also prevent __________ disorders. With regular brain training, you will notice that you have better memory and greater creativity in your daily life. Train your brain by doing different types of brain questions on a daily basis or by approaching daily problems **in a way you're not** __________ **to**. Just make a conscious effort to think of different ways of doing things.

남: 좋은 몸매를 유지하는 법을 아세요? 아마도 여러분은 운동하는 걸 생각할 겁니다. 하지만 여러분이 두뇌 운동에 대해 생각해 본 적이 마지막으로 언제인가요? 두뇌를 훈련하는 것은 건강한 몸을 유지하는 것만큼 중요합니다. 연구에 따르면 일주일에 한 시간 정도의 뇌 운동으로도 여러분이 매일 사용하는 사고 능력을 향상시킬 수 있을 뿐만 아니라 기억 장애를 예방할 수 있다고 합니다. 규칙적인 두뇌 훈련을 통해 여러분은 기억력이 나아지고 또한 매일의 삶에서 더 큰 창의성을 갖게 되는 걸 알게 될 것입니다. 매일 다른 두뇌 훈련 문제를 풀어봄으로써 또는 여러분이 익숙하지 않은 방법으로 매일의 문제를 접근함으로써 여러분의 뇌를 훈련해 보세요. 단지 어떤 일을 하는 (이전과) 다른 방법에 대해 생각하려고 의식적으로 노력해 보세요.

대화상황
- 두뇌 운동의 필요성과 효과에 대해 얘기하면서 창의성 신장에 대한 의식적 노력의 중요성을 강조하고 있다.

표현정리
- Training your brian is just as important as maintaining ~: 「just as + 형용사 + as」는 '~만큼 …한'이라는 뜻의 원급 비교구문으로, 여기서는 두뇌 훈련이 신체 훈련만큼 중요하다는 말을 하고 있다.
- in a way you're not used to : 「be used to + -ing」는 '익숙하다'라는 뜻으로 「be accustomed to + -ing」와 바꿔 쓸 수 있다.

정답 workout / memory / used

DIALOGUE

M: Hey, Grace. Did you watch that documentary about Jeong Yakyong last night?

W: You mean the late Joseon dynasty scholar? — the one who wrote *Mokminsimseo*?

M: That's right. He also built the Hwaseong Fortress in Suwon with his creative invention.

W: I haven't seen the documentary, **but I did read a book about him**. His creativity was __________. I was particularly impressed reading about the system he invented to handle heavy building materials. What was it called... *Geojunggi*?

M: That's the one. And I agree — I think *geojunggi* is his greatest invention. What a brilliant idea it is, right?

W: **You can say that again**. Do you know how to ____________ it? I was surprised to see it lifting huge stones.

M: Yes, actually, I saw one once at a folk village and tried it out.

W: That sounds pretty cool. I'm interested in engineering. If you have a moment, can you tell me more about it?

M: Sure. Let's talk about it during lunch time.

W: Thanks. See you soon.

남: 안녕, Grace. 너 어젯밤 정약용에 관한 다큐멘터리 봤니?

여: 조선 왕조 후기 학자를 말하는 거야? 목민심서 썼던 그 사람?

남: 맞아. 그는 또한 창의적인 발명으로 수원 화성을 건축했어.

여: 그 다큐멘터리는 못 봤지만 그에 관한 책은 읽었어. 그의 창의성은 정말 대단해. 난 그가 무거운 건축 자재를 다루기 위해 발명한 그 시스템에 관해 읽으면서 특별히 감명 받았어. 그게 뭐였더라.. 거중기?

남: 그래, 그거야. 그리고 나도 거중기가 그의 가장 훌륭한 발명품이라는 데 동의해. 정말 기막힌 아이디어야, 그렇지?

여: 그래 맞아. 너 그거 작동하는 법 아니? 그게 무거운 돌들을 들어 올리는 걸 보고 놀랐어.

남: 그래, 정말이지, 나도 그걸 민속촌에서 보고 한 번 시도해 봤었어.

여: 재미있었겠다. 내가 엔지니어링에 관심이 있어서 그러는데 시간 좀 있으면 그것에 관해 나에게 좀 얘기해 줄 수 있어?

남: 물론이지. 점심시간에 얘기하자.

여: 고마워. 이따 봐.

대화상황
- 정약용에 관한 다큐멘터리 프로그램 시청에 관해 얘기하면서 그가 발명한 거중기에 관해 Grace가 큰 관심을 나타내고 있다.

표현정리
- I haven't seen the documentary, but I did read a book about him.: 조동사 did는 여기서 동사 read를 강조하기 위한 용법으로 쓰였다.
- You can say that again. : 상대방의 말에 적극 동의하는 표현으로서 '정말 그렇다.' 정도의 뜻이다.

정답 incredible / operate

Into Real Life

W: Ladies and gentlemen, welcome to the *Creativity Talk Show*. Have you ever heard of the Six Thinking Hats strategy? Well, let me introduce a psychologist, Dr. de Bono, who can help everyone think more creatively.

Dr. de Bono: Thank you for inviting me. One day, I was trying to solve a problem. I found myself thinking about many things at the same time and got confused with no solutions. So, I tried to think about one thing at a time and each time, in a __________ way. That helped me a lot, and I was able to come up with the Six Thinking Hats strategy. **Let's suppose you wear six hats**, each with a different color: white, red, blue, green, yellow, and black, and the way you think changes with each hat. Wouldn't it be fun?

여: 신사 숙녀 여러분, Creativity Talk Show에 오신 것을 환영합니다. 여러분 혹시 6개의 생각하는 모자 전략이라는 것에 관해 들어보신 적 있으신가요? 여러분이 좀 더 창의적으로 생각할 수 있게 도와 줄 심리학자 de Bono 박사님을 소개합니다.

de Bono 박사: 초대해 주셔서 감사합니다. 어느 날 제가 문제를 하나 풀려고 하고 있었어요. 그러다 동시에 많은 것들을 생각하느라 해결책도 없이 혼란스럽기만 했죠. 그래서 다른 방식으로 한 번에 한 가지만 생각해 보려고 했어요. 그게 큰 도움이 되었고 6개의 생각하는 모자 전략을 생각해 낼 수 있게 되었던 거죠. 여러분이 흰색, 빨간색, 파란색, 초록색, 노란색, 그리고 검은색의 각기 다른 색깔을 가진 6개의 모자를 쓰고 있고, 여러분이 생각하는 방식이 각각의 모자에 따라 달라진다고 가정합시다. 재미있지 않겠어요?

W: Indeed. So each hat would make a person think in a different way. Is that right?

Dr. de Bono: Yes. Let's start with the white hat. It remembers all information you need and deals with facts. The red hat, on the other hand, loves feelings and emotions.

W: What about the green one?

Dr. de Bono: The most important hat you wear is the green one. It focuses on new ideas and ________. **With this hat on, any thought is welcome!**

W: What a brilliant idea!

Dr. de Bono: Also, you get to think positively and explore the bright side of things with the yellow hat on. The black hat gives warnings and makes you think ________ about things. Above all, there is a hat that manages and balances the whole process — a blue hat. It is the boss of all hats.

W: How interesting! How can we apply this strategy in real life? Please give us an example.

여: 정말 그렇겠네요. 그럼 각각의 모자가 우리가 다른 방식으로 생각하게 만들어 준다는 거죠? 맞나요?

de Bono 박사: 네. 우선 흰색 모자부터 시작합시다. 그것은 당신이 필요로 하는 모든 정보를 기억하고 사실을 다루는 거예요. 반면에, 빨간 모자는 감정과 느낌을 사랑하죠.

여: 초록색 모자는요?

de Bono 박사: 당신이 쓰는 가장 중요한 모자가 바로 초록색 모자예요. 그것은 새로운 아이디어와 창의성에 초점을 맞추죠. 이 모자를 쓰고 있으면 어떤 생각이든 환영이에요!

여: 정말 기가 막힌 아이디어네요!

de Bono 박사: 또한, 노란 모자를 쓰면 여러분은 긍정적으로 생각하게 되고 사물의 밝은 면을 탐구하게 되죠. 까만 모자는 경고를 주고 사물에 대해 비판적으로 생각할 수 있게 해 줘요. 무엇보다, 이 모든 과정을 관리하고 조율해 주는 모자가 있는데 그게 바로 파란 모자예요. 모든 모자 중 대장이죠.

여: 정말 흥미롭네요! 이 전략을 어떻게 실생활에 적용할 수 있을까요? 예를 하나 들어 주시죠.

표현정리
- Let's suppose ~ : 「let's suppose (that) + 절」은 '~라고 가정해 보자'라는 의미로 상대방에게 어떤 상황을 가정해서 상상해 보라는 뜻이다.
- With this hat ~ welcome! : 「with + 옷/모자/신발 등 + on」은 '~ 을 입은 상태에서'라는 뜻이며, 'any ~ welcome'은 '어떤 생각이든 다 할 수 있다'라는 뜻이다.

정답 different / creativity / critically

Check Your Progress

W: Chris, did you see the *Creativity Talk Show* yesterday? It included a new brain question.

M: No, what is the question about?

W: It was such a brilliant question. According to the show, you are likely to have a high IQ if you solve this question.

M: I love such challenges! Bring it on!

W: All right. Listen. John's father has five sons. Four are ________ Ten, Twenty, Thirty, and Forty. **Can you guess what the name of the fifth son would be?**

M: Easy! **His name must be Fifty, right?**

W: Wrong! Since it's John's father, he needs a son named John. So the fifth son's name is John.

M: Wow, that's so obvious but also so hard at the same time. I want to be good at these things, but my brain moves too slowly. Do you know how to improve brain ________?

W: Well, actually, the show gave some tips on how to boost brain power, and one of them was eating a lot of fish. Fish have special chemicals that help your brain to work faster.

M: Oh, that's awesome! I love eating fish.

W: It will also help you lower your ________ of developing memory disorders.

M: Well, I should go and eat some fish for dinner right now!

여: Chris, 너 어제 Creativity Talk Show 봤니? 새로운 창의력 문제가 나왔어.

남: 아니. 뭐에 관한 문제였는데?

여: 정말 기막힌 질문이었어. 그 쇼에 따르면, 네가 이 문제를 풀면 넌 높은 지능을 가졌을 확률이 높아.

남: 나 그런 도전적인 것 좋아해. 해봐!

여: 그래. 잘 들어봐. John의 아버지에게는 아들이 다섯 있어. 네 명의 이름은 Ten, Twenty, Thirty, Forty야. 다섯 번째 아들의 이름은 뭐 일것 같아?

남: 너무 쉽다! 당연히 Fifty겠지, 맞지?

여: 틀렸어! 이 사람은 John의 아버지이기 때문에 John이라는 이름을 가진 아들이 한 명 있어야 해. 그렇다면 다섯째 아들의 이름은 John이지.

남: 와우, 너무 뻔한 건데 동시에 너무 어렵다. 나 이런 퀴즈 잘 맞추고 싶은데 내 두뇌가 너무 느려. 두뇌 기능을 향상시키는 법 알고 있니?

여: 글쎄, 사실은 그 쇼에서 두뇌 힘을 증강시키는 법에 관한 몇 가지 팁을 줬는데 그 중에 하나가 생선을 많이 먹는 거였어. 생선에는 뇌를 더 빨리 작동하게 하는 특별한 화학물질이 들어있거든.

남: 그것 참 잘됐네. 난 생선 먹는 걸 엄청 좋아하거든.

여: 생선이 기억 장애가 생길 위험성을 줄여주는 데도 도움이 될 거야.

남: 가서 오늘 저녁에 당장 생선을 먹어야겠어!

표현정리
- Can you guess what the name of the fifth son would be?: 'What would the name of the fifth son be?'라는 직접의문문의 구조가 Can you guess의 목적어가 되면서 간접의문문(「의문사+주어+동사」)으로 전환된 형식이다.
- His name must be Fifty, right?: must be는 '~임에 분명하다'라는 의미로 강한 추측을 표현한다.

정답 named / function / risk

교과서 핵심 정리

Reading Comprehension

*해석을 참조하여 빈칸에 알맞은 말을 쓰거나 괄호에서 알맞은 말을 고르시오.

P.115 L.1~10

Brain Games

Start Thinking Outside the Box

What word in the English language is always spelled incorrectly? If long and difficult words come to mind, take another guess. Any ideas? The answer is the word "incorrectly" __________! Although this may seem to be just a nonsense question, there is much more to it than meets the eye. The way most people approach this question shows that they tend to think "inside the box," which means thinking in a __________ way. Sometimes, however, this doesn't help you solve challenging problems. Try stepping outside your imaginary box and solve problems in a way you've never thought about before. Let your creativity fly.

두뇌 게임

틀에서 벗어나 생각하기를 시작하라.

영어에서 어떤 단어가 항상 부정확하게(incorrectly) 써지는가? 길고 어려운 단어가 생각난다면, 다른 것을 생각해 보라. 알겠는가? 정답은 '부정확하게(incorrectly)'라는 그 단어 자체다. 이게 단순히 난센스 퀴즈로 보일 수도 있지만 여기에는 보이는 것 이상의 뭔가가 더 있다. 대부분의 사람들이 이 질문에 접근하는 방식은 사람들이 '틀 안에서' 생각하는 경향, 즉 전통적인 방식으로 생각하는 경향이 있다는 것을 보여준다. 하지만 가끔 이 방식은 도전적인 문제들을 해결하는 데 도움이 되지 못한다. 여러분의 상상 속의 그 상자에서 한 걸음 나와 이전에는 한 번도 생각해 보지 않았던 방식으로 문제들을 풀어보라. 여러분의 창의력에 날개를 달아라.

단락요약
- 틀 안에서 주어진 문제를 생각하지 말고 틀 밖에서 생각해 볼 때 난제를 해결할 수 있다.

구문정리
- ~ there is much more to it than meets the eye.: 'more than meets the eye'는 '보이는 것 이상의 어떤 것'이라는 뜻으로 겉으로 드러나지 않은 중요한 무엇인가를 의미한다.
- The way most people approach this question shows that ~: 'the way (how) most people approach this question'이 이 문장의 주어이다. 긴 주어의 핵심요소인 the way가 3인칭 단수여서 동사 show에 -s가 붙은 형태가 온다.

정답 itself / traditional

P.115 L.11~22

First Round: Go Beyond What You Are Used to

Going beyond what you are used to can be the first step in becoming __________. Here is question number one. A great golfer can only successfully hit the ball 3, 5, 7, or 11 yards. On the final hole of the game, he's on his last shot. Now, he has to make a 20-yard swing. If the ball doesn't directly go in, it will roll past the __________. What is the lowest number of swings that it would take for him to successfully put the ball in the hole? Here's a clue. What about thinking outside the concept of the golfer hitting in a __________ direction — he can hit diagonally, as well. Did you get the answer? Is your answer four times? Actually, by swinging two times for 11 yards in a diagonal direction, the golfer could successfully finish the game!

1라운드 : 익숙한 것 너머로 가라.

익숙한 것 너머로 가는 것이 창의적이 되는 첫 번째 단계일 수 있다. 여기 1번 문제가 있다. 한 위대한 골프 선수가 3, 5, 7, 11 야드만 공을 성공적으로 칠 수 있다. 경기 마지막 홀에서 그가 마지막 샷을 치게 되었다. 이제, 그는 20 야드 스윙을 해야만 한다. 만약 공이 곧장 들어가지 않으면 그것은 구멍을 지나 굴러가게 될 것이다. 그가 공을 구멍에 성공적으로 넣으려면 최소한 몇 번의 스윙을 해야 하는가? 힌트가 있다. 골프 선수가 공을 직선 방향으로 친다는 관념에서 벗어나 생각해 보는 건 어떨까? 즉, 그는 사선 방향으로도 칠 수 있다는 것이다. 답을 생각해 냈는가? 당신의 답이 '네 번'인가? 사실, 11야드씩을 사선 방향으로 두 번만 스윙하고서도 골프 선수는 성공적으로 경기를 끝낼 수 있었다.

단락요약
- 익숙하고 습관적인 사고방식에서 벗어나 다른 각도에서 창의적으로 생각해 보면 문제는 쉽게 풀릴 수 있다.

구문정리
- Going beyond what you are used to can be ~ : 관계사 what은 '~한 것'이라는 의미로 'what you are used to'는 '네가 익숙해져 있는 것'이라고 해석된다.
- What is the lowest number of swings that it would take for him to successfully put ~: 「it(가주어) would take ~ for + 목적격(의미상 주어) + to 부정사(진주어)」는 '~가 …하는 데 ~가 걸리다'라는 의미이다.

정답 creative / hole / straight

P.116 L.1~13

Are you ready for the next question? One day, a farmer challenged an engineer, a physicist, and a mathematician to a game in which the person who fenced off the largest area with the __________ amount of wire would win. It seemed that everyone had his or her own way of thinking. The engineer made a large circle with her wire. The physicist made a long fence, using less wire than the engineer's. He said that the fence could be an infinitely long straight line and would fence in half of the earth. Finally, the mathematician laughed at the other two and presented her idea to the farmer. Quite surprised, the farmer announced that the mathematician was the __________. What was the mathematician's idea?

The mathematician had made a tiny fence around herself and said, "I fenced off the entire world except for this little piece of land that I'm standing on." None of the other challengers had expected her to say this because they had only focused on what was __________ the fence and not the other way around.

다음 질문에 관한 준비가 되었는가? 어느 날, 한 농부가 기술자와 물리학자, 그리고 수학자를 데리고 가장 적은 양의 철삿줄로 가장 넓은 면적에 울타리를 치는 사람이 이기는 시합을 시켰다. 모두 각자만의 생각하는 방식이 있는 것 같았다. 기술자는 자신의 철사를 가지고 커다란 원을 만들었다. 물리학자는 기술자의 철사보다 더 적은 양을 쓰면서 긴 울타리를 만들었다. 그는 그 울타리가 끝없이 긴 직선일 수 있고 그러면 땅의 절반을 울타리 칠 수 있을 거라고 말했다. 마지막으로 수학자는 그 두 사람을 비웃으며 자신의 아이디어를 농부에게 말했다. 깜짝 놀라며 농부는 수학자가 이겼다고 발표했다. 이 수학자의 아이디어는 무엇이었을까?

그 수학자는 자신의 둘레에 작은 울타리를 치고 말했다. "나는 내가 서 있는 이 작은 한 조각 땅을 제외한 세상 전체에 울타리를 쳤어요." 다른 도전자들은 그녀가 이렇게 말할 줄이라고는 예상하지 못했었다. 왜냐하면 그들은 울타리 안에 있는 것에만 중점을 두었고 그 반대의 것에는 주목하지 않았기 때문이다.

단락요약
- 틀에서 벗어난 사고를 통해 가장 적은 양의 철사로 가장 넓은 면적에 울타리를 친 수학자의 이야기

구문정리
- and a mathematician to a game in which the person who fenced off the largest area with the smallest amount of wire would win.: 선행사 a game을 설명하는 관계대명사 절이 이어지고 있고, 이때 in which는 where로 바꿔 쓸 수 있다.
- Quite surprised, the farmer announced that ~ : (Being) Quite surprised는 being이 생략된 분사구문으로, 여기서는 As the farmer was quite surprised를 분사구문으로 바꿔 쓴 것이다.

정답 smallest / winner / inside

P.116 L.14-20

You might remember the story of the egg of Columbus. People told Columbus that his discovery of the New World was not a big deal. So he asked them to do the very simple task of making an egg __________ upright. After a while, everyone gave up. Clearly making his point, Columbus got the egg to stand on its end by tapping it on the table. When something like this is shown to you, it seems to be easy at first glance. However, the hard part is to be the first to think __________ what you are used to. By thinking in a different way, you will find yourself at a whole new level of creativity.

여러분은 Columbus의 달걀에 관한 이야기를 기억할 것이다. 사람들은 Columbus에게 그의 신대륙 발견은 대단한 일이 아니었다고 말했다. 그래서 그는 그들에게 달걀을 똑바로 세우는 아주 간단한 과제를 해 보라고 요청했다. 잠시 후 모두가 포기했다. 자신의 입장을 명확하게 표명하면서, Columbus는 달걀을 탁자에 톡톡 두드림으로써 그것을 서게 했다. 이런 일이 여러분에게 보여질 때, 처음 언뜻 보기에는 쉬워 보일 수 있다. 하지만, 어려운 것은 여러분이 익숙해져 있는 것 그 이상의 것을 생각해내는 첫 번째 사람이 되는 것이다. 다른 방식으로 생각함으로써, 여러분은 자신이 온전히 창의성의 새로운 수준에 있음을 알게 될 것이다.

단락요약
- 콜럼버스처럼 익숙한 틀에서 생각하는 것을 벗어나 다른 방식으로 생각해 보는 첫 번째 사람이 되는 것에 관해 말하고 있다.

구문정리
- Clearly making his point, Columbus got the egg to stand on its end ~ : 'make one's point'는 '자신의 입장/주장을 표명하다'라는 뜻으로 여기서는 분사 구문(~하면서)의 형태로 쓰였다.
- When something like this is shown to you, ~ : something like this(이와 같은 것)가 주어로 쓰였고 동사 is shown은 수동태로서 '보여지다'라는 뜻이다.

정답 stand / beyond

P.117 L.1~13

Second Round: Use Your Imagination to Expand What You Can See

It is also helpful to step out of your comfort zone and look beyond what you can see. In other words, use your imagination! Your final brain game begins with a __________ story.

There once lived a rich king. Loving his wife so much, he wanted to be with her forever. One day, he asked an artist to paint a painting of himself and the queen. The painting the artist drew, "A Beautiful Queen," is pictured above. Here is your question: where is the queen? You'll need to use your creativity to see her!

It is not until you divide the __________ into four squares that you can solve the question. To find the queen, you have to turn the squares upside down or switch their places. Now, do you see the queen's beautiful outline? Neither looking closely at the king nor staring at the yellow background can help you answer the question. However, by using your imagination, you can see a lady in the portrait.

2라운드: 볼 수 있는 것을 넓히기 위해 상상력을 사용하라

안주해 있는 영역에서 한 걸음 물러 나와 볼 수 있는 것 이상을 보는 것도 도움이 될 수 있다. 다른 말로 하면, 상상력을 사용해 보라는 것이다! 여러분의 마지막 두뇌 게임은 로맨틱한 이야기를 가지고 시작한다.

옛날에 한 부유한 왕이 살았다. 부인을 너무 사랑한 그는 그녀와 영원히 함께 있고 싶었다. 어느 날 그는 화가를 불러 자신과 왕비의 초상화를 그려달라고 했다. 그 화가가 그린 "아름다운 왕비"라는 그림이 위에 그려져 있다. 여기 질문이 있다: 왕비는 어디 있는가? 그녀를 보려면 여러분의 상상력이 필요할 것이다.

이 초상화를 4등분해야 문제를 풀 수 있게 된다. 왕비를 찾으려면 여러분은 그 사각형들을 뒤집거나 순서를 바꾸거나 해야 한다. 자, 이제 왕비의 아름다운 윤곽이 보이는가? 왕을 가까이 쳐다본다거나 노란 배경을 뚫어져라 보는 것은 당신이 이 질문에 답하는 데 도움을 주지 못한다. 하지만, 여러분의 상상력을 이용하면 이 초상화에 한 부인의 모습이 보일 것이다.

단락요약

- 상상력을 활용하여 보이지 않는 것을 볼 수 있게 하는 방법에 관한 이야기이다.

구문정리

- It is not until you divide the portrait into four squares that you can solve the question.: 'It is not until ~ that...'은 '~하고 나서야 비로소 …할 수 있다'라는 의미의 구문이다.
- Neither looking closely at the king nor staring at the yellow background can help. : 'neither *A* nor *B*'는 'A도 B도 둘 다 ~하지 않다'라는 의미로 둘 다에 대한 부정이다. 이때 A와 B는 어형이 같아야 한다. (looking – staring)

정답 romantic / portrait

P.118 L.1~11

Solving this problem requires imagination. Imagination is the ability to make a mental picture of something in your mind. What's so interesting about this ability, however, is that it is not limited only to seeing images in your head. It can include all the five __________ and feelings — so going well beyond what can be seen. Training your imagination to combine all the five senses and emotions will help you to strengthen your creativity.

Did you enjoy pumping up your brain with these brain games? Thinking __________ the box might seem difficult at first. However, it gets easier as you try to break the boundaries of your old thinking __________. When you face a problem, don't give up too quickly. Open your mind and let your creativity work for you!

이 문제를 풀기 위해서는 상상력이 필요하다. 상상력은 마음속으로 어떤 것에 관한 그림을 그릴 줄 아는 능력이다. 하지만 이 능력이 매우 흥미로운 점은 이게 머릿속에서 어떤 이미지를 보는 것에만 국한되지 않는다는 것이다. 여기에는 오감과 느낌들 - 볼 수 있는 것을 넘어서 가는 것 - 이 포함될 수도 있다는 것이다. 여러분의 상상력이 모든 오감과 감정들과 결합하도록 훈련하는 것은 여러분의 창의력을 강화하는 데 도움이 될 것이다. 이 두뇌 게임을 하면서 여러분의 두뇌를 강화시키는 게 즐거웠는가? 틀에서 벗어난 생각을 하는 것이 처음에는 어려워 보일 수도 있다. 하지만, 여러분의 오래된 생각의 패턴의 경계를 깨뜨리려고 노력할 때 이것은 좀 더 쉬워진다. 문제에 직면했을 때, 너무 빨리 포기하지 말라. 마음을 열고 여러분의 창의력이 여러분을 위해 작동하게 하라.

단락요약

- 상상력에 오감 및 감정들을 결합하여 생각하는 훈련을 하다보면 더욱 창의적인 사고가 가능하다는 주장이다.

구문정리

- What's so interesting about this ability, however, is that ~ : 여기서 what은 '~한 것'이라는 의미의 관계사이고, that절은 be동사 is의 보어로 쓰였다.
- Open your mind and let your creativity work for you! : 「사역동사(let) + 목적어(your creativity) + 동사원형(work)」의 구문으로, '~로 하여금 …하게 해 주어라.'라는 뜻이다.

정답 senses / outside / patterns

Focus on Structure

P.116 L.3 It seemed | **that** everyone had his or her own way of thinking.
가주어 / 접속사(진주어 절을 이끔)

➔ 동사 seem(~인 것으로 보이다)은 가주어 it을 주어로 하여 「It seems/seemed (that) + 주어 + 동사」의 구문으로 쓰여서 '~인 것으로 보인다/보였다' 또는 '~인 것 같다/같았다'의 의미를 나타낸다. 가주어 it을 쓰지 않고 나타낼 때는 「주어 + seem(s/ed) + to 부정사」의 형태로 쓸 수 있다.

ex. **It** seems **that** she is unable to create a stable relationship with anyone.

= She seems **to be** unable to create a stable relationship with anyone.
주어 seem(s) to 부정사

cf. It seems that ~구문에서 동사 seem의 시제와 that 절의 동사 시제가 다를 경우, 「주어+seem(s/ed) + to have p.p.」 형태의 완료부정사를 쓴다.

ex. It seems that the dog had lots of snack. 그 개는 간식을 많이 먹었던 것으로 보인다.
현재 / 과거

= The dog seems to have had lots of snack.
완료 부정사

P.116 L.8 Quite **surprised,** | the farmer announced | that the mathematician was the winner.
과거분사 (분사구문), 주어 / 동사 / 동사의 목적어가 되는 절

➔ 주어의 태도나 상태 및 상황 또는 동시 동작을 나타내는 분사구문은 일반적으로 주절 앞에 위치한다. 주절에 있는 주어의 입장에서 능동적인 동작이나 행동인 경우는 현재분사(-ing)를 쓰고, 수동적인 상태나 감정의 경우에는 과거분사(-ed/en)를 쓴다. 과거분사인 경우는 Being이 생략된 것으로 본다.

ex. As Andrew was very disappointed, he resigned today. 너무 실망해서, Andrew는 오늘 사임했다.
접속사 주어 동사

→ (Being) Very disappointed, Andrew resigned today. : 분사 Being이 생략되어 과거분사 disappointed가 남음.

cf. As the king loved his wife so much, he wanted to be with her forever.

→ Loving his wife so much, the king wanted to be with her forever.
*분사구문에서 주어가 생략되기 때문에 주절에서 대명사를 명사로 바꿔 주어야 한다.

Check-Up

정답 P. 240

1 다음 문장을 주어진 단어로 시작하여 의미가 같도록 다시 쓰시오.

(1) It seems that Emma is jealous of her younger sister.
= Emma ______________________.

(2) Miriam seemed to be aware of the situation.
= It ______________________.

2 다음 문장의 밑줄 친 부분을 분사구문으로 나타내시오.

(1) As Kate was deeply concerned about her safety, she wanted to stay home.
→ ______________________, Kate wanted to stay home.

(2) The dog barked loudly and it scared us.
→ ______________________, the dog scared us.

Tip

❶ (1) 「It seems + that 절」 = 「주어 + seem(s/ed) + to 부정사」
(2) 「주어 + seemed + to 부정사」 = 「It seems/seemed + that 절」
jealous 질투하는, 부러워하는
be aware of ~를 인식하다, 알다

❷ (1) being이 생략된 분사구문
(2) 접속사와 (주절의 주어와 같은) 주어가 생략되고 동사를 분사(-ing)로 바꾸면 됨
bark (개가) 짖다

언어 기능별 집중 대비

Listen and Speak/Into Real Life

정답 P. 240

1 대화를 듣고, 여자가 가장 관심 있고 알고 싶어 하는 것을 고르시오.

① 목민심서의 내용
② 정약용의 정치 철학
③ 거중기의 작동 방식
④ 조선시대 건축물의 특징
⑤ 수원 화성의 설계와 건축

2 다음을 듣고, 남자가 주장하는 내용의 핵심을 고르시오.

① Exercise regularly to get in shape.
② Make an effort to improve your critical reading skills.
③ Prevent memory disorders by asking creative questions.
④ Solve as many math questions as possible on a daily basis.
⑤ Train your brain and think of different ways of doing things.

3 대화를 듣고, 여자가 조언해 주는 내용으로 맞는 것을 고르시오.

① 세탁물 탈색 방지법
② 수저의 녹을 제거하는 법
③ 옷에 묻은 음식물 얼룩 제거법
④ 다량의 소금을 빨리 녹이는 방법
⑤ 식사 중 소금 섭취를 줄이는 방법

4 대화를 듣고, 물음에 답하시오.

(1) Dr. de Bono가 말하는 the Six Thinking Hats 전략에 대해 바르게 말한 것은?
① It can help people feel less nervous in the interview.
② It can help people choose a hat that suits their clothes.
③ It can encourage people to be more engaged in psychological findings.
④ It can cause people to feel more confused, not knowing which hat to wear.
⑤ It can help people think in a different way and come up with creative ideas.

(2) the Six Thinking Hats의 색상별 특징에 대해 <u>틀리게</u> 말한 것은?
① 흰색 – 사실과 관련된 정보를 기억하는 두뇌
② 빨강 – 감정이나 느낌을 다루는 두뇌
③ 녹색 – 새로운 아이디어와 창의력을 담당하는 두뇌
④ 노랑 – 전체적인 균형을 이루고 관리하는 두뇌
⑤ 검은색 – 비판적으로 사고하거나 경고하는 두뇌

Tip

❶ 화자의 관심 파악하기
출처: Listen In_Dialogue

❷ 대화의 주제 파악하기
출처: Listen In_Monologue
on a daily basis 매일

❸ 조언의 내용 파악하기
출처: Get Ready_3

❹ Into Real_Life
(1) 주제 고르기
(2) 구체적인 정보 파악하기
출처: Into Real Life Step 1
suit 어울리다, 들어맞다
come up with (생각이) 떠오르다

Read and Think

정답 P. 241

1 다음 글의 ①~⑤ 중 아래의 문장이 들어가기에 가장 알맞은 곳은?

Sometimes, however, this doesn't help you solve challenging problems.

Start Thinking Outside the Box

What word in the English language is always spelled incorrectly? If long and difficult words come to mind, take another guess. Any ideas? ① The answer is the word "incorrectly" itself! ② Although this may seem to be just a nonsense question, there is much more to it than meets the eye.

③ The way most people approach this question shows that they tend to think "inside the box," which means thinking in a traditional way. ④ Try stepping outside your imaginary box and solve problems in a way you've never thought about before. ⑤ Let your creativity fly.

[2-3] 다음 글을 읽고, 물음에 답하시오.

__________________ can be the first step in becoming creative.

(A) Actually, by swinging two times for 11 yards in a diagonal direction, the golfer could successfully finish the game!

(B) Here's a clue. What about thinking outside the concept of the golfer hitting in a straight direction — he can hit diagonally, as well. Did you get the answer? Is your answer four times?

(C) Here is question number one. A great golfer can only successfully hit the ball 3, 5, 7, or 11 yards. On the final hole of the game, he's on his last shot. Now, he has to make a 20-yard swing.

(D) If the ball doesn't directly go in, it will roll past the hole. What is the lowest number of swings that it would take for him to successfully put the ball in the hole?

2 윗글의 주어진 문장에 이어질 글의 순서로 알맞은 것은?

① (B) – (C) – (A) – (D)
② (B) – (C) – (D) – (A)
③ (C) – (B) – (A) – (D)
④ (C) – (D) – (A) – (B)
⑤ (C) – (D) – (B) – (A)

3 윗글의 빈칸에 가장 알맞은 것은?

① Borrowing ideas from golfers
② Going beyond what you are used to
③ Training your body as well as your brain
④ Sticking to the traditional way of thinking
⑤ Solving difficult math problems on a daily basis

Tip

❶ 출처: P.115 L.1-10
유형: 문장의 위치 파악

❷-❸ 출처: P.115 L.11-22
유형: 2. 글의 순서 파악하기
3. 빈칸 추론
stick to ~에 달라붙다, 고수하다

Tip

[4-5] 다음 글을 읽고, 물음에 답하시오.

> One day, a farmer challenged an engineer, a physicist, and a mathematician to a game ① in which the person who fenced off the largest area with the smallest amount of wire would win. It seemed that everyone had his or her own way of thinking. The engineer made a large circle with her wire. The physicist made a long fence, ② used less wire than the engineer's. He said that the fence could be an infinitely long straight line and would fence in half of the earth. Finally, the mathematician laughed at the other two and presented her idea to the farmer. ③ Quite surprised, the farmer announced that the mathematician was the winner. What was the mathematician's idea? The mathematician had made a tiny fence around ④ herself and said, "I fenced off the entire world except for this little piece of land that I'm standing on." ⑤ None of the other challengers had expected her to say this because they had only focused on what was inside the fence and ⓐ not the other way around.

4-5 출처: P.116 L.1-13
유형: 4. 문법성 판단
5. 어구의 의미 파악
consider 간주하다, 고려하다

4 윗글의 밑줄 친 ①~⑤ 중 어법상 어색한 것은?

5 윗글의 밑줄 친 ⓐ가 의미하는 것은?

① they did not fence off the entire world
② they did not focus on what was outside
③ they did not make a fence around themselves
④ they did not consider each other's idea creative
⑤ they did not turn around to see how large the area was

6 다음 글에서 Columbus가 사람들에게 말하려고 했던 것은?

> You might remember the story of the egg of Columbus. People told Columbus that his discovery of the New World was not a big deal. So he asked them to do the very simple task of making an egg stand upright. After a while, everyone gave up. Clearly making his point, Columbus got the egg to stand on its end by tapping it on the table. When something like this is shown to you, it seems to be easy at first glance. However, the hard part is to be the first to think beyond what you are used to. By thinking in a different way, you will find yourself at a whole new level of creativity.

6 출처: P.116 L.14-20
유형: 의도 파악하기

① It was not easy at all to make an egg stand upright.
② Tapping the egg on the table to make it stand was a brilliant idea.
③ Don't give up doing something that seems to be difficult to do at first.
④ The great discovery he made was something that nobody thought of doing.
⑤ He discovered the New World because he had been used to thinking critically.

Tip

[7-8] 다음 글을 읽고, 물음에 답하시오.

It is also helpful to step out of ⓐ <u>your comfort zone</u> and look beyond what you can see. _____ⓑ_____, use your imagination! Your final brain game begins with a romantic story.

There once lived a rich king. Loving his wife so much, he wanted to be with her forever. One day, he asked an artist to paint a painting of himself and the queen. The painting the artist drew, "A Beautiful Queen," is pictured above. Here is your question: where is the queen? You'll need to use your creativity to see her!

It is not until you divide the portrait into four squares that you can solve the question. To find the queen, you have to turn the squares upside down or switch their places. Now, do you see the queen's beautiful outline? Neither looking closely at the king nor staring at the yellow background can help you answer the question. ___ⓒ___, by using your imagination, you can see a lady in the portrait.

7 윗글에서 밑줄 친 ⓐ에 해당하는 것은?

① looking beyond what you can see
② using your creativity to see the queen
③ dividing the king's portrait into four squares
④ turning the squares upside down or switching their places
⑤ looking closely at the king or staring at the yellow background

8 윗글의 빈칸 ⓑ와 ⓒ에 들어갈 말이 바르게 연결된 것은?

① Otherwise — Therefore
② In addition — In conclusion
③ On the other hand — So far
④ In other words — However
⑤ On the contrary — For instance

9 다음 글의 빈칸에 가장 알맞은 것은?

Thinking outside the box might seem difficult at first. However, it gets easier as you try to break the boundaries of your old thinking patterns. When you face a problem, don't give up too quickly. Open your mind and let your _________ work for you!

① creativity
② intuition
③ positivity
④ compassion
⑤ expectation

7-8 출처: P.117 L.1-13
유형: 7. 어구의 의미 파악
8. 연결어 파악
so far 지금까지
on the contrary 반대로, 대조적으로
in other words 다른 말로 하자면
otherwise 만약 그렇지 않으면
in conclusion 결론적으로

9 출처: P.118 L.7-10
유형: 핵심어 파악
intuition 본능, 직감
compassion 공감, 온정
expectation 기대감

언어 기능별 집중 대비

Language Notes Write It Right

정답 P. 241

1 다음 우리말에 맞게 괄호 안의 말을 이용하여 문장을 완성하시오.

(1) 수업 중에는 교사가 학생의 말을 경청하는 게 아니라 학생이 교사의 말을 경청하도록 되어 있다.
In class, students are supposed to ____________. (the other way around)

(2) 안주하는 곳에서 나올 때까지는 너의 삶을 변화시키지 못할 것이다.
You will never change your life ________________. (comfort zone)

(3) 떠오르는 생각을 적어 놓을 수 있도록 공책을 한 권 가지고 다녀라.
Carry a notebook so that you can ________________. (come to mind)

(4) 사진 속 그 아기는 기저귀만 빼고는 아무것도 입지 않고 있었다.
The baby in the picture ______________________________. (except for)

(5) 나는 아이들의 놀이공간을 마당과 분리해서 울타리를 쳐야 한다고 생각한다.
I think we should ________________________ from the yard. (fence off)

2 다음 문장을 주어진 단어로 시작하여 쓰시오.

(1) It seems that Jasmin is upset about the decision.
→ Jasmin seems ____.

(2) It seemed that there was plenty to eat in the kitchen.
→ There seemed ____.

(3) Paul seemed to have been ill for quite a long time.
→ It seemed that ____.

3 분사구문을 이용하여 두 문장을 한 문장으로 바꿀 때 빈칸에 알맞은 말을 쓰시오.

(1) He had curiosity about daydreaming. He studied the act of daydreaming.
→ ____________________________, he studied the act of daydreaming.

(2) We were eaten by mosquitoes. We wished we had made a hotel reservation.
→ ____________________________, we wished we had made a hotel reservations.

(3) The dog was frightened by the loud fireworks. It hid under the couch.
→ ____________________________, the dog hid under the couch.

(4) Mike was injured during the soccer match. He had to leave the field.
→ Injured during the soccer match, ____________________________.

Tip

❶ 출처: P.77 L.2-16
1. 표현 익히기
be supposed to ~해야 한다, ~하기로 되어 있다
come to mind (생각이) 떠오르다
write down 적다
diaper 기저귀
play area 놀이 공간

❷ 「it seems/seemed (that) + 절」
= 「주어 seem(s)/seemed + to 부정사」
plenty 풍부한 양

❸ 주어가 일치하는 경우 앞 문장의 동사를 현재분사(-ing) 형태로 고쳐서 분사구문으로 나타낸다. be동사가 있는 경우 being으로 나타내는데 이는 생략할 수 있다. 따라서 being이 생략되고 남은 과거분사로 시작하는 분사구문이 생긴다.
reservation 예약
frightened 겁에 질린

Basic

정답 P. 241

1 대화를 듣고, 여자의 마지막 말에 이어질 남자의 응답으로 가장 적절한 것을 고르시오.

① Yes, let's ask someone nearby.
② No, but I know how to find the way.
③ Yes, we should go to the police office.
④ No, let's not waste time with the map.
⑤ Yes. I received a training in map-reading.

2 대화를 듣고, 여자의 조언으로 맞는 것을 고르시오.

① Washing clothes in salty water will remove food stains on them.
② Brushing your teeth with a spoonful of salt will keep your teeth clean.
③ Washing in salty water will help you maintain good skin conditions.
④ Using warm salty water in washing socks will remove the bad smell of them.
⑤ Making the overall dish less salty will keep you from having heart diseases.

[3~4] 다음 중 나머지 넷과 연결 관계가 다른 것을 고르시오.

3

① finite – infinite
② divide – combine
③ brilliant – stupid
④ include – exclude
⑤ diagonal – circular

4

① discover – discovery
② creative – creativity
③ expect – expectation
④ imagine – imagination
⑤ announce – announcement

5 다음 중 〈보기〉의 밑줄 친 말과 의미가 가장 가까운 것은?

> 보기 Thinking outside the box usually helps you to solve challenging problems.

① To think for fun
② To think clearly
③ To partially daydream
④ To limit your imagination
⑤ To find new ways of doing things

6 다음 문장의 빈칸에 가장 알맞은 것은?

> The pop singer is trying to ____________ album sales with an extended publicity tour.

① set up
② pull up
③ light up
④ make up
⑤ pump up

7 다음 글의 밑줄 친 ①~⑤ 중 어법상 잘못된 것을 찾아 바르게 고쳐 쓰시오.

> Solving this problem ① require imagination. Imagination is the ability to make a mental picture of something in your mind. ② What's so interesting about this ability, however, is that it is not limited only to ③ seeing images in your head. It can include all the five senses and feelings — so going well beyond ④ what can be seen. Training your imagination to combine all the five senses and emotions will help you to ⑤ strengthen your creativity.

____________ → ____________

8 다음 글의 밑줄 친 말과 문맥상 의미가 가장 가까운 것은?

What word in the English language is always spelled incorrectly? The answer is the word "incorrectly" itself! Although this may seem to be just a nonsense question, there is much more to it than meets the eye. The way most people approach this question shows that they tend to think "inside the box," which means thinking in a <u>traditional</u> way. Sometimes, however, this doesn't help you solve challenging problems. Try stepping outside your imaginary box and solve problems in a way you've never thought about before.

① familiar ② practical
③ educational ④ modern
⑤ handed-down

[9~10] 다음 글을 읽고, 물음에 답하시오.

You might remember the story of the egg of Columbus. People told Columbus that his discovery of the New World was not a big deal. So he asked them to do the very simple task of making an egg ___ⓐ___(stand) upright. After a while, everyone gave up. Clearly making his point, Columbus got the egg to stand on its end by tapping it on the table. When something like this is ___ⓑ___(show) to you, it seems to be easy at first glance. However, the hard part is to be the first ______ⓒ______. By thinking in a different way, you will find yourself at a whole new level of creativity.

9 윗글의 빈칸 ⓐ~ⓑ에 알맞은 말을 쓰시오.

ⓐ ______________ ⓑ ______________

10 윗글의 빈칸 ⓒ에 알맞은 말을 〈보기〉의 단어들을 사용하여 완성하시오.

보기 beyond / used / you / are / to / to / think / what

→ ______________________________.

[11~12] 다음 중 어법상 <u>어색한</u> 문장을 고르시오.

11

① Most of the employees seemed to be tired.
② It seems my mother to know what is bothering me.
③ There seems to be some misunderstanding on both sides.
④ Does it seem that Ethan can be a successful leader?
⑤ What seems to be a problem between you and your dad?

12

① Quite surprised, Miriam hurried to open the door.
② Not knowing what to do, Leo asked her for help.
③ Barking loudly, the dog ran after the stranger.
④ Received the phone call, Miriam began to cry.
⑤ Terrified by the gunfire, people screamed and ran.

[13~14] 다음 〈보기〉의 우리말과 같도록 괄호 안의 단어를 사용하여 빈칸을 완성하시오. (필요한 경우 형태를 바꾸시오)

13

보기 그 양로원은 즐겁고 편안한 곳인 것 같았다.
(pleasant / and / comfort / place)

→ The nursing home ______________________________.

14

보기 서둘러 인쇄되느라, 그 책에는 오류가 많다.
(print / in / haste)

→ ______________________, the book contains many errors.

Advanced

정답 P. 242

[1~2] 다음 대화를 듣고, 물음에 답하시오.

1 **What is the most impressive thing about Jeong Yakyong to Grace?**

① his creativity shown in the field of engineering
② a great number of books he wrote about architecture
③ the documents he collected on a variety of topics
④ the system he invented to break huge stones into small pieces
⑤ the fact that he was a great scholar in the late Joseon Dynasty

2 **What are the speakers going to talk about during lunch time?**

① when to visit the Hwaseong Fortress
② what to do in the folk village next week
③ how the stone lifting system is operated
④ other great inventions of Jeong Yakyong
⑤ what to include in their documentary review

3 다음을 듣고, 남자가 말하고 있는 주제를 고르시오.

① Maintain balance between work and play.
② Improve your memory through daily workout.
③ Prevent memory loss by exercising your brain.
④ Practice thinking outside the box for your brain.
⑤ Challenge your brain with various open questions.

4 다음 글의 밑줄 친 부분 중 문맥상 어색한 문장은?

What word in the English language is always spelled incorrectly? If long and difficult words come to mind, take another guess. ① Any ideas? ② The answer is the word "incorrectly" itself! ③ Although this may seem to be just a nonsense question, there is much more to it than meets the eye. ④ The way most people approach this question shows that they tend to think "inside the box," which means thinking in a traditional way. ⑤ Many times, this approach pumps up your critical thinking ability and helps you solve the challenging problems. Try stepping outside your imaginary box and solve problems in a way you've never thought about before. Let your creativity fly.

[5~6] 다음 글을 읽고, 물음에 답하시오.

ⓐ Going beyond what you are used to can be the first step in becoming creative. Here is question number one. A great golfer can only successfully hit the ball 3, 5, 7, or 11 yards. On the final hole of the game, he's on his last shot. Now, he has to make a 20-yard swing. If the ball doesn't directly go in, it will roll past the hole. What is the lowest number of swings that it would take for him to successfully put the ball in the hole? Here's a clue. What about thinking outside the concept of the golfer hitting in a straight direction — he can hit diagonally, as well. Did you get the answer? ⓑ Is your answer four times? Actually, by swinging two times for 11 yards in a diagonal direction, the golfer could successfully finish the game!

5 윗글의 밑줄 친 ⓐ의 예시로 쓰인 표현을 본문에서 찾아 영어로 쓰시오.

⊖ ______________________

6 윗글에서 글쓴이가 밑줄 친 ⓑ라고 말하는 이유를 우리말로 쓰시오.

⊖ ______________________

[7~9] 다음 글을 읽고 물음에 답하시오.

One day, a farmer challenged an engineer, a physicist, and a mathematician to a game in which the person who fenced off the largest area with ① the small amount of wire ② would win. It seemed that everyone had his or her own way of thinking. The engineer made a large circle with her wire. The physicist made a long fence, using less wire than the engineer's. He said that the fence ③ could be an infinitely long straight line and would fence in half of the earth. Finally, the mathematician laughed at the other two and ④ presented her idea to the farmer. Quite surprised, the farmer announced that ⓐ the mathematician was the winner. What was the mathematician's idea?

The mathematician had made a tiny fence around herself and said, ⓑ "I fenced off the entire world except for this little piece of land that I'm standing on." None of the other challengers had expected her ⑤ to say this because they had only focused on what was inside the fence and not the other way around.

7 윗글의 ①~⑤ 중 어법상 잘못된 것을 고르시오.

8 윗글의 밑줄 친 ⓐ에 대한 이유로 알맞은 것은?

① She successfully fenced off half of the earth.
② She did not use any wire in fencing off the area.
③ She fenced off the largest area with the smallest amount of wire.
④ She focused on what was inside the fence, not outside the fence.
⑤ She finished fencing off the largest area in the shortest time among the three contestants.

9 윗글의 밑줄 친 ⓑ가 의미하는 것은?

① 울타리의 바깥이 내가 울타리 친 면적이다.
② 울타리의 안쪽은 내가 혼자 서 있기에도 작다.
③ 울타리의 안쪽에 더 중요한 것이 자리 잡고 있다.
④ 울타리의 바깥쪽은 안쪽에 비해 면적이 엄청 작다.
⑤ 울타리의 안과 밖을 구별하는 것은 의미 없는 일이다.

[10~11] 다음 글을 읽고 물음에 답하시오.

There is a great story about creativity at a Japanese soap company. The company had received a (A)(complaint / compliment) from a customer who had bought a box of soap that was empty. Having discovered that some boxes left the factory without any soap, the company decided to solve the problem. How? The company (B)(produced / purchased) an expensive scanner to scan every box that was on the assembly line and had two engineers look at each package. This seemed to work, but it was very expensive. One day, a regular employee at the factory came up with the brilliant idea to simply put an electric fan at the end of the assembly line, which would ______ away any empty boxes. Boxes that were full would be too (C) (large / heavy) and would not be affected by the fan. Thanks to his idea, the company was able to completely solve the problem at a low cost.

10 윗글의 괄호 안의 (A)~(C)에 알맞은 말이 차례대로 연결된 것은?

① complaint – produced – large
② complaint – purchased – heavy
③ compliment – purchased – heavy
④ compliment – produced – large
⑤ compliment – purchased – large

11 윗글의 빈칸에 알맞은 말을 주어진 철자로 시작하여 쓰시오.

⊖ b ______________________

주관식 서술형 대비

12 역사적으로 훌륭한 창의적 발명품이라고 생각되는 것 하나를 정하여 왜 그렇게 생각하는지 이유를 포함하여 3문장 내외의 글을 쓰시오.

I think one of the best inventions in history is
____
____
____
______________________.

UNIT 7

The Name of the Game in Creative Industries

교과서 핵심 정리

Words & Phrases

Listen and Speak ~ Into Real Life

- ☐ popularity *n.* 인기 (popular *adj.* 인기 있는)
- ☐ prefer *v.* 선호하다 (preference *n.* 선호도)
  cf. prefer *A* to *B* = like *A* better than *B*
- ☐ indicate* *v.* 가리키다, 나타내다 *cf.* indicator 지표
- ☐ take part (in) ~에 참가하다(=participate in)
- ☐ afterwards *ad.* 이후에
- ☐ grateful *adj.* 감사하는(=thankful)
- ☐ meaningful *adj.* 의미 있는 (↔ meaningless)
- ☐ influence* *v.* 영향을 미치다 *n.* 영향
  influential *adj.* 영향력 있는
- ☐ reveal *v.* 드러내다, 밝히다 (revelation *n.* 폭로, 적발)
- ☐ account for* ~를 설명하다, ~를 차지하다
- ☐ remaining *adj.* 남아 있는, 나머지의 (remain v. 남아 있다)
- ☐ survey *n.* (여론) 조사, 연구 *v.* 조사하다

Read and Think

- ☐ release* *v.* (영화를) 개봉하다, 발표하다, 발매하다
- ☐ revive* *v.* 소생시키다, 되살아나게 하다 (revival *n.* 회복)
- ☐ phenomenon *n.* 현상 (*pl.* phenomena 현상들)
- ☐ icon *n.* 아이콘, 상징, 우상시 되는 인물
- ☐ economy* *n.* 경제 (economic *a.* 경제의, 경제성이 있는)
- ☐ attract *v.* 매혹하다, 끌어당기다 (attraction *n.* 매력)
- ☐ storytelling *n.* 스토리텔링, 이야기하기
- ☐ a great number of* 엄청난 수의
  (*cf.* a number of=many)
- ☐ give life to* ~에게 활기를/생명력을 불어넣다
- ☐ glamor(또는 glamour) *n.* 화려함, 화려한 아름다움
  adj. glamourous 화려한, 매력적인
- ☐ make use of* ~를 활용하다
- ☐ feature* *v.* ~의 특징을 그리다 *n.* 특징, 용모
- ☐ costume *n.* 의상, 복장
- ☐ terrific* *adj.* 멋진, 훌륭한 *cf.* terrible 끔찍한
- ☐ phantom *n.* 유령, 환영, 허깨비
- ☐ estimate *v.* 추정하다, 어림짐작하다, 평가하다
- ☐ decade *n.* 10년간
- ☐ profit* *n.* 수익, 이득 *adj.* profitable 이익이 되는
- ☐ hologram *n.* 홀로그램, 홀로그래피로 만든 입체 영상
- ☐ audience *n.* 청중 *cf.* spectator 관중
- ☐ uniqueness* *n.* 독특함, 독창성 (unique *adj.* 독창적인)
- ☐ marketing *n.* 마케팅, 홍보 영업
- ☐ advantage *n.* 이익 (↔disadvantage 불이익)
- ☐ manufacture *v.* 제조하다
- ☐ daydreamer *n.* 공상가, 몽상가 (daydream *v.* 공상하다)

Language Notes

- ☐ earn *v.* (돈을) 벌다
- ☐ anticipate *v.* 기대하다, 예상하다 (anticipation *n.* 기대)
- ☐ wisely *ad.* 현명하게 (wise *adj.* 현명한, wisdom *n.* 지혜)
- ☐ billion *n.* 10억
  cf. trillion 1조

Write It Right

- ☐ advertise* v. 광고하다 (advertisement = ad n. 광고)
- ☐ brochure* *n.* 소책자, 안내서
- ☐ dynamic* *adj.* 역동적인 (dynamically *ad.* 역동적으로)
- ☐ a wide range of* 광범위한, 넓은 범위의
- ☐ meet expectations* 기대를 충족시키다
- ☐ descriptive *adj.* 묘사하는 (describe *v.* 묘사하다)

Around the World

- ☐ entertaining *adj.* 즐겁게 해주는, 오락을 제공하는
- ☐ represent *v.* 나타내다, 상징하다
- ☐ plot *n.* 줄거리
- ☐ outline *n.* 개요, 윤곽 *v.* 윤곽을 그리다
- ☐ by accident 우연히 (=accidentally)
- ☐ illustrate *v.* 설명하다, 삽화를 넣다
  cf. illustrator 삽화가

Check-Up

정답 P. 243

1 다음 문장의 빈칸에 알맞은 말을 <보기>에서 골라 쓰시오. (필요한 경우 어형을 바꾸시오.)

보기 >> make use of / take part in / give life to
a great number of / a large amount of / account for

(1) The festival is supposed to ______________ the area.
(2) We could ______________ our resources in a more efficient way.
(3) The Chinese market ______________ 35% of the company's revenue.
(4) The company has created ______________ job opportunities in urban areas.
(5) Many celebrities ______________ the Ice Bucket Challenge to help the people living with Lou Gehrig's Disease.

2 다음 뜻풀이에 해당하는 말을 주어진 철자로 시작하여 쓰시오.

(1) i __________ : a widely known symbol
(2) g __________ : a very exciting and attractive quality
(3) r __________ : to make something available to the public
(4) r __________ : to make something or someone strong, healthy, or active again
(5) p __________ : a fact or an event that is observed and studied and that is typically unusual or difficult to understand fully

주관식 서술형

3 우리말에 맞게 괄호 안의 단어들을 사용하여 문장을 완성하시오.

(1) 이 주제에 관해서는 의견들의 폭넓은 다양성이 존재한다.
There is ______________________________ on this issue.
(a / range / wide / of / opinions)

(2) 우리의 예상과는 반대로, 그녀는 그 음악원에 입학했다.
______________________, she was accepted by the music academy.
(our / to / expectation / contrary)

(3) 정부는 그 프로젝트에 수십억 달러를 투자했다.
The government has invested ______________________________.
(in / the / project / of / dollars / billions)

(4) 사회 보안이 총 공공 지출의 약 1/3을 차지한다.
Social security ______________________ total public spending.
(a third / for / about / accounts / of)

Tip

❶ 주요 숙어표현 익히기
resource 자원
revenue 수입
urban 도시의
Lou Gehrig's Disease 루게릭병

❷ 영영사전풀이
fully 완벽하게, 온전히

❸ 핵심어휘를 사용한 영작
invest 투자하다
spending 지출

교과서 핵심 정리

Dialogues & Monologue

Listen and Speak | *해석을 참조하여 빈칸에 알맞은 말을 쓰시오.

GET READY

1 W: How may I help you?
M: I'm looking for a birthday present for my friend.
W: How about this one? These days, **nothing __________ to the popularity of this little character.**
M: I'm sure my friend will like it. Thanks for your help.

여: 무얼 도와드릴까요?
남: 친구에게 줄 생일 선물을 찾고 있어요.
여: 이건 어떠세요? 요즘 이 작은 캐릭터 인형의 인기와 견줄만한 게 없어요.
남: 제 친구가 정말 좋아할 것 같네요. 감사합니다.

2 W: What are you reading?
M: I'm reading *The Hunger Games*. Have you ever read it?
W: No, I haven't. But I've seen the movie.
M: Me, too. But I __________ the books because nothing compares to the original.

여: 뭘 읽고 있니?
남: 'The Hunger Games'를 읽고 있어. 너 이거 읽어봤어?
여: 아니. 하지만 영화로는 봤어.
남: 나도 봤어. 하지만 원작과는 비교가 안 되기 때문에 난 책이 더 좋아.

3 W: I'm really into musicals. What is popular these days?
M: Let me search the Internet. This website has a chart of this month's top five musicals.
W: **This chart indicates that *Hero* is ranked first!**
M: Do you want to go see it together?
W: Sounds great.

여: 난 정말 뮤지컬 좋아하는데, 요즘 뭐가 인기 있니?
남: 인터넷 검색해볼게. 이 웹사이트에 이번 달 상위 1위부터 5위까지 뮤지컬 차트가 나와.
여: 이 차트에는 '영웅'이 1위를 했다고 나오네.
남: 함께 보러 갈래?
여: 좋지.

표현정리
- These days, nothing compares to the popularity of this little character. : 'nothing compares to ~'는 '~와 비교할 수 있는 것은 없다' 또는 '~가 가장 …하다'라는 의미로 최상급의 의미를 갖는다.
- This chart indicates that ~: 자료나 통계를 인용할 때 주로 「출처 + indicates that ~」의 구문을 써서 '~에 …로 나와 있다'라는 의미를 표현한다.

정답 compares / prefer

LISTEN IN

DIALOGUE 1

W: You look quite excited today. What's up?
M: My favorite band YBB is going to the Edinburgh Festival Fringe!
W: Congratulations! But what is the Fringe?
M: Oh, the Edinburgh Festival Fringe is a huge arts festival __________ in Edinburgh, Scotland every August.
W: Cool! Nothing compares to attending an arts festival. So is it for bands only?
M: No. **This festival includes plays, comedy, dance, and concerts.**
W: So it's a festival for all the performing arts?
M: Exactly. Several Korean performers have taken part so far. A few years ago, *Nanta* performed there and was invited to Broadway afterwards.
W: This must be a great __________ for your favorite band then!
M: Yes, it is. Oh, I really want to fly to Edinburgh!
W: Where can you buy tickets?
M: You can buy them from the website or from street musicians there.

여: 너 오늘 굉장히 흥분된 것처럼 보이네. 무슨 일이야?
남: 내가 제일 좋아하는 YBB 밴드가 에든버러 프린지 페스티벌에 오거든!
여: 축하해! 그런데 그 프린지라는 게 뭐야?
남: 아, 에든버러 프린지 페스티벌은 매년 8월에 스코틀랜드의 에든버러에서 열리는 큰 예술 축제야.
여: 멋있겠다! 예술 축제에 참여하는 것 만한 것도 없지. 그런데 그게 밴드들만 오는 거니?
남: 아니. 이 축제에는 연극, 코미디, 춤, 그리고 연주회가 다 있어.
여: 그럼 모든 공연 예술을 위한 축제인 거니?
남: 맞아. 지금까지 한국인 공연가도 몇 명 참가했어. 몇 년 전에는 '난타'도 거기서 공연을 했고 그 후에 브로드웨이에 초대받았었지.
여: 그럼 네가 좋아하는 그 밴드에게도 이 축제는 엄청난 기회겠네!
남: 그렇지. 아, 정말 에든버러로 날아가고 싶다!
여: 표는 어디에서 살 수 있는 거야?
남: 웹사이트나 그 곳에 있는 길거리 음악가들에게서 살 수 있어.

대화상황
- 모든 종류의 공연 예술을 볼 수 있는 에든버러 프린지 페스티벌과 거기에 참가하는 한 밴드에 관한 이야기를 하고 있다.

표현정리
- This festival includes plays, comedy, ~: 이 축제에 참여하는 다양한 장르의 공연 예술을 열거하고 있다.

정답 held / opportunity

Into Real Life

W: Okay, Jihun. Let's get started on our newspaper article about movies. Look at this pie chart.
M: Is this the one about students' favorite movies?
W: Yes. The graph reveals that 40% of students chose __________ movies as their favorite.
M: Interesting. It also says here that sci-fi movies account for 35%.
W: And the most popular movie was *The Admiral*. It seems like __________ compares to the dynamics of movies about Korean history.
M: I can't believe *The Admiral* beat *Interstellar*.
W: ***Interstellar* came in second by only five votes.**
M: What about the remaining 25%?
W: They chose action movies, animations, or others.
M: This will be a great article for the school newspaper.

여: 지훈아, 영화에 관한 신문 기사에 대해 시작해 보자. 이 파이 차트를 봐.
남: 이게 학생들이 가장 좋아하는 영화에 대한 차트야?
여: 응. 이 그래프에는 40%의 학생들이 가장 좋아하는 영화로 역사 영화를 뽑았다고 나와 있어.
남: 재미있네. 그리고 여기 보면 공상 과학 영화가 35%를 차지한다고 나와 있어.
여: 그리고 가장 인기 있는 영화는 '장군'이었어. 한국 역사에 관한 영화만큼 역동적인 것은 없는 것 같아.
남: '장군'이 '인터스텔라'를 이겼다는 걸 믿을 수가 없어.
여: '인터스텔라'가 겨우 5표 차이로 2위를 했어.
남: 나머지 25%는 뭐야?
여: 액션 영화랑 애니메이션 그리고 나머지 다른 장르들이야.
남: 이거 학교 신문에 내기 딱 좋은 기사가 되겠어.

담화주제 • 학교 신문에 실을 영화 관련 설문 조사의 결과에 관해 얘기하고 있다.

표현정리
- The graph reveals that ~ : '그래프에 따르면 ~ 라고 되어 있다.'라는 의미로, 자료를 인용할 때 쓰는 표현이다.
- *Interstellar* came in second by only five votes.: 「come in second by + 수치」는 '~만큼 수치의 차이로 2위가 되다'라는 뜻이다.

정답 history / nothing

Check Your Progress

M: Hello, Daehan High School students. Today in our weekly school news, we'd like to show you the results of the school __________ "What is your favorite genre of the performing arts?" Our club members asked more than 200 students in the school to participate in this survey. Please take a look at this pie chart. This chart indicates that 50% of students chose concerts while 35% chose musicals. **The remaining 15% chose dance, plays, and others.** It was good to see that Daehan High School students have a variety of __________ in the performing arts. Next week, we will bring you more interesting news about our school. See you then!

남: 안녕하세요, 대한 고등학교 학생 여러분. 오늘 주간 학교 뉴스에서는 "공연 예술 중에 가장 좋아하는 장르는 무엇입니까?"라는 학교 설문조사의 결과를 알려드리도록 하겠습니다. 우리 동아리 부원들이 이 설문조사에 참여한 200여명 학생들에게 물었습니다. 이 파이 차트를 봐 주세요. 이 차트에서 보면 50%의 학생들이 콘서트를, 35%의 학생들이 뮤지컬을 꼽은 것을 알 수 있습니다. 나머지 15%는 춤, 연극, 그리고 기타 장르입니다. 대한 고등학교 학생들이 공연 예술에 관해 다양한 취향을 가지고 있다는 것을 알게 되어 좋았습니다. 다음 주에는 우리 학교에 관한 더 흥미로운 뉴스를 가지고 오도록 하겠습니다. 다음 주에 만나요!

담화주제 • 학교 주간 뉴스에서 선호하는 공연예술 장르에 관한 학생 설문 조사의 결과를 발표하고 있다.

표현정리
- The remaining 15% chose dance, plays, and others.: 여기서 the remaining은 콘서트를 꼽은 50%의 학생들과 뮤지컬을 꼽은 35%의 학생을 제외한 나머지 학생들을 가리킨다.

정답 survey / tastes

교과서 핵심 정리

Reading Comprehension

***해석을 참조하여 빈칸에 알맞은 말을 쓰거나 괄호에서 알맞은 말을 고르시오.**

P.135 L.1~7

Money Talks? Culture Talks!

Do you know Frodo? He is a character from the movie *The Lord of the Rings*. After the movie was released, a great __________ of people visited New Zealand, where the movie was filmed, reviving the nation's economy. It was (very / so) successful that this phenomenon got its own name – the "Frodo economy." The industries that involve this kind of __________ content are called "creative industries." Creative industries are economic activities that are related to using human knowledge and imagination.

Frodo를 아는가? 그는 영화 '반지의 제왕'에 나오는 인물이다. 그 영화가 개봉된 후, 엄청나게 많은 사람들이 그 영화가 촬영되었던 뉴질랜드를 방문했고 이것이 그 나라의 경제를 활성화시켰다. 그것은 굉장히 성공적이었고 이 현상을 '프로도 경제(효과)'라고 이름을 붙이기까지 했다. 이러한 문화 컨텐츠를 포함하는 산업들은 '창조적 산업'이라고 불린다. 창조적 산업은 인간의 지식과 상상력을 사용하는 것과 관련된 경제 활동이다.

단락요약

- 프로도 경제 효과와 창의적 산업의 정의에 관해 소개하고 있다.

구문정리

- After the movie was released, a great number of people visited New Zealand, where the movie was filmed, reviving the nation's economy.: 관계부사 where는 선행사 New Zealand를 수식하는 절을 이끌고 있다. 이때의 where는 in which로 바꿔 쓸 수 있다. reviving은 문장 뒤에 추가된 분사구문으로서 and it revived로 풀어 쓸 수 있다.
- Creative industries are economic activities that are related to using human knowledge and imagination: related to ~는 '~와 관련된'이라는 뜻으로 여기서 to는 전치사이므로 뒤에 명사류(명사 / 대명사 / 동명사)가 온다. 여기서는 using이라는 동명사 형태가 쓰였다.

정답 number / so / cultural

P.135 L. 8~23

U.K.

The U.K.'s creative industries are largely based on its imaginative __________. The very writer who gave life to Frodo was British, along with the icon of classic literature — Shakespeare. One of the most successful writers of all time (are / is) British as well. J.K. Rowling's work has attracted millions of people to visit London to see the Harry Potter Studios, Platform $9\frac{3}{4}$ at King's Cross Station, and the cafe (which / where) the series was written. The Harry Potter series is known to have earned the U.K. a large amount of money so far. One unique aspect of the U.K.'s culture is its storytelling clubs. In storytelling clubs, people gather to share interesting stories, feeding children's __________. Combined with such creativity, some of these stories are beautifully translated into books, films, and the performing arts.

영국의 창조적 산업들은 크게 자국의 상상력 뛰어난 문학작품에 바탕을 두고 있다. Frodo에게 생명력을 불어넣은 바로 그 작가도 고전 문학의 아이콘인 셰익스피어와 함께 영국인이었다. 전 세대를 통틀어 가장 성공적인 작가들 중 한 명도 영국인이다. J.K. Rowling의 작품은 수백만의 사람들을 매료시켜 해리포터 스튜디오, 킹스 크로스 역에 있는 플랫폼 $9\frac{3}{4}$, 그리고 그 시리즈를 집필했던 카페 등을 방문하도록 했다. 해리포터 시리즈로 인해 영국이 벌어들인 돈은 지금까지 막대하다고 알려져 있다. 영국 문화의 한 가지 독특한 측면은 그 나라의 스토리텔링 클럽들이다. 스토리텔링 클럽에서 사람들은 모여서 재미있는 이야기를 나누고, 아이들의 상상력을 채워준다. 그러한 창의력과 결합되어 이러한 이야기들 중 일부는 책과 영화와 그리고 공연 예술로 아름답게 번역되어진다.

단락요약

- 영국의 창조적 산업에서 문화 컨텐츠의 바탕은 상상력이 풍부한 문학 작품에 기반을 두고 있다.

구문정리

- The Harry Potter series is known to have earned the U.K. a large amount of money so far.: 「be known to have + p.p.」는 '~했다고 알려져 있다'라는 뜻으로, 어떤 일이 일어난 것이 알려진 것 보다 먼저 일어난 일임을 나타내는 완료부정사가 쓰였다. (= It is known that the Harry Potter series have earned (또는 earned) the U.K. a large amount of money so far.)
- Combined with such creativity, some of these stories are ~: Being이 생략되어 과거분사로 시작되는 분사구문으로서 '~와 결합되어'라고 해석한다. (= Some of these stories are combined with such creativity. + They are ~)

정답 literature / is / where / imagination

P.136 L.1~20

U.S.A.

The United States of America is another country whose cultural attractions have earned major tourism dollars. Its greatest strength [lies / lays] in its glamor. Hollywood studios create some of the most fantastic and dynamic movies in the world, making use of their fine computer graphics. Not only that, people can enjoy Universal Studios, a theme park based on the famous ________ industry. Here, visitors can enjoy fun rides as well as fantastic shows based on real Hollywood movies such as *Shrek*. Culturally, the U.S.A. also features Broadway in New York. If you had the chance to visit Broadway, you would be amazed by the glamor of the musicals. You could enjoy the realistic make-up and costumes in *The Lion King*, the fun dance and music of *Mamma Mia!*, and the terrific songs and plot of *The Phantom of the Opera*. Broadway shows are (estimating / estimated) to have gained more than 1.3 billion dollars in 2015-2016.

미국도 문화적 명소들이 주요 관광 수입을 벌어들여주는 또 다른 나라다. 미국의 가장 큰 강점은 그 화려한 매력에 있다. 할리우드 스튜디오들은 그들의 섬세한 컴퓨터 그래픽을 활용하여 세계에서 가장 환상적이고 역동적인 영화들을 만들어 낸다. 그뿐만 아니라, 사람들은 유명한 영화 산업에 기반을 둔 테마 공원인 유니버설 스튜디오를 즐길 수도 있다. 여기에서, 방문객들은 슈렉과 같은 실제 할리우드 영화에 기반을 둔 환상적인 쇼뿐 아니라 재미있는 놀이기구도 탈 수 있다. 문화적으로, 미국은 또한 뉴욕에 있는 브로드웨이가 특징적이다. 만약 브로드웨이를 방문할 기회를 갖게 된다면, 여러분은 아마 뮤지컬의 화려함에 경탄할 것이다. 여러분은 라이언 킹의 실제적인 분장과 의상, 맘마미아의 재미있는 춤과 음악, 그리고 오페라의 유령에서의 환상적인 노래와 줄거리를 즐길 수 있을 것이다. 브로드웨이 쇼는 2015년에서 2016년 사이에 13억 달러를 벌어들인 것으로 추정된다.

단락요약
- 미국 문화 관광의 특징은 화려함과 영화산업에 기반을 둔 환상적인 쇼에 있으며 또한 뉴욕 브로드웨이에서 그것을 체험할 수 있다.

구문정리
- The United States of America is another country whose cultural attractions have earned major tourism dollars.: 선행사 another country를 수식하는 whose는 소유격 관계대명사로서 여기서는 접속사와 소유격 대명사 its를 대신해서 쓰였다.
- If you had the chance to visit Broadway, you would be amazed by the glamor of the musicals. : '만약 ~한다면 …할 것이다'라는 의미의 가정법 과거의 문장으로, 「if + 주어 + 동사의 과거형 ~ 주어 + should / could / would / might + 동사원형」의 형태다.

정답 lies / movie / estimated

P.137 L.1~10

KOREA

If you were (asking / asked) to name one successful creative industry in Korea, what would you choose? It would be a hard question because there are so many. In fact, Korea's creative industries are reported to have been internationally successful for more than a decade. Nowadays, the economic impact of the "Korean Wave" is increasing by using new technology and good strategies. In particular, K-pop is gaining large profits (using / used) advanced technologies. A new type of concert, a combination of K-pop and hologram technology, is quite profitable. In this concert the audience feels as if the singer were actually on stage. (Attracted / Attracting) to its uniqueness, more and more K-pop fans flock to hologram concert halls.

만약 여러분에게 한국에서 성공적인 창조적 산업을 하나 명명하라면 무엇을 고르겠는가? 너무 많아서 어려운 질문일 것이다. 사실, 한국의 창조적 산업들은 10여 년간 국제적으로 성공적이었다고 보도되고 있다. 요즈음, '한류'의 경제적 영향력은 새로운 기술과 좋은 전략을 사용함으로써 더 증가하고 있다. 특히, K-pop은 진보된 기술들을 사용하여 큰 수익을 얻고 있다. K-pop과 홀로그램의 결합이라는 새로운 형태의 콘서트는 꽤 수익이 크다. 이 콘서트에서 청중들은 마치 가수가 무대에 있는 것처럼 느끼게 된다. 이 독특함에 매료되어 점점 더 많은 K-pop 팬들이 홀로그램 콘서트 장으로 몰려들고 있다.

단락요약
- 한류의 영향력 증대와 진보된 기술을 사용한 K-pop의 시장 확대에 대해 얘기하고 있다.

구문정리
- Korea's creative industries are reported to have been internationally successful ~: 완료 부정사 to have been은 보도되는(are reported) 시점보다 더 이전에 발생한 일임을 나타낸다. (= It is reported that Korea's creative industries have been successful.)
- In this concert the audience feels as if the singer were actually on stage.: 「as if + 주어 + 동사의 과거형」은 가정법 과거 구문으로 '마치 ~가 …인/한 것처럼'이라는 뜻이다.

정답 asked / using / Attracted

P.137 L.11-18

Marketing strategies are another key to the success of the Korean Wave. In the character industry, some characters are first introduced in an animated series before they are made into toys, theme parks, and other products. This way, the characters can __________ into other fields once they prove to be popular. Many companies also use a marketing strategy called product placement for indirect advertising on TV shows. These companies take advantage of the fact that Korean Wave fans abroad pay close attention to what products Korean celebrities use on TV shows and try to purchase the __________ items as they do.

마케팅 전략들은 한류의 성공에 있어서 또 하나의 열쇠다. 캐릭터 산업에 있어서, 어떤 캐릭터들은 장난감이나 테마 공원 그리고 제품들로 만들어지기 전에 만화 영화 시리즈에서 처음 소개된다. 이런 방식으로 해서, 그 캐릭터들은 일단 유명해지면 다른 분야로 확장해 가는 것이다. 많은 회사들도 TV 쇼에서 간접적인 광고를 위해 간접 광고라고 불리는 마케팅 전략을 사용한다. 이런 회사들은 외국에 있는 한류 팬들이 한국의 유명 연예인들이 TV 쇼에서 어떤 제품을 사용하는 지 눈여겨보다가 그들이 사는 것과 똑 같은 제품을 사려고 한다는 사실을 이용한다.

단락요약
- 한국의 캐릭터 산업과 연예인들을 통한 간접 광고 등 마케팅 전략의 확산성에 관해 얘기 하고 있다.

구문정리
- Many companies also use a marketing strategy called product placement for indirect advertising on TV shows.: called 앞에는 「주격 관계대명사 + be동사」가 생략되어 있다(which(that) is). called 이하는 선행사 marketing strategy를 수식하는 형용사절이다.

정답 expand / same

P.138 L.1~13

Other Countries

Along with the U.K., the U.S.A., and Korea, many other countries around the world are promoting their creative industries. Bollywood in India, the largest movie industry in the world, is attracting more and more fans with its __________ products. China, a country with rich cultural and historical resources, is introducing policies to support its creative industries. Japan has (launched / launching) its own brand "Cool Japan" to promote Japanese creative industries such as animation and J-pop.

As some scholars predict, creative industries may be the next global industry, just like farming or manufacturing was in the past. Who knows? The next generation's leading CEOs may be imaginative __________ or romantic writers.

영국, 미국, 그리고 한국과 함께, 세계의 많은 다른 나라들도 그들의 창조적 산업을 홍보하고 있다. 세계에서 가장 큰 영화 산업인 인도의 볼리우드는 그 독특한 상품들을 가지고 점점 더 많은 팬들을 끌어들이고 있다. 풍부한 문화적, 역사적 자원을 가진 나라 중국도 자국의 창조적 산업을 후원하기 위한 정책들을 도입하는 중이다. 일본은 '멋진 일본'이라는 자체 브랜드명을 출시해서 애니메이션이나 J-pop 같은 일본의 창조적 산업을 홍보하고 있다.

몇몇 학자들이 예측한 것처럼, 창조적 산업은, 과거에 농업이나 제조업이 그랬던 것처럼, 차세대 글로벌 산업이 될 것이다. 다음 세대의 선두 최고 경영인들이 상상력 풍부한 공상가들이나 낭만적인 작가들이 될지 누가 알겠는가?

단락요약
- 인도와 중국, 일본의 창조적 문화 산업의 특징 및 차세대 창조적 산업의 선두 주자의 특징에 대해 이야기를 하고 있다.

구문정리
- As some scholars predict, creative industries may be the next global industry, just like farming or manufacturing was in the past.: just like farming or manufacturing was (the next global industry) in the past에서 중복되는 표현이 생략된 구문이다.
- Who knows? : '누가 알겠는가?'는 'Nobody knows.'와 비슷한 의미로, 어떤 일이 벌어질 가능성이 있음을 시사하는 표현이다.

정답 unique / launched / daydreamers

Focus on Structure

P. 135 L.14 The Harry Potter series is known | **to have earned** the U.K. | a large amount of money | so far.
주어 동사(수동태) 완료부정사 (to have p.p.)

→ 「주어 + be 동사 + known / reported / estimated / believed… + to have p.p.」 구문은 '~가 …했다/이었다는 것이 알려지다 / 보도되다 / 추정되다 / 믿어지다…'라는 의미로서, …완료부정사로 표현된 사실이나 사건이 be동사의 시제보다 이전에 발생한 것이라는 시제의 차이를 나타낸다. 또한, 이 구문은 가주어 It을 사용하여 「It is + known / reported / estimated (that) 주어 + 현재완료 또는 과거형」구문으로 바꿔 쓸 수 있다.

ex. He **is** known **to have been** involved with printing and coloring William's work.
(그는 William의 작품을 인쇄하고 색칠하는 데 관여해 왔다고 알려져 있다.)
= It **is** known that he **has been** involved with printing and coloring William's work.
가주어 is보다 한 시제 앞선 현재완료 시제 (또는 과거형 was도 가능)

cf. 단순부정사를 쓰는 경우는 be동사의 시제와 같은 경우이다.
ex. The magical sign **is** believed **to give** power to become invisible.
(그 마법의 표시는 보이지 않게 되는 능력을 준다고 믿어진다.)
= It **is** believed that the magical sign **gives** power to become invisible.
be동사 is와 같은 현재형 시제

P. 136 L.14 If you **had** the chance to visit Broadway, | you **would be** amazed by the glamor of the musicals.
과거형 동사 「조동사의 과거형 + 동사원형」

→ 현재 사실이나 상태와는 다른 어떤 상황을 가정하여 말할 때 쓰는 가정법 과거 구문은 「If + 주어 + 동사의 과거형~, 주어 + 조동사의 과거형 + 동사원형」의 형태로 나타낸다.

cf. 과거 사실이나 상태와 다른 어떤 상황을 가정하여 '~했었다면 …했을 텐데'라는 의미를 나타낼 때는 「If + 주어 + had + p.p. …, 주어 + 조동사의 과거형 + have + p.p.」 형태인 가정법 과거완료를 사용한다.
ex. If she **had attended** the union meeting, she **would have met** him in person. (그녀가 조합 회의에 참석했더라면 그를 직접 만났을 텐데.)

Check-Up

정답 P. 243

1 다음 문장을 주어진 단어로 시작하여 의미가 같도록 빈칸을 완성하시오.

(1) It is known that she wrote for newspapers for more than a decade.
= She is known ______________ for more than a decade.

(2) The spy is believed to have sent messages via Facebook to his girlfriend.
= It is believed that the spy ______________.

2 다음 문장을 가정법 문장으로 바꿔 쓰시오.

(1) He does not know the formula for the volume of a sphere. He cannot solve the math problem.
→ If he ______________, he ______________.

(2) It's raining. + I can't go golfing.
→ If ______________, I could ______________.

Tip

❶ (1) is known의 현재시제와 wrote의 과거시제가 서로 다르므로 완료부정사를 사용한다.
(2) via ~를 통해

❷ (1) 현재사실과 반대되는 상황을 가정할 때는 가정법 과거 구문을 사용한다.
formula 공식
volume 부피
sphere 구 *cf.* hemisphere 반구

언어 기능별 집중 대비

Listen and Speak/Into Real Life

정답 P. 243

Tip

1 대화를 듣고, 두 사람이 보고 있는 도표의 주제를 고르시오.

① 영화 인기 순위 도표
② 뮤지컬 인기 순위 도표
③ 영화 관람의 목적 순위 도표
④ 뮤지컬 시청 횟수 조사 도표
⑤ 공연 예술 관람 평균 비용 도표

❶ 대화의 주제 파악하기
출처: Get Ready_3

2 대화를 듣고, 남자가 말하고 있는 페스티벌에 대해 맞지 않는 것을 고르시오.

① 매년 8월에 에든버러에서 개최된다.
② 연극, 코미디, 춤, 콘서트 등이 공연된다.
③ 예술 공연이 주를 이루는 축제다.
④ 한국 뮤지컬 '난타'도 여기서 공연한 적이 있다.
⑤ 입장권 및 관람권 예매는 온라인으로만 가능하다.

❷ 내용 일치 불일치 파악하기
출처: Listen In_Dialogue 1

3 대화를 듣고, 여자가 특별히 의미 있는 경험이라고 한 것을 고르시오.

① selling the most concert tickets in Indonesia
② singing in front of her international fans
③ listening to her fans singing her songs in Korean
④ visiting a Korean language center in Vietnam
⑤ being greeted by her European fans wearing *hanbok*

❸ 특정 경험 파악하기
출처: Listen In_Dialogue 2

4 대화를 듣고, 물음에 답하시오.

(1) 설문 조사에서 학생들에게 했던 주된 질문은?

① How often do you read a newspaper?
② What kind of movies do you like best?
③ Why do you think Korean history movies are popular?
④ Which newspaper do you think is not biased?
⑤ Who do you like to go to the movies with?

(2) 두 사람이 학교 신문에 실으려고 하는 기사 내용으로 맞는 것을 고르시오.

① History movies are the most popular type of movie.
② More than half of the students chose hitory movies as their favorite.
③ Less than 30% of the students chose sci-fi movies as their favorite.
④ *Interstellar* was much more popular than *The Admiral*.
⑤ A quarter of the students answered that their favorite movie was *Interstellar*.

❹ (1) 주제 파악하기
(2) 구체적인 정보 파악하기
출처: Into Real Life_Step 1
biased 편견이 있는
quarter 1/4

언어 기능별 집중 대비

Read and Think

정답 P. 244

Tip

❶ 출처: P.135 L.2-7
유형: 적절한 제목 고르기
side effect 부작용

1 다음 글의 제목으로 가장 알맞은 것은?

Do you know Frodo? He is a character from the movie *The Lord of the Rings*. After the movie was released, a great number of people visited New Zealand, where the movie was filmed, reviving the nation's economy. It was so successful that this phenomenon got its own name – the "Frodo economy." The industries that involve this kind of cultural content are called "creative industries." Creative industries are economic activities that are related to using human knowledge and imagination.

① Side Effects of "Frodo Economy"
② Roles of Characters in Movies
③ Definition of Creative Industry
④ Characteristics of Fantasy Movies
⑤ Origin of Creative Industries Using Movies

[2-3] 다음 글을 읽고, 물음에 답하시오.

❷❸ 출처: P.135 L. 9-23
유형: 2. 빈칸 추론
3. 문법성 판단
literacy (글을) 읽고 쓸 줄 아는 능력
cf. literate 읽고 쓸 줄 아는
illiterate 문맹의
literary 문학의

The U.K.'s creative industries are largely based on ______ⓐ______. The very writer who gave life to Frodo was British, along with the icon of classic literature—Shakespeare. One of the most successful writers of all time ⓑ <u>is</u> British as well. J.K. Rowling's work has attracted millions of people ⓒ <u>to visit</u> London to see the Harry Potter Studios, Platform $9\frac{3}{4}$ at King's Cross Station, and the cafe ⓓ <u>where</u> the series was written. The Harry Potter series is known ⓔ <u>to have earned</u> the U.K. a large amount of money so far. One unique aspect of the U.K.'s culture is its storytelling clubs. In storytelling clubs, people gather to share interesting stories, feeding children's imagination. ⓕ <u>Combining</u> with such creativity, some of these stories are beautifully translated into books, films, and the performing arts.

2 윗글의 빈칸 ⓐ에 가장 알맞은 것은?

① the public libraries
② its magical landscape
③ its imaginative literature
④ the film studios of fantasy movies
⑤ the high literacy levels of the people

3 윗글의 밑줄 친 ⓑ~ⓕ 중 어법상 어색한 것은?

① ⓑ ② ⓒ ③ ⓓ ④ ⓔ ⑤ ⓕ

[4-5] 다음 글을 읽고, 물음에 답하시오.

The United States of America is another country whose cultural attractions have earned major tourism dollars. (①) Hollywood studios create some of the most fantastic and dynamic movies in the world, (A)(made / making) use of their fine computer graphics. (②) Not only that, people can enjoy Universal Studios, a theme park based on the famous movie industry. (③) Here, visitors can enjoy fun rides as well as fantastic shows based on real Hollywood movies such as *Shrek*. (④) Culturally, the U.S.A. also features Broadway in New York. (⑤) If you (B) (have / had) the chance to visit Broadway, you would be amazed by the glamor of the musicals. You could enjoy the realistic make-up and costumes in *The Lion King*, the fun dance and music of *Mamma Mia*!, and the terrific songs and plot of *The Phantom of the Opera*. Broadway shows are estimated to (C) (gain / have gained) more than 1.3 billion dollars in 2015-2016.

4-5 출처: P.136 L.2-20
유형: 4. 문장의 위치 파악
5. 문법성 판단

4 윗글의 괄호 안의 ①~⑤ 중에서 아래의 문장이 들어 가기에 가장 알맞은 곳은?

Its greatest strength lies in its glamor.

5 윗글의 괄호 안의 (A)~(C)에 알맞은 말을 골라 쓰시오.

6 다음 글의 요지로 가장 알맞은 것은?

If you were asked to name one successful creative industry in Korea, what would you choose? It would be a hard question because there are so many. In fact, Korea's creative industries are reported to have been internationally successful for more than a decade. Nowadays, the economic impact of the "Korean Wave" is increasing by using new technology and good strategies. In particular, K-pop is gaining large profits using advanced technologies. A new type of concert, a combination of K-pop and hologram technology, is quite profitable. In this concert the audience feels as if the singer were actually on stage. Attracted to its uniqueness, more and more K-pop fans flock to hologram concert halls.

6 출처: P.137 L.2-10
유형: 글의 요지 파악
combination 결합
downturn 하락, 침체

① K-pop's international success was something unexpected.
② The economic impact of culture on music industry is huge.
③ The combination of K-pop and hologram technology resulted in the Korean Wave.
④ Despite the international economic downturn, K-pop music industry is gaining more profit than ever.
⑤ The "Korean Wave", combined with the introduction of advanced technology and good strategies, is becoming more profitable than before.

[7-8] 다음 글을 읽고, 물음에 답하시오.

In the character industry, some characters are first introduced in an animated series before they are made into toys, theme parks, and other products. ⓐ This way, the characters can expand into other fields once they prove to be popular. Many companies also use a marketing strategy called product placement for indirect advertising on TV shows. These companies take advantage of the fact that Korean Wave fans abroad pay close attention to what products Korean celebrities use on TV shows and __________ⓑ__________.

7-8 출처: P.137 L.11-18
유형: 7. 지칭어 파악
8. 빈칸 추론
so far 지금까지
on the contrary 반대로, 대조적으로
in other words 다른 말로 하자면

7 윗글의 밑줄 친 ⓐThis way가 가리키는 것은?

① 애니메이션 제작 방식
② 한류 홍보의 성공 방식
③ 캐릭터 산업의 마케팅 방식
④ 애니메이션 영화의 광고 방식
⑤ 다양한 캐릭터 상품의 간접광고 방식

8 윗글의 빈칸 ⓑ에 가장 알맞은 것은?

① ask the companies not to advertise them
② study hard to learn the Korean language
③ try to purchase the same items as they do
④ send a review on the shows and other TV programs
⑤ compare them with the products made in their own countries

9 다음 글에서 글쓴이가 밑줄 친 부분을 예로 든 이유로 가장 적절한 것은?

Along with the U.K., the U.S.A., and Korea, many other countries around the world are promoting their creative industries. Bollywood in India, the largest movie industry in the world, is attracting more and more fans with its unique products. China, a country with rich cultural and historical resources, is introducing policies to support its creative industries. Japan has launched its own brand “Cool Japan” to promote Japanese creative industries such as animation and J-pop.

As some scholars predict, creative industries may be the next global industry, just like farming or manufacturing was in the past. Who knows? The next generation’s leading CEOs may be <u>imaginative daydreamers or romantic writers.</u>

9 출처: P.138 L.1-13
유형: 글쓴이의 의도 파악

① 직업에는 귀천이 따로 없다는 것을 강조하기 위해
② 모든 국가의 제조업의 주역은 이런 사람들이었음을 상기시키기 위해
③ 과거의 노동 시장에서 살아남을 수 있었던 직업의 특징을 부각시키기 위해
④ 농업과 제조업에서 요구하던 자질과는 전혀 다른 사람을 부각시키기 위해
⑤ 미래 창조 산업의 발달은 과거 농업과 제조업의 발달을 기반으로 하고 있음을 강조하기 위해

언어 기능별 집중 대비

Language Notes / Write It Right

정답 P. 244

1 다음 우리말에 맞게 괄호 안의 말을 이용하여 문장을 완성하시오.

(1) 많은 기자들이 그 정치가 주변으로 몰려들었다.
____________________ around the politician. (a great number of)

(2) 모든 사람이 이 강당을 이용할 수 있는 것은 아니다.
Not everyone ____________________. (make use of)

(3) 40%의 실험 대상자들이 체중이 늘어난 것으로 추정되었다.
40% of the subjects ____________________ (estimate, gain weight)

(4) 그녀는 전에 심장마비를 겪었던 것으로 보도되고 있다.
She is reported ____________________. (suffer from)

(5) 만약 당신에게 말할 기회가 한 번 더 주어진다면, 무엇을 말하겠습니까?
If you ____________________, what would you say? (one more chance)

2 다음 문장을 주어진 단어로 시작하여 쓰시오.

(1) It seems that her boyfriend quit the job.
→ Her boyfriend ____________________.

(2) It is believed that the war went on for ten days.
→ The war ____________________.

(3) The caterpillar is known to have a sting equivalent to a mild electrical shock.
→ It is known that ____________________.

(4) Last year, the U.K. economy was estimated to have grown by 2.6%.
→ Last year, it was estimated that ____________________.

3 다음 문장을 가정법 문장으로 바꾸어 쓰시오.

(1) I ate a lot and so I felt sick.
→ If I ____________________.

(2) She does not study hard and she cannot pass the exam.
→ She could ____________________.

(3) He is always late for work and, because of that, he cannot be promoted.
→ If he ____________________.

Tip

❶ a great number of 많은, 다수의
heart attack 심장 마비

❷ 완료부정사 (시제의 차이)
quit 그만두다
caterpillar 애벌레
sting (찌르는) 침
equivalent to ~와 대등한

❸ 가정법 과거: 현재 사실의 반대 상황
가정법 과거완료: 과거 사실의 반대 상황
promote 승진시키다, 홍보하다

Basic

정답 P. 244

1 대화를 듣고, 축제에 대해 언급되지 않은 것을 고르시오.

① 축제가 열리는 도시
② 축제가 열리는 달
③ 축제 행사 공연의 종류
④ 축제에 참가한 한국 공연 팀의 수
⑤ 축제 표를 구매할 수 있는 방법

2 대화를 듣고, 남자의 견해로 맞는 것을 고르시오.

① The original books are better than the movies.
② Reading books is not as fun as watching movies.
③ *The Hunger Games* is the best movie ever made.
④ The plot of *The Hunger Games* is very complicated.
⑤ The movies, in general, are better than the books.

3 다음 밑줄 친 부분 중 어법상 잘못된 것은?

① The number of lions are stable or even rising.
② There were a great number of bikes in the store.
③ A large amount of sugar leads to various diseases.
④ The amount of salt varies widely from one cheese to another.
⑤ Last night, a number of swans were found dead in the park.

4 다음 중 나머지 넷과 다른 하나는?

① life – lives
② mice – mouse
③ child – children
④ medium – media
⑤ phenomenon – phenomena

5 다음 중 반의어끼리 연결된 것은?

① terrific – terrible
② phantom – ghost
③ glamorous – fancy
④ advantage – benefit
⑤ audience – spectator

6 다음 문장의 빈칸에 가장 알맞은 것은?

The company remains moderately ________, but it is not making as much money as it should.

① reliable
② bankrupt
③ profitable
④ glamorous
⑤ economical

[7~8] 다음 글을 읽고, 물음에 답하시오.

Along with the U.K., the U.S.A., and Korea, many other countries around the world are ⓐ promoting their creative industries. Bollywood in India, the largest movie industry in the world, is ⓑ attracting more and more fans with its unique products. China, a country with rich cultural and historical resources, is introducing policies ⓒ to withhold its creative industries. Japan has launched its own brand "Cool Japan" ⓓ to promote Japanese creative industries such as animation and J-pop.

As some scholars predict, creative industries may be the next global industry, just like farming or manufacturing was in the past. ① Who knows? The next generation's leading CEOs may be ⓔ imaginative daydreamers or romantic writers.

7 윗글의 밑줄 친 ⓐ~ⓔ 중 문맥상 쓰임이 어색한 것은?

① ⓐ ② ⓑ ③ ⓒ ④ ⓓ ⑤ ⓔ

8 윗글의 밑줄 친 ① **Who knows?**의 의미로 가장 알맞은 것은?

① I don't care.
② Anything is possible.
③ It's a tough question.
④ Everyone knows it.
⑤ It's not likely to happen.

[9~10] 다음 글을 읽고, 물음에 답하시오.

The United States of America is another country whose cultural attractions have earned major tourism dollars. Its greatest strength lies in its glamor. Hollywood studios create some of the most fantastic and dynamic movies in the world, making use of their fine computer graphics. Not only that, people can enjoy Universal Studios, a theme park based on the famous movie industry. Here, visitors can enjoy fun rides as well as fantastic shows based on real Hollywood movies such as *Shrek*. Culturally, the U.S.A. also features Broadway in New York. If you had the chance to visit Broadway, you would be amazed by the glamor of the musicals. You could enjoy the realistic make-up and costumes in *The Lion King*, the fun dance and music of *Mamma Mia!*, and the terrific songs and plot of *The Phantom of the Opera*. Broadway shows are estimated to have gained more than 1.3 billion dollars in 2015-2016.

9 According to the passage above, what are the two main features of the American cultural industry?

① film studios and classic music halls
② glamorous shows and dynamic concerts
③ fine computer graphics and theme parks
④ Hollywood movies and Broadway musicals
⑤ realistic musicals and modern operas

10 윗글의 내용과 일치하지 않는 것은?

① 미국의 문화 산업은 큰 수익을 창출하고 있다.
② 미국의 문화 산업의 강점은 화려함에 있다.
③ 환상적이고 역동적인 할리우드 영화에는 정교한 컴퓨터 그래픽 기술이 사용된다.
④ 미국 브로드웨이 뮤지컬은 화려한 할리우드 영화와 달리 소박한 멋을 추구한다.
⑤ 2015년에서 2016년까지 뉴욕 브로드웨이 쇼를 통해 벌어들인 소득은 13억 달러 이상이었다.

[11~12] 다음 글을 읽고, 물음에 답하시오.

__________ are another key to the success of the Korean Wave. In the character industry, some characters are first introduced in an animated series (a)(after / before) they are made into toys, theme parks, and other products. This way, the characters can (b)(expend / expand) into other fields once they prove to be popular. Many companies also use a marketing strategy called product placement for (c) (direct / indirect) advertising on TV shows.

11 윗글의 빈칸에 가장 알맞은 것은?

① Marketing strategies
② Diversifying characters
③ Creative ideas in design
④ Promotions of characters
⑤ Advertisement platforms

12 윗글의 괄호 안의 (a)~(c)에 들어갈 말이 차례대로 연결된 것은?

① after – expend – direct
② after – expand – direct
③ before – expand – direct
④ before – expend – indirect
⑤ before – expand – indirect

13 다음 <보기>의 문장을 주어진 어구로 시작하여 가정법 문장으로 바꾸어 쓰시오.

보기 I want to make clothes for myself, but I don't have a sewing machine.

→ If I ______________________________ .

14 다음 <보기>의 우리말과 같도록 괄호 안의 단어를 사용하여 빈칸을 완성하시오. (필요한 경우 어형을 바꾸시오.)

보기 그 남자는 지난 10년 동안 최소한 다섯 개의 가짜 이름을 사용해 왔다고 알려져 있다. (fake name / at least)

→ The man is known ______________________ during the last decade.

수준별 단원평가

Advanced

정답 P. 245

[1~2] 다음 대화를 듣고, 물음에 답하시오.

1 남자가 신문을 가지고 온 이유를 고르시오.

① 관련 기사에 실린 자료를 인용하려고
② 전날 다 못 읽은 부분을 마저 읽기 위해
③ 수지의 해외 콘서트 일정을 확인하기 위해
④ 수지에 대한 잘못된 기사 수정을 요청하려고
⑤ 국내 신문과 국외 신문의 차이를 비교하려고

2 **Which of the following did Suji do or happened to Suji in Europe?**

① Her concert sold the most tickets in the European countries.
② She thanked her international fans for singing along with her.
③ She paid a short visit to a Korean language center.
④ She became interested in performing arts as well as in learning a foreign language.
⑤ Some of her fans, who were wearing the traditional Korean clothes, greeted her in the airport.

3 다음을 듣고, 남자의 어조로 맞는 것을 고르시오.

① analytical
② persuasive
③ anticipating
④ encouraging
⑤ sentimental

4 다음 글을 통해 알 수 있는 사실을 아래 문장으로 요약할 때 빈칸 (a)와 (b)에 알맞은 말을 주어진 철자로 시작하여 쓰시오.

Do you know Frodo? He is a character from the movie *The Lord of the Rings*. After the movie was released, a great number of people visited New Zealand, where the movie was filmed, reviving the nation's economy.

J.K. Rowling's work has attracted millions of people to visit London to see the Harry Potter Studios, Platform $9\frac{3}{4}$ at King's Cross Station, and the cafe where the series was written. The Harry Potter series is known to have earned the U.K. a large amount of money so far.

→ Creative industries, which refer to (a) e________ activities that are related to using cultural content and imagination, are quite (b) p________.

5 다음 글에서 할리우드 영화와 브로드웨이 뮤지컬의 공통점으로 말하고 있는 것은?

Hollywood studios create some of the most fantastic and dynamic movies in the world, making use of their fine computer graphics. Not only that, people can enjoy Universal Studios, a theme park based on the famous movie industry. Here, visitors can enjoy fun rides as well as fantastic shows based on real Hollywood movies such as *Shrek*. Culturally, the U.S.A. also features Broadway in New York. If you had the chance to visit Broadway, you would be amazed by the glamor of the musicals. You could enjoy the realistic make-up and costumes in *The Lion King*, the fun dance and music of *Mamma Mia!*, and the terrific songs and plot of *The Phantom of the Opera*. Broadway shows are estimated to have gained more than 1.3 billion dollars in 2015-2016.

① They are glamorous.
② They use fine computer graphics.
③ Their plots are usually unrealistic.
④ Most of them are adapted from novels.
⑤ They have become the icon of performing arts.

[6~7] 다음 글을 읽고 물음에 답하시오.

If you were asked to name one successful creative industry in Korea, what would you choose? (A) It would be a hard question because there are so many. (B) Nowadays, the economic impact of the "Korean Wave" is increasing by using new technology and good strategies. (C) In particular, K-pop is gaining large profits using advanced technologies. (D)A new type of concert, a combination of K-pop and hologram technology, is quite profitable. (E) In this concert the audience feels as if the singer were actually on stage. Attracted to its uniqueness, more and more K-pop fans flock to hologram concert halls.
Marketing strategies are another key to the success of the Korean Wave. In the character industry, some characters are first introduced in an animated series before they are made into toys, theme parks, and other products. This way, the characters can expand into other fields once they prove to be popular. Many companies also use a marketing strategy called product placement for indirect advertising on TV shows. These companies take advantage of the fact that Korean Wave fans abroad pay close attention to what products Korean celebrities use on TV shows and try to purchase the same items as they do.

6 윗글의 (A)~(E) 중 아래의 문장이 들어가기에 가장 알맞은 곳은?

In fact, Korea's creative industries are reported to have been internationally successful for more than a decade.

① (A) ② (B) ③ (C) ④ (D) ⑤ (E)

7 윗글의 내용과 일치하지 않는 것은?

① Combined with advanced technology, K-pop is making more money than before.
② K-pop hologram concerts are popular among K-pop fans because they can meet the singers on stage.
③ The character industry produces character-related products after the animated series is introduced.
④ Many companies advertise a product by supplying it for use in TV shows.
⑤ Korean Wave fans abroad are affected by the marketing strategy called product placement.

[8~9] 다음 글을 읽고 물음에 답하시오.

Stories have power. (①) They not only can change people's lives ⓐ <u>but</u> can also change the world. (②) One story that is known ⓑ <u>to change</u> the history of America is *Uncle Tom's Cabin*. (③) This sensational, yet ⓒ <u>touching</u>, story upset many Americans and started a debate over the freedom of American slaves. (④) These days, stories ⓓ <u>affect</u> the world in a different way: well-made stories can expand to other industries such as movies, characters, and tourism, ⓔ <u>making</u> a large amount of money. (⑤)

8 윗글의 괄호 안의 ①~⑤ 중 아래 문장이 들어가기에 가장 알맞은 곳은?

This story realistically describes the hard lives of American slaves.

① ② ③ ④ ⑤

9 윗글의 밑줄 친 ⓐ~ⓔ 중 어법상 어색한 것은?

① ② ③ ④ ⑤

주관식 서술형 대비

10 한류와 관련하여 외국인들에게 홍보하고 싶은 문화 컨텐츠를 정하고 이를 소개하는 글을 간단히 쓰시오. (3-4 문장 정도)

Welcome to the new center of the Korean Wave. I'd like to introduce you to ________________
____
____
____
____________________________________.

UNIT 8

What Makes a Good Citizen?

내신체크 01 교과서 핵심 정리 > Go to p. 154

- 어휘 총정리
- 대본 정리
  질서를 지키지 않거나 법규를 위반했을 때의 위험성에 대한 경고
- 본문 정리
  법과 질서를 지키고 다른 사람을 배려하는 성숙한 시민 의식을 갖자

내신체크 02 언어 기능별 집중 대비 > Go to p. 164

- **듣기와 말하기** 대본별 필수 출제 유형
- **읽기** 각 단락별 필수 점검 유형
- **언어 재료 및 쓰기** 어휘 및 구문, 주관식 서술형 대비 문제

내신체크 03 수준별 단원 평가 > Go to p. 169

- **Basic** 지식, 사실적 이해 대비 문제
- **Advanced** 추론적 이해 및 감상, 주관식 서술형 대비 문제

교과서 핵심 정리

Words & Phrases

Listen and Speak ~ Into Real Life

- ☐ absolutely *ad.* 완전히, 정말로, 절대적으로
- ☐ due* *adj.* 기한이 된, 만기의, ~ 할 예정인
  cf. due to ~때문에
- ☐ shame *n.* 수치, 치욕 *v.* 부끄럽게 하다
  cf. What a shame!* 유감이다! 참 부끄러운 일이다!
- ☐ illegal* *adj.* 불법의 (↔ legal 합법적인)
- ☐ penalty* *n.* 처벌, 벌(금), 불이익 (=fine 벌금)
- ☐ embarrassing* *adj.* 난처하게 하는, 당혹스러운
- ☐ ruin *v.* 망치다 *n.* 유적, 폐허
- ☐ transfer* *v.* 옮기다, ~로 바꾸다, 전가하다
- ☐ jaywalk* *v.* 무단 횡단하다
- ☐ detect* *v.* 발견하다, 탐지하다
  (detection *n.* 발견, 탐지) *cf.* detective 탐정
- ☐ exit *n.* 출구 *v.* 나가다, 퇴장하다
- ☐ janitor *n.* 수위, (빌딩 등의) 관리인
- ☐ treatment* *n.* 치료, 처리 (treat *v.* 치료하다, 처리하다)
- ☐ operate on* ~를 수술하다
- ☐ fake *adj.* 가짜의, 위조한

Read and Think

- ☐ frown *v.* 눈살을 찌푸리다, 찡그리다 *n.* 언짢은 기색
- ☐ civic* *adj.* 시민의, 도시의
  cf. civil 시민다운, 국내의 civil war 내전
- ☐ regulation* *n.* 규제, 법규 (regulate *v.*해 규제하다)
- ☐ pedestrian *n.* 보행자, 도보 여행자
- ☐ push aside* (한쪽으로) 밀치다
- ☐ make way for* 길을 열어주다, 자리를 내주다
- ☐ be ashamed of ~ for -ing* …한 것에 대해 ~를 부끄럽게 여기다
- ☐ public *adj.* 공공의, 공적인 *n.* 일반 사람, 대중
- ☐ firework *n.* 불꽃(놀이)
- ☐ misbehavior *n.* 잘못된 행동, (위법한) 부정행위
- ☐ garbage *n.* (주로 부엌에서 나오는)쓰레기 (= rubbish)
- ☐ keep order 질서를 유지하다
  cf. out of order 고장이 난(= broken)
- ☐ care about ~를 신경 쓰다, 배려하다
- ☐ firefighter 소방관, 소방수
- ☐ rescue* *v.* 구하다 *n.* 구조
- ☐ extinguisher* *n.* 소화기 (= f ire extinguisher)
  (extinguish *v.* (불을) 끄다, 소화하다 (=put out))
- ☐ trap* *v.* 가두다 *n.* 덫, 올가미
- ☐ relieve* *v.* 완화시키다, 안도하게 하다
  (relief *n.* 구조, 완화)
- ☐ disaster *n.* 재난, 재해 (disastrous *adj.* 파괴적인)
- ☐ be faced with* ~에 직면하다 (=confront with)
- ☐ keep *A* from -ing A가 ~하지 못하게 막다
- ☐ potential *adj.* 잠재적인 *n.* (잠재된) 가능성
- ☐ noticeably* *ad.* 눈에 띄게, 두드러지게
  (notice *v.* 알아차리다)
- ☐ contribute to* ~에 공헌하다, 기여하다
- ☐ be willing to + 동사원형 기꺼이 ~하다

Language Notes

- ☐ observe* *v.* 준수하다, 관찰하다
  (observance *n.* 준수 observation 관찰)
- ☐ neglect *v.* 무시하다, 방치하다
- ☐ severe *adj.* 심한, 가차 없는
- ☐ occur *n.* 발생하다, 일어나다 (=happen)
  (occurrence *n.* 발생, 사건)

Write It Right

- ☐ put ~ in (the correct) order ~를 순서에 맞게 놓다
- ☐ careless *adj.* 경솔한, 부주의한 (↔ careful)

Around the World

- ☐ watch out (for ~)* (~를) 조심하다, 경계하다
  (= look out for~)
- ☐ unfenced *adj.* 울타리가 없는, 무방비의
- ☐ unexpectedly *ad.* 예상치 않게, 뜻밖에, 불쑥
- ☐ give way to* ~ 에게 (길을) 양보하다, 굴복하다

Check-Up

정답 P. 246

1 다음 문장의 빈칸에 알맞은 말을 〈보기〉에서 골라 알맞은 형태로 쓰시오.

보기 >> push aside / be faced with / be ashamed of
be willing to / watch out for

(1) He ___________ the janitor and opened the door.

(2) She ___________ her father's being alcoholic and didn't tell anybody about it.

(3) You need to ___________ the children playing in the street.

(4) If you ___________ fly at night, you can get a much cheaper ticket.

(5) We ___________ the task of balancing the needs of younger generations and older generations.

2 다음 뜻풀이에 해당하는 말을 주어진 철자로 시작하여 쓰시오.

(1) f ___________ : to view with disapproval or to have an angry look

(2) j ___________ : to cross a street at a place other than a regular crossing

(3) m___________ : improper, inappropriate, or bad behavior

(4) r ___________ : a law, rule, or other order prescribed by authority

(5) e ___________ : to put out (a fire, light, etc.)

주관식 서술형

3 우리말에 맞게 괄호 안의 단어들을 사용하여 문장을 완성하시오.

(1) 경찰은 사고가 발생하지 않도록 하기 위해 최선을 다했다.
The police tried their best ___________________________.
(accidents / keep / to / from / occurring)

(2) 나는 그런 어리석은 실수를 한 내 자신이 매우 부끄러웠다.
I ___________________________ such a stupid mistake.
(making / for / of / myself / so / felt / ashamed)

(3) 착한 시민은 어려움에 처한 이웃을 무시하지 않고 도와준다.
Good citizens do not ___________________________.
(help / need / in / neglect / their neighbors / but)

(4) 여행하는 동안 우리들은 예상하지 못한 도전들에 직면했다.
During the trip, we ___________________________.
(challenges / unexpected / were / with / faced)

Tip

1 주요 숙어표현 익히기
alcoholic 알코올 중독의

2 영영사전풀이
crossing 횡단보도
inappropriate 부적절한
prescribe 처방하다, 규정하다
put out 끄다

3 핵심어휘를 사용한 영작
occur 발생하다
neglect 무시하다

교과서 핵심 정리

Dialogues & Monologue

Listen and Speak | *해석을 참조하여 빈칸에 알맞은 말을 쓰시오.

GET READY

1 M: Mom, do you really have to drive so slowly?
W: I'm just trying to be safe!
M: But we are late!
W: Trust me. **It's always better to be ________ than sorry.**

남: 엄마, 이렇게 천천히 운전해야만 해요?
여: 안전하게 하려고 하는 거야!
남: 하지만 우리 늦었잖아요!
여: 엄마를 믿어. 나중에 후회하는 것보다 안전한 게 항상 나아.

2 W: Let's get going!
M: Before we start, you should wear this helmet.
W: Dad, do I really have to wear this funny-looking helmet when I ride my bike?
M: Absolutely. It will keep you safe.

여: 자, 가요.
남: 출발하기 전에 너 이 헬멧 써야지.
여: 아빠, 자전거 탈 때 이렇게 웃기게 생긴 헬멧을 정말로 써야 하는 거예요?
남: 물론이지. 이게 널 안전하게 지켜줄 거야.

3 W: Taylor, will you borrow some books from the library for me?
M: Why can't you do that yourself?
W: Last time, I returned some books ________ **the due date.** So I can't borrow books for the next ten days.
M: **What a shame!**

여: Taylor, 내 대신 도서관에서 책 좀 빌려다 줄래?
남: 왜 네가 직접 빌릴 수 없어?
여: 지난번에 반납 기한 지나서 책을 반납했거든. 앞으로 10일 간 책을 빌릴 수가 없어.
남: 이런, 유감이네.

표현정리
- It's always better to be safe than sorry.: 「better *A* than *B*」는 'B하느니 A하는 게 낫다'라는 뜻이고, 많이 쓰이는 표현으로는 "Better late than never."(늦더라도 하는 것이 안하는 것보다 더 낫다)가 있다.
- past the due date는 '정해진 날짜가 지나서'라는 뜻으로 'overdue(연체된)'라는 표현으로 대체할 수 있다.
- What a shame!: '창피한 일이다!/유감이다!/안됐다!' 등 어떤 일에 대한 유감을 표현할 때 많이 쓰는 표현이다.

정답 safe / past

LISTEN IN

DIALOGUE 1

W: How was your first week in Singapore as an exchange student, Ed?
M: Great. I noticed that the country is so clean.
W: Throwing trash on the street is illegal here.
M: Many other countries have that law, too. But **I feel like it's** much better kept in Singapore.
W: Maybe it's because of the ________. When you are caught three times, you have to clean the city once a week wearing certain clothes.
M: **That must be embarrassing.** (pause) Will you hold my stuff while I drink some water?
W: You mean, you want to drink it here on the subway? If I were you, I'd wait until we get off the subway.
M: Do I really have to do that? I'm thirsty.
W: Drinking and eating on the subway are ________ in Singapore.
M: Really? I didn't know that. Is there anything else I should know?
W: Let me tell you one more thing. Bringing smelly fruit on the subway is illegal, too.
M: You mean like strong-smelling fruit? Thanks for telling me.

여: Ed, 교환학생으로서 싱가포르에서 보낸 첫 주 어땠어?
남: 좋아. 이 나라가 참 깨끗하다는 것을 알게 됐어.
여: 거리에 쓰레기 버리는 게 여기서는 불법이야.
남: 다른 많은 나라들도 그 법이 있긴 해. 하지만 그 법이 싱가포르에서 훨씬 더 잘 지켜지고 있는 것 같아.
여: 어쩌면 처벌 때문이겠지. 세 번 걸리면 특정한 옷을 입고 일주일에 한 번 도시를 청소해야 해.
남: 그거 참 당혹스럽겠네. (잠시 후) 나 물 마시는 동안 내 물건 좀 들고 있어줄래?
여: 여기 지하철에서 그것을 마신다고? 내가 너라면, 우리가 지하철에서 내릴 때까지 난 기다리겠어.
남: 정말 그래야 하나? 나 목마른데.
여: 싱가포르에서는 지하철에서 마시거나 먹는 게 불법이야.
남: 정말? 난 몰랐어. 내가 알아야 할 게 또 있니?
여: 한 가지만 더 말해 줄게. 지하철에 냄새나는 과일을 가지고 타는 것도 불법이야.
남: 강한 냄새가 나는 과일 같은 거 말하는 거지? 말해 줘서 고마워.

대화상황
- 싱가포르에 교환학생으로 온 Ed에게 싱가포르에서 지켜야 할 다양하고 엄격한 법규에 대해 알려주고 있다.

표현정리
- I feel like it's much better kept in Singapore.: I feel like ~'나는 ~인 것 같다'라는 뜻으로 상황에 대한 자신의 느낌을 표현한다.
- That must be embarrassing.: 여기에 쓰인 must be는 '분명 ~일 것이다'라는 뜻의 강한 추측을 나타낸다.

정답 penalty / illegal

DIALOGUE 2

M: Hi, Suji. What did you do last weekend?
W: I went to my favorite singer's concert.
M: That sounds exciting. **How did you like it**?
W: The concert itself was very good, but the audience's bad __________ ruined my day.
M: Oh, no. What was the matter?
W: The man behind me kept kicking my seat, and the man in front of me stood up, blocking my view.
M: What a shame!
W: **Not only that**, the people at the front pushed the fence so hard that one woman fell and hurt herself.
M: That sounds terrible. What happened to her, then?
W: Fortunately, she was __________ to the hospital immediately, but the concert wasn't the same as before.
M: I'm sorry to hear that.

남: 안녕, 수지야. 지난 주말에 뭐 했어?
여: 내가 좋아하는 가수 콘서트 갔었어.
남: 재미있었겠다. 어땠어?
여: 콘서트 자체는 아주 좋았는데, 관객들의 무례한 매너 때문에 하루를 다 망쳤어.
남: 이런. 무슨 일이 있었어?
여: 내 뒤에 있던 사람은 계속 발로 내 좌석을 차는가 하면, 내 앞에 있는 사람은 일어서서 내 시야를 막아버리는 거야.
남: 이런!
여: 그것뿐만이 아니야. 앞에 있었던 사람들이 펜스를 너무 세게 밀어서 한 여자가 넘어져서 다치기까지 했어.
남: 끔찍했겠다. 그럼, 그 여자는 어떻게 됐어?
여: 다행히 곧장 병원으로 옮겨지긴 했어. 하지만 콘서트는 (여자가 다치기) 그 전이랑 같진 못했지.
남: 유감이다.

대화상황
• 사람들이 질서를 지키지 않아 안전사고가 나고 엉망이 되어버린 콘서트 관람 경험에 대해 얘기하고 있다.

표현정리
• How did you like it? : '그거 어땠어?'라는 의미로 소감을 물어보는 말이다.
• Not only that, ~: '그것만이 아니라'라는 의미로, 추가적인 정보나 사실을 전달할 때 쓴다.

정답 manners / transferred

DIALOGUE 3

W: Jinu, you have to wait for the green light.
M: Do I really have to do that? I'm late!
W: Didn't you hear the news about Mingming?
M: What happened to her?
W: Last Friday, she got hit by a car while __________ and broke her arm.
M: That's terrible news!
W: **No kidding**. I also recently saw on the news that out of all the causes of teenage traffic accidents, jaywalking ranked __________.
M: What a shame!
W: **It seems like a little thing to** just wait for the light, but if you don't, you could face serious problems.
M: You're right. And I hope Mingming gets better soon.
W: I'm going to visit her this weekend. Will you join me?
M: Absolutely!
W: Oh, let's go. The light's green.

여: 진우야, 초록불이 켜질 때까지 기다려야지.
남: 꼭 그래야 해? 나 늦었어!
여: 너 Mingming에 대한 뉴스 못 들었어?
남: 걔한테 무슨 일이 났어?
여: 지난 금요일에 무단 횡단하다가 차에 치여서 팔이 부러졌어.
남: 끔찍한 소식이네!
여: 맞아. 또 최근에 뉴스에서 들었는데 10대의 교통사고의 모든 원인들 중 무단 횡단이 1위를 차지했어.
남: 이런!
여: 신호를 기다리는 게 사소한 일 같이 보이긴 하지만 그렇게 하지 않으면 너도 심각한 문제에 직면하게 될 수도 있어.
남: 네 말이 맞아. Mingming이 곧 회복되었으면 좋겠다.
여: 이번 주말에 그녀를 병문안 갈 거야. 너도 같이 갈래?
남: 물론이지!
여: 어, 가자. 초록불이야.

대화상황
• 신호를 지키지 않고 횡단보도를 건너려는 친구를 제지하며 무단 횡단의 위험성에 대해 얘기하고 있다.

표현정리
• No kidding.: 원래의 의미는 '농담 하지 마.'라는 뜻이지만, 여기서는 '정말 그래.(=Truly/Seriously.)'라는 의미로 쓰였다.
• It seems like a little thing to ~: It은 여기서 가주어로 쓰였고 진주어는 to 이하이다.

정답 jaywalking / first

Into Real Life

STEP 1

(Siren sounds.)

M: Ladies and gentlemen, your attention, please. We have detected signs of a fire on the fifth floor of the building. Please leave the auditorium immediately through the doors on the right. Use the exit stairs to the ground level. Please follow the safety instructions and do not ________. **Make sure you do not use the elevators.** Stay close to the floor, and if possible, cover your mouth and nose with ________ tissues.
Your attention, please. We would like to inform you again that we have detected signs of a fire ....

(사이렌이 울린다.)

남: 여러분, 주목해 주시기 바랍니다. 건물 5층에서 화재 신호가 감지되었습니다. 오른 쪽에 있는 문을 통해 강당을 즉시 나가 주십시오. 1층으로 가는 비상계단을 이용해 주십시오. 안전 수칙을 따라 주시고 당황하지 마십시오. 엘리베이터는 절대 타시면 안 됩니다. 마룻바닥 가까이 몸을 대시고 가능하면 젖은 물수건으로 입과 코를 막으십시오.
주목해 주세요. 화재 신호가 감지되었음을 다시 한 번 알려드리겠습니다. ...

담화주제
- 화재 신호가 감지된 건물 안에서 비상계단을 통해 신속히 건물 밖으로 나가라는 방송 내용이다.

표현정리
- Make sure you do not use the elevators ~ : make sure는 '~하도록 명심하라'는 의미로 경고나 당부의 표현이다.
- Stay close to the floor.: 화재 발생 시 최대한 몸을 낮추어 피신해야 하므로'몸을 바닥과 가까이 하라'는 표현을 쓴다.

정답 panic / wet

Write It Right

W: Last Saturday, a high school student was walking down the stairs looking at her smartphone. As a ________, she fell down the stairs and broke her leg. Fortunately, Mr. Park, a janitor who was in the building discovered her. After checking her leg, he called 119. The emergency rescue team arrived at the building **shortly afterwards** and gave the girl emergency ________. After she was transferred to the hospital, a doctor operated on the girl successfully. The girl said, "I thank everyone. I thank the janitor for staying with me until the ambulance came. **Thanks to the rescue team,** I received emergency treatment. Thanks to the doctor, my leg is ________."

여: 지난 토요일, 한 고등학생이 스마트폰을 보면서 계단을 내려 걸어가고 있었습니다. 그 결과, 그 학생은 계단에서 굴러 떨어졌고 다리를 다쳤습니다. 다행히 박 씨 경비 아저씨께서 건물 안에 계시던 중이라 그 학생을 발견하셨습니다. 다리가 괜찮은지 살펴본 후 아저씨는 119를 불렀습니다. 얼마 지나지 않아 응급 구조팀이 도착했고 그 여학생에게 응급 처치를 해 주었습니다. 병원으로 옮겨진 후, 의사가 성공적으로 그 여학생을 수술했습니다. 그 학생은 "모든 분들께 고맙습니다. 구급차가 올 때까지 제 옆에 계셔주신 경비 아저씨에게도 감사드립니다. 구조팀 덕분에 응급 처치도 받을 수 있었습니다. 의사 선생님 덕분에 제 다리는 회복되고 있는 중입니다."라고 말했습니다.

담화주제
- 스마트폰을 보며 계단을 내려가다 굴러 떨어져서 다친 여학생이 어떻게 응급조치를 받게 되었는지에 관한 이야기이다.

표현정리
- The emergency rescue team arrived ~ shortly afterwards and gave ~: shortly afterwards는 '얼마 지나지 않아 곧'이라는 뜻으로 시간이 많이 경과되지 않았음을 나타내는 표현이다.
- Thanks to the rescue team, I received emergency treatment.: thanks to는 '~덕분에'라는 뜻으로, 대상에 대한 감사나 어떤 일이 생긴 원인을 나타낸다.

정답 result / treatment / recovering

교과서 핵심 정리

Reading Comprehension

***해석을 참조하여 빈칸에 알맞은 말을 쓰거나 괄호에서 알맞은 말을 고르시오.**

P.155 L.1~6

Back to Basics

Have you ever frowned at thoughtless people who were talking loudly in the library? Have you ever felt threatened by people pushing you aside on the subway? Did you jaywalk on the way to school today? All of these are related to (city / civic) life. (Responsible / Irresponsible) citizens form a safer, cleaner community where members contribute to one another's happiness and comfort. The three examples below show how a responsible citizen should act.

기본으로 돌아가라

도서관에서 시끄럽게 얘기하는 생각 없는 사람들에게 인상을 찌푸린 적이 있나요? 지하철에서 여러분을 옆으로 밀치는 사람들에게 위협받는 느낌을 느껴본 적 있나요? 오늘 등굣길에 무단 횡단했나요? 이런 모든 것들이 시민 생활과 관련되어 있습니다. 책임감 있는 시민은 사회 구성원들이 서로 서로의 행복과 안위를 위해 기여하는 더 안전하고 더 깨끗한 공동체를 형성합니다. 아래 세 가지 예시들은 책임감 있는 시민이 어떻게 행동해야 할지를 보여줍니다.

단락요약

- 타인을 배려하지 않는 무책임한 시민의 행동을 먼저 예로 들고 난 후, 책임감 있는 시민의 행동 사례를 소개하고 있다.

구문정리

- Responsible citizens form a safer, cleaner community where members contribute ~: 관계부사 where는 선행사인 community를 수식하며 in which로 바꿔 쓸 수 있다.

정답 civic / Responsible

P.155 L.7~25

Civic awareness begins when people follow simple rules such as traffic regulations. However, many ambulance drivers (compliment / complain) of selfish drivers and careless pedestrians.

"Please move over. This is an emergency!"

Even though an ambulance driver shouted this to the cars nearby and the siren was ringing, only some cars were slowly changing their lanes. According to traffic regulations, drivers must make way for __________ vehicles.

Pedestrians also caused difficulties. Several pedestrians who crossed the street at a red light blocked the way, (delayed / delaying) the ambulance's arrival.

When the ambulance finally arrived at the destination, the driver said, "It is very fortunate that we made it in time! But the people who didn't make __________ for us should be ashamed of themselves for having broken traffic laws."

시민 의식은 사람들이 교통 법규와 같은 단순한 규칙들을 따를 때 시작된다. 하지만, 많은 구급차 운전자들은 이기적인 운전자들과 부주의한 보행자들에 대해 불만을 표한다.

"비켜 주세요. 응급 상황입니다!"

구급차 운전자가 근처 차량들에게 소리치고 사이렌이 울리고 있었지만, 몇몇 차량만이 천천히 차선을 바꿀 뿐이었다. 교통 법규에 따르면, 차량 운전자들은 응급 차량들에게 길을 양보해 주어야 한다. 보행자들도 어려움을 야기했다. 빨간 불에 길을 건너는 몇 몇 보행자들이 길을 가로 막아 구급차의 도착을 지연시켰다. 구급차가 결국 목적지에 도착했을 때 운전자가 말했다. "시간 내에 도착해서 운이 좋았어요. 하지만 우리에게 길을 양보해주지 않은 사람들은 교통 법규를 어긴 것에 대해 부끄러워해야 해요."

단락요약

- 응급 차량에게 길을 내주어야 한다는 교통 법규를 어기는 차량 운전자들 때문에 구급차가 시간 내에 도착하지 못하는 경우가 있다.

구문정리

- Civic awareness begins when people follow~: 「begin when + 주어 +동사」는 '~ 가/이 …할 때 시작된다'라는 뜻이다.
- It is very fortunate that we made it in time!: It은 가주어이고 that 이하의 절이 진주어인 구문이다. (= That we made it in time is very fortunate. = We were fortunate enough to make it in time. = It is very fortunate for us to make it in time.)
- But the people ~ should be ashamed of themselves for having broken traffic laws. : 「be ashamed of + … + for + having + p.p.」는 '~ 한 것에 대해 …를 부끄럽게 여기다'라는 의미이다. 여기서 완료형 동명사 'having broken'이 쓰인 이유는 교통 법규를 어긴 사람이 부끄러워 해야 할 시점보다 이전에 일어났거나 이미 완료된 일이기 때문이다.

정답 complain / emergency / delaying / way

Caution

Don't you realize?
The sound is leaking.

Please do it at the beach

Garbage
Can't
Walk!

P.156 L.1~11

Responsible citizens also show good manners. When they are in public places, they keep __________ and clean up after themselves.

Last Saturday, thousands of people flocked to a fireworks festival. Even though the fireworks were beautiful, some people's misbehavior made it (easy/ hard) to fully enjoy the beauty of the fireworks. Most people observed the law. However, some people pushed one another, (hurt / hurting) others. The police reported that more than a hundred people had been hurt and fourteen of them had been taken to hospital that day. Furthermore, volunteer workers had a very hard time cleaning up the area as it was full of __________. "I wish people cared more about others than just about themselves," said a volunteer worker.

책임감 있는 시민은 또한 예의 있게 행동한다. 공공장소에 있을 때, 그들은 질서를 지키고 자신이 있던 자리를 깨끗이 치운다.

지난 토요일, 수천 명의 사람들이 불꽃놀이 축제에 모여들었다. 불꽃놀이는 아름다웠지만, 어떤 사람들의 잘못된 행동은 그 불꽃놀이의 아름다움을 온전히 즐기는 걸 어렵게 만들었다. 대부분의 사람들은 법규를 지켰다. 하지만, 어떤 사람들은 서로 밀치다가 다른 사람들을 다치게 했다. 경찰은 100여 명의 사람들이 다쳤고 그 중 14명은 그 날 병원에 실려 갔다고 보도했다. 더군다나, 자원 봉사자들은 쓰레기로 가득 찬 그 지역 일대를 치우느라 엄청 애를 먹었다. "사람들이 자기 자신만큼이나 다른 사람들을 신경 썼으면 좋겠어요."라고 한 자원봉사자가 이야기 했다.

단락요약

- 일부 사람들이 불꽃놀이 축제에서 서로 밀치고 쓰레기를 함부로 버리는 등 무책임한 시민 행동을 한 것에 대해 개탄하고 있다.

구문정리

- Even though the fireworks were beautiful, some people's misbehavior made it hard to fully enjoy ~ fireworks: 「주어 + make it + 형용사 + to부정사」는 '~가 …하는 것을 ~하게 만들다'라는 의미로 여기서는 to fully enjoy하는 것을 어렵게 만들었다는 뜻이다. (=We couldn't fully enjoy the beauty of the fireworks because of some people's misbehavior.)
- The police reported that more than a hundred people had been hurt~: 경찰이 보도한(reported) 것이 과거시제라면 사람들이 다친(had been hurt) 시점은 그 이전에 일어난 일이기 때문에 과거완료(had + p.p.)시제가 쓰였다.
- I wish people cared more about others ~: 「I wish + 주어 + 과거형 동사」는 가정법 과거형의 표현으로 '~하면/한다면 좋겠다'라는 의미이다.

정답 order / hard / hurting / garbage

P.157 L.1-19

Last, but not least, good citizens do not neglect but help their neighbors in need.

On February 14th at 6:20 a.m., the 119 emergency center received an urgent call. "There is a fire in the building! And there are people inside!"

When the firefighters and the 119 rescue team arrived at the scene, the firefighters were not faced with the usual __________ problem. The neighbors (has / had) already moved their cars to make space for the fire engine. When the rescue team arrived on the fifteenth floor, they saw some neighbors (tried / trying) to put out the fire with fire extinguishers.

With the neighbors' help, the 119 team rescued the family who had been trapped inside. The neighbor who called 119 said, "I was so __________ to see them safe." The head officer of the emergency center said, "The neighbors' help and our team's quick response kept the fire from turning into a bigger disaster. We'd like to thank the neighbors for having helped the rescue."

마지막으로, 하지만 앞의 것들과 마찬가지로 중요하게도, 좋은 시민은 도움을 필요로 하는 이웃을 무시하지 않고 돕는다.

2월 14일 오전 6시 20분, 119 긴급 센터에서 한 통의 응급 전화를 받았다. "건물에 불이 났어요. 그리고 사람들이 그 안에 있어요!"

소방관들과 119 구조 팀이 현장에 도착했을 때, 소방관들은 평상시의 주차 문제에 직면하지 않았다. 이웃 주민들이 이미 소방차가 있을 자리를 마련해 주기 위해 자신들의 차량을 옮겨 놓은 상태였다. 구조팀이 15층에 도착했을 때, 그들은 몇 몇 이웃 주민들이 소화기로 불을 끄려고 애쓰고 있는 모습을 보았다. 이웃들의 도움으로, 119 팀은 안에 갇혔던 그 가족을 구할 수 있었다. 119에 신고 전화를 했던 이웃 주민은 "그 사람들이 안전한 걸 봐서 안심이 됩니다."라고 말했다. 응급 센터 소장은 이렇게 말했다. "이웃의 도움과 우리 팀의 재빠른 대처가 그 불이 더 큰 재난으로 변하는 걸 막아주었습니다. 이 구조를 도와 준 이웃 주민분들께 감사드리고 싶습니다."

단락요약

- 이웃 주민들의 성숙한 시민 의식과 소방대원들의 신속한 진화 작업으로 인해 건물의 화재가 크게 번지는 걸 막을 수 있었다.

구문정리

- they saw some neighbors trying to put out the fire ~: 「지각동사(saw) + 목적어(some neighbors) + 현재분사(trying)」 구문으로 '~가 …하고 있는 것을 보다'라는 뜻이다. 이 구문에서 현재분사 대신 동사원형을 사용할 수도 있다.
- The neighbors' help ~ kept the fire from turning into a bigger disaster.: 「keep + 목적어 + from + -ing」는 '~가 …하는 것을 막다'라는 뜻의 구문으로 keep 대신 prevent를 쓸 수도 있다.

정답 parking / had / trying / relieved

P.158 L.1~9

These three examples show simple ways to become a responsible citizen. __________ simple regulations, showing good manners in public, and helping neighbors in need can prevent a lot of tragic accidents. Each individual has the potential to contribute to making the world a better place. These days, more and more drivers are making way for __________ vehicles. Our manners are noticeably improving. There are many volunteers who are more than willing to help those in __________.

Becoming a responsible citizen and making the community a better place are not difficult. Observe the law. Keep order. Care about others. In other words, just go back to __________.

이 세 가지 예시는 책임감 있는 시민이 되는 간단한 방법을 보여주고 있다. 간단한 법규를 지키는 것, 공중도덕을 지키는 것, 그리고 어려운 이웃을 돕는 것은 수많은 비참한 사고를 예방할 수 있게 한다. 각 개인은 이 세상을 좀 더 나은 곳으로 바꾸도록 공헌할 잠재적 능력을 가지고 있다. 요즈음 점점 더 많은 운전자들이 긴급 차량을 위해 길을 내어주고 있다. 우리의 예의범절도 눈에 띄게 향상되고 있다. 곤궁에 처한 사람들을 도와주는 것 이상으로 하려는 많은 자원봉사자들이 있다.

책임감 있는 시민이 되고 지역 사회를 좀 더 나은 곳으로 만드는 것은 그다지 어렵지 않다. 법을 지키도록 하라. 질서를 지켜라. 다른 사람을 배려하라. 다른 말로 하자면, 기본으로 돌아가라.

단락요약

- 앞서 든 세 가지 예시를 종합하여 책임감 있는 시민의 세 가지 기본적 태도에 대해 말하고 있다.

구문정리

- Each individual has the potential to contribute to making the world a better place.: each 다음에는 단수명사가 오고 따라서 동사도 3인칭 단수형태(여기서는 has)가 된다. 'contribute to + 명사구(명사/대명사/동명사)'는 '-에 헌신하다'라는 뜻으로 여기서는 동명사 making이 목적어로 온 경우다.
- Becoming a responsible citizen and making the community a better place are not difficult.: 문장의 주어가 동명사 형태인 becoming과 making 둘이므로 복수 주어가 되어 이에 맞게 복수 동사 are가 쓰였다.

정답 Observing / emergency / need / basics

Focus on Structure

P. 155 L.22 They should be ashamed of themselves | **for having broken** traffic laws.
S V 「전치사 + 완료형 동명사」

「전치사 + 동명사」의 구문에서 단순 동명사가 아닌 완료형 동명사 「having + p.p.」가 쓰인 경우, 주절의 동사 시제보다 동명사로 표현된 사건이나 상태의 시제가 먼저 일어났거나 이미 완료되었다는 것을 나타낸다. 하지만 일반적으로 동명사를 목적어로 취하는 동사(remember, complain, deny 등)의 목적어로 쓰인 경우, 단순 동명사와 완료 동명사의 구분에 큰 의미가 없는 경우도 있다.

ex. He complained **of being** treated unfairly.
(= He complained that he was treated unfairly.)
과거 과거
그는 부당한 대우를 받은 것을 불평했다.

He complained **of having been** treated unfairly.
(= He complained that he had been treated unfairly.)
과거 과거완료

ex. She denied taking the money. (= She denied that she took the money.)
She denied having taken the money. (= She denied that she had taken the money.)
그녀는 그 돈을 받았다는 것을 부인했다.

P. 156 L.6 The police reported | that more than a hundred people **had been hurt** | that day.
S V (과거) S 동사(과거완료수동태) 부사구

과거완료수동태는 「had been + p.p.」의 형태로 나타내며, 같은 문장에 쓰인 다른 동사의 시제(과거)보다 이전에 일어났거나 이루어진 일을 묘사하거나 설명하기 위해 쓰인다.

ex. We found that the window **had been broken** by someone. (과거완료 – 수동태)
우리는 누군가 그 창문을 깼다는 것을 알았다.
cf. We found that someone **had broken** the window. (과거완료 – 능동태)

P. 156 L.9 **I wish** | people **cared** more about others | than just about themselves.
I wish S V(과거)

I wish 가정법 과거 구문은 「I wish + 주어 + 동사 과거형」형태로 쓰여서 '~라면/한다면 좋겠다'라는 뜻의 소망이나 현재 사실에 대한 유감을 나타낸다.

ex. **I wish** I **knew** what I did. (= I feel sorry that I don't know what I did.)
내가 무엇을 했는지 안다면 좋을 텐데.

Check-Up

정답 P. 246

1 다음 두 문장의 뜻이 같도록 빈칸에 알맞은 말을 쓰시오.

(1) Emma didn't talk about having been a beauty queen.
= Emma didn't talk that ______________________.

(2) Ted was blamed for having neglected his duty.
= Ted was blamed because he ______________________.

2 다음 밑줄 친 부분을 바르게 고쳐 쓰시오.

(1) The team rescued the family who <u>have been trapped</u> inside.
(2) I interviewed two females who <u>had adopted</u> to Europe.
(3) I wish <u>I can go</u> to the concert with you.

Tip

❶ 완료형 동명사: 주절의 시제보다 먼저 일어난 일을 묘사함
blame 비난하다
neglect 게을리 하다
duty 의무

❷ (1) 과거완료수동태
(2) 과거완료수동태
(3) I wish 가정법 과거
trap (덫이나 올무 등에) 가두다
adopt 입양하다, 채택하다

언어 기능별 집중 대비

Listen and Speak/Into Real Life

정답 P. 246

Tip

1 대화를 듣고, 여자의 마지막 말이 의미하는 바로 알맞은 것을 고르시오.

① I'm sorry for being late.
② Don't say sorry for being late.
③ Being safe is not as important as being on time.
④ Being safe is more important than being on time.
⑤ You always have to choose to be late than to be safe.

❶ 표현의 의미 파악하기
출처: Get Ready_1
be on time 제시간에 가다/도착하다

2 대화를 듣고 여자의 마지막 말에 대한 남자의 응답으로 가장 알맞은 것을 고르시오.

① No kidding!
② What a shame!
③ How silly I am!
④ How embarrassing!
⑤ What a coincidence!

❷ 마지막 말에 대한 응답 고르기
출처: Get Ready_3

3 대화를 듣고, 대화의 내용과 일치하지 않는 것을 고르시오.

① Jinu is in a hurry and doesn't want to wait for the green light.
② Jinu did not know what had happened to Mingming.
③ Mingming had a car accident last Friday.
④ Mingming had her leg broken in the accident.
⑤ Jaywalking is a major cause of teenage traffic accidents.

❸ 일치/불일치 파악하기
출처: Listen In_Dialogue 3

4 대화를 듣고, 물음에 답하시오.

(1) 대화가 일어나고 있는 장소로 알맞은 것은?
① on the subway
② in the cafeteria
③ in the grocery store
④ in the travel agency
⑤ in the currency exchange office

(2) 대화를 듣고 싱가포르에서 법규에 어긋나는 행동으로 언급되지 않은 것은?
① Littering
② Wearing certain costumes
③ Drinking on the subway
④ Eating on the subway
⑤ Bringing smelly fruit on the subway

❹ (1) 대화 장소 파악하기
(2) 언급되지 않은 내용 파악하기
출처: Listen In_Dialogue1
money exchange office 환전소

언어 기능별 집중 대비

Read and Think

정답 P. 246

1 다음 글의 밑줄 친 **All of these**가 가리키는 것으로 가장 알맞은 것은?

> Have you ever frowned at thoughtless people who were talking loudly in the library? Have you ever felt threatened by people pushing you aside on the subway? Did you jaywalk on the way to school today? All of these are related to civic life. Responsible citizens form a safer, cleaner community where members contribute to one another's happiness and comfort.

① good manners in public
② impressive experiences
③ behaviors against rules
④ things that are legally okay
⑤ responsible behaviors of civic people

Tip

❶ 출처: P.155 L.1-5
유형: 지칭어 파악하기
against rules 규칙에 어긋난
legally 법적으로

[2-3] 다음 글을 읽고, 물음에 답하시오.

> Even though an ambulance driver shouted this to the cars nearby and the siren ① was ringing, only some cars were slowly changing their lanes. According to traffic regulations, drivers must make way for emergency vehicles.
>
> Pedestrians also ② caused difficulties. Several pedestrians who crossed the street at a red light blocked the way, ③ delaying the ambulance's arrival.
>
> When the ambulance finally arrived at the destination, the driver said, "It is very ④ fortunately that we made it in time! But the people who didn't make way for us should be ashamed of themselves for ⑤ having broken traffic laws."

2 윗글의 밑줄 친 ①~⑤ 중 어법상 어색한 것은?

3 윗글에서 마지막에 인용한 **the driver**의 태도로 가장 알맞은 것은?

① complaining
② regretting
③ encouraging
④ apologizing
⑤ complimenting

❷❸ 출처: P.155 L.10-24
유형: 2. 문법성 판단
3. 어조 파악하기
regretting 후회하는
apologizing 사과하는
complimenting 칭찬하는

4 다음 글의 빈칸 ⓐ와 ⓑ에 알맞은 말이 바르게 연결된 것은?

> Even though the fireworks were beautiful, some people's misbehavior made it hard to fully enjoy the beauty of the fireworks. Most people observed the law. ___ⓐ___, some people pushed one another, hurting others. The police reported that more than a hundred people had been hurt and fourteen of them had been taken to hospital that day. ___ⓑ___, volunteer workers had a very hard time cleaning up the area as it was full of garbage.

① Therefore – However
② Additionally – Therefore
③ Likewise – Otherwise
④ However – Furthermore
⑤ Otherwise – Furthermore

❹ 출처: P.156 L.3-9
유형: 연결어 파악
otherwise 그렇지 않다면, 반대로
likewise 비슷하게

Tip

[5-6] 다음 글을 읽고, 물음에 답하시오.

(A) The neighbor who called 119 said, "I was so relieved to see them safe." The head officer of the emergency center said, "The neighbors' help and our team's quick response kept the fire from turning into a bigger disaster. We'd like to thank the neighbors for having helped the rescue."

(B) "There is a fire in the building! And there are people inside!" When the firefighters and the 119 rescue team arrived at the scene, the firefighters were not faced with ____________________. The neighbors had already moved their cars to make space for the fire engine.

(C) When the rescue team arrived on the fifteenth floor, they saw some neighbors trying to put out the fire with fire extinguishers. With the neighbors' help, the 119 team rescued the family who had been trapped inside.

5-6 출처: P.157 L.2-19
유형: 5. 글의 순서
6. 빈칸 추론
suffocate 질식시키다
reserve 예약하다

5 윗글에서 아래의 문장 다음에 이어질 글의 순서로 가장 알맞은 것은?

On February 14th at 6:20 a.m., the 119 emergency center received an urgent call.

① (A)–(C)–(B)
② (B)–(A)–(C)
③ (B)–(C)–(A)
④ (C)–(A)–(B)
⑤ (C)–(B)–(A)

6 윗글의 빈칸에 가장 알맞은 것은?

① the usual parking problem
② the problem of stopping the fire
③ a high risk for being suffocated
④ a noisy crowd blocking the exits
⑤ a space reserved for the firefighters

7 다음 글에서 아래 주어진 문장이 들어가기에 가장 알맞은 곳은?

* There are many volunteers who are more than willing to help those in need.

7 출처: P.158 L.1-9
유형: 문장이 들어갈 위치 파악

These three examples show simple ways to become a responsible citizen. Observing simple regulations, showing good manners in public, and helping neighbors in need can prevent a lot of tragic accidents. (A) Each individual has the potential to contribute to making the world a better place. (B) These days, more and more drivers are making way for emergency vehicles. (C) Our manners are noticeably improving. (D) Becoming a responsible citizen and making the community a better place are not difficult. (E) Observe the law. Keep order. Care about others. In other words, just go back to basics.

① (A) ② (B) ③ (C) ④ (D) ⑤ (E)

8 다음 글의 빈칸에 가장 알맞은 것은?

During the 2022 Qatar World Cup, thousands of people in red clothes gathered at City Hall to watch the Russia vs. Korea match. Not only the huge red wave itself, but also ______________________ impressed the world. The police later reported that there had been almost no accidents during the game and the street had been cleaned up by the citizens. "I am proud of the citizens for having kept order throughout the game," said a police officer.

① the passionate cheer
② people's good manners
③ the attitude of the foreigners
④ the ethnic diversity of the people
⑤ the teamwork of the Korean players

8 출처: P.161
유형: 빈칸 추론
ethnic 민족의, 인종의
diversity 다양성

[9-10] 다음 글을 읽고, 물음에 답하시오.

It has been discovered that the Titanic accident resulted from a number of little things that added up. According to a survivor, that night was especially dark with little moon light. (A) Furthermore, the person in charge of watching for danger at night was not wearing his glasses. (B) All these conditions were bad enough, but worse was to come. (C) When warnings were finally issued, nearly half of the passengers did not come on the deck because people had confidence in the ship. (D) So, when passengers were told to leave the ship on lifeboats, many didn't feel the need to leave the "unsinkable" ship. (E) Due to such ignorance, 473 lifeboat seats remained empty and more than 1,500 people drowned.

9-10 출처: P.167 L.3-11
유형: 9. 문장이 들어갈 위치 파악
10. 요지 파악
afloat (가라앉지 않고) 떠 있는

9 윗글의 (A) ~ (E) 중 아래 문장이 들어가기에 가장 알맞은 곳을 고르시오.

The ship had been praised for its strength and security by the news magazines back then.

① (A) ② (B) ③ (C) ④ (D) ⑤ (E)

10 According to the passage, which was the most important cause of the Titanic accident?

① The night when the accident happened was dark with little moon light.
② The man in charge of watching for danger did not wear his glasses.
③ Passengers who thought the Titanic was unsinkable would not leave the ship on lifeboats.
④ There were not enough life boats in the ship for all the passengers.
⑤ Passengers had a false sense of hope that the ship might stay afloat a little bit longer.

언어 기능별 집중 대비

Language Notes Write It Right

정답 P. 246

Tip

❶ (1),(2) 전치사 +완료형 동명사
(3),(4),(5) 과거완료 수동태: had been +p.p.
hive 벌집

1 다음 우리말에 맞게 괄호 안의 말을 이용하여 문장을 완성하시오.

(1) 너는 너의 책임을 다하지 않았던 것에 대해 부끄럽게 생각해야 한다.
You should be ashamed of yourself ______________________________.
(do responsibility)

(2) 그 환자들은 그 두 명의 수녀가 자신들을 돌봐 주었던 것에 대해 감사했다.
The patients thanked the two nuns for ______________________.
(take care)

(3) 나는 그 소화기가 이전에 분실되었다는 사실을 깨달았다.
I realized that the fire extinguisher __________________ before. (lose)

(4) 그 양봉가는 커다란 벌집에 갇혀 있었던 벌들을 꺼냈다.
The beekeeper took out the bees __________________ in a large hive.
(keep)

(5) 그녀는 할머니에 의해 씻겨 있었던 접시들을 다시 씻었다.
She washed the dishes again ________________________________
by her grandmother. (wash)

2 다음 글을 읽고, 물음에 답하시오.

❷ (1) 사고의 경위
(2) 지칭어 내용 파악

Dear, Mr. Park,

I am the girl who got the leg operation last Saturday. I'd like to thank you for having rescued me that day.

Just before the accident, I had been looking at my smartphone as usual while walking. So I didn't see the stairs in front of me and fell. After falling, I could feel that my leg had been broken.

Fortunately, you found me, checked my condition, and called the rescue services. You also stayed with me until the rescue team came. Thanks to you, I could be transferred to the hospital and got the treatment at the right time. I would like to thank you once again for helping me that day. I am ashamed of myself for having been so careless. I will never make the same mistake again.

Once again, thank you!

Best regards,

Suji Kim

(1) How did Suji have her leg broken?

____

(2) What does the underlined phrase "the same mistake" refer to?

____

Basic

정답 P. 247

1 대화를 듣고, 여자의 심정으로 알맞은 것을 고르시오.

① She is afraid of riding a bike.
② She feels safe to wear a helmet.
③ She feels comfortable to wear a helmet.
④ She is willing to learn how to ride a bike.
⑤ She is not willing to wear a funny-looking helmet.

2 대화를 듣고, 여자의 상황으로 맞는 것을 고르시오.

① She wants to go to the library with Taylor.
② She wants Taylor to return some books for her.
③ She completely forgot the due date of the books she had borrowed.
④ She returned some books after the due date, so she can't borrow books right now.
⑤ She has lost some of the books she had borrowed from the library.

3 다음 〈보기〉의 밑줄 친 표현과 바꿀 수 있는 것은?

> 보기
> *A:* Sam had to miss the concert because he was ill.
> *B:* <u>What a shame!</u>

① Good for him!
② He deserves it.
③ That's too bad.
④ He didn't mean it.
⑤ He should be ashamed of himself.

4 다음 단어의 뜻이 <u>잘못</u> 연결된 것은?

① relieve: 완화하다
② extinguish: 점화하다
③ regulation: 규제, 법규
④ pedestrian: 보행자
⑤ noticeably: 눈에 띄게

5 다음 중 유의어끼리 바르게 연결된 것은?

① detect – conceal
② severe – harsh
③ fake – genuine
④ public – private
⑤ neglect – consider

6 다음 중 밑줄 친 숙어의 뜻이 <u>잘못</u> 연결된 것은?

① <u>put out</u> the fire: 불을 지피다
② <u>keep order</u>: 질서를 유지하다
③ <u>care about</u> others: 남을 고려하다
④ <u>watch out for</u> dogs: 개를 조심하다
⑤ <u>those in need</u> : 어려움에 처한 사람들

7 다음 글의 밑줄 친 부분의 사례에 해당하지 <u>않는</u> 것은?

> Have you ever frowned at thoughtless people who were talking loudly in the library? Have you ever felt threatened by people pushing you aside on the subway? Did you jaywalk on the way to school today? All of these are related to civic life. <u>Responsible citizens</u> form a safer, cleaner community where members contribute to one another's happiness and comfort. The three examples below show how a responsible citizen should act.

① the citizens who quickly made way for emergency vehicles
② the people who cleaned up the public park for themselves
③ the citizens who called 119 to report that there was a fire and who took care of the victims
④ the car drivers who delayed the arrival of the ambulance by not changing their lanes quickly
⑤ the neighbors who helped 119 team rescue the family who had been trapped inside

[8~9] 다음 글을 읽고, 물음에 답하시오.

"Please move over. This is an emergency!"
Even though an ambulance driver shouted this to the cars nearby and the siren was ringing, only some cars were slowly changing their lanes. According to traffic regulations, drivers must ___ⓐ___ for emergency vehicles.
Pedestrians also caused difficulties. Several pedestrians ___________ⓑ___________ (the / street / blocked / crossed / the / way / at / a / red / light / who), delaying the ambulance's arrival.
When the ambulance finally arrived at the destination, the driver said, "It is very fortunate that we made it in time! But the people who didn't ______ⓒ______ for us should be ashamed of themselves for having broken traffic laws."

8 윗글의 밑줄 친 빈칸 ⓐ 와 ⓒ에 공통으로 들어갈 말을 두 단어로 쓰시오.

→ ______________________

9 윗글의 빈칸 ⓑ에 들어갈 말을 괄호 안의 단어들을 이용하여 문장을 완성하시오.

→ ______________________

10 다음 중 어법상 어색한 문장은?

① Everybody wishes they had more free time.
② I feel ashamed of myself for having lied to him.
③ The police reported that hundreds of people had been hurt in the car accident.
④ The song that she had been composed received mixed reviews.
⑤ I took the medicine that had been prescribed by the physician for me.

11 다음 글의 괄호 안의 ⓐ와 ⓑ의 단어를 활용하여 알맞은 형태를 쓰시오.

Last Saturday, thousands of people flocked to a fireworks festival. Even though the fireworks were beautiful, some people's misbehavior made it hard to fully enjoy the beauty of the fireworks. Most people observed the law. However, some people pushed one another, hurting others. The police reported that more than a hundred people ⓐ(hurt) and fourteen of them ⓑ(take) to hospital that day. Furthermore, volunteer workers had a very hard time cleaning up the area as it was full of garbage.

→ ⓐ ______________
ⓑ ______________

12 다음 <보기>의 우리말과 같도록 괄호 안의 단어를 활용하여 문장을 완성하시오.

보기 공동체를 좀 더 나은 곳으로 만드는 것은 어렵지 않다. (better)

→ Making the community ______________.

13 다음 <보기>의 우리말을 괄호 안의 단어들을 사용하여 영어로 쓰시오.

보기 그들의 도움이 그 불이 더 큰 재난으로 바뀌는 것을 막았다.
(the / fire / their / help / kept / a / bigger / disaster / from / turning / into)

→ ______________________

Advanced

정답 P. 247

[1~2] 다음 방송을 듣고, 물음에 답하시오.

1 방송의 내용과 일치하지 않는 것은?

① The girl was looking at her smartphone when she fell down the stairs.
② The janitor, who found the girl with the broken leg, gave her emergency treatment.
③ The janitor called 119 after he checked the girl's condition.
④ It didn't take long for the emergency rescue team to get to the building.
⑤ The girl had to undergo an operation in the hospital for the broken leg.

2 이 방송의 끝부분에서 인용한 여학생 말의 어조로 가장 알맞은 것은?

① grateful ② regretful
③ apologetic ④ overwhelmed
⑤ disappointed

3 대화를 듣고, 두 사람이 보고 있는 사진에 대해 바르게 말한 것을 고르시오.

① The picture was taken in a dangerous place.
② The man in the picture looks very scared.
③ The cliff on which the man is hanging is not real.
④ The people take risks to have a look at the picture.
⑤ The fake cliff in the picture makes the viewers feel at ease.

4 다음 대화의 빈칸에 가장 알맞은 것은?

A: I recently read the news that out of all the causes of teenage traffic accidents, ________ ranked first.
B: What a shame!
A: It seems like a little thing to just wait for the light, but if you don't, you could face serious problems.
B: You're right. Oh, let's go. The light's green.

① speeding ② texting
③ smoking ④ littering
⑤ jaywalking

[5~6] 다음 글을 읽고, 물음에 답하시오.

It has been discovered that the Titanic accident resulted from a number of little things that added up. (A) According to a survivor, that night was especially dark with little moon light. (B) Furthermore, the person in charge of watching for danger at night was not wearing his glasses. (C) When warnings were finally issued, nearly half of the passengers did not come on the deck because people had confidence in the ship. (D) The ship had praised for its strength and security by the news magazines back then. (E) So, when passengers were told to leave the ship on lifeboats, many didn't feel the need to leave the "unsinkable" ship. Due to such ignorance, 473 lifeboat seats remained ___ⓐ___ and more than 1,500 people ___ⓑ___.

5 윗글의 (A)~(E) 중 아래의 문장이 들어가기에 가장 알맞은 것은?

All these conditions were bad enough, but worse was to come.

① (A) ② (B) ③ (C) ④ (D) ⑤ (E)

6 윗글의 빈칸 ⓐ와 ⓑ에 들어갈 말을 각각 쓰시오.

ⓐ: ________ ⓑ: ________

7 다음 글의 밑줄 친 ①~⑤ 중 어법상 어색한 것은?

Observing simple regulations, showing good manners in public, and ①helping neighbors in need can prevent a lot of tragic accidents. Each individual has the potential to contribute to ②making the world a better place. These days, more and more drivers are making way for emergency vehicles. Our manners ③are noticeably improving. There are many volunteers who are more than willing ④helping those in need.

Becoming a responsible citizen and making the community a better place ⑤are not difficult. Observe the law. Keep order. Care about others. In other words, just go back to basics.

[8~9] 다음 글을 읽고, 물음에 답하시오.

On February 14th at 6:20 a.m., the 119 emergency center received an urgent call. (A)"There is a fire in the building! And there are people inside!"
(B) When the firefighters and the 119 rescue team arrived at the scene, the firefighters were not faced with the usual parking problem. (C) When the rescue team arrived on the fifteenth floor, they saw some neighbors trying to put out the fire with fire extinguishers. (D) With the neighbors' help, the 119 team rescued the family who had been trapped inside. (E) The neighbor who called 119 said, "I was so relieved to see them safe." The head officer of the emergency center said, "The neighbors' help and our team's quick response kept the fire from turning into a bigger disaster. We'd like to thank the neighbors for having helped the rescue."

8 윗글의 (A)~(E) 중 아래의 문장이 들어가기에 가장 알맞은 곳은?

The neighbors had already moved their cars to make space for the fire engine.

① (A) ② (B) ③ (C) ④ (D) ⑤ (E)

9 윗글을 읽고 알 수 있는 것으로 알맞은 것은?

① Fire engine drivers seldom have a parking problem.
② It is hard for firefighters to get help from rescue team members.
③ The family had been trapped inside the building long before the fire started.
④ The neighbors were quite helpful in putting out the fire in the building.
⑤ The fire turned into a bigger disaster due to the slow response of the rescue team.

[10~11] 다음 글을 읽고, 물음에 답하시오.

Last Saturday, thousands of people flocked to a fireworks festival. Even though the fireworks were beautiful, some people's misbehavior made it hard to fully enjoy the beauty of the fireworks. Most people observed the law. However, some people pushed one another, hurting others. The police reported that more than a hundred people had been hurt and fourteen of them had been taken to hospital that day. Furthermore, volunteer workers had a very hard time cleaning up the area as it was full of garbage. "I wish people cared more about others than just about themselves," said a volunteer worker.

10 다음 질문에 알맞은 답을 완전한 문장으로 쓰시오.

Q. What caused the accident of people getting hurt in the fireworks festival?

→ ____________________

11 윗글의 밑줄 친 부분과 비슷한 의미가 되도록 빈칸에 알맞은 말을 주어진 철자로 시작하여 쓰시오.

→ I wish people would behave as r__________ c__________.

주관식 서술형 대비

12 화재 발생 시 기본적인 안전 수칙을 세 가지만 추가하여 쓰시오.

- When the fire alarm sounds, act immediately to ensure your safety.
- ____________________
- ____________________
- ____________________

2학기 중간고사

[1~6] 잘 듣고, 물음에 답하시오.

01. 대화를 듣고, 여자의 마지막 말에 이어질 남자의 응답으로 가장 적절한 것을 고르시오.

① Wow, what a brilliant idea!
② Can you pass me the salt, please?
③ I'm afraid it won't work this time.
④ That sounds wonderful. I'd love to.
⑤ I'd love to do you a favor, but I'm busy.

02. 다음을 듣고, 내용의 주제로 가장 적절한 것을 고르시오.

① effects and types of brain training
② misunderstandings about the brain power
③ importance of maintaining a healthy body
④ how to prevent memory disorder in old age
⑤ different types of approach to our daily problems

03. 대화를 듣고, 도표의 내용과 일치하지 않는 것을 고르시오.

① History movies are the most popular movies.
② The second most popular movies are movies.
③ Action movies are less popular than sci-fi movies.
④ *Interstellar* got five more votes than *The Admiral.*
⑤ The second most favorite movie was *Interstellar*.

04. 대화를 듣고, 설문조사의 결과와 일치하지 않는 것을 고르시오.

① 좋아하는 공연예술의 유형에 대한 설문조사이다.
② 설문에 참가한 인원은 교내 학생 200명이다.
③ 가장 인기 있는 공연예술 유형은 연주회이다.
④ 뮤지컬을 고른 학생의 비율은 35%이다.
⑤ 연주회나 뮤지컬 이외의 공연예술 선호도는 10% 이하다.

05. 다음 대화를 듣고, 여자의 마지막 말에 이어질 남자의 응답으로 가장 알맞은 것을 고르시오.

① Banning fruit? It is not good for our health.
② Is it? Actually, nobody seems to like smelly fruit.
③ They sell lots of smelly fruit on the street. It's awful.
④ I'm afraid you should keep yourself away from smelly fruit.
⑤ You mean like strong-smelling fruit? Thanks for telling me.

06. 다음을 듣고, 안내 방송 내용과 일치하지 않는 것을 고르시오.

① 화재가 감지된 곳은 건물 5층이다.
② 강당 오른쪽 문을 통해 신속히 빠져나가도록 한다.
③ 1층으로 내려오는 비상계단을 사용하지 않도록 한다.
④ 가급적 지면과 몸을 가까이 하여 신속히 이동한다.
⑤ 물티슈로 입과 코를 가리도록 한다.

07. 다음 글의 빈칸에 가장 알맞은 것은?

What word in the English language is always spelled incorrectly? If long and difficult words come to mind, take another guess. Any ideas? The answer is the word "incorrectly" itself! Although this may seem to be just a nonsense question, there is much more to it than meets the eye. The way most people approach this question shows that they tend to think "inside the box," which means thinking in a traditional way. Sometimes, however, this doesn't help you solve challenging problems. Try stepping outside your imaginary box and solve problems in a way ________________________. Let your creativity fly.

① you are quite used to
② you approach other problems
③ you've never thought about before
④ you challenge and overcome problems
⑤ you think of the answers to funny questions

08. 다음 글에서 전하고자 하는 메시지로 가장 알맞은 것은?

Here is question number one. A great golfer can only successfully hit the ball 3, 5, 7, or 11 yards. On the final hole of the game, he's on his last shot. Now, he has to make a 20-yard swing. If the ball doesn't directly go in, it will roll past the hole. What is the lowest number of swings that it would take for him to successfully put the ball in the hole? Here's a clue. What about thinking outside the concept of the golfer hitting in a straight direction — he can hit diagonally, as well. Did you get the answer? Is your answer four times? Actually, by swinging two times for 11 yards in a diagonal direction, the golfer could successfully finish the game!

① Change the direction of hitting the golf ball to swing well.
② To solve challenging problems, think beyond what you are used to.
③ Diagonal direction is preferred by most professional golfers.
④ It is unusual for golfers not to hit in a straight direction.
⑤ Finishing the game is always more important than winning it.

09. 다음 밑줄 친 ①~⑤ 중 어법상 어색한 것은?

You might remember the story of the egg of Columbus. People told Columbus that his discovery of the New World was not a big deal. So he asked them to do the very simple task of making an egg ① stand upright. After a while, everyone gave up. Clearly ② making his point, Columbus got the egg to stand on its end by tapping it on the table. When something like this ③ shows to you, it seems to be easy at first glance. However, the hard part is to be the first to think beyond ④ what you are used to. By thinking in a different way, you will find ⑤ yourself at a whole new level of creativity.

10. 다음 밑줄 친 ①~⑤의 it이 가리키는 것이 나머지와 다른 것은?

> Creative people daydream. Viewing daydreaming as a waste of time, noncreative people usually stop doing ① it when they find themselves exploring imaginative worlds. Having curiosity about ② it, however, a group of scientists studied the act of daydreaming and suggested that ③ it is a source of creativity. They also said that daydreaming can lead to sudden insights because ④ it is related to our ability to remember information. In addition, the scientists have found that a brain goes through the same process when it daydreams and when ⑤ it comes up with creative ideas.

[11-12] 다음 괄호 안의 (A)~(C) 에 들어갈 말이 바르게 연결된 것을 고르시오.

11.

> Do you know Frodo? He is a character from the movie *The Lord of the Rings*. After the movie was released, a great number of people visited New Zealand, (A)(which / where) the movie was filmed, reviving the nation's economy. It was so successful that this phenomenon got its own name – the "Frodo economy." The industries that involve this kind of cultural content (B)(are / is) called "creative industries." Creative industries are economic activities that are related to (C)(use / using) human knowledge and imagination.

① which – are – use
② where – is – use
③ which – is – use
④ where – are – using
⑤ which – is – using

12.

> The United States of America is another country (A)(where / whose) cultural attractions have earned major tourism dollars. Its greatest strength (B)(lays / lies) in its glamor. Hollywood studios create some of the most fantastic and dynamic movies in the world, (C)(made / making) use of their fine computer graphics. Not only that, people can enjoy Universal Studios, a theme park based on the famous movie industry.

① where – lays – made
② where – lies – made
③ whose – lies – made
④ whose – lays – making
⑤ whose – lies – making

[13-14] 다음 밑줄 친 ①~⑤ 중 어법상 어색한 것을 고르시오.

13.

> If you were asked to name one successful creative industry in Korea, what would you choose? It would be a hard question because there are so many. In fact, Korea's creative industries are reported to ① have been internationally successful for more than a decade. Nowadays, the economic impact of the "Korean Wave" ② is increasing by using new technology and good strategies. In particular, K-pop is gaining large profits ③ using advanced technologies. A new type of concert, a combination of K-pop and hologram technology, is quite profitable. In this concert the audience feels as if the singer ④ were actually on stage. ⑤ Attracting to its uniqueness, more and more K-pop fans flock to hologram concert halls.

14.

Marketing strategies are another key to the success of the Korean Wave. In the character industry, some characters are first ① introduced in an animated series before they are ② made into toys, theme parks, and other products. This way, the characters can expand into other fields once they prove ③ to be popular. Many companies also use a marketing strategy called product placement for indirect advertising on TV shows. These companies take advantage of the fact that Korean Wave fans abroad ④ paying close attention to what products Korean celebrities use on TV shows and try to purchase the same items as they ⑤ do.

15. 다음 글의 ①~⑤ 중 전체 흐름과 관계없는 문장은?

①Along with the U.K., the U.S.A., and Korea, many other countries around the world are promoting their creative industries. ② Bollywood in India, the largest movie industry in the world, is attracting more and more fans with its unique products. ③ China, a country with rich cultural and historical resources, is introducing policies to support its creative industries. ④ Spain is holding the Tomatina Festival, the world's biggest food fight, every year. ⑤ Japan has launched its own brand "Cool Japan" to promote Japanese creative industries such as animation and J-pop.

16. 다음 글의 밑줄 친 **the driver**의 어조로 가장 알맞은 것은?

"Please move over. This is an emergency!"

Even though an ambulance driver shouted this to the cars nearby and the siren was ringing, only some cars were slowly changing their lanes. According to traffic regulations, drivers must make way for emergency vehicles.

Pedestrians also caused difficulties. Several pedestrians who crossed the street at a red light blocked the way, delaying the ambulance's arrival.

When the ambulance finally arrived at the destination, the driver said, "It is very fortunate that we made it in time! But the people who didn't make way for us should be ashamed of themselves for having broken traffic laws."

① ashamed
② fanciful
③ sarcastic
④ annoyed
⑤ determined

17. 다음 괄호 안의 (A)~(C)에 들어갈 말이 바르게 연결된 것은?

Last Saturday, thousands of people flocked to a fireworks festival. Even though the fireworks were beautiful, some people's (A) (misbehavior / misunderstanding) made it hard to fully enjoy the beauty of the fireworks. Most people (B) (observed / violated) the law. However, some people pushed one another, hurting others. The police reported that more than a hundred people had been hurt and fourteen of them had been taken to hospital that day. (C) (Furthermore / Nonetheless), volunteer workers had a very hard time cleaning up the area as it was full of garbage. "I wish people cared more about others than just about themselves," said a volunteer worker.

① misbehavior – observed – Furthermore
② misbehavior – violated – Furthermore
③ misbehavior – observed – Nonetheless
④ misunderstanding – violated – Nonetheless
⑤ misunderstanding – observed – Nonetheless

[18-19] 다음 글을 읽고, 물음에 답하시오.

(A) On February 14th at 6:20 a.m., the 119 emergency center received an urgent call. "There is a fire in the building! And there are people inside!"

(B) The head officer of the emergency center said, "The neighbors' help and our team's quick response kept the fire from turning into a bigger disaster. We'd like to thank the neighbors for having helped the rescue."

(C) When the firefighters and the 119 rescue team arrived at the scene, the firefighters were not faced with the usual parking problem. The neighbors had already moved their cars ________________.

(D) When the rescue team arrived on the fifteenth floor, they saw some neighbors trying to put out the fire with fire extinguishers. With the neighbors' help, the 119 team rescued the family who had been trapped inside. The neighbor who called 119 said, "I was so relieved to see them safe."

18. 윗글의 (A)에 이어질 내용을 순서에 맞게 배열한 것으로 가장 알맞은 것은?

① (B) – (C) – (D)
② (B) – (D) – (C)
③ (C) – (B) – (D)
④ (C) – (D) – (B)
⑤ (D) – (B) – (C)

19. 윗글의 빈칸에 가장 알맞은 것은?

① to make space for the fire engine
② to give way to emergency vehicles
③ to escape from the fire immediately
④ to avoid a crash with the fire engine
⑤ to let the rescue team enter the building

20. 다음 글의 제목으로 가장 알맞은 것은?

Observing simple regulations, showing good manners in public, and helping neighbors in need can prevent a lot of tragic accidents. Each individual has the potential to contribute to making the world a better place. These days, more and more drivers are making way for emergency vehicles. Our manners are noticeably improving. There are many volunteers who are more than willing to help those in need.

Becoming a responsible citizen and making the community a better place are not difficult. Observe the law. Keep order. Care about others. In other words, just go back to basics.

① Basic Rules to Follow in the Emergency
② Simple Ways to Become a Responsible Citizen
③ The Cause of Irresponsibility of the Citizens
④ Fostering a Deep Sense of Justice in the Citizens
⑤ A Simple Guide to Recover Trust between Individuals

서술형

[21-22] 다음 빈칸에 알맞은 말을 〈보기〉의 단어들을 사용하여 완성하시오.

21.

Imagination is the ability to make a mental picture of something in your mind. What's so interesting about this ability, however, is that ______________ ______________ in your head. It can include all the five senses and feelings — so going well beyond what can be seen. Training your imagination to combine all the five senses and emotions will help you to strengthen your creativity.

보기 images / seeing / is / it / only / to / not / limited

22.

Have you ever frowned at thoughtless people who were talking loudly in the library? Have you ever felt threatened by people pushing you aside on the subway? Did you jaywalk on the way to school today? All of these are related to civic life. Responsible citizens form a safer, cleaner community ______________ ______________ and comfort.

보기 members/where/happiness/contribute/to /one/another's

서술형

23. 다음 괄호 안의 단어들을 사용하여 우리말을 영어로 쓰시오.

(1) 너는 교통 법규를 어긴 것에 관해 자신에게 부끄러워해야 한다. (ashamed / violate / traffic laws)

⊖ ______________

(2) 만약 내게 좀 더 많은 시간이 있다면, 이 도시에 좀 더 오래 머무를 텐데. (stay/ longer)

⊖ ______________

서술형

24. 다음 두 문장의 의미가 같도록 빈칸에 알맞은 말을 쓰시오.

(1) It seems that Mr. Han is an honest accountant.
= Mr. Han seems ______________
______________.

(2) As the king loved his wife so much, he wanted to be with her forever.
= ______________, the king wanted to be with her forever.

(3) It is known that the patient had been exposed to the disease while traveling.
= The patient is known ______________
______________.

논술형

25. 다음 조건에 맞게 주어진 질문에 대한 답을 3~4 문장으로 쓰시오.

Q. Volunteering is a great way to make a difference in your community. Write your own experience of volunteering for your community.

조건> 1. 자원봉사 활동의 내용과 본인의 역할이 드러나도록 쓸 것
2. 자원봉사 활동을 통해 느낀 점을 포함할 것

____
____
____
____
____

UNIT 9

Maps Used to the Max

내신체크 01 교과서 핵심 정리 > Go to p. 180

어휘 총정리

대본 정리
옛 지도와 현재 지도를 비교하며 지도가 삶에 미치는 영향에 관한 대화

본문 정리
지도의 발전 역사와 미래의 지도가 줄 수 있는 정보에 대해 이야기

내신체크 02 언어 기능별 집중 대비 > Go to p. 188

듣기와 말하기 대본별 필수 출제 유형

읽기 각 단락별 필수 점검 유형

언어 재료 및 쓰기 어휘 및 구문, 주관식 서술형 대비 문제

내신체크 03 수준별 단원 평가 > Go to p. 193

Basic 지식, 사실적 이해 대비 문제

Advanced 추론적 이해 및 감상, 주관식 서술형 대비 문제

교과서 핵심 정리

Words & Phrases

Listen and Speak ~ Into Real Life

- ☐ look up ~를 찾아보다
- ☐ route *n.* 경로, 길
- ☐ transportation *n.* 교통(수단), 수송(운송)
  cf. public transportation 대중교통(수단)
- ☐ reasonable* *adj.* 합리적인, 타당한
- ☐ spot *n.* 지점, 장소, 점 *cf.* tourist spot 관광지
- ☐ constantly *ad.* 계속해서, 끊임없이(=unceasingly)
- ☐ means *n.* 수단, 방법(=method)
- ☐ investigate* *v.* 탐사하다, 조사하다 (investigation *n.* 탐사)
- ☐ similarity *n.* 유사성, 비슷한 점 (similar *adj.* 비슷한)
- ☐ explore* *v.* 탐사하다, 탐험하다 (exploration *n.* 탐험)
- ☐ as well as ~: ~와 마찬가지로, ~뿐만 아니라
- ☐ category *n.* 범주, 카테고리 (categorize *v.* 범주에 넣다)
- ☐ accommodate* *v.* 공간을 제공하다, 수용하다
  (*n.* accommodation 숙박시설, 수용)
- ☐ lesser *adj.* 덜한, 더 적은

Read and Think

- ☐ navigation *n.* 운항, 항해 (navigate *v.* 항해하다)
- ☐ examine *v.* 살펴보다, 조사하다 (=scrutinize)
  n. examination 검사, 조사, 시험(=exam)
- ☐ geographical* *adj.* 지리의, 지리적인
  n. geography 지리(학) *cf.* geology 지질학
- ☐ distribute *v.* 배분하다, 나눠주다 (distribution *n.* 분배)
- ☐ clay* *n.* 진흙
- ☐ represent *v.* 나타내다, 상징하다 (representation *n.* 묘사)
- ☐ mythical* *adj.* 신화적인, 가공의 (myth *n.* 신화)
- ☐ illustrate *v.* 보여주다, 삽화를 넣다
  n. illustrator 삽화가
- ☐ compass *n.* 나침반
- ☐ projection* *n.* 투사, 투영 (project *v.* 투영하다)
- ☐ devise *v.* 고안하다, 창안하다
- ☐ commercial *adj.* 상업의, 상업적인 (commerce *n.* 상업) *cf.* commercial film (=CF) 광고, 상업적 영화
- ☐ contour* *n.* (사물의) 윤곽, 등고선
- ☐ widespread *adj.* 널리 퍼진, 광범위한
- ☐ map-making* *n.* 지도 제작
- ☐ observation* *n.* 관찰 (observe *v.* 관찰하다, 준수하다)
- ☐ hardware *n.* (컴퓨터) 하드웨어
- ☐ spatial *adj.* 공간의, 공간적인 (space *n.* 공간)
- ☐ be based on* ~에 기초하다, ~에 근간을 두다
- ☐ be composed of* ~로 구성되다 (=consist of)
- ☐ revolutionize *v.* 혁신하다, 대혁명을 일으키다
- ☐ prediction *n.* 예상, 예측 (predict *v.* 예상하다)
- ☐ drone *n.* 드론, 무인비행기
- ☐ augment* *v.* 증강하다, 강화하다 (augmentation *n.* 증강)
- ☐ rely on* ~에 의존하다 (reliance *n.* 의존)

Language Notes

- ☐ path* *n.* 경로, 길, (행동) 계획
- ☐ narrow *adj.* 좁은 (↔ wide)
- ☐ proof *n.* 증거 (prove *v.* 증명하다, 입증하다)
- ☐ memorable *adj.* 기억할 만한, 인상적인, 중요한

Write It Right

- ☐ parking lot* 주차장, 주차 구역
- ☐ construction *n.* 건설, 공사(construct *v.* 건설하다)
- ☐ period *n.* 기간
- ☐ notify* *v.* 공지하다, 알리다 (notification, notice *n.* 공지)
- ☐ inconvenience *n.* 불편함 (↔ convenience 편리)

Around the World

- ☐ coincide with* ~와 (우연히) 일치하다
  cf. What a coincidence! 이런 우연이 또 있나!
- ☐ numerical *adj.* 숫자상의
- ☐ region *n.* 지역 (regional *adj.* 지역의, 지역에 관한)
- ☐ statistics* *n.* 통계(학) (statistical *adj.* 통계적인)
- ☐ cooperation *n.* 협조, 협력 (cooperative *adj.* 협조적인)

☑ Check-Up

정답 P. 250

1 다음 문장의 빈칸에 알맞은 말을 〈보기〉에서 골라 넣으시오.

보기 >> look it up / as well as / based on / composed of / rely on

(1) The film is ____________ a short story by Thomas Mann.

(2) The audience was ____________ poor and old people.

(3) My homeroom teacher is witty ____________ intelligent.

(4) If you don't know what the word means, ____________ in the dictionary.

(5) It's natural that they ____________ their money and manpower during the election.

2 다음 뜻풀이에 해당하는 말을 주어진 철자로 시작하여 쓰시오.

(1) r ____________: to depend confidently

(2) s ____________: relating to the position, area, and size of things

(3) r ____________: to show or describe something or someone; to be a sign or symbol of something

(4) n ____________: the act of directing a ship, aircraft, etc. from one place to another

(5) a ____________: to increase the size or value of something by adding something to it

주관식 서술형

3 우리말에 맞게 괄호 안의 단어들을 사용하여 문장을 완성하시오.

(1) 초기 지도들은 손으로 그려지고 삽화가 넣어졌다.
The early maps were ______________________________.
(hand / by / drawn / and / illustrated)

(2) 우리는 어쩌면 증강현실 지도 안으로 걸어 들어갈 수 있을지도 모른다.
We might even be able to walk ______________________________.
(into / the / map / reality / augmented)

(3) 우리는 우리의 목적지로 가는 최단경로를 찾기 위해 GPS 내비게이션을 쓴다.
We use a GPS navigation to find ______________________________.
(to / our / destination / the / shortest / route)

(4) 항공사진의 광범위한 사용은 지도제작 기술에 엄청난 도약을 가져왔다.
The widespread use of air photos ______________________________.
(a / great / in / leap / map-making / brought / about / skills)

Tip

❶ 주요 숙어표현 익히기
witty 재치 있는
election 선거

❷ 영영사전풀이
confidently 자신있게, 확신을 갖고

❸ 핵심어휘를 사용한 영작
GPS (=Global Positioning System)
by hand 손으로, 수작업으로
bring about ~를 가져오다

교과서 핵심 정리

Dialogues & Monologue

Listen and Speak | *해석을 참조하여 빈칸에 알맞은 말을 쓰시오.

LISTEN IN

DIALOGUE 1

M: Excuse me.
W: Good morning. How can I help you?
M: I'd be interested to know about tourist spots in Seoul.
W: There are many beautiful places you can visit in Seoul. The nearest one is *Gyeongbokgung*. It's a famous __________.
M: Great! I've always wanted to visit a palace in Korea. **Can you tell me how to get there**?
W: Turn right at the next corner and walk __________ to the end of the block.
M: Okay. Let me write that down.
W: Then turn left and go straight for about 10 meters. **You'll see the palace on your right.**
M: Great! Thank you for your help.
W: You're welcome. Enjoy your tour!

남: 실례합니다.
여: 안녕하세요. 무엇을 도와드릴까요?
남: 서울의 관광 명소에 대해 알고 싶은데요.
여: 서울에는 방문할 아름다운 곳이 많아요. 가장 가까운 곳은 경복궁이에요. 유명한 궁전이죠.
남: 멋지네요. 항상 한국의 고궁을 방문하고 싶었어요. 거기에 가는 법을 알려주실 수 있나요?
여: 다음 모퉁이에서 우회전하시고 블록이 끝나는 지점까지 직진하세요.
남: 알겠습니다. 적을게요.
여: 그런 다음 좌회전하고 약 10미터 정도 직진하세요. 그러면 오른쪽에 고궁이 있어요.
남: 알겠어요. 도와줘서 감사해요.
여: 뭘요. 즐거운 여행 되세요.

대화상황
- 관광객에게 서울의 관광 명소에 대한 추천과 길 안내를 해주고 있다.

표현정리
- Can you tell me how to get there?: '목적지까지 가는 길을 알려달라'는 부탁의 표현이다.
- You'll see the palace on your right. : '오른쪽에 궁이 보일 거예요.'라는 뜻이다.

정답 palace / straight

DIALOGUE 2

W: Hey, how was your trip?
M: It was great except that my friends and I constantly argued over __________.
W: Oh, no. Didn't you have a map with you?
M: Of course we did. We just had different opinions about which was the fastest way.
W: **That happens quite frequently when** you are traveling with a lot of people.
M: I guess so. But arguing about the shortest __________ made us spend more time getting to places.
W: That's too bad. The journey to a place should be a fun part of traveling.
M: **I totally agree with you.** I'd be interested to know how people traveled thousands of years ago.
W: I'm sure traveling was more difficult then. **By the way, did you know that maps existed** even in the 6th century B.C.?
M: Really? That's quite a long time ago.
W: Yes. I'm surprised that they had the __________ to develop maps at that time.
M: Me, too.

여: 안녕. 여행은 어땠어?
남: 다 좋았는데 친구들이랑 길 찾는 것 때문에 계속 싸웠어.
여: 이런. 지도 안 갖고 갔어?
남: 물론 갖고 갔지. 다만 어느 길이 가장 빠른 길인지에 대해 의견이 달랐어.
여: 많은 사람들이랑 여행하다 보면 흔히 그런 일이 생기지.
남: 그런 것 같아. 하지만 최단 경로를 가지고 싸우다 보니 어떤 장소로 가는데 더 많은 시간이 걸렸어.
여: 참 아쉽다. 어떤 곳으로 가기까지의 여정이 여행의 재미있는 부분 중 하나인데.
남: 전적으로 동의해. 수천 년 전 사람들은 어떻게 여행했을지 궁금해.
여: 분명히 그때는 지금보다 더 힘들었겠지. 그런데 말이야, 너 기원전 6세기에도 지도가 있었다는 것 알고 있었어?
남: 정말? 꽤 오래 전인데.
여: 맞아. 그 당시에 지도를 개발할 수단이 있었다는 게 놀라워.
남: 나도 놀랍네.

대화상황
- 여행에서 목적지까지의 최단 경로를 찾으며 다니느라 친구들과 끊임없이 말다툼을 한 경험을 얘기하다가 지도의 역사에 대해 화제를 전환하고 있다.

표현정리
- That happens quite frequently when ~: '~할 때(하다보면) 흔히 생기는 일이다'라는 표현이다.
- I totally agree with you.: '상대방의 의견에 전적으로 동의한다'는 표현으로 I cannot agree more.라는 표현으로도 사용한다.
- By the way, did you know that maps existed ~: 'by the way'는 화제를 전환할 때 쓰는 표현으로 '그건 그렇고' 또는 '그런데'로 해석한다.

정답 directions / route / means

MONOLOGUE

W: Good morning, everyone. For next week's __________ class, we are going to examine the old maps of our city. We will also compare them with the city's latest maps. You'll be very surprised to see **how much the city's __________ have changed** in the past few decades. But before we investigate maps next week, today we are going to look at some old photos of our city. First, find some pictures of the city from the past on the Internet. Then, write down some similarities and differences between the city's past and present. **Lastly, I want you to share** what you found with the rest of the class. I'd be interested to know what kind of things you can learn just by looking at the photos.

여: 안녕하세요, 여러분. 다음 주 지리 수업에서 우리 도시의 오래된 지도를 조사하려고 합니다. 그리고 그 지도들을 우리 도시의 최신 지도들과도 비교해 볼 예정입니다. 도시의 모습이 지난 수십 년 동안 얼마나 많이 바뀌었는지 보면 무척 놀라게 될 겁니다. 하지만 다음 주에 지도들을 조사해보기 전에, 오늘 우리는 우리 도시의 과거 사진 몇 장을 먼저 보려고 합니다. 먼저, 인터넷에서 과거 우리 도시의 사진들을 찾아보세요. 그러고 나서 우리 도시의 과거와 현재의 유사점과 차이점을 적어보세요. 마지막으로, 자신이 찾은 것을 친구들과 공유해 보세요. 사진을 보는 것만으로도 여러분이 어떤 종류의 것들을 배울 수 있는지 궁금해집니다.

대화상황
- 도시의 옛 지도와 현재 지도를 비교해 보는 지리 수업에서 교사가 학생들에게 수업 중 과제를 제시하고 있는 상황이다.

표현정리
- You'll be very surprised to see how much the city's features have changed ~: 「의문사(how much) + 주어(the city's features) + 동사(have changed)」의 구문으로 된 간접의문문이 see의 목적어로 쓰였다.
- Lastly, I want you to share what you found ~: 「I want you to + 동사원형」은 상대방에게 가볍게 그러나 공손하게 명령하는 표현으로, 수업 중 교사의 지시 상황에 많이 쓰인다.

정답 geography / features

Into Real Life

M: Hello, and welcome to *All About Eating Out*. Today, we're going to explore good Korean restaurants in the neighborhood. Our first choice is *Seoulite*. This restaurant ________ over 70 different kinds of Korean food in 10 different categories. The menu includes popular dishes like *bulgogi* and *bibimbap* **as well as** some lesser known but equally good ones. This restaurant can comfortably ________ 200 guests. And it's always full! Let me talk to one of the customers waiting here.

M: Hello. What's your name?

W: I'm Sarah.

M: Sarah, I'm surprised that this huge restaurant can be so full of people! Are you a ________ customer here?

W: Yes. I've been coming here regularly since the restaurant opened three years ago.

M: I'd be interested to know why you like this place so much.

W: I can always enjoy a great variety of delicious Korean food at reasonable prices.

남: 안녕하세요, 외식의 모든 것에 오신 걸 환영합니다. 오늘 저희는 주변 지역에 있는 좋은 한국 식당들을 탐사하려고 합니다. 저희가 첫 번째로 선택한 곳은 서울라이트입니다. 이 식당은 10개의 범주에 70여 가지나 되는 한국 음식을 제공하고 있습니다. 식단에는 덜 알려졌으나 동일하게 맛있는 요리들뿐만 아니라 불고기와 비빔밥 같은 인기 있는 요리도 있습니다. 이 식당은 200명의 손님들을 넉넉히 수용할 수 있습니다. 또한 항상 만원입니다! 여기서 기다리고 있는 고객 한 분과 이야기를 나눠보겠습니다.

남: 안녕하세요? 이름이 어떻게 되나요?

여: Sarah입니다.

남: Sarah, 이렇게 큰 식당이 이렇게 사람들로 꽉 차 있는 걸 보고 놀랐는데요. 혹시 여기 단골이신가요?

여: 네. 저는 3년 전 이 식당이 개업한 이래 꾸준히 오고 있어요.

남: 이 식당을 왜 그렇게 좋아하는지 궁금한데요.

여: 항상 합리적인 가격에 엄청나게 다양한 맛있는 한국 음식들을 먹을 수 있어서죠.

담화주제
- 손님이 많고 인기 있는 한식당을 찾아가 손님과 그 식당의 장점에 대해 인터뷰하는 내용이다.

표현정리
- The menu includes popular dishes like *bulgogi* and *bibimbap* as well as some lesser known but equally good ones.: 「*A* as well as *B*」는 'B뿐 아니라 A도'라는 뜻이다. 여기서 good ones라는 것은 good dishes를 지칭하는 말로 대명사 one/ones는 불특정 명사를 대신할 때 쓰인다.
- ~ at reasonable prices: 가격에 대한 주관적 견해를 나타낼 때 비싼 경우는 expensive, 싼 경우는 cheap, 적절한 경우는 reasonable을 쓴다.

정답 offers / accommodate / regular

교과서 핵심 정리
Reading Comprehension

*해석을 참조하여 빈칸에 알맞은 말을 쓰거나 괄호에서 알맞은 말을 고르시오.

P.175 L.1~11

The History of Maps

What Is a Map?

Hannah is a college student who likes to hang out with her friends. She woke up late this morning, so she took a cab to get to class (on/ in) time. The cab driver used a GPS navigation system to find the __________ route to her school. For lunch, Hannah took her friends to one of the places she found through an online map of good restaurants. After her afternoon classes, she learned how she could get to the city library through an online map service. (On/In) her way to the library, a group of foreign tourists asked for directions to a famous park. Hannah used the subway map to give them __________. When she got home in the evening, she turned on her computer and examined several tourist information maps on the Internet for a family trip.

지도의 역사

지도는 무엇인가?

한나는 친구들과 어울리기를 좋아하는 대학생이다. 그녀는 오늘 아침 늦게 일어났고, 학교에 제 시간에 가기 위해 택시를 탔다. 택시 기사는 그녀의 학교로 가는 최단 경로를 찾기 위해 내비게이션을 사용했다. 점심을 먹으려고, 한나는 좋은 식당에 대한 온라인 지도를 통해 찾은 장소들 중 하나로 친구들을 데리고 갔다. 오후 수업이 끝난 후, 그녀는 온라인 지도 서비스를 통해 시립 도서관 가는 법을 배웠다. 도서관 가는 길에, 한 무리의 외국 관광객들이 그녀에게 한 유명한 공원으로 가는 길을 물었다. 한나는 그들에게 길을 가르쳐 주려고 지하철 지도를 사용했다. 저녁에 집에 왔을 때, 그녀는 컴퓨터를 켜서 가족 여행 갈 때 필요한 몇 가지 관광 정보 지도를 검색해 보았다.

단락요약
- 일상의 삶에서 지도가 얼마나 다방면에 쓰이는 지에 대해 한나의 하루를 통해 알아본다.

구문정리
- Hannah took her friends to one of the places she found through an online map~: the places와 she 사이에 관계대명사 which/that이 생략된 구문이다.
- On her way to the library, ~: 「on one's way to + 장소명사」는 '~로 가는 길에'라는 뜻의 부사구이다.

정답 on / shortest / On / directions

P.175 L.12~19

There is no denying the fact that maps are more than just pieces of paper with __________ information on them. They are a big part of people's daily lives. They are (used / using) for simple tasks like finding a good restaurant in the neighborhood, as well as for business, security, and medical and academic purposes. Ever since the development of maps, people have been using them to exchange __________, describe imaginary worlds, control their land, distribute their ideas, and (pass/ passed) their thoughts on to future generations. Let's take a look at the __________ of maps to see how they have been developed and used.

지도가 지리적 정보를 포함한 몇 장의 종이 그 이상이라는 사실은 부인할 수 없다. 지도는 우리의 일상적 삶의 큰 부분을 차지한다. 사업, 보안, 그리고 의료적이거나 학문적인 목적을 위해서만이 아니라 근처에 있는 좋은 식당을 찾는 간단한 일에서도 지도가 사용된다. 지도가 개발된 이후, 인간은 정보를 교환하거나 상상의 세계를 묘사하거나 자신들의 영토를 관리하거나 아이디어를 전파하거나 다음 세대에 자신들의 사상을 전달하기 위해 지도를 사용해 왔다. 지도가 어떻게 개발되고 사용되어 왔는지를 보기 위해 지도의 역사에 대해 살펴보자.

단락요약
- 지도의 다양한 쓰임에 대한 설명과 함께, 이어질 글이 지도의 역사에 대한 글임을 말하고 있다.

구문정리
- There is no denying the fact that maps are ~: 「there is no -ing」는 '~하는 것은 불가능하다, ~할 수 없다'라는 의미로 「we cannot + 동사원형」으로 바꾸어 표현할 수 있다.
- ~finding a good restaurant in the neighborhood, as well as for business, security, and medical and academic purposes.: '*A* as well as *B*'는 'B뿐만 아니라 A도'라는 뜻으로 'in addition to' 또는 'and also'와 비슷한 의미를 갖는다.

정답 geographical / used / information / pass / history

P.176 L.1~17

Early Maps

The earliest surviving map of the world is preserved on a clay tablet made in ancient Babylonia in about 6th century B.C. It represents the earth as a flat circle with oceans and mythical islands around it. The European maps made during the Middle Ages were heavily (influencing /influenced) by religious views.

초기의 지도들

현존하는 세계 최초의 지도는 진흙 판에 (새겨진 상태로) 보존되어 있는데 이것은 기원전 약 6세기에 고대 바빌로니아에서 만들어진 것이다. 이 지도에는 지구가 대양과 신화적 섬들에 둘러싸인 평평한 원으로 나타나 있다. 중세 시대에 만들어진 유럽의 지도들은 종교적 관점에 의해 크게 영향을 받았다.

For example, a map of the world created in the 6th century shows that the world is flat, and the heavens are shaped like a box with a curved lid. All of these early maps were, of course, drawn and illustrated by __________.

The invention of printing made maps much more widely __________ in the 15th century. Map-making skills advanced during the Age of Exploration in the 15th and 16th centuries. Coast lines, islands, rivers, and harbors were (described / describing) on maps. Compass lines and other navigation aids were included, and new map projections were devised. People at the time had the belief that such maps had great value for military and economic purposes and often treated them as national or commercial __________. Whole-world maps that resemble (that / those) of today began to appear in the early 16th century, following voyages by Columbus and others to the New World.

예를 들면, 6세기에 제작된 한 지도에는 세상은 평평하고 하늘은 구부러진 뚜껑을 가진 상자 같은 모양으로 나와 있다. 물론 이 초기 지도들은 모두 손으로 그려지고 삽화를 넣은 것이다.

15세기 인쇄술의 발달은 지도가 훨씬 더 광범위하게 사용될 수 있도록 해 주었다. 지도 제작 기술은 15세기와 16세기 탐험의 시대 동안에 발전했다. 해안선과 섬들과 강들과 항구들이 지도상에 묘사되어 있다. 컴퍼스 기본선들과 다른 내비게이션 도구들이 도입되었고 새로운 지도 투영법들이 고안되었다. 그 당시 사람들은 그러한 지도가 군사적 경제적 목적을 위한 엄청난 가치를 지니고 있다고 믿었고 그래서 지도를 국가적 또는 상업적 비밀로 취급했다. 오늘날의 지도와 비슷한 세계 지도는 16세기 초에 등장하기 시작했는데 이것은 신세계로 향했던 콜럼버스와 다른 여러 사람들의 항해에 잇따른 것이었다.

단락요약

- 현존하는 세계 최초의 지도로부터 16세기 지도에 이르기까지 지도에서 볼 수 있는 당대의 가치관 및 지도의 가치

구문정리

- made maps much more~: 「make+목적어+목적격보어」의 구문으로, '~를 ...하게 만들다'라는 뜻이다. 여기서 목적격 보어는 형용사인 (much more widely) available이다.
- ~maps that resemble those~ : '대명사 that(단수)/those(복수)'는 앞에 제시된 명사를 대신하는 것으로, 여기서는 maps가 복수이므로 복수 대명사 those로 받는다.
- ~ following voyages by Columbus and others to the New World.: 현재분사로 시작하는 분사구문으로서 추가적인 정보를 덧붙이고 있다. following은 의미상으로 and (they) followed와 비슷한 뜻이다.

정답 hand / available / described / secrets / those

P.177 L.1-23

Modern Maps

Maps became increasingly accurate and factual during the 17th, 18th, and 19th centuries with the application of scientific methods. First introduced in 1500, the bird's-eye view, or a view from a great __________, became widely used in the 17th and 18th centuries. Shading and contour lines were used to show geographical features in more __________. The widespread use of air photos following World War I brought about a great __________ in map-making skills. This technology revealed even the most remote places to the rest of the world. Modern map-making skills are based on a combination of ground observation and remote sensing.

The advancement of science and increased exchanges among people and countries have led to the development of more advanced technologies for making maps. No other technology has been as revolutionary as the geographic information system (GIS), which (merged / emerged) in the 1970s and 1980s. This system, which is composed of computer hardware, software, and digital information, makes it possible for people to create searches, analyze spatial information, and __________ map information on their own. It is used nowadays for maps, navigation systems, transportation information, analysis of business zones, and other purposes.

근대의 지도들

지도는 과학적 방법의 적용과 함께 17, 18 19세기 동안 점점 더 정확하고 사실적이 되었다. 1500년에 소개된 조감도 또는 굉장히 높은 곳에서 보는 법은 17세기와 18세기에 널리 쓰이게 되었다. 조금 더 자세히 지형적 특징을 나타내기 위해 음영과 등고선이 사용되었다. 1차 대전에 뒤따른 항공사진의 폭넓은 사용은 지도 제작 기술에 있어서 획기적인 도약을 가져왔다. 이 기술은 심지어 가장 멀리 떨어진 장소들까지도 전 세계에 드러내 주었다. 현대 지도제작 기술은 지상 관측과 원격계측탐지 기술의 결합에 기초를 두고 있다.

과학의 발전과 사람들과 국가 간 교류의 증가는 지도 제작에 있어서 더욱 진보된 기술의 발전을 이끌어내었다. 1970년대와 80년대에 등장한 지리정보체계(GIS)보다 더 혁명적인 것은 없었다. 컴퓨터 하드웨어와 소프트웨어 및 전자 정보로 구성된 이 체계는 사람들로 하여금 검색을 만들어내고 공간적 정보를 분석하며 스스로 지도 정보를 편집할 수 있도록 해주었다. 이것은 오늘날 지도들, 내비게이션 시스템, 교통 정보, 사업 지역에 대한 분석 및 여러 다른 목적들을 위해 쓰이고 있다.

단락요약

- 현대 지도의 역사와 지도 제작 기술의 발전의 바탕이 된 기술 과학에 대해 말하고 있다.

구문정리

- First introduced in~ : (Being) First introduced로 시작하는 분사구문으로 '분사구문에 주어가 없는 경우는 주절의 주어와 일치해서 생략한 것으로 보면 된다.
- The advancement of ~ have led to~: '*A* lead to *B*'는 'A가 (~를) B로 이끌다'또는 'A가 B를 이끌어내다'라는 뜻으로, 과학의 발전과 교류의 증가가 (~의) 발전을 이끌어 냈다'는 뜻이다.
- No other technology has been as revolutionary as the geographic information system ~: 부정어 no로 시작하여 비교의 표현인 as ~as가 오는 경우, 외양은 원급 비교이지만 의미는 최상급이다. 즉, 이 문장은 The geographic information system is the most revolutionary. 라는 최상급의 문장과 의미가 같다.

정답 height / detail / leap / emerged / edit

P.177 L.13~22

Sinjeungdonggukyeojiseungram

The map-making business in Korea began in full scale in the 15th century. While many books from that era contained detailed maps, no other geography book was as comprehensive as *Sinjeungdonggukyeojiseungram*. Published in 1530, the 55-volume book contains very detailed maps of the country such as *Paldochongdo*. There is no denying the fact that Ulleungdo and Dokdo are described as a part of Korea's __________.

신증동국여지승람

우리나라의 지도 제작 사업은 15세기에 본격적으로 시작되었다. 그 당시의 많은 책들이 자세한 지도들을 포함하고 있긴 하지만, 신증동국여지승람만큼 포괄적인 지도책은 없다. 1530년에 출판된 이 55권 분량의 책은 팔도총도와 같은 우리나라의 아주 세밀한 지도들을 포함하고 있다. 울릉도와 독도가 우리나라 영토의 일부로 나와 있다는 사실도 부인할 수 없다.

단락요약
- 조선시대 지리서인 신증동국여지승람에 대한 설명이다.

구문정리
- no other geography book was as comprehensive as ~: 부정 주어 no other geography book과 원급 비교 표현인 'as ~ as'가 같이 쓰이면 의미상으로는 최상급이 된다. (= ~was the most comprehensive geography book)
- There is no denying the fact that ~: 「there is no + -ing」 구문은 '~할 수 없다'라는 뜻이다. 따라서 주어진 구문은 Nobody can deny ~, It's impossible to deny ~ 등과 같은 의미이다. 여기 쓰인 that 절은 the fact와 동격인 절을 이끄는 접속사이다.

정답 territory

P.178 L.1~14

Future Maps

People have long been developing maps to graphically describe the place (which / where) we live. Scientists have been using the old ideas of maps for more creative functions to __________ the way we live. These days, people rely heavily on maps for business activities, national defense, the exploration of the human body, academic research, and the prediction of geographical changes. It won't be long before many companies have their products delivered to customers with the help of drones and robots __________ with GPS navigation systems. In the future, more advanced technology will be used for making maps. There is a great possibility that future maps will contain information about everything in physical space, including indoor areas. So you may get directions not only to a shopping center, but also to the inside of the stores. What is more, you might even be able to walk into an __________ reality map to go shopping. You'll be surprised to see (how / what) future maps will look like!

미래의 지도

사람들은 오랫동안 우리들이 살고 있는 장소를 지리적으로 묘사하기 위해 지도를 개발해왔다. 과학자들은 우리가 사는 방식을 개혁하기 위한 좀 더 창의적인 기능들을 위해 지도에 관한 오래된 아이디어들을 사용해 오고 있다. 요즈음, 사람들은 사업 활동, 국가적 방위, 인간 신체에 대한 탐구, 학문적 연구, 그리고 지리학적 변화에 대한 예측 등을 위한 목적으로 지도에 크게 의존하고 있다. 많은 회사들이 조만간에 GPS 내비게이션 시스템이 장착된 드론이나 로봇을 통해 고객들에게 상품을 전달하게 될 것이다. 미래에는 좀 더 진보된 기술이 지도 제작에 쓰이게 될 것이다. 미래의 지도는 내부적 영역을 포함해 물리적 공간 안에 있는 모든 것에 대한 정보를 포함할 확률이 높다. 따라서 여러분은 쇼핑센터로 가는 길 안내뿐 아니라 그 가게들 안에 들어가는 길까지 안내받을 지도 모른다. 더 나아가, 여러분은 쇼핑을 하러 증강 현실 속으로 걸어 들어갈 수 있게 될 지도 모른다. 미래의 지도가 어떨지 알게 되면 정말 놀랄 것이다.

단락요약
- 미래의 지도는 어떤 정보를 줄 수 있을지에 대한 전망을 얘기하고 있다.

구문정리
- People have long been developing maps ~: 「have been -ing」는 현재완료진행형으로서 '(계속) ~해오고 있는 중이다'라고 해석한다.
- ~the way we live. : '우리가 사는 방법'이라는 뜻으로, 선행사 the way는 관계부사 how를 생략한 채로 쓰인다.
- It won't be long before many companies have their products delivered ~: 「it won't be long before + 주어 + 동사」는 '~가 …하는데 오래 걸리지 않을 것이다'라는 뜻으로 '곧 (얼마 지나지 않아) ~할 것이다'와 같은 의미이다. 또한 여기 쓰인 동사 have는 사역동사로서 「have + 목적어 + 과거분사」 구문이며 '~를 …되도록 만들다/시키다'의 의미를 표현한다.
- What is more, you might even be able to walk ~: 'what is more'는 '더욱이' 또는 '게다가'라는 뜻으로 수준이 더 높아지거나 정도가 커지는 경우를 표현한다.

정답 where / revolutionize / equipped / augmented / what

Focus on Structure

P. 175 L.12 There is no denying **the fact** | **that** maps are more than just pieces of paper.
동격어구 동격절을 이끄는 접속사

⊖ idea, opinion, fact, belief 등에 대한 구체적인 내용을 나타내고자 할 때 that으로 시작하는 동격절을 사용한다. 이때 쓰인 접속사 that은 생략할 수 없다.

동격의 명사절을 이끄는 접속사 that	형용사절을 이끄는 관계대명사 that
that 이하의 절이 완전한 문장임	that 이하의 절이 불완전함 (주어나 목적어가 없음)
that 절은 명사절	that 절은 형용사절 (앞의 선행사를 수식)
I heard the news that she retired. 나는 그녀가 은퇴했다는 소식을 들었다. (the news = she retired)	I heard the news that she reported. 나는 그녀가 보도한 소식을 들었다. (the news ≠ she reported)

cf. 「There is no + 동명사(-ing)」는 '~할 수 없다' 또는 '~할 방법이 없다'라는 뜻으로 불가능함을 나타내며, 「We cannot + 동사원형」 또는 「It is impossible to + 동사원형」으로 바꾸어 표현할 수 있다.

ex. There is no telling how she will react. : 그녀가 어떻게 반응할지 알 수가 없다.
(= We cannot [Nobody can] tell how she will react.)

P. 177 L.14 **No other** technology has been **as** revolutionary | **as** the geographic information system.
S(부정어구) V as 형용사 / 부사 as 비교 대상

⊖ 부정어구(no one / nobody / nothing / no + (other) + 명사)가 주어로서 원급 비교 표현과 같이 쓰인 경우 최상급의 의미를 갖는다.

ex. **Nothing** is **as** important **as** health. (건강만큼 중요한 것은 없다. : 원급 비교)
= Health is **more important than** anything else. (건강은 다른 어떤 것보다 더 중요하다. : 비교급 비교)
= Health is **the most important** thing. (건강이 가장 중요한 것이다. : 최상급 비교)

☑ Check-Up

정답 P. 250

1 다음 괄호 안의 단어들을 바르게 배열하여 문장을 완성하시오.

(1) She hid the fact (she / with / anxiety / that / struggles)
(2) He argued (the / belief / against / that) vaccines caused autism.

2 다음 문장의 뜻이 같도록 빈칸에 알맞은 말을 쓰시오.

(1) No other man was as strong as Hercules.
= Hercules was stronger ______________________.
= Hercules was the ______________________.

(2) No other person in our class is as intelligent as Monica.
= Monica is more ______________________.
= Monica is the most ______________________.

Tip

❶ (1) the fact와 동격인 명사절
(2) the belief와 동격인 명사절
struggle with ~로 어려움을 겪다
autism 자폐증

❷ 부정어구가 주어인 원급 비교
= 비교급 ~than any (other)
= 최상급
Hercules 헤라클레스
intelligent 똑똑한, 지식이 많은

언어 기능별 집중 대비

Listen and Speak/Into Real Life

정답 P. 250

1 대화를 듣고, 남자가 알고 싶어 하는 것을 고르시오.

① He wants to know how the map application works.
② He wants to know what time the library closes today.
③ He wants to know what the fastest route to the museum is.
④ He wants to know why people use map applications every day.
⑤ He wants to know whether he can use the Internet in the library.

2 대화를 듣고, 여행 중 남자가 목적지까지 가는 데 더 많은 시간이 걸린 이유를 고르시오.

① He didn't have a map with him.
② He wanted to enjoy the journey itself.
③ He and his friends argued about which route to take.
④ He couldn't find the way to the destination easily.
⑤ He couldn't understand the language of the local people.

3 대화를 듣고, 내용과 일치하지 않는 것을 고르시오.

① The show host is introducing Seoulite to the audience.
② Seoulite serves only a few popular Korean dishes such as *Bibimbap*.
③ Seoulite is big enough to accommodate 200 people.
④ Sarah is waiting in line in Seoulite because it is full now.
⑤ Sarah has been a regular customer to Seoulite for about three years.

4 대화를 듣고, 물음에 답하시오.

(1) 다음 주 지리 수업의 주제로 가장 알맞은 것은?

① 지도 읽는 법에 대한 기초 지식 쌓기
② 학생들이 사는 지역의 자연적 특징 조사하기
③ 지도 작성법의 원리에 따라 향토지도 그리기
④ 학생들이 사는 지역의 옛 지도 비교 조사하기
⑤ 지도를 보며 길 찾는 법을 배우고 길안내 하기

(2) 다음 중 이번 시간 학생들이 해야 할 학습 활동으로 바르게 언급된 것은?

① 인터넷에서 유명한 도시들의 랜드마크 조사하기
② 인터넷에서 도시의 지도를 찾아 공책에 모사하기
③ 사는 도시의 역사 유적지를 주어진 지도에 표시하기
④ 지도상에 나타난 도시와 시골의 특징 비교하여 말하기
⑤ 사는 도시의 옛 사진을 찾아보고 현재와 과거 비교하기

Tip

❶ 글의 대의 파악하기
출처: Get Ready_1

❷ 이유 파악하기
출처: Listen In_Dialogue 2
destination 목적지
local people 지역 주민들

❸ 일치 / 불일치 파악하기
출처: Into Real Life_step 1
wait in line 줄서서 기다리다

❹ (1) 주제 파악하기
(2) 구체적인 정보 파악하기
출처: Listen In_Monologue

언어 기능별 집중 대비

Read and Think

정답 P. 251

Tip

1 다음 글의 주제로 가장 알맞은 것은?

Hannah is a college student who likes to hang out with her friends. She woke up late this morning, so she took a cab to get to class on time. The cab driver used a GPS navigation system to find the shortest route to her school. For lunch, Hannah took her friends to one of the places she found through an online map of good restaurants. After her afternoon classes, she learned how she could get to the city library through an online map service. On her way to the library, a group of foreign tourists asked for directions to a famous park. Hannah used the subway map to give them directions. When she got home in the evening, she turned on her computer and examined several tourist information maps on the Internet for a family trip.

① how to read maps ② limited types of maps
③ our daily use of maps ④ how to give directions
⑤ quality of map services

❶ 출처: P.175 L.3-11
유형: 주제 파악하기
limited 제한된
give directions 길을 안내하다

2 다음 글에서 지도의 사용 목적으로 직접적으로 언급되지 않은 것은?

There is no denying the fact that maps are more than just pieces of paper with geographical information on them. They are a big part of people's daily lives. They are used for simple tasks like finding a good restaurant in the neighborhood, as well as for business, security, and medical and academic purposes. Ever since the development of maps, people have been using them to exchange information, describe imaginary worlds, control their land, distribute their ideas, and pass their thoughts on to future generations. Let's take a look at the history of maps to see how they have been developed and used.

① 인근에 있는 좋은 식당 찾기 ② 다음 세대에 사상 전수하기
③ 자신들의 토지를 관리하기 ④ 인구 밀집 지역 파악하기
⑤ 상상의 세계를 묘사하기

❷ 출처: P.175 L.12-19
유형: 언급되지 않은 내용 찾기

3 다음 글의 밑줄 친 ①~⑤ 중 어법상 어색한 것은?

The earliest ① surviving map of the world is preserved on a clay tablet made in ancient Babylonia in about 6th century B.C. It ② represents the earth as a flat circle with oceans and mythical islands around it. The European maps ③ were made during the Middle Ages were heavily influenced by religious views. For example, a map of the world ④ created in the 6th century shows that the world is flat, and the heavens are shaped like a box with a curved lid. All of these early maps were, of course, ⑤ drawn and illustrated by hand.

❸ 출처: P.176 L. 2-8
유형: 문법성 판단하기

Tip

4 다음 글의 빈칸에 가장 알맞은 것은?

Map-making skills advanced during the Age of Exploration in the 15th and 16th centuries. Coast lines, islands, rivers, and harbors were described on maps. Compass lines and other navigation aids were included, and new map projections were devised. People at the time had the belief that such maps had great value for military and economic purposes and often treated them as ________________________.

① an interpreter of the nature
② national or commercial secrets
③ good records of natural environment
④ virtual observations made by the experts
⑤ priceless treasure of individual map-makers

❹ 출처: P.176 L.10-17
유형: 빈칸 추론하기
interpreter 통역가, 번역가
commercial 상업의, 상업적인
virtual 사실상의
priceless 아주 귀중한

5 다음 글의 (A)~(E) 중 아래의 문장이 들어가기에 가장 알맞은 곳은?

* This technology revealed even the most remote places to the rest of the world.

Maps became increasingly accurate and factual during the 17th, 18th, and 19th centuries with the application of scientific methods. (A) First introduced in 1500, the bird's-eye view, or a view from a great height, became widely used in the 17th and 18th centuries. (B) Shading and contour lines were used to show geographical features in more detail. (C) The widespread use of air photos following World War I brought about a great leap in map-making skills. (D) Modern map-making skills are based on a combination of ground observation and remote sensing. (E)

❺ 출처: P.177 L. 2-10
유형: 문장이 들어갈 위치 파악하기

6 다음 글의 (a)~(d)에 알맞은 말이 차례대로 연결된 것은?

The advancement of science and increased exchanges among people and countries have (a)(followed / led) to the development of more advanced technologies for making maps. No other technology has been (b)(as / more) revolutionary as the geographic information system (GIS), which emerged in the 1970s and 1980s. This system, which is (c)(composed / consisted) of computer hardware, software, and digital information, makes it possible for people (d)(creating / to create) searches, analyze spatial information, and edit map information on their own.

① followed — as — composed — creating
② led — more — consisted — to create
③ followed — more — consisted — creating
④ led — as — composed — to create
⑤ led — as — composed — creating

❻ 출처: P.177 L.11-22
유형: 어법과 어휘 적절성 파악하기

Tip

[7-8] 다음 글을 읽고, 물음에 답하시오.

(A) What is more, you might even be able to walk into an augmented reality map to go shopping. You'll be surprised to see what future maps will look like!

(B) In the future, more advanced technology will be used for making maps. There is a great possibility that future maps will contain information about everything in physical space, including indoor areas. So you may get directions not only to a shopping center, but also to the inside of the stores.

(C) These days, people rely heavily on maps for business activities, national defense, the exploration of the human body, academic research, and the prediction of geographical changes. It won't be long before many companies have their products delivered to customers with the help of drones and robots equipped with GPS navigation systems.

(D) People have long been developing maps to graphically describe the place where we live. Scientists have been using the old ideas of maps for more creative functions ____________________.

7-8 출처: P.178 L.2-12
유형: 7. 글의 순서 파악(논리적 흐름)
8. 빈칸 추론

7 윗글의 괄호 안의 (A)~(D) 를 순서대로 바르게 배열하시오.

8 윗글의 빈칸에 가장 알맞은 것은?

① to make more profit
② to live in an augmented reality
③ to sustain our materialized life
④ to prevent geographical changes
⑤ to revolutionize the way we live

[9-10] 다음 글을 읽고, 물음에 답하시오.

Sinjeungdonggukyeojiseungram

The map-making business in Korea began ___ⓐ___ full scale in the 15th century. While many books from that era contained detailed maps, no other geography book was as comprehensive as *Sinjeungdonggukyeojiseungram*. Published in 1530, the 55-volume book contains very detailed maps of the country such as *Paldochongdo*. There is no denying the fact that Ulleungdo and Dokdo are described ___ⓑ___ a part of Korea's territory.

9-10 출처: P.177
유형: 9. 알맞은 전치사
10. 세부 사항 파악

9 윗글의 ⓐ와 ⓑ에 알맞은 말을 쓰시오.

ⓐ ____________ ⓑ ____________

10 윗글의 내용과 일치하지 않는 것은?

① 신증동국여지승람의 출판 연도
② 신증동국여지승람의 책 권수
③ 신증동국여지승람의 제작 동기
④ 신증동국여지승람에 포함된 지도 이름
⑤ 신증동국여지승람에 독도가 표기되어있는지 여부

언어 기능별 집중 대비

Language Notes / Write It Right

정답 P.251

1 다음 우리말에 맞게 괄호 안의 말을 이용하여 문장을 완성하시오.

(1) 다른 어떤 영화도 타이타닉만큼 로맨틱하지는 못하다.
______________________ as Titanic. (romantic)

(2) 나는 기업들이 사회적 책임을 다해야 한다는 의견에 동의한다.
I agree with the opinion ______________________.
(social responsibilities)

(3) 다른 어떤 군인도 그만큼 용감하지는 않았다.
No other soldier ______________________. (brave)

(4) 소금물에 담그는 것보다 더 효과적인 것은 없는 것 같다.
Nothing seems to be ______________________. (soak in salt water)

(5) 흡연이 해롭다는 사실은 부인할 수 없다.
There is no denying the fact ______________________. (harmful)

Tip

❶ (1), (3), (4) 「부정주어 + 원급 비교 = 최상급」
(2) 동격의 that
(5) 동격절을 이끄는 접속사 that

2 다음 글을 읽고, 물음에 답하시오.

The invention of printing made maps much more widely available in the 15th century. Map-making skills advanced during the Age of Exploration in the 15th and 16th centuries. Coast lines, islands, rivers, and harbors were described on maps. Compass lines and other navigation aids were included, and new map projections were devised. People at the time had the belief that such maps had great value for military and economic purposes and often treated them as national or commercial secrets. Whole-world maps that resemble those of today began to appear in the early 16th century, following voyages by Columbus and others to the New World.

(1) What features were included in the maps in the 15th and the 16th centuries?

____

(2) Why were maps in the 16th century treated national and commercial secrets?

____

❷ (1) 세부 사항 파악
(2) 이유 파악

Basic

정답 P.251

1 대화를 듣고, 여자가 남자에게 권하는 것을 고르시오.

① 지도 앱 사용하여 길 찾기
② 사전 앱 사용하여 단어 찾기
③ 인터넷에서 도서관 정보 찾기
④ 앱을 이용한 메일 검색하기
⑤ 인터넷에서 교통 정보 찾기

2 대화를 듣고, 대화의 장소로 가장 알맞은 것을 고르시오.

① a tourist spot
② a famous palace
③ a travel agency
④ the subway station
⑤ the tourist information center

3 다음 대화의 밑줄 친 ① ~ ⑤ 중 문맥상 어색한 것은?

W: I'd be interested to know where I can buy clothes ① at reasonable prices in Busan.
M: ② Why don't you go to Seomyeon? It's not far from here.
W: Seomyeon? ③ Let me take a look at the subway map. Oh, I just have to take line number 1.
M: Right. ④ After getting on at Seomyeon Station, just check the tourist information map ⑤ to find shopping centers.

4 다음 단어의 뜻이 잘못 연결된 것은?

① spatial: 공간의
② augment: 약화시키다
③ distribute: 분배하다
④ illustrate: 삽화를 넣다
⑤ widespread: 널리 퍼진

5 다음 중 반의어끼리 연결된 것은?

① path – route
② rely – depend
③ investigate – explore
④ similarity – difference
⑤ reasonable – acceptable

6 다음 글의 빈칸에 알맞은 말을 〈보기〉의 단어들을 사용하여 쓰시오.

보기 as / was / comprehensive / other / no / book / geography

The map-making business in Korea began in full scale in the 15th century. While many books from that era contained detailed maps, ______________________ as *Sinjeungdonggukyeojiseungram*.

→ ______________________

7 다음 중 밑줄 친 부분의 우리말 해석이 잘못된 것은?

① If you come across a new word, look it up in the dictionary. (찾아보다)
② The band's performance was scheduled to coincide with the fireworks. (~와 일치하다)
③ Water is composed of hydrogen and oxygen. (분해되다)
④ Diet plays a great role in curing depression as well as bone problems. (~뿐만 아니라⋯도)
⑤ The success of this project relies on everyone making an effort. (~에 달려있다)

8 다음 영영풀이에 해당하는 단어로 알맞은 것은?

a device for finding direction with a needle that can move easily and that always points to magnetic north

① compass
② drone
③ calculator
④ cellphone
⑤ thermometer

9 다음 글의 내용과 일치하지 않는 것은?

The earliest surviving map of the world is preserved on a clay tablet made in ancient Babylonia in about 6th century B.C. It represents the earth as a flat circle with oceans and mythical islands around it. The European maps made during the Middle Ages were heavily influenced by religious views. For example, a map of the world created in the 6th century shows that the world is flat, and the heavens are shaped like a box with a curved lid. All of these early maps were, of course, drawn and illustrated by hand.

① World maps were not available in ancient Babylonia in the 6th century B.C.
② People in old times used clay tablets to draw maps.
③ The ancient Babylonians believed that the earth was surrounded with mythical islands.
④ The European people in the Middle Ages believed that the earth was flat.
⑤ The old maps show us what belief about the world the people had at that time.

10 다음 중 밑줄 친 부분의 용법이 나머지 넷과 다른 것은?

① She hid the fact <u>that</u> she had a child.
② These are examples of bias <u>that</u> women face at work.
③ The book changed my thought <u>that</u> people are selfish.
④ The research supports the idea <u>that</u> animals can be depressed.
⑤ I agree with the opinion <u>that</u> all students should take P.E. every day.

11 다음 중 〈보기〉의 문장과 의미가 같은 것은?

보기 No other subject is as interesting as geography.

① Geography is not an interesting subject.
② Geography is the most interesting subject.
③ Geography is interesting, but it is not a subject.
④ Geography is not as interesting as other subjects.
⑤ There is no subject that is not as interesting as geography.

12 다음 〈보기〉의 우리말과 같도록 괄호 안의 단어를 활용하여 빈칸에 알맞은 말을 쓰시오.

보기 그것은 지구가 우주의 중심이라는 믿음을 깨뜨렸다.

→ It destroyed ______________ of the universe. (center)

13 다음 〈보기〉의 우리말을 주어진 단어들을 사용하여 완성하시오.

보기 이 주차장만큼 많은 차를 수용할 수 있는 다른 주차장은 없다.
(this / one / can / as / many / cars / as / accommodate)

→ No other parking lot ______________.

수준별 단원평가

Advanced

정답 P. 252

[1~2] 다음 방송을 듣고, 물음에 답하시오.

1 대화의 내용과 일치하지 않는 것을 고르시오.

① The construction site is near the park.
② A community center will be built in the town.
③ The construction period is about two months long.
④ The construction will take place the day after tomorrow.
⑤ Suji has taken the route through the park from school to her house.

2 수지가 불만을 표현하는 사항을 고르시오.

① 공원 시설 이용이 어려워지는 것
② 공사에 대한 공지가 되지 않은 것
③ 지역에 불필요한 건물이 지어지는 것
④ 공사 기간이 예상한 것보다 길어지는 것
⑤ 주차 시설이 차량 대수에 비해 부족한 것

3 대화를 듣고, 여자가 자신이 보고 있는 지도를 신뢰하는 이유를 고르시오.

① 음식 비평 전문가가 제작했기 때문에
② 최첨단 기술을 사용하여 만들었기 때문에
③ 최근에 생긴 식당 정보를 수록했기 때문에
④ 지리 선생님이 추천해 주신 것이기 때문에
⑤ 설문조사의 결과를 충실히 반영했기 때문에

4 다음 글의 제목으로 가장 알맞은 것은?

There is no denying the fact that maps are more than just pieces of paper with geographical information on them. They are a big part of people's daily lives. They are used for simple tasks like finding a good restaurant in the neighborhood, as well as for business, security, and medical and academic purposes. Ever since the development of maps, people have been using them to exchange information, describe imaginary worlds, control their land, distribute their ideas, and pass their thoughts on to future generations. Let's take a look at the history of maps to see how they have been developed and used.

① The Roles of Maps
② The History of Maps
③ The Process of Map-making
④ The Necessity of Developing Maps
⑤ The Exchange of Ideas Through Maps

[5~6] 다음 글을 읽고, 물음에 답하시오.

The earliest surviving map of the world is preserved on a clay tablet made in ancient Babylonia in about 6th century B.C. It represents the earth as a flat circle with oceans and mythical islands around it. The European maps made during the Middle Ages were ① <u>heavily influenced</u> by religious views. For example, a map of the world created in the 6th century shows that the world is flat, and the heavens are shaped like a box with a curved lid. All of these early maps were, of course, drawn and ② <u>illustrated by hand</u>.

The invention of printing made maps much ③ <u>more widely available</u> in the 15th century. Map-making skills advanced during the Age of Exploration in the 15th and 16th centuries. Coast lines, islands, rivers, and harbors were described on maps. Compass lines and other navigation aids were included, and new map projections were devised. People at the time had the belief that such maps ④ <u>had little value</u> for military and economic purposes and often treated them as national or commercial secrets. Whole-world maps that resemble those of today began to appear in the early 16th century, ⑤ <u>following voyages</u> by Columbus and others to the New World.

5 What do the maps drawn in the 6th century B.C. in ancient Babylonia and those drawn in the Middle Ages in Europe have in common?

→ ______________________

6 윗글의 밑줄 친 ①~⑤ 중 문맥상 어색한 것을 찾아 바르게 고쳐 쓰시오.

__________ → __________

7 다음 〈보기〉의 단어들을 배열하여 아래 글의 내용을 포괄적인 한 문장으로 요약하시오.

보기 our / daily / maps / part / a / big / lives / are / of

Hannah is a college student who likes to hang out with her friends. She woke up late this morning, so she took a cab to get to class on time. The cab driver used a GPS navigation system to find the shortest route to her school. For lunch, Hannah took her friends to one of the places she found through an online map of good restaurants. After her afternoon classes, she learned how she could get to the city library through an online map service. On her way to the library, a group of foreign tourists asked for directions to a famous park. Hannah used the subway map to give them directions. When she got home in the evening, she turned on her computer and examined several tourist information maps on the Internet for a family trip.

⊖ ______________________________

8 다음 글을 요약할 때 빈칸에 알맞은 말을 쓰시오.

The advancement of science and increased exchanges among people and countries have led to the development of more advanced technologies for making maps. No other technology has been as revolutionary as the geographic information system (GIS), which emerged in the 1970s and 1980s. This system, which is composed of computer hardware, software, and digital information, makes it possible for people to create searches, analyze spatial information, and edit map information on their own. It is used nowadays for maps, navigation systems, transportation information, analysis of business zones, and other purposes.

⊖ Creating searches, analyzing spatial information, and editing map information on our own are made possible through ______________ ______________.

[9~10] 다음 글을 읽고, 물음에 답하시오.

People have long been developing maps to graphically describe the place where we live. Scientists have been using the old ideas of maps for more creative functions to revolutionize the way we live. (A) These days, people rely heavily on maps for business activities, national defense, the exploration of the human body, academic research, and the prediction of geographical changes. (B) It won't be long before many companies have their products delivered to customers with the help of drones and robots equipped with GPS navigation systems. (C) In the future, more advanced technology will be used for making maps. (D) So you may get directions not only to a shopping center, but also to the inside of the stores. (E) What is more, you might even be able to walk into an augmented reality map to go shopping. You'll be surprised to see what ______________ will look like!

9 윗글의 (A)~(E) 중 아래의 문장이 들어가기에 가장 알맞은 곳은?

There is a great possibility that future maps will contain information about everything in physical space, including indoor areas.

① (A) ② (B) ③ (C) ④ (D) ⑤ (E)

10 윗글의 빈칸에 알맞은 말을 두 단어로 쓰시오.

⊖ ______________________________

주관식 서술형 대비

11 다음 지시문을 잘 읽고 지리적으로 학교를 묘사하는 글을 3~4 문장으로 쓰시오.

Describe your school including the following information.

1. the location of the school, such as what it is near and how far most students travel to get to it
2. information about the school itself, such as what its name is and what it looks like.

⊖ ______________________________

____

UNIT 10

What Matters Most in Life

내신체크 01 교과서 핵심 정리 > Go to p. 198

 **어휘 총정리**

대본 정리
우리에게 소중한 것들에 관한 대화와 Tolstoy에 관한 강연

본문 정리
인생의 목표와 삶의 의미를 찾아가는 왕의 이야기

내신체크 02 언어 기능별 집중 대비 > Go to p. 208

듣기와 말하기 대본별 필수 출제 유형

 **읽기** 각 단락별 필수 점검 유형

언어 재료 및 쓰기 어휘 및 구문, 주관식 서술형 대비 문제

내신체크 03 수준별 단원 평가 > Go to p. 213

 **Basic** 지식, 사실적 이해 대비 문제

Advanced 추론적 이해 및 감상, 주관식 서술형 대비 문제

교과서 핵심 정리

Words & Phrases

Listen and Speak ~ Into Real Life

- ☐ favor* *n.* 호의, 부탁 *v.* 선호하다 (favorite *adj.* 좋아하는)
- ☐ stuff *n.* 물건, 물질, (종류를 막론한 어떤) 것
- ☐ help out (어려운 일을) 거들다, 도와주다
- ☐ recommend* *v.* 추천하다 (recommendation *n.* 추천)
- ☐ take action 행동(조치)을 취하다
- ☐ have a long face* 우울한 얼굴(표정)을 하다
- ☐ rude *adj.* 무례한 (↔ polite)
- ☐ easier said than done 행동보다 말이 쉽다 (=말은 쉽지만 행동은 어렵다)
- ☐ adapt* *v.* 적응시키다, 개작(번안)하다 (adaptation *n.* 적응) *cf.* adopt 채택하다, 입양하다 (adoption *n.* 채택)
- ☐ novelist *n.* 소설가
- ☐ literary* *adj.* 문학의 (literature *n.* 문학) *cf.* literate 글을 읽고 쓸 줄 아는 (↔ illiterate 문맹의)
- ☐ philosophical *adj.* 철학적인 (philosophy *n.* 철학)

Read and Think

- ☐ hermit *n.* 은자, 세속을 떠나 사는 사람
- ☐ bearded *adj.* 수염이 있는 (beard *n.* 수염)
- ☐ bodyguard *n.* 경호원, 호위병
- ☐ declare* *v.* 선언하다, 공포하다 (declaration *n.* 선언)
- ☐ common* *adj.* 평범한, 일반의, 공통의
- ☐ dig* *v.* 파다 채굴하다 (dig–dug–dug)
- ☐ deserve* *v.* ~할 만하다, ~할 가치가 있다
- ☐ spade *n.* 삽, 가래, (카드놀이에서의) 스페이드
- ☐ possess* *v.* 소유하다(=own) (possession *n.* 소유)
- ☐ lose oneself in* ~에 열중하다(=be absorbed in)
- ☐ unsteady *adj.* 불안정한, 휘청거리는 (↔ steady)
- ☐ unconscious* *adj.* 의식이 없는 (unconsciousness *n.*)
- ☐ wound* *n.* 상처 *v.* 부상을 입히다 (=injure)
- ☐ bleed *v.* 피를 흘리다 (blood *n.* 피)
- ☐ majesty *n.* 위엄, 장엄, 주권 *cf.* Your Majesty 폐하
- ☐ have mercy on* ~에게 자비를 베풀다
- ☐ weapon *n.* 무기 (=arms)
- ☐ forgive* *v.* 용서하다(forgive–forgave–forgiven) (forgiveness *n.* 용서)
- ☐ property* *n.* 재산, 소유물, 부동산
- ☐ take away 빼앗다, 없애다
- ☐ get back at ~에게 복수하다, 보복하다
- ☐ mean *v.* 의미하다 *n.* 수단 *adj.* 불친절한 *cf.* means 수단
- ☐ attack* *v.* 공격하다 *n.* 공격 (↔ defend 방어하다)
- ☐ make peace* 화해하다
- ☐ grant* *v.* 수여하다, 부여하다 *cf.* take something for granted ~를 당연히 여기다
- ☐ make up one's mind 다짐하다, 결정하다(=decide)

Language Notes

- ☐ specific* *adj.* 특정한, 구체적인
- ☐ occupy* *v.* 차지하다, 점령하다 *cf.* occupied 사용 중인 occupation 직업
- ☐ seek* *v.* 추구하다(seek–sought–sought)
- ☐ injury *n.* 부상 (injure *v.* 부상을 입히다)

Write It Right

- ☐ heading *n.* 표제, 제목
- ☐ encounter* *n.* (우연한) 만남 *v.* (우연히) 만나다
- ☐ remind* *v.* 상기시키다, 기억나게 해주다
- ☐ touching* *adj.* 감동적인, 감정적이 되게 하는

Around the World

- ☐ annual* *adj.* 일 년의, 해마다 하는 (=yearly)
- ☐ play *n.* 연극
- ☐ cast member 배역
- ☐ establish* *v.* 설립하다 (establishment *n.* 설립)

Check-Up

정답 P. 252

1 다음 문장의 빈칸에 알맞은 말을 〈보기〉에서 골라 넣으시오. (필요한 경우 형태를 바꾸시오.)

보기 >> take away / take action / help out
lose oneself in / have mercy on / get back at

(1) As soon as we get his decision, we will ___________.
(2) Paul ___________ his elderly neighbor ___________ by clearing the snow from her path.
(3) My mother didn't hear me because she ___________ the music.
(4) She appealed to the judge to ___________ her husband.
(5) I think he's trying to ___________ her for what she said in the meeting.
(6) I was a bit worried when an official came and ___________ my passport ___________.

Tip

❶ 주요 숙어표현 익히기
elderly 나이든
clear 치우다
appeal 호소하다

2 다음 뜻풀이에 해당하는 말을 주어진 철자로 시작하여 쓰시오.

(1) h___________: a person who lives alone and apart from the rest of society, especially for religious reasons
(2) d___________: to announce something clearly, firmly, publicly, or officially
(3) p___________: to have or own something, or to have a particular quality
(4) p___________: a thing or things belonging to someone
(5) g___________: to give or allow someone something, usually in an official way

❷ 영영사전풀이
publicly 공개적으로
officially 공식적으로

주관식 서술형

3 우리말에 맞게 괄호 안의 단어들을 사용하여 문장을 완성하시오.

(1) 그 개는 뼈를 숨기려고 구멍을 파고 있었다.
The dog was ______________________________________.
(a / hole / hide / its / bone / in / digging / to)

(2) 그 경찰관은 폭발 사고에서 심하게 부상을 입었다.
The police man was ______________________________________.
(the / explosion / in / wounded / badly)

(3) 그는 죽기 전에 자신의 아들과 화해하고 싶어 했다.
He wanted ______________________________________.
(his / son / with / before / he / died / peace / make / to)

(4) 나는 아직 어디로 가야할지 결정을 내리지 않았다.
I haven't ______________________________________.
(mind / yet / about / to / go / where / made / up / my)

❸ 핵심어휘를 사용한 영작
explosion 폭발
(explode v.)
badly 심하게, 몹시

교과서 핵심 정리

Dialogues & Monologue

Listen and Speak | *해석을 참조하여 빈칸에 알맞은 말을 쓰시오.

GET READY

1 W: **Can I ask you a favor?**
M: Of course. How can I help you?
W: I have to move some stuff this weekend, but I need a helper. Some of my stuff is way too __________.
M: It sounds like you need more than just one helper. Let's get Jinu, too.

여: 부탁 좀 들어줄래?
남: 물론이지. 뭘 도와줄까?
여: 이번 주말에 물건 좀 옮겨야 하는데 도와 줄 사람이 필요해. 내 물건 중 몇은 너무 무겁거든.
남: 한 사람 이상이 필요할 것 같은데. 진우에게도 도와달라고 하자.

2 W: **May I ask a favor of you?**
M: Of course. What do you need?
W: My computer keeps giving me the "blue screen of death."
M: Let me __________ and find out what the problem is.

여: 부탁 좀 들어줄래?
남: 물론이지. 무슨 도움이 필요한데?
여: 컴퓨터에 계속해서 "죽음의 블루 스크린"이 떠.
남: 한번 살펴보고 무슨 문제가 있나 볼게.

3 W: **Can you do me a favor?**
M: Sure. I'd be glad to help out.
W: Can you __________ me? I can't find my cell phone anywhere.
M: I'll call you now!

여: 부탁 좀 들어줄래?
남: 물론이지. 도와 줄 수 있으면 좋은 거지.
여: 나한테 전화 좀 걸어줄래? 내 휴대전화를 아무데서도 못찾겠어.
남: 지금 곧 걸게!

표현정리
- May / Can I ask you a favor? : 상대에게 부탁을 할 때 많이 쓰이는 표현이다. May I ask a favor of you? 또는 Can/Could you do me a favor?와 같은 표현으로도 쓸 수 있다.

정답 heavy / check / call

LISTEN IN

DIALOGUE 1

M: Hi, Leah. Can I ask you a favor?
W: Sure, how can I help you?
M: I know you like reading books. Can you __________ a good book?
W: No problem. What kind of books do you like to read?
M: I like to read novels.
W: What about this novel written by a French author?
M: Can you tell me more about it?
W: Hector, the main character, travels to find the answer to **the question of when the most important time in a person's life is.** Have you ever thought about this question before?
M: Well... I think the past is the most important **given the fact that we learn a lot from** __________ in the past.
W: Of course. History is important, but the past is the past.
M: What about the future? The future is full of excitement and __________.
W: The future is also important, but it hasn't come yet.
M: Oh, I see. You mean that the most important time is now because in the present we can take action.
W: Yes, you got it. That's what this book is about.

남: 안녕, Leah. 부탁 하나만 들어줄래?
여: 물론이지. 무슨 부탁인데?
남: 너 책읽기 좋아하는 거 알아. 좋은 책 한 권만 추천해 줄래?
여: 물론이지. 어떤 종류의 책을 읽고 싶은데?
남: 소설을 읽고 싶어.
여: 프랑스 작가가 쓴 이 소설은 어때?
남: 그 책에 대해 좀 더 알려줄래?
여: 남자 주인공인 Hector가 한 사람의 인생에서 가장 중요한 시간이 언제인지에 관한 물음에 대해 답을 찾는 여행을 해. 이 질문에 대해 이전에 생각해본 적 있니?
남: 글쎄... 과거의 경험에서 많은 걸 배우니까 과거가 가장 중요할 것 같은데.
여: 물론이야. 역사는 매우 중요해. 하지만 과거는 과거일 뿐이야.
남: 미래는 어때? 미래는 흥미진진한 것과 가능성으로 가득 차 있잖아.
여: 미래도 역시 중요하지만 아직 오지 않았어.
남: 아, 알겠다. 네 말은 현재 우리가 행동을 취할 수 있기 때문에 가장 중요한 시간은 지금이라는 말이지?
여: 그래, 맞았어. 바로 이 책이 그것에 관한 거야.

대화상황
- 삶에서 가장 중요한 시간이 언제인지에 관한 소설을 친구에게 추천하는 대화이다.

표현정리
- ~the question of when the most important time in a person's life is.: the question과 when 이하의 절은 동격이며(~라는 질문), when 이하의 의문문은 간접 의문문의 형식「의문사+주어+동사」을 취하고 있다.
- ~given the fact that we learn a lot from experience: 'given the fact that 절'은 '~라는 사실을 감안하면/고려하면'이라는 뜻이다.

정답 recommend/experience/possibilities

DIALOGUE 2

W: Edward, may I ask you a favor?
M: I'd be glad to help out. What is it?
W: I argued with my mom this morning. And I don't know what to do.
M: Oh, I was wondering why you **had such a long** __________. What happened exactly?
W: I went to bed late last night because I **was playing online games until late, which my mom really hates.** Then I got up late this morning. My mom was really mad at me as if I _______ a little girl.
M: Your mom was really mad at you because she worries about you.
W: I know, but I also know that I kept being ___________. This made her even angrier.
M: You should always remember that the most important person is the one closest to you.
W: I know. But **it's easier said than done.**
M: You'd better go and say sorry to her as soon as possible.
W: Okay, I will. Thank you for your advice.

여: Edward, 부탁 하나만 들어줄래?
남: 물론이지, 들어 주고말고. 뭔데?
여: 나 오늘 아침 우리 엄마랑 싸웠는데 어떻게 해야 할지 모르겠어.
남: 아, 안 그래도 왜 이렇게 우울한 표정인가 궁금했었어. 정확히 무슨 일이 있었던 거야?
여: 어젯밤에 엄마가 싫어하는 온라인 게임을 늦게까지 하다가 늦게 잠자리에 들었거든. 아침에 늦게 일어나니까 엄마가 마치 내가 어린 애인 것처럼 나에게 화를 내시잖아.
남: 엄마는 네 걱정이 돼서 화가 나신 거야.
여: 알아. 하지만 나도 계속 엄마에게 못되게 굴었어. 그래서 엄마는 더 화가 나셨고.
남: 너랑 가장 가까운 사람이 가장 중요한 사람이라는 거 너 기억해야해.
여: 알아. 하지만 말하는 건 쉬운데 행동으로 하는 건 어렵더라고.
남: 가능하면 빨리 가서 엄마한테 사과 하는게 좋을 것 같아.
여: 알았어. 그럴게. 충고 고마워.

대화상황
- 엄마와 심하게 싸운 친구에게 가장 가까이 있는 사람이 가장 소중한 사람임을 얘기하며 먼저 사과하라고 충고하고 있다.

표현정리
- I was wondering why you had such a long face.: have a long face는 '우울하게 보이다'라는 의미로 'look sad/unhappy'와 같은 뜻이다.
- I was playing online games until late, which my mom really hates.: 콤마 다음에 위치한 which는 앞 문장 전체를 선행사로 하는 계속적 용법의 관계대명사이다. 즉 '늦게까지 온라인 게임을 하는 것'이 관계대명사 which의 선행사이다.
- ~ it's easier said than done.: 「easier *A* than *B*」는 'B보다 A가 쉽다'또는 'A는 쉽지만 B는 어렵다'라는 의미로, 여기서는 말하는 건 쉽지만 행동으로 옮기는 것은 어렵다는 뜻으로 쓰였다.

정답 face / were / rude

DIALOGUE 3

W: Chris! You're late again.
M: Sorry, I'm late.
W: What happened this time?
M: I met Edward on my way here and **stopped to talk** with him for a second. I didn't know that I would be late for this meeting.
W: Oh, Chris. **It sounds like you don't know when to do what with whom.**
M: You're right, Seonmi. I often get __________ when deciding what I need to do first, and then I make mistakes.
W: You'd better __________ with the plan you made in the first place. Otherwise, you'll get behind your schedule.
M: Thanks, Seonmi. I'll keep that in mind.
W: So let's start working on this team project. If we don't, we're not going to be able to meet the due date.
M: Okay. Let's get started. And thank you for your advice.

여: Chris! 너 또 늦었어.
남: 미안, 늦어서.
여: 이번엔 무슨 일이 있었어?
남: 여기 오는 길에 Edward를 만나서 잠깐 얘기하다가 왔는데 이 모임에 늦을 줄은 몰랐어.
여: 이런, Chris. 너는 언제 무엇을 누구랑 할지 모르는 것 같아.
남: 네 말이 맞아, 선미야. 난 종종 내가 먼저 해야 할 일을 결정할 때 헷갈려서 실수를 하고 말아.
여: 넌 네가 처음 정한 계획을 고수하는 게 좋을 것 같아. 안 그러면, 넌 계획에 뒤쳐지게 될 거야.
남: 고마워, 선미야. 명심할게.
여: 자, 그럼 이 팀 프로젝트 시작하자. 지금 시작하지 않으면 정해진 날짜에 못 맞추게 될지도 몰라.
남: 알았어. 시작하자. 그리고 충고해줘서 고마워.

대화상황
- 회의 시간에 늦은 친구에게 계획한 우선순위에 따라 생활할 것을 충고하는 대화이다.

표현정리
- ~and stopped to talk with him for a second.: 「stop + to부정사」는 '~하기 위해 하던 행동을 멈추다'라는 의미이고, 「stop + 동명사」는 '~하는 것을 멈추다/그만두다'라는 뜻이다.
- It sounds like you don't know when to do what with whom.: It sounds like~는 상대방에게 자신의 생각이나 느낌을 다소 완곡하게 표현할 때 쓴다. you don't know when to do what with whom은 when to do와 what to do와 whom to do with를 한꺼번에 연결한 표현으로, '언제 해야 할지, 무엇을 해야 할지, 누구와 해야 할지'를 의미한다.

정답 confused / stick

Into Real Life

M: Good morning, students. Today we are going to read a great play that was adapted from a story written by Leo Tolstoy. So we need to learn about its author. **As you may know**, Leo Tolstoy was a Russian novelist, regarded as one of the greatest novelists of all time. He is best **known for** *War and Peace* and *Anna Karenina*.

W: **I've heard of** those. They sound like great novels.

M: Yes, he first achieved literary fame in his twenties.

W: May I ask a question?

M: Sure. What is it?

W: Did he write any plays or short stories?

M: That's a good question. He wrote plays and several philosophical short stories. Until his __________ from a serious disease at the age of 82, Tolstoy consistently attempted to find the truth __________ his works and in his real life.

남: 안녕하세요, 학생 여러분. 오늘 우리는 Leo Tolstoy가 쓴 이야기를 각색해서 만든 위대한 극본을 읽을 거예요. 따라서 작가에 대해 배울 필요가 있어요. 여러분도 알다시피, Leo Tolstoy는 전 시대에 걸쳐 가장 위대한 소설가들 중 한 명으로 여겨지는 러시아의 작가예요. 전쟁과 평화, 안나 카레니나로 가장 잘 알려져 있는 작가이고요.

여: 저도 그 소설들 들어봤어요. 훌륭한 소설들 같아요.

남: 맞아요. Tolstoy는 20대에 처음으로 문학적 명성을 얻었죠.

여: 질문해도 될까요?

남: 물론이죠. 무슨 질문이죠?

여: Tolstoy가 극본이나 단편 소설도 썼나요?

남: 좋은 질문입니다. Tolstoy는 극본도 썼고 몇 편의 철학적인 단편 소설도 썼어요. 82세의 나이에 심각한 질병으로 죽음을 맞이하기 전까지, 그는 지속적으로 자신의 작품 활동과 자신의 실제 삶에서 진리를 찾으려고 노력했어요.

대화상황
- Tolstoy의 작품을 읽기 전 작가인 Tolstoy에 관해 설명하고 있다.

표현정리
- As you may know, ~: 일반적으로 잘 알려진 사실을 말하고자 할 때 많이 쓰는 표현이다.
- He is best known for ~: 「be known for」는 '~로 알려지다'라는 의미로서 알려지게 된 계기를 말한다. 여기서는 be best known for의 최상급 형태로 쓰였다. 한편 「be known as」는 '~로서 알려지다'라는 의미이고, 「be known to」는 '~에게 알려지다'라는 뜻이다.
- I've heard of those ~: hear of는 '~에 대해 들어보다'라는 의미로, 여기서는 「have heard of~」의 형태로 들어본 경험을 말하고 있다.

정답 death / through

Check Your Progress

W: Chris, are you going to give your presentation next week?

M: Yes. It is my turn to present for the project work.

W: Are you ready for your presentation?

M: Well... I'm working on it.

W: I know you've got a really __________ schedule.

M: No problem. I'm going to complete the project on time. By the way, may I ask you a __________ ?

W: Sure. What is it?

M: I decided to change my presentation topic to tsunamis.

W: That sounds great! That's a really interesting topic.

M: I searched on the Internet for more information, but actually, I couldn't find much information on tsunamis.

W: **It sounds like you need some help**. Don't worry. I think I can help you with your new topic.

M: Thank you, Ms. Smith.

여: Chris, 너 다음 주에 발표 할 거니?

남: 네. 제가 프로젝트 활동에 대한 발표를 할 차례예요.

여: 너 발표 준비는 된 거니?

남: 음… 아직 준비하고 있는 중이에요.

여: 내가 알기로 너 스케줄이 엄청 빡빡한 것 같은데.

남: 걱정 마세요. 제 시간에 프로젝트 완수할 거예요. 그런데, 부탁 하나만 들어주실래요?

여: 물론이지. 뭔데?

남: 제가 발표 주제를 쓰나미로 바꾸려고 결정했거든요.

여: 그것 참 멋지겠다! 그건 정말 재미있는 주제야.

남: 좀 더 많은 정보를 찾으려고 인터넷을 검색했는데 사실 쓰나미에 대해 많은 정보를 못 찾았어요.

여: 도움이 좀 필요한 것 같구나. 그 새로운 주제에 대해 내가 좀 도와줄 수 있을 것 같아.

남: 고마워요, Smith 선생님.

대화상황
- 발표할 주제를 바꾸고 자료를 검색하다가 선생님에게 도움을 요청하고 있는 대화이다.

표현정리
- It sounds like you need some help.: You need some help.라고 단정지어 말하는 것이 아니라 It sounds like you need some help.라고 말함으로써 '~한 것 같다'라는 의미의 자신의 생각이나 느낌을 전달한다.

정답 tight / favor

교과서 핵심 정리

Reading Comprehension

*해석을 참조하여 빈칸에 알맞은 말을 쓰거나 괄호에서 알맞은 말을 고르시오.

P.195 L.4~12

The Three Most Important Things in Life

Characters : King, Hermit, Bearded Man, Doctor, Bodyguard

A certain king wanted to know the answers to three key questions: First, what is the most important thing to accomplish in life? Second, when should he accomplish the most important thing? And third, who are the right people to help him accomplish that task? He thought that if he knew the answers to these questions, he (will / would) never fail in anything. So he ________ throughout his kingdom that he would give a large reward to anyone who could answer the three questions. However, no one in the country was able to give him (satisfied / satisfying) answers. The king then decided to consult a wise hermit. The hermit only received common people, so the king visited him (wearing / to wear) simple clothes.

등장인물: 왕, 은자, 수염 난 사람, 의사, 경호원

한 어떤 왕이 세 가지 중요한 질문에 대한 답을 알고 싶었다. 첫째, 인생에서 성취해야 할 가장 중요한 것은 무엇인가? 둘째, 그 가장 중요한 것을 언제 성취해야 하는 것인가? 셋째, 그 일을 성취하는 것을 도와 줄 적합한 사람은 누구인가? 그는 만약 이 세 가지 질문에 대한 답을 알 수 있다면 그가 어떤 일에서도 절대 실패하지 않을 것이라고 생각했다. 그래서 그는 자신의 왕국 전체에 이 세 가지 질문에 답할 수 있는 사람에게 큰 포상을 할 것이라고 공표했다. 하지만, 그 나라의 어느 누구도 왕에게 만족할 만한 답을 하지 못했다. 그러자 이 왕은 현명한 은자에게 자문을 구하기로 결심했다. 그 은자는 평민들만 받아주었기 때문에 왕은 소박한 옷을 입고 그를 방문했다.

단락요약
- 왕은 인생에서 가장 중요한 일, 그 일을 할 시기, 그 일을 하는 것을 도울 적합한 사람이 누군지에 대한 답을 얻고자 은자를 찾아가기로 한다.

구문정리
- He thought that if he knew the answers to these questions, he would never fail in anything.: 가정법은 간접 화법으로 바꿀 때 시제의 영향을 받지 않는다. 따라서 이 문장은 He thought, "If I knew the answers to these questions, I would never fail in anything."을 간접 화법으로 바꾼 문장이다.
- he declared throughout his kingdom that he would give ~: 간접 화법으로 바뀌면서 시제일치(declared – would)를 이룬다. (= he said, "I will give ~)

정답 would / declared / satisfying / wearing

P.196 L.1~12

Act 1, Scene 1

The king meets the hermit, who is digging the ground in front of his hut. Glancing at the king, the hermit greets him and goes on digging.

King: *(Approaching)* I have come to you, wise hermit, to ask you to answer three questions: What is the most important thing that deserves my attention? When is the right time to do that important thing? And who are the people I need most to help me accomplish it?

(Without saying a word, the hermit continues ________ as if he had heard nothing.)

King: You look tired. *(Reaching for the hermit)* Let me take the spade and work (while / awhile) for you.

Hermit: Thanks!

(Giving the spade to the king, he sits down on the ground.)

1막 1장

왕은 자신의 오두막 앞에서 땅을 일구고 있는 은자를 만난다. 왕을 흘끗 보고서 은자는 인사를 하더니 계속 땅을 일군다.

왕: (다가서며) 현명한 은자여, 저는 세 가지 질문을 하기 위해서 왔습니다. 제가 주목해야 할 가치가 있는 가장 중요한 것은 무엇인지요? 그 중요한 것을 해야 할 적절한 때는 언제입니까? 그 일을 성취하기 위해 저에게 필요한 사람들은 누구인지요?

(아무 말도 하지 않고 은자는 마치 아무 말도 못 들었던 것처럼 계속 땅만 일군다.)

왕: 피곤해 보이시는 군요. (은자에게 다가가며) 제가 삽을 가지고 당신을 위해 잠시 일을 하겠습니다.

은자: 고맙습니다!

(삽을 왕에게 주고 그는 땅에 앉는다.)

단락요약
- 은자를 찾아간 왕은 은자가 하던 땅 일구는 일을 대신하며 자신의 질문에 대답해 주기를 기다리고 있다.

구문정리
- Glancing at the king, the hermit gives ~ : 분사구문으로 시작되는 구문으로서 Glancing의 주체는 the hermit이다.
- ~ the hermit continues digging as if he had heard nothing: 「as if + 주어 + had p.p.」구문은 '마치 ~했던 것처럼'이라는 뜻이다.

정답 digging / awhile

P.196 L.13~21

Act 1, Scene 2

Hermit: *(Watching the king digging the ground)* To be honest, I know who you are. I think you __________ everything you want. Are you still not satisfied?

King: Of course not!

Hermit: *(Losing himself in thought for a while and rising from his seat)* Now rest awhile and let me work a bit. I have to get this job done.

(Not giving him the spade, the king continues to dig. The sun begins to set behind the trees.)

King: I came to you, wise man, for answers to my questions. If you can give me (any/none), tell me so, and I will return home.

1막 2장

은자: (왕이 땅을 일구는 것을 보면서) 솔직히 말하면, 난 당신이 누군지 알고 있습니다. 당신은 원하는 것을 다 소유하고 있는 것 같은데 아직도 만족하지 못 하시는 건가요?

왕: 물론 아닙니다!

은자: (잠시 생각에 잠기더니 앉은 자리에서 일어서며) 이제 좀 쉬시죠. 제가 좀 일하겠습니다. 이 일을 끝내야 하거든요.

(삽을 주지 않고 왕은 계속 땅을 일군다. 해가 나무 뒤로 기울기 시작한다.)

왕: 현자여, 난 당신에게 제 질문들에 대한 답을 얻기 위해 왔소. 답을 줄 수 없다면 그렇다고 말해 주시오. 그러면 집으로 돌아가겠습니다.

단락요약
- 왕은 은자가 자신의 질문에 대답해주기를 기다렸으나 아무 답이 없자 포기하고 돌아가려 하고 있다.

구문정리
- Watching the king digging the ground ~ : '지각동사(watching)+목적어(the king)+현재분사(digging)'의 구문이다.

정답 possess / none

P.197 L.1~16

Act 2, Scene 1

A sound is (hearing / heard) in the woods. A bearded man appears.

Hermit: Here comes someone walking. Let us see who it is.

Bearded man: *(Walking unsteadily, in an __________ voice)* Help me, please. Have mercy on me. *(Falling down on the ground unconsciously)*

King: *(Finding a large __________ on the man's stomach)* What happened to you? Come on! Are you okay? *(Putting his hand on the unconscious man's neck to see if he is alive)* (Judging/Judged) from your wound, I need to do something to stop the bleeding! Doctor! Doctor! *(Carrying the wounded man into the hut)*

Act 2, Scene 2

In the hut, a doctor is __________ for the bearded man who fell down on the ground unconscious.

King: Is he going to make it?

Doctor: I am not sure, Your Majesty.

King: I wonder who this man is. Anyway, there's no time for that now. You must do your best to __________ his life.

Doctor: Yes, Your Majesty. I will do my best.

2막 1장

숲에서 어떤 소리가 들린다. 수염 난 남자가 등장한다.

은자: 누군가가 여기로 걸어오는군요. 누군지 봅시다.

수염 난 남자: (위태롭게 걸어오며 다급한 목소리로) 제발 도와주세요. 자비를 베풀어 주세요. (의식을 잃고 땅에 쓰러진다.)

왕: (남자의 배에 난 큰 상처를 발견하고) 무슨 일이오? 이봐요! 괜찮아요? (남자가 살아있는지 보려고 자신의 손을 의식을 잃은 남자의 목에다 대어보며) 부상당한 걸로 보건데 지혈을 하기 위해 뭔가 해야 할 것 같군. 의사! 의사! (부상당한 남자를 오두막으로 옮긴다.)

2막 2장

오두막 안에서 의사가 의식을 잃고 쓰러졌던 수염 난 남자를 돌보고 있다.

왕: 살 수 있을 것 같은가?

의사: 잘 모르겠습니다, 폐하.

왕: 이 자가 누군지 궁금하군. 어쨌든, 지금 그걸 알아볼 시간은 없고. 이 자의 목숨을 살리기 위해 최선을 다하게.

의사: 예, 폐하. 최선을 다하겠습니다.

단락요약
- 정체는 모르지만 배에 부상을 당해 의식을 잃고 쓰러진 남자를 살리기 위해 최선을 다하라고 왕이 의사에게 명령하고 있다.

구문정리
- ~ to see if he is alive: 접속사 if는 '~인지 아닌지'라는 의미로 whether와 바꿔 쓸 수 있다.
- Judging from your wound, I need ~ : judging from ~은 '~로 판단해 보건데'라는 뜻으로 독립 분사구문으로 쓰인다.
- Is he going to make it? : make it은 여기서 '버텨내다' 또는 '힘든 상태에서 살아남다'라는 뜻으로 쓰였다.
- I wonder who this man is.: 'Who is this man?'이라는 의문문이 I wonder의 목적어로 쓰이면서 간접의문문의 순서 「who(의문사) + this man(주어) + is(동사)」의 순서로 바뀌었다.

정답 heard / urgent / wound / Judging / caring / save

P.198 L.1-25

Act 3, Scene 1

The hermit wakes up early the next morning and leaves for work. After the hermit is gone, the king's bodyguards rush to the king.

Bodyguard: *(Rushing to the king, in an urgent voice)* Your Majesty, I'm ________ this place is dangerous for you.

King: Why?

Bodyguard: Last night, we found a strange man (carried / carrying) a weapon. I think we had better leave this place as soon as possible.

King: Okay. I'll return to my palace after I meet the hermit.

Act 3, Scene 2

The king sees the bearded man awake.

Bearded man: *(In a weak voice)* Forgive me!

King: Are you okay now?

Bearded man: Forgive me!

King: What do you mean? I have nothing to forgive you for.

Bearded man: Yes, Your Majesty. You do not know me, but I know you. Seeing that you took away my ________ and put my brother to death, I was an enemy of yours who sought to get back at you. Knowing you had gone alone to see the hermit, I planned to kill you on your way back. But on my way here, I came upon your soldiers, who wounded me. I would not have survived if you had not saved my life. If you allow it, I will serve you as your most faithful ________. Forgive me, Your Majesty!

King: I forgive you! And I also accept you as one of my men.

3막 1장

은자는 다음 날 아침 일찍 일어나 일하러 나간다. 은자가 나가자 왕의 호위병이 왕에게 급히 온다.

호위병: (왕에게 급히 다가오며 다급한 목소리로) 폐하, 이 곳은 폐하께 위험한 장소인 것 같습니다.

왕: 어째서인가?

호위병: 어젯밤에 무기를 가지고 다니는 수상한 자를 발견했습니다. 가급적 빨리 이곳을 떠나는 게 좋을 것 같습니다.

왕: 알겠다. 은자를 만나고 나서 궁으로 돌아가겠다.

3막 2장

왕이 수염 난 자가 깨어 있는 것을 본다.

수염 난 남자: (작은 목소리로) 저를 용서해 주십시오!

왕: 이제 괜찮은가?

수염 난 남자: 저를 용서해 주십시오.

왕: 무슨 말인가? 난 자네를 용서할 게 없네.

수염 난 남자: 있습니다, 폐하. 왕께서는 저를 모르시지만 저는 폐하를 알고 있습니다. 왕께서 제 재산을 몰수하고 제 형을 죽이는 걸 보고 저는 폐하에게 복수를 하고자 하는 폐하의 원수가 되었습니다. 폐하께서 은자를 만나러 혼자 가셨다는 걸 알고 저는 폐하가 돌아오는 길에 죽이려고 계획을 했습니다. 하지만 여기 오는 길에 병사들을 만났고 부상을 입었습니다. 폐하께서 제 목숨을 구해주지 않으셨더라면 저는 살지 못했을 것입니다. 허락하시면 폐하에게 가장 충성스런 신하로서 섬기겠습니다. 저를 용서해 주십시오, 폐하!

왕: 용서하도록 하겠다. 그리고 너를 내 신하로 받아들이도록 하마.

단락요약

- 수염 난 남자가 왕이 은자를 만나고 돌아가는 길에 왕을 죽이려고 계획하고 있었던 것을 고백하고 용서를 구하면서, 자신을 살려준 왕에게 충성을 맹세하고 있다.

구문정리

- I'm afraid this place is dangerous ~ : 「I'm afraid + (that) 주어 +동사」는 '~할까 두렵다'라는 뜻으로, 좋지 않은 일을 예측하거나 예상할 때 쓰는 표현이다.
- Seeing that you took away my property and put my brother to death, ~ : Seeing으로 시작하는 분사구문은 'When I saw that ~'에서 접속사와 주어를 생략하고 saw를 현재분사인 seeing으로 바꿔서 만들어졌다.
- Knowing you had gone alone to see the hermit, I planned ~ : 앞 문장과 마찬가지로 현재분사 Knowing으로 시작하는 분사구문은 'When/As I knew (that) you had gone…'에서 접속사와 주어를 생략한 후 knew의 현재분사인 knowing을 써서 만들어졌다.

정답 afraid / carrying / property / servant

P.199 L.11~15 **P.200** L.1~17

Act 4, Scene 1

The hermit is outside, planting seeds in the ground that had been dug the day before.

King: (Approaching the hermit) For the last time, I beg you to answer my questions, wise man.

Hermit: Your questions were answered only when the wounded man appeared.

King: What do you mean?

Hermit: If you (had/have) not dug these beds for me, that man would have attacked you. You might have been killed. So the most important time was (what /when) you were digging the beds, and I was the most important man, and helping me was your most important task. Afterwards, when that man ran to us, the most important time was when you were attending to him. If you had not had the doctor (save/saving) his life, the bearded man would have died without having made __________ with you. So he was the most important man, and what you did for him was the most important thing for you to do.

King: You're right. You're right. I didn't know anything about that at that time.

Hermit: Yes, none of us knows what the future has in store for us.

King: You speak words of __________, old man.

Hermit: Remember that there is only one time that is important: that time is now. Seeing that the present is the only time you are granted that you have control over, it is the most important time. The most important person is the one you are __________, for you will never know whether you will ever have dealings with anyone else.

King: *(Looking into the eyes of the hermit)* Oh, I should have been wiser to realize this. I am grateful for the answers you have given to me. I have now found all three answers!

Act 4, Scene 2

King: *(Excited)* Bodyguard, bodyguard!

Bodyguard: *(Running out of the woods)* Yes, Your Majesty.

King: Thanks to this man, I have all the answers to the three questions. Call my men from the palace and have them (grant/granting) him anything that he wishes for.

Bodyguard: *(Lowering his head)* Yes, Your Majesty.

With his questions fully answered, the king makes up his mind to live by the hermit's great teachings.

4막 1장

은자는 밖에서 그 전날 갈아놓았던 땅에 씨를 심고 있다.

왕: (은자에게 다가가서) 마지막으로 간청하건데 현자여, 제 질문에 답을 해 주시오.

은자: 그 수염 난 자가 나타났을 때 당신의 질문은 모두 대답됐소.

왕: 무슨 말이오?

은자: 만약 당신이 제 대신에 이 모판을 갈지 않았었더라면, 그 자는 당신을 공격했었을 것이고 당신은 죽었을 수도 있었소. 그러니 가장 소중한 시간은 당신이 이 모판을 갈고 있었던 때이고, 가장 중요한 사람은 나였고, 나를 돕는 게 당신의 가장 중요한 일이었소. 그 다음에, 그 남자가 우리에게 달려왔을 때, 가장 중요한 시간은 당신이 그를 돌보고 있었던 때요. 만약 당신이 의사에게 그를 살려내도록 하지 않았더라면 그는 당신과 화해하지 못한 상태로 죽었을 것이오. 그러니 가장 중요한 사람은 그였고, 당신이 그를 위해 한 일이 당신이 해야 할 가장 중요한 일이었소.

왕: 그렇군, 당신 말이 맞소. 난 당시에는 그걸 전혀 모르고 있었소.

은자: 맞소. 미래가 우리를 위해 무엇을 준비해 놓고 있는지는 아무도 모르지요.

왕: 늙은 자여, 지혜의 말씀을 하시는 군요.

은자: 중요한 시간은 유일하게 하나라는 걸 기억하시오. 그리고 그건 바로 지금입니다. 바로 지금이 당신이 통제할 수 있도록 주어진 오직 하나밖에 없는 시간이기 때문에 그게 가장 중요한 시간인 거죠. 가장 중요한 사람은 당신과 지금 함께 있는 사람입니다. 왜냐하면 당신이 (그가 아닌) 다른 어떤 사람과 거래를 하게 될지 아닐지는 아무도 모르는 일이기 때문입니다.

왕: (은자의 눈을 쳐다보며) 오, 이걸 깨달았을 만큼 더 현명했어야 했는데. 이런 답을 주셔서 감사하오. 세 가지 답을 이제 다 찾았소.

4막 2장

왕: (흥분되어) 호위병, 호위병!

호위병: (숲에서 뛰어 나오며) 예, 전하!

왕: 이 사람 덕분에 내가 그 세 가지 질문에 대한 답을 얻었으니 성에서 사람들을 불러 와 이 자에게 그가 바라는 것은 무엇이든 주도록 하라.

호위병: (머리를 조아리며) 예, 전하!

자신의 질문들이 모두 완벽히 답변되자, 왕은 그 은자의 위대한 가르침을 따라 살기로 결심한다.

단락요약

- 왕은 현자에게서 지혜의 말을 듣고 세 개의 질문에 대한 완벽한 답을 얻은 뒤 그 깨달음을 따라 살기로 한다.

구문정리

- ~ planting seeds in the ground that had been dug the day before.: 관계대명사 that 절에 쓰인 「had been dug」은 과거완료 수동태로서 '(그 전날에 이미) 일구어져 있었던'이라는 의미이다.
- If you had not dug these beds for me, that man would have attacked you.: 가정법 과거완료 구문 「if + 주어 + had p.p. ~, 주어 + would/should/could/might have + p.p.」은 과거 사실에 대한 반대 상황을 가정하여 말할 때 쓰인다.
- for you will never know whether you will ~: 접속사 for는 이유를 나타내는 말로서 '~이므로'라고 해석한다.
- ~ have them grant him anything that he wishes for.: 「사역동사(have)+목적어(them)+동사원형(grant)」의 구문으로서, '~로 하여금 ...하도록 하다'라는 뜻이다.

정답 had / when / save / peace / wisdom / with / grant

Focus on Structure

P. 76 L.17 **To be honest,** | I know | who you are.
부사구(독립부정사) *S* *V* *O*

→ to 부정사가 들어간 관용적 표현이 부사구로 쓰여 문장 전체를 수식하는데 이를 독립부정사라고 부른다. 이런 독립부정사는 문장의 앞, 중간, 끝 등에 비교적 자유롭게 위치한다. 많이 쓰이는 관용적 표현들은 다음과 같다.

to be honest	솔직히 말하자면	strange to say	이상한 말이지만
to tell the truth	사실을 말하자면	so to speak	말하자면, 이를테면
to begin with	우선, 무엇보다도	needless to say	말할 필요도 없이
to be brief	간단히 말해서	to make matters worse	설상가상으로
to conclude	결론적으로	to do him/her justice	정당히 평가하자면

ex. To make matters worse, it began to rain hard. (설상가상으로, 비가 세차게 내리기 시작했다.)

ex. The hotel was awful! To begin with, our room was too small.
(그 호텔은 끔찍했다! 무엇보다 우리 방이 너무 작았다.)

P. 76 L.19-20 I **would** not **have survived** | **if** you **had** not **saved** my life.
S 조동사(과거형) have p.p. if *S* had p.p.

→ 과거 상황이나 사건의 반대를 가정하여 말할 때 가정법 과거완료 구문을 사용한다. 「If + 주어 + had + p.p. … 주어 + would/should/could/might + have p.p.」, 또는 순서를 바꾸어 「주어 + would/should/could/might + have p.p... if +주어 + had p.p.」의 형태로 쓰며, '~했었다면 …했었을 텐데'라는 의미로 해석한다.

ex. The king had the doctor care for the soldier. + The soldier did not die. (과거 사실)
(왕이 의사에게 그 병사를 돌보도록 했다. + 그 병사는 죽지 않았다.)
→ If the king **had not had** the doctor care for the soldier, the soldier **would have died**.
(만약 왕이 의사에게 그 병사를 돌보도록 하지 않았더라면 그 병사는 죽었을 것이다.)

Check-Up

정답 P. 253

1 다음 우리말에 맞게 빈칸에 알맞은 말을 쓰시오.

(1) 무엇보다도 그것은 전혀 필요하지 않은 것이었다.
→ It was totally unnecessary, ______________________.

(2) 솔직히 말해서, 우리는 그 결과에 대해 다소 실망했다.
→ ______________, we were somewhat disappointed with the result.

2 주어진 문장을 가정법 문장으로 바꿔 쓰시오.

(1) Sarah helped me with the project so I could finish it.
→ If Sarah ______________________.

(2) I didn't have any money with me so I couldn't buy him a birthday present.
→ ______________________ him a birthday present.

(3) Jason was not smart enough to solve the problem.
→ If Jason ______________________.

Tip

❶ (1) 독립부정사가 문미에 위치한 경우
(2) 독립부정사가 문두에 위치한 경우
somewhat 다소, 어느 정도

❷ (1) 과거 사실이 긍정문이므로 가정법 문장은 부정문이 된다.
(2) 과거 사실이 부정문이므로 가정법 문장은 긍정문이 된다.
(3) 형용사+ enough to 부정사: ~할 만큼 충분히 …한

Listen and Speak/Into Real Life

정답 P. 253

1 다음을 듣고, 여자가 남자에게 부탁하려는 것을 고르시오.

① to move some heavy stuff
② to buy her some good stuff
③ to get her a stronger helper
④ to get along with his friends
⑤ to help the neighbor move some stuff

2 대화를 듣고, 내용과 일치하지 않는 것을 고르시오.

① 남자는 여자에게 책 추천을 부탁하고 있다.
② 여자는 프랑스 작가의 책을 추천해 준다.
③ 여자는 남자에게 책의 주제를 설명해 준다.
④ 남자는 경험을 통해 배우므로 과거를 중요하게 생각한다.
⑤ 여자는 가능성으로 가득 찬 미래의 중요성을 강조한다.

3 대화를 듣고, 여자가 엄마를 더욱 화나게 한 이유를 고르시오.

① She didn't know what she did wrong.
② She played online games late again at night.
③ She didn't do her homework that was due today.
④ She didn't apologize to her mom and kept being rude.
⑤ She told her a lie that she didn't play the online game.

4 다음을 듣고, 물음에 답하시오.

(1) 남자가 하고 있는 강의의 주제로 가장 알맞은 것은?

① 톨스토이의 작품이 인기 있는 이유
② 톨스토이의 대표작에 대한 내용 소개
③ 톨스토이의 사상에 영향을 준 요인들
④ 톨스토이가 작품 활동을 했던 시대적 배경
⑤ 톨스토이와 그의 작품에 대한 간략한 소개

(2) 남자가 언급한 내용이 아닌 것은?

① 톨스토이의 대표적 작품
② 톨스토이가 문학적 명성을 얻은 시기
③ 톨스토이의 철학적인 단편 소설들
④ 톨스토이가 노년에 쓴 작품들의 특징
⑤ 톨스토이가 작가활동을 통해 추구했던 것

Tip

❶ 중심 내용 파악하기
출처: Get Ready_1

❷ 일치/불일치 파악하기
출처: Listen In_Dialogue 1

❸ 이유 파악하기
출처: Listen In_Dialogue 2
due (제출) 기한이 된

❹ (1) 주제 고르기
(2) 구체적인 정보 파악하기
출처: Into Real Life_Step 1

언어 기능별 집중 대비

Read and Think

정답 P. 253

Tip

[1-2] 다음 글을 읽고, 물음에 답하시오.

Characters: King, Hermit, Bearded Man, Doctor, Bodyguard

A certain king wanted to know the answers to three key questions: First, what is the most important thing ① to accomplish in life? Second, when should he accomplish the most important thing? And third, who are the right people to help him ② accomplishing that task? He thought that if he knew the answers to these questions, he ③ would never fail in anything. So he declared throughout his kingdom that he ④ would give a large reward to anyone who could answer the three questions. However, no one in the country was able to give him ⑤ satisfying answers. The king then decided to consult a wise hermit. The hermit only received common people, so the king visited him wearing simple clothes.

1-2 출처: P.195 L.2-12
유형: 1. 문법성 판단
2. 세부 사항 파악하기

1 윗글의 밑줄 친 ①~⑤ 중 어법상 어색한 것은?

2 윗글을 통해 알 수 있는 사실이 아닌 것은?

① He didn't want to waste time doing unimportant things.

② He thought that he would need someone to help him accomplish the important task.

③ He was afraid of doing things because he had many experiences of failure.

④ He was not satisfied with the answers he got from the people in the country.

⑤ He thought that the answers to the questions deserved a large reward.

3 다음 대화에 나타난 **Hermit**의 태도를 표현한 말로 가장 알맞은 것은?

The king meets the hermit, who is digging the ground in front of his hut. Glancing at the king, the hermit greets him and goes on digging.

King: *(Approaching)* I have come to you, wise hermit, to ask you to answer three questions: What is the most important thing that deserves my attention? When is the right time to do that important thing? And who are the people I need most to help me accomplish it?

(Without saying a word, the hermit continues digging as if he had heard nothing.)

King: You look tired. *(Reaching for the hermit)* Let me take the spade and work awhile for you.

Hermit: Thanks!

(Giving the spade to the king, he sits down on the ground.)

① desperate ② curious ③ frustrated
④ arrogant ⑤ indifferent

3 출처: P.196 L.2-12
유형: 인물의 태도 파악
desperate 필사적인
frustrated 좌절한, 분노한
arrogant 거만한
indifferent 무관심한

Tip

[4-5] 다음 대화를 읽고, 물음에 답하시오.

Hermit: *(Watching the king digging the ground)* To be honest, I know who you are. I think you possess everything you want. Are you still not ⓐ satisfied?

King: Of course not!

Hermit: *(Losing himself in thought for a while and ⓑ rising from his seat)* Now rest awhile and let me work a bit. I have to get this job ⓒ doing.

(ⓓ Not giving him the spade, the king continues to dig. The sun begins to set behind the trees.)

King: I came to you, wise man, for answers to my questions. If you can give me ⓔ none, tell me so, and I will return home.

4-5 출처: P.196 L.13-21
유형: 4. 문법성 판단
5. 인물의 심정 파악
puzzled 혼란한
perplexed 당황스러운
impatient 참을성 없는
melancholy 울적한

4 위 대화의 밑줄 친 ⓐ~ⓔ 중 어법상 어색한 것은?

① ⓐ ② ⓑ ③ ⓒ ④ ⓓ ⑤ ⓔ

5 위 대화의 마지막 부분에 나타난 왕의 심정으로 가장 알맞은 것은?

① lonely
② puzzled
③ perplexed
④ impatient
⑤ melancholy

[6-7] 다음 대화를 읽고, 물음에 답하시오.

Act 2, Scene 1

A sound is heard in the woods. A bearded man appears.

Hermit: Here comes someone walking. (A) Let us see who it is.

Bearded man: *(________________, in an urgent voice)* Help me, please. Have mercy on me. *(Falling down on the ground unconsciously)*

King: *(Finding a large wound on the man's stomach)* What happened to you? Come on! Are you okay? (B) Judging from your wound, I need to do something to stop the bleeding! (C) Doctor! Doctor! *(Carrying the wounded man into the hut)*

Act 2, Scene 2

In the hut, a doctor is caring for the bearded man who fell down on the ground unconscious.

King: (D) Is he going to make it?

Doctor: I am not sure, Your Majesty.

King: (E) I wonder who this man is. Anyway, there's no time for that now. You must do your best to save his life.

Doctor: Yes, Your Majesty. I will do my best.

6-7 출처: P.197 L.2ㅅ-16
유형: 6. 문장의 위치 파악
7. 빈칸 추론
sympathy 동정(심)

Tip

6 위 대화의 (E) 중 아래의 지문이 들어가기에 가장 알맞은 곳은?

> (A)*~* Putting his hand on the unconscious man's neck to see if he is alive

① (A) ② (B) ③ (C) ④ (D) ⑤ (E)

7 위 대화의 빈칸에 가장 알맞은 것은?

① Walking unsteadily
② Greeting the king
③ Staring at the king
④ Showing a sign of sympathy
⑤ Putting his finger on his lips

[8-9] 다음 대화를 읽고, 물음에 답하시오.

Act 3, Scene 2

The king sees the bearded man awake.

Bearded man: *(In a weak voice)* Forgive me!

King: Are you okay now?

Bearded man: Forgive me!

King: What do you mean? I have nothing to forgive you (A)(for / from).

Bearded man: Yes, Your Majesty. You do not know me, but I know you. Seeing that you took away my property and put my brother to death, I was an enemy of yours who sought to get back at you. (B)(Known / Knowing) you had gone alone to see the hermit, I planned to kill you on your way back. But on my way here, I came upon your soldiers, who wounded me. I would not have survived if you (C)(had / have) not saved my life. If you allow it, I will serve you as your most faithful servant. Forgive me, Your Majesty!

King: I forgive you! And I also accept you as one of my men.

8-9 출처: P.198 L.13-25
유형: 8. 내용 파악 하기
9.일치/불일치 파악

8 위 대화의 괄호 안의 (A) ~ (C)에 들어갈 말이 차례대로 연결된 것은?

① for – Known – had
② for – Knowing – had
③ for – Knowing – have
④ from – Known – have
⑤ from – Knowing – had

9 위 대화의 수염 난 남자에 대한 내용과 일치하지 않는 것은?

① He is asking the king for forgiveness.
② His brother was killed by the king.
③ He tried to take a revenge on the king.
④ He could save his life thanks to the king.
⑤ He was once a faithful servant of the king.

언어 기능별 집중 대비

Language Notes Write It Right

정답 P. 254

Tip

❶ (1), (2) 독립부정사
(3)~(5) 가정법 과거완료
major in ~을 전공하다

1 다음 우리말에 맞게 괄호 안의 단어들을 이용하여 문장을 완성하시오.

(1) 무엇보다도 우선, 나는 출혈을 멈추기 위해 뭔가를 해야 한다.
________________, I need to do something to stop the bleeding. (begin)

(2) 솔직히, 그 스프는 너무 짜서 먹을 수 없을 정도였다.
________________, the soup was too salty to eat. (honest)

(3) 내가 물리학을 공부했더라면 훌륭한 우주비행사가 되었을 텐데.
________________, I would have become a great astronaut. (physics)

(4) 그녀가 지혜로웠다면 그런 큰 실수를 하지 않았을 것이다.
________________, she would not have made such a big mistake. (wise)

(5) 내가 20대에 이 책을 읽었더라면 철학을 전공했을 텐데.
If I had read this book when I was in my 20s, ________________. (major)

2 다음 글을 읽고, 물음에 답하시오.

❷ pity 동정, 불쌍히 여기다
dress (상처부위를) 싸매다
purpose 목적

"Do you not see?" replied the hermit. "If you had not pitied my weakness yesterday and had not dug these beds for me, you would have gone away. Then that man would have attacked you and you would have wished you had stayed with me. So the most important time was when you were digging the beds. And I was the most important man and to do me good was your most important business. Afterwards, when the man ran to us, the most important time was when you were caring for him, because if you had not dressed his wounds he would have died without having made peace with you. So he was the most important man and what you did for him was your most important business. Remember then, there is only one time that is important and that time is Now. It is the most important time because it is the only time we have any power to act. The most necessary person is the person you are with at a particular moment for no one knows what will happen in the future and whether we will meet anyone else. The most important business is to do that person good because we were sent into this world for that purpose alone."

(1) What are the three questions the hermit is answering to?

____

(2) What are the answers of the hermit to each question?

____

Basic

정답 P. 254

1 대화를 듣고, 여자의 마지막 말에 이어질 남자의 응답으로 알맞은 것을 고르시오.

① I'm afraid I can't.
② That's okay. Be careful next time.
③ Never mind. Everything will be okay.
④ Send me the message by email, please.
⑤ Let me check and find out what the problem is.

2 대화를 듣고, 여자가 Chris에게 한 충고의 요지로 맞는 것을 고르시오.

① 지키지 못할 약속은 하지 마라.
② 처음 계획한 대로 행동에 옮기라.
③ 자신과 비슷한 성격의 사람과 친해져라.
④ 우선순위를 정할 때 긴급한 것을 먼저 하라.
⑤ 상대방이 말할 때 중요한 것은 기록하라.

3 다음 대화의 빈칸에 가장 알맞은 것은?

A: ______________________________
B: Of course. I'd be glad to help out.

① I beg your pardon?
② Do you need some help?
③ May I ask you a favor?
④ Would you like me to help you?
⑤ Would you mind helping me out?

4 다음 중 〈보기〉의 밑줄 친 단어와 같은 의미로 쓰인 것은?

보기 He was mean to his friends.

① I didn't mean to upset you.
② It was mean of him not to invite her.
③ The GDP of this state was below the mean.
④ Does the name Miriam mean anything to you?
⑤ With children, if you say no, you have to mean it.

5 다음 중 반의어끼리 연결된 것은?

① grant – offer
② weapon – arms
③ injure – wound
④ declare – announce
⑤ merciful – cruel

6 다음 글의 빈칸 ⓐ와 ⓑ에 들어갈 말을 주어진 단어들을 사용하여 완성하시오. (필요하면 어형을 바꾸시오.)

A certain king wanted to know the answers to three key questions: First, what is the most important thing to accomplish in life? Second, when should he accomplish the most important thing? And third, who are the right people to help him accomplish that task? He thought that if he ______ⓐ______ to these questions, ______ⓑ______ in anything. So he declared throughout his kingdom that he would give a large reward to anyone who could answer the three questions. However, no one in the country was able to give him satisfying answers. The king then decided to consult a wise hermit. The hermit only received common people, so the king visited him wearing simple clothes.

ⓐ ________________ (know / answer)
ⓑ ________________ (not / fail)

7 다음 중 밑줄 친 부분의 쓰임이 어색한 것은?

① He is, so to speak, a grownup baby.
② To be honest, I don't think she deserves it.
③ There are problems. To start with, I can't cook.
④ It was difficult, to be sure, but we managed to finish the job.
⑤ We arrived on time. To make matters worse, we could see the sunrise.

8 다음 문장의 빈칸에 가장 알맞은 것은?

She was trying to __________ him for humiliating her.

① pay for
② send for
③ get back at
④ take advantage of
⑤ take good care of

[9~10] 다음 대화를 읽고, 물음에 답하시오.

King: *(Approaching the hermit)* For the last time, I beg you ① to answer my questions, wise man.

Hermit: Your questions were answered only when the wounded man appeared.

King: What do you mean?

Hermit: If you ② did not dig these beds for me, that man would have attacked you. You might have been killed. So the most important time was when you ③ were digging the beds, and I was the most important man, and helping me was your most important task. Afterwards, when that man ran to us, the most important time was when you were attending to him. If you had not had the doctor save his life, the bearded man would have died without ④ having made peace with you. So he was the most important man, and ⑤ what you did for him was the most important thing for you to do.

King: You're right. You're right. I didn't know anything about that at that time.

9 위 대화의 밑줄 친 ①~⑤ 중 어법상 어색한 것을 찾아 바르게 고쳐 쓰시오.

_______________ → _______________

10 Hermit이 한 말을 다음과 같이 요약할 때 빈칸 ⓐ와 ⓑ에 알맞은 것은?

> The most important time is now and the most necessary person is the one ____ⓐ____ at a particular moment, and the most important business is ____ⓑ____ to that person.

① you are with – to do good
② who is noble – to do good
③ whom you trust – to do justice
④ who looks poor – to pay attention
⑤ you met before – to carefully listen

11 다음 문장과 의미가 가장 가까운 것은?

> If we had taken a taxi, we wouldn't have missed the plane.

① We missed the plane though we took a taxi.
② We didn't miss the plane because we took a taxi.
③ We missed the plane because we didn't take a taxi.
④ We missed the plane, but we don't regret not taking a taxi.
⑤ We could have missed the plane if we had not taken a taxi.

[12~13] 다음 우리말과 같도록 괄호 안의 단어를 사용하여 문장을 완성하시오.

12

> 만약 당신이 나를 돌봐주지 않았더라면 나는 죽었을 것입니다. (care / for / I / me / should / died / have)

→ If you had not ______________________.

13

> 솔직히 말하자면, 나는 내가 유명해질 거라고 생각해 본 적이 없다. (honest/ never/ to/ thought/ I/ be)

→ ______________________ I would be famous.

14 다음 글의 빈칸에 알맞은 단어를 쓰시오.

> Hermit: Remember that there is only one time that is important: that time is now. Seeing that the ________ is the only time you are granted that you have control over, it is the most important time.

수준별 단원평가

Advanced

정답 P. 254

1 대화를 듣고, 남자가 Smith 선생님에게 부탁한 것을 고르시오.

① to lend him some books on tsunamis
② to recommend a good presentation topic
③ to help him to work on the team project
④ to give feedback on his first presentation
⑤ to find more information on tsunamis for him

2 대화를 듣고, 내용을 통해 답할 수 없는 질문을 고르시오.

① Where is Tolstoy from?
② What are Tolstoy's famous books?
③ When did Tolstoy first gain his literary fame?
④ What did Tolstoy seek through his works and in his life?
⑤ Which of Tolstoy's works best represents his philosophy about life?

3 대화를 듣고, 남자가 여자에게 한 충고로 맞는 것을 고르시오.

① Be kind to someone who is closest to you.
② Don't put off things you need to do today.
③ Do to others as you do to your parents or family.
④ Don't do things your parents do not want you to.
⑤ Accept your parent's apology as soon as possible.

4 다음 글의 빈칸 ⓐ~ⓒ에 들어갈 말이 차례대로 연결된 것은?

Elements of a Play
- What happens? : ____ⓐ____ is composed of clearly defined problems for the characters to solve.
- To whom does it happen? : ____ⓑ____ provide the reasons for the events in the plot.
- What does a play require? : For all of the arts, public performance is essential. The ____ⓒ____ can inspire actors.

① text – characters – plot
② plot – narrators – event
③ plot – script – motive
④ script – characters – audience
⑤ text – motives – characters

5 다음 글의 (A)~(E) 중 아래의 문장이 들어가기에 가장 알맞은 곳은?

He thought that if he knew the answers to these questions, he would never fail in anything.

A certain king wanted to know the answers to three key questions: First, what is the most important thing to accomplish in life? Second, when should he accomplish the most important thing? And third, who are the right people to help him accomplish that task? (A) So he declared throughout his kingdom that he would give a large reward to anyone who could answer the three questions. (B) However, no one in the country was able to give him satisfying answers. (C) The king then decided to consult a wise hermit. (D) The hermit only received common people, so the king visited him wearing simple clothes. (E)

① (A) ② (B) ③ (C) ④ (D) ⑤ (E)

[6~7] 다음 대화를 읽고, 물음에 답하시오.

A sound is heard in the woods. A bearded man appears.

Hermit: Here comes someone walking. Let us see who it is.

Bearded man: (Walking unsteadily, in an urgent voice) Help me, please. Have mercy on me. (Falling down on the ground unconsciously)

King: (Finding a large wound on the man's stomach) What happened to you? Come on! Are you okay? (Putting his hand on the unconscious man's neck to see if he is alive) ___ⓐ___, I need to do something to stop the bleeding! Doctor! Doctor! (Carrying the wounded man into the hut)

In the hut, a doctor is caring for the bearded man who fell down on the ground unconscious.

King: Is he going to ___ⓑ___?

Doctor: I am not sure, Your Majesty.

King: I wonder who this man is. Anyway, there's no time for that now. You must do your best to save his life.

Doctor: Yes, Your Majesty. I will do my best.

6 위 대화의 ⓐ와 ⓑ에 들어갈 말이 차례대로 연결된 것은?

① To be honest – get it
② Not to mention – beat it
③ Generally speaking – take it
④ Judging from the wound – make it
⑤ To make matters worse – turn it

7 위 대화의 내용과 일치하지 <u>않는</u> 것은?

① The king does not know who the bearded man is.
② The bearded man faints because he bleeds too much.
③ The king does not seem to think that the wound of the bearded man is serious.
④ The king orders the doctor to do his best to cure the bearded man.
⑤ The doctor is not sure about whether the bearded man can make it or not.

[8~10] 다음 대화를 읽고, 물음에 답하시오.

Bearded man: Forgive me!

King: What do you mean? I have nothing to forgive you for.

Bearded man: ⓐ <u>Yes</u>, Your Majesty. You do not know me, but I know you. Seeing that you took away my property and put my brother to death, I was an enemy of yours ⓑ (you / who / back / at / sought / to / get). Knowing you had gone alone to see the hermit, I planned to kill you on your way back. But on my way here, I came upon your soldiers, who wounded me. I would not have survived if you had not saved my life. If you allow it, I will serve you as your most faithful servant. Forgive me, Your Majesty!

King: I forgive you! And I also accept you as one of my men.

8 위 대화의 밑줄 친 ⓐ가 의미하는 것을 완전한 영어 문장으로 쓰시오.

→ ______________________________

9 위 대화의 괄호 안의 ⓑ의 단어들을 알맞게 배열하시오.

주관식 서술형 대비

10 자신이 읽었던 단편 소설에 대해 아래의 요소가 들어가도록 내용을 요약하여 5문장 내외로 쓰시오.

- Book title
- Introduction: What is the story about?
- Body: What does the story show or tell?
- Conclusion: What lesson does the story give to you? or What does it remind you of?

Title: ______________

The story is about ______________________________.

The story shows ______________________________.

This book made me think about ______________________________.

2학기 기말고사

[1~6] 잘 듣고, 물음에 답하시오.

01. 대화를 듣고, 남자의 여행에 관한 불만 사항으로 맞는 것을 고르시오.

① 친구들과 최단 경로에 대해 논쟁하느라 시간 낭비한 것
② 여행지 선정 과정에서 자신의 의견을 제시하지 못한 것
③ 지도를 준비하지 않아서 길을 찾느라 시간을 허비한 것
④ 여행지 숙소가 광고에 나온 것과 달라 실망스러웠던 것
⑤ 시간이 없어서 중요한 유적지들을 다 둘러보지 못한 것

[2~3] 대화를 듣고, 물음에 답하시오.

02. 대화의 마지막 부분에 여자가 언급한 것과 관련 있는 문장을 고르시오.

① Watch out for rock falling.
② Littering is not allowed here.
③ Please slow down at animal crossing.
④ Under construction. Drive safely, please.
⑤ Drivers must drive at the speed of 30km per hour.

03. 대화에서 남자가 여자에게 권유한 귀가 길 경로로 맞는 것을 고르시오.

① 공원을 가로질러 가는 길
② 주차장을 돌아서 가는 길
③ 시청을 통과해서 가는 길
④ 지역 복지 센터를 돌아서 가는 길
⑤ 시청과 지역 복지 센터 사이로 난 길

04. 대화를 듣고, 남자가 지도를 보며 놀라는 이유로 맞는 것을 고르시오.

① 많은 식당에 대한 정보가 들어 있어서
② 식당마다의 특징에 대한 설명이 들어 있어서
③ 자신이 사는 인근 지역 식당 정보도 들어 있어서
④ 식당 음식들에 대한 많은 리뷰가 포함되어 있어서
⑤ 식당 손님들의 호감도가 맛과 가격별로 되어 있어서

05. 대화를 듣고, 선미가 Chris에게 한 충고로 맞는 것을 고르시오.

① 우선순위로 정한 것을 먼저 해라.
② 제출 기한을 지켜서 과제를 제출하라.
③ 사소한 약속도 소중히 지키도록 해라.
④ 말보다 실천이 중요하다는 것을 잊지 마라.
⑤ 다른 사람들의 기준에 맞춰 살지 않도록 하라.

06. 다음을 듣고, 주어진 질문에 대한 맞는 답을 고르시오.

Q. What is the characteristic of Tolstoy's short stories?

① They focus on the origin of evil.
② They contain philosophical questions.
③ They pay much attention to the life of nobles.
④ They display lots of sympathy toward human life.
⑤ They show the pessimistic view about human nature.

07. 다음 글의 주제로 가장 알맞은 것은?

Hannah is a college student who likes to hang out with her friends. She woke up late this morning, so she took a cab to get to class on time. The cab driver used a GPS navigation system to find the shortest route to her school. For lunch, Hannah took her friends to one of the places she found through an online map of good restaurants. After her afternoon classes, she learned how she could get to the city library through an online map service. On her way to the library, a group of foreign tourists asked for directions to a famous park. Hannah used the subway map to give them directions. When she got home in the evening, she turned on her computer and examined several tourist information maps on the Internet for a family trip.

① Advantages of Using Maps for Your Business
② Ways of Using Online Thematic Mapping Software
③ How Maps Can Be Made Available to Foreign Tourists
④ Various Types of Map and Their Uses in Our Daily Lives
⑤ A Massive Difference between Regular Maps and Online Maps

08. 다음 글의 밑줄 친 ①~⑤ 중 가리키는 대상이 나머지와 다른 것은?

There is no denying the fact that maps are more than just pieces of paper with geographical information on them. ① They are a big part of people's daily lives. ② They are used for simple tasks like finding a good restaurant in the neighborhood, as well as for business, security, and medical and academic purposes. Ever since the development of maps, people have been using ③ them to exchange information, describe imaginary worlds, control ④ their land, distribute their ideas, and pass their thoughts on to future generations. Let's take a look at the history of maps to see how ⑤ they have been developed and used.

09. 다음 글의 (A)~(E) 중 아래의 문장이 들어가기에 가장 알맞은 곳은?

All of these early maps were, of course, drawn and illustrated by hand.

The earliest surviving map of the world is preserved on a clay tablet made in ancient Babylonia in about 6th century B.C. It represents the earth as a flat circle with oceans and mythical islands around it. (A) The European maps made during the Middle Ages were heavily influenced by religious views. (B) For example, a map of the world created in the 6th century shows that the world is flat, and the heavens are shaped like a box with a curved lid.

(C) The invention of printing made maps much more widely available in the 15th century. (D) Map-making skills advanced during the Age of Exploration in the 15th and 16th centuries. (E) Coast lines, islands, rivers, and harbors were described on maps.

① (A) ② (B) ③ (C) ④ (D) ⑤ (E)

10. 다음 글의 괄호 안의 ⓐ와 ⓑ에 알맞은 말이 차례대로 연결된 것은?

Maps became increasingly accurate and factual during the 17th, 18th, and 19th centuries with the ⓐ (application / appliances /adoption) of scientific methods. First introduced in 1500, the bird's-eye view, or a view from a great height, became widely used in the 17th and 18th centuries. Shading and contour lines were used to show ⓑ (geological / geographical/geography) features in more detail.

① application – geological
② application – geographical
③ appliances – geological
④ appliances – geography
⑤ adoption – geographical

11. 다음 글의 ①~⑤ 중 전체 흐름과 관계없는 문장은?

① The advancement of science and increased exchanges among people and countries have led to the development of more advanced technologies for making maps. ② No other technology has been as revolutionary as the geographic information system (GIS), which emerged in the 1970s and 1980s. ③ This system, which is composed of computer hardware, software, and digital information, makes it possible for people to create searches, analyze spatial information, and edit map information on their own. ④ If you are considering jobs related to GIS, you should study programming remote sensing, and web development. ⑤ It is used nowadays for maps, navigation systems, transportation information, analysis of business zones, and other purposes.

① ② ③ ④ ⑤

[12-14] 다음 글을 읽고, 물음에 답하시오.

(A) Scientists have been using the old ideas of maps for more creative functions to revolutionize ⓐ the way we live.
(B) In the future, more advanced technology will ⓑ be used for making maps. There is a great possibility that future maps will contain information about everything in physical space, including indoor areas.
(C) So you may get directions not only to a shopping center, but also to the inside of the stores. ⓒ What is more, you might even be able to walk into an augmented reality map to go shopping. You'll be surprised to see what future maps will look like!
(D) These days, people rely ⓓ heavily on maps for business activities, national defense, the exploration of the human body, academic research, and the prediction of geographical changes. It won't be long before many companies have their products ⓔ deliver to customers with the help of drones and robots equipped with GPS navigation systems.

12. 윗글의 밑줄 친 ⓐ~ⓔ 중 어법상 어색한 것을 고르시오.

13. 윗글 (A)에 이어질 글의 순서를 바르게 배열하시오.

14. 윗글의 내용과 일치하지 않는 것은?

① The old idea that a map can only be useful if it is complete and accurate has been discarded.
② Maps that are being developed can dramatically change the way we live.
③ Combined with the advanced technology, future maps will provide us with new experience.
④ Augmented reality maps will allow us to shop around sitting in our homes and offices.
⑤ Drones equipped with GPS navigation systems are being used to deliver products to the customers.

15. 다음 밑줄 친 ①~⑤ 중 어법상 어색한 것은?

A certain king wanted to know the answers to three key questions: First, what is the most important thing ① to accomplish in life? Second, when should he accomplish the most important thing? And third, who are the right people to help him ② accomplish that task? He thought that if he knew the answers to these questions, he ③ would never fail in anything. So he declared throughout his kingdom that he would give a large reward to anyone who could answer the three questions. However, no one in the country was able to give him ④ satisfying answers. The king then decided to consult a wise hermit. The hermit only received common people, so the king visited him ⑤ to wear simple clothes.

16. 다음 대화에서 King과 Hermit의 표면적 태도를 각각 가장 잘 묘사한 것은?

The king meets the hermit, who is digging the ground in front of his hut. Glancing at the king, the hermit greets him and goes on digging.

King: *(Approaching)* I have come to you, wise hermit, to ask you to answer three questions: What is the most important thing that deserves my attention? When is the right time to do that important thing? And who are the people I need most to help me accomplish it?

(Without saying a word, the hermit continues digging as if he had heard nothing.)

King: You look tired. *(Reaching for the hermit)* Let me take the spade and work awhile for you.

Hermit: Thanks! *(Giving the spade to the king, he sits down on the ground.)*

	King		Hermit
①	arrogant	–	humble
②	proud	–	determined
③	critical	–	passionate
④	desperate	–	indifferent
⑤	optimistic	–	pessimistic

17. 다음 대화의 밑줄 친 ①~⑤를 연기할 때 주의할 점으로 적절하지 않은 것은?

A sound is heard in the woods. A bearded man appears.

Hermit: Here comes someone walking. ① Let us see who it is.

Bearded man: *(Walking unsteadily, in an urgent voice)* Help me, please. ② Have mercy on me. *(Falling down on the ground unconsciously)*

King: *(Finding a large wound on the man's stomach)* What happened to you? Come on! Are you okay? *(Putting his hand on the unconscious man's neck to see if he is alive)* Judging from your wound, ③ I need to do something to stop the bleeding! Doctor! Doctor! *(Carrying the wounded man into the hut)*

In the hut, a doctor is caring for the bearded man who fell down on the ground unconscious.

King: ④ Is he going to make it?

Doctor: I am not sure, Your Majesty.

King: I wonder who this man is. ⑤ Anyway, there's no time for that now. You must do your best to save his life.

Doctor: Yes, Your Majesty. I will do my best.

① 궁금한 표정으로 말한다.
② 쓰러져가며 힘없이 말한다.
③ 긴박한 어조로 혼잣말처럼 한다.
④ 염려하는 기색이 역력한 상태로 말한다.
⑤ 의사를 나무라면서 아주 강경하게 말한다.

[18-19] 다음 대화를 읽고, 물음에 답하시오.

The hermit wakes up early the next morning and leaves for work. After the hermit is gone, the king's bodyguards rush to the king.

Bodyguard: *(Rushing to the king, in an urgent voice)* Your Majesty, I'm afraid this place is dangerous for you.

King: Why?

Bodyguard: Last night, we found a strange man ① carrying a weapon. I think we had better ② leave this place as soon as possible.

King: Okay. I'll return to my palace after I meet the hermit.

The king sees the bearded man awake.

Bearded man: *(In a weak voice)* Forgive me!

King: Are you okay now?

Bearded man: Forgive me!

King: What do you mean? I have nothing to forgive you for.

Bearded man: Yes, Your Majesty. You do not know me, but I know you. Seeing that you took away my property and put my brother to death, I was an enemy of ③ yours who sought to get back at you. Knowing you ④ had gone alone to see the hermit, I planned to kill you on your way back. But on my way here, I came upon your soldiers, who wounded me. I would not have survived if you ⑤ did not save my life. If you allow it, I will serve you as your most faithful servant. Forgive me, Your Majesty!

King: I forgive you! And I also accept you as one of my men.

18. 위 대화의 밑줄 친 ①~⑤ 중 어법상 어색한 것은?

① ② ③ ④ ⑤

19. 위 대화의 내용과 일치하지 않는 것은?

① The bodyguard urges the king to leave the place immediately.
② The king wants to invite the hermit to his palace when he returns.
③ The bearded man asks the king for forgiveness for attempting to kill him.
④ The bearded man got an attack from the king's soldiers and was severely wounded.
⑤ The bearded man says that he owes his life to the king.

[20-21] 다음 대화를 읽고, 물음에 답하시오.

Act 4, Scene 1

The hermit is outside, planting seeds in the ground that had been dug the day before.

King: *(Approaching the hermit)* For the last time, I beg you to answer my questions, wise man.

Hermit: Your questions were answered only when the wounded man appeared.

King: What do you mean?

Hermit: If you had not dug these beds for me, that man would have attacked you. You might have been killed. So the most important time was when you were digging the beds, and I was the most important man, and helping me was your most important task. Afterwards, when that man ran to us, the most important time was ______ⓐ______ ____________.(attend) If you had not had the doctor save his life, the bearded man would have died without having made peace with you. So he was the most important man, and what you did for him was the most important thing for you to do.

King: You're right. You're right. I didn't know anything about that at that time.

Hermit: Yes, none of us knows what the future has in store for us.

King: You speak words of wisdom, old man.

Hermit: Remember that there is only one time that is important: that time is now. Seeing that the present is the only time you are granted that you have control over, it is the most important time. The most important person is ___ⓑ___ ________(one), for you will never know whether you will ever have dealings with anyone else.

King: *(Looking into the eyes of the hermit)* Oh, I should have been wiser to realize ⓒ this. I am grateful for the answers you have given to me. I have now found all three answers!

서술형

20. 위 대화의 빈칸 ⓐ와 ⓑ에 들어갈 말을 괄호 안의 단어를 사용하여 쓰시오.

⊖ ⓐ ______________________

ⓑ ______________________

서술형

21. 위 대화의 밑줄 ⓒ this를 요약한 아래의 문장을 읽고, 빈칸에 공통으로 들어갈 표현을 쓰시오.

> ______________ time is now, that the person you are with now is ______________ person, and that the things you do for someone are ______________ thing to do.

⊖ ______________________

서술형

[22-23] 다음 〈보기〉의 문장과 의미가 같도록 빈칸에 알맞은 말을 쓰시오.

22.

> 보기 There is no telling what the outcome will be.

= It ______________ what the outcome will be.

23.

> 보기 No other architect was as creative as Gaudi.

= Gaudi was ______________________ .

서술형

24. 다음 〈보기〉의 우리말과 같도록 괄호 안의 단어들을 사용하여 영어로 쓰시오.

> 보기 오늘날의 지도들과 닮은 세계 지도는 16세기 초에 등장하기 시작했다. (whole-world maps / those)

⊖ ______________________

논술형

25. 다음 조건에 맞게 주어진 질문에 대한 답을 3~4 문장으로 쓰시오.

> **Q.** What is one thing you regret doing or not doing?

> 조건> ① 언제, 무엇을 했는지가 드러나게 쓸 것
> ② 가정법 과거완료 구문을 1문장 포함시킬 것
> ③ 3문장 모두 full sentence로 쓸 것

____

____

____

정답과 해설

UNIT 1 Getting Off to a Great Start

교과서 핵심 정리 Check-Up

Words & Phrases

1. (1) take part in (2) By the way (3) in the end
   (4) from scratch (5) search for (6) In brief
2. (1) participate (2) session (3) display
   (4) expert (5) reward
3. (1) when he is in need (2) too large to deliver
   (3) was fascinated by his performance
   (4) too large to display

1

(1) 나는 그 모임에 참석할 거라고 벌써 약속을 했다.
(2) 그런데, 너는 아직도 공공도서관에서 일하고 있는 중이니?
(3) 그가 결국에는 승리할 것을 의심하지 않는다.
(4) 이제 나는 모든 것을 처음부터 시작해야만 한다.
(5) 책을 찾는 데는 두 가지 다른 방법이 있다.
(6) 간단히 말해 너는 받은 만큼 주어야 한다.

2

(1) 참석하다: 모임 같은 특정한 목적을 위해 그룹에 함께 하다
(2) 회의: 의회나 다른 행정 조직의 모임
(3) 전시하다: 사람들이 쉽게 볼 수 있도록 어떤 장소에 어떤 것을 두다
(4) 전문가: 어떤 것을 하는 데 있어서 매우 솜씨가 좋은 사람, 또는 어떤 주제에 관해 많이 알고 있는 사람
(5) 보상: 예를 들어, 행동을 잘 하거나, 열심히 일하거나 어떤 단체에 공헌을 하여 받는 것

Reading Comprehension(Focus on Structure)

1. (1) friend to help her (2) has been sleeping since
2. (1) to leave (2) has been working (3) correct

1

(1) 내 여동생은 도와줄 친구가 없다.: 명사를 수식하는 to부정사구
(2) 내 남동생은 귀가 후 계속 잠을 자고 있다.: 과거의 일정 시점에서부터 현재까지 계속되는 동작을 나타내는 현재완료진행형 시제

2

(1) 사무실을 마지막에 나가는 사람은 소등을 해야 합니다.: 명사를 수식하는 to부정사구
(2) 내 남동생은 대학 졸업 후 은행에서 근무하고 있다.: 현재완료진행형 시제의 형태는 「have/has+been -ing」이다.
(3) 나는 문제가 무엇인가를 파악하고 고치려고 해 보았지만 실패했다.: 밑줄 친 correct는 의미상 tried to 뒤에 and로 연결되는 병렬 구조를 이루고 있으므로 동사원형을 써야 한다.

언어 기능별 집중 대비

Listen and Speak / Into Real Life

1. ① 2. ③ 3. ⑤ 4. (1) ② (2) ⑤

1

W: What are you interested in?
M: I am interested in bowling.
W: Then why don't you join our school's bowling club? They're seeking some new students.
M: Oh, really? I didn't know that our school had a bowling club. Thanks for letting me know.

여자가 주는 정보에 대해 알려줘서 고맙다는 인사를 하는 것이 자연스럽다.

① 알려줘서 고마워.
② 고마워. 3시까지 올 수 있겠니?
③ 사실, 나는 다른 사람을 돕는 것을 좋아하지 않아요.
④ 와, 잘됐다. 너도 그곳의 친구들을 좋아하게 될 거야.
⑤ 그게 좋겠어요. 충고해주셔서 고맙습니다. 김 선생님.

2

W: What do you want to do when the new semester starts?
M: I want to read as many books as possible.
W: Are you interested in reading?
M: Sure, I am. I especially like to read detective novels.
W: Oh, really? I like detective stories, too.

추리 소설을 좋아한다는 남자의 말에 자신도 추리 소설을 좋아한다는 동감의 표현이 오는 것이 자연스럽다.

① 그럼, 그 동아리에 가입해 보렴.
② 물론이지, 책은 마음의 양식이야.
③ 아, 그래? 나도 추리 소설을 좋아해.
④ 그게 좋겠다. 언제 만날까?
⑤ 그렇게 하지 마. 네 건강에 안 좋아.

3

M: Sumi, is that you?
W: Hi, Eddy. Are you in this class, too?
M: Yes, I am. I didn't expect to see you here.
W: Me, neither. I'm so happy we're in the same class at the same school.
M: Me, too. By the way, did you hear that we need to choose an elective subject by the end of this week?
W: Yes, I did. I've already decided to take physics.
M: Really? Physics is the most challenging subject for me.
W: I know it won't be easy, but I do like science and math. How about you? What are you interested in?
M: I'm interested in languages, so I think I'll go for either Spanish or Japanese.
W: Oh, that's cool.

여자는 선택 과목으로 이미 물리학을 정했고, 남자는 스페인어나 일본어를 선택할 생각이다.

4

W: Welcome, freshmen! I am Jiwon, the head of the student council. What do you want to do in your free time? What are you most interested in? Our school clubs are looking forward to meeting all of you. Our school has 35 clubs, and you're welcome to join any of them. The application period starts from this Wednesday and ends on Tuesday next week. You can get information about all our clubs on our school website. You can get the application form from your homeroom teacher and hand it in to each club room. When you choose a school club, you need to think about your hobbies and interests. You also need to consider your aptitude and dream job. Finding the right club is the key to a happy school life for the next three years. Think it through and then hurry to sign up!

(1) 학생회장이 신입생들에게 학교 동아리에 가입할 것을 권유하는 방송이다.
(2) ⑤ 동아리 가입의 제한 사항은 말하지 않았다.

Read and Think

1. ④ 2. ④ 3. ① 4. ⑤ 5. ③ 6. ⑤
7. ④ 8. ② 9. ② 10. ④

1 ④에서 동사 advised의 목적격보어로는 to부정사가 쓰이므로 log를 to log로 고쳐야 한다.

2 글의 마지막 문장에서 지수가 학교 동아리에 대한 흥미로운 정보를 찾았다고 했으므로 그에 관한 내용이 이어지는 것이 가장 적절하다.

3 No Limits는 영화 동아리이므로 매년 학교 축제에 발표하기 위해 제작할 것으로는 ① short films(단편영화)가 가장 적절하다.

4 앞부분에 나오는 Do you want~의 다섯 문장에서 영화감독, 영화 대본, 음향효과, 영화배우(액션배우와 로맨틱영화배우)에 대해 언급하고 있다. ⑤ 티켓 판매에 관해서는 언급되지 않았다.

5 ③ 모형 비행기나 차를 만들면서 집중력을 향상시키는 것이 자연스러우므로 decrease(줄다)가 아니라 improve(향상시키다)가 쓰인다.

6 제빵클럽의 설립 취지와, 주요 활동, 주위의 평가, 참여행사 등을 설명하고 있지만 동아리 구성인원에 대한 언급은 없다.

7 학교 축제에서 제빵 가판대를 설치하는 것은 빵을 팔기 위한 것이므로 buy(사다)가 아니라 sell(팔다)이 쓰여야 한다.

8 제시된 문장의 so에 해당하는 내용이 글의 앞부분에 연이어 나오는 의문문 들임을 파악할 수 있다. (B) 뒤의 결과를 나타내는 내용은 주어진 문장과 인과 관계이다.

9 글 뒤에 나오는 설명으로 보아 Little Helpers는 자원봉사활동 동아리이며, 따라서 빈칸에는 ② helping others (남을 돕는 것)가 들어가야 한다.
① 운동을 하는 것
③ 돈을 버는 것
④ 친구를 사귀는 것
⑤ 건강한 음식을 먹는 것

10 글의 최종 결론에 해당하는 문장을 이끄는 접속사로 ④ In the end(결국에는)가 들어가야 한다.
① 그렇지만 ② 그러나 ③ 사실 ⑤ 무엇보다도

Language Notes / Write It Right

1. (1) have been waiting (2) to avoid (3) go
(4) without using (5) Why should
2. (1) Anyone who can sing or play an instrument.
(2) It brings great rewards and helps form stronger bonds with the other members.

1
(1) '~해오고 있는 중이다'의 현재완료진행 시제를 「have been -ing」로 쓴다.
(2) '~하도록'의 목적을 나타낼 때 to 부정사를 쓴다.
(3) 「let+목적어+원형부정사」: ~를 …하도록 허락하다
(4) '~ 하지 않고'는 without -ing를 써서 나타낸다.
(5) 조동사가 들어간 의문문의 어순은 「의문사+조동사+주어~?」이다.

수준별 단원평가 Basic

1. ③ 2. ⑤ 3. ① 4. ③ 5. ②
6. ② 7. Finding the right club 8. ③ 9. ④, ⑤
10. ⑤ 11. ④ 12. in control of
13. Search for / the volunteering clubs

1
W: What are you interested in?
M: I am interested in bowling.
W: Then why don't you join our school's bowling club? They're seeking some new students.
M: Oh, really? I didn't know that our school had a bowling club. Thanks for letting me know.
무엇에 관심이 있느냐는 여자의 질문에 남자는 볼링에 흥미가 있다고 답하고 있다.

2
M: Hi, Hwajin. How was your first week at school?
W: Well, everything is new to me. A week has passed so quickly. But I found my new homeroom teacher and classmates to be nice and friendly.
M: That's good. By the way, do you have any plans for this weekend?
W: Yeah, I teach Korean to Vietnamese children every Saturday.
M: Oh, is it part of a community service?
W: Yes, it is. I have worked as a volunteer teacher for two years at the community center. I think it's meaningful, and I am also really interested in teaching languages.
M: Of course. You can speak both Vietnamese and Korean. That's a perfect kind of volunteer work for you. Can I join you this weekend?
W: Sure, you can. What do you want to do for them?
M: I'm interested in mathematics, so I think I can teach them math.
W: Oh, that sounds good.
남학생과 여학생은 학교에서의 첫 주에 관한 대화를 나누고 있다. 남학생은 수학을 좋아하며 여학생은 지역 문화 센터에서 매주 토요일에 2년 째 베트남 아이들에게 한글을 가르치고 있다.

3 vehicle은 '차량'이라는 뜻이다.

4 take part in은 participate in과 같은 뜻으로 '~에 참가하다'라는 뜻이다.

5 regular에 ir을 붙여서 반의어가 되었다. '불규칙한'이라는 뜻이다.

6 ②는 to부정사의 부사적 용법으로(~하기 위해서) 쓰인 반면, 나머지는 명사적 용법으로 쓰였다.

7 Finding ~ 이하가 문장의 주어이며 여기서 finding은 동명사로 쓰였다.

8 동사 want, with, hope 등은 목적어로 to부정사의 형태를 취하며 visit는 '방문하다'라는 뜻이다.

9 ④ 지원자들은 반드시 연주하고자 하는 악기를 가지고 와야 한다.
⑤ 3학년 선배들이 멋진 공연을 하기로 되어 있다.

10 ⑤ 현재완료진행형은 종료된 시점을 나타낸 표현과 함께 쓸 수 없다.

11 ④는 내 취미가 무엇인지 아느냐고 묻는 표현이다.

12 in control of는 '~를 관리하고 있는'의 의미이다.

13 명령문은 동사원형으로 문장을 시작한다.

수준별 단원평가 Advanced

1. ④ 2. ③ 3. ⑤ 4. ③
5. community service
6. I have worked as a volunteer teacher for two years at the community center. 7. ① strengthen→ relieve
8. By making your own
9. producing short films every year for the school festival
10. happiness 11. ④ 12. 해설 참조

[1-2]

W: Welcome, freshmen! I am Jiwon, the head of the student council. What do you want to do in your free time? What are you most interested in? Our school clubs are looking forward to meeting all of you. Our school has 35 clubs, and you're welcome to join any of them. The application period starts from this Wednesday and ends on Tuesday next week. You can get information about all our clubs on our school website. You can get the application form from your homeroom teacher and hand it in to each club room. When you choose a school club, you need to think about your hobbies and interests. You also need to consider your aptitude and dream job. Finding the right club is the key to a happy school life for the next three years. Think it through and then hurry to sign up!

1 학생회 회장인 지원은 신입생들에게 학교의 동아리에 가입하라는 방송을 하고 있다. 3년 간 행복한 학교생활을 위해 본인에게 맞는 동아리를 선택하라고 권하고 있다.

2 담임 선생님께 동아리 가입 신청서를 받아 각 동아리 교실에 제출하라고 했다.

3

W: Freshmen, your attention, please. I am Lee Sia, the head of the school orchestra. What do you want to do for extracurricular activities? If you are interested in playing any musical instrument, why don't you try out for the school orchestra? Tomorrow we are going to have auditions for new members of the orchestra in the auditorium after school at 5 p.m. There will be a brief introduction to our club and some great performances by senior students. Each individual audition will last about 10 minutes. Don't forget to bring the musical instrument you want to play. For more information, please visit our club room. We hope to see you at the auditions. Thank you for your attention.

오케스트라 단장이 신입생들을 대상으로 말하고 있다.

4 물리학을 선택 과목으로 선택했다는 여학생의 말에 남학생은 깜짝 놀라며 물리학은 자신에게 어려운 과목이라고 말하고 있다.

5 community service는 '봉사활동'이라는 뜻이다.

6 it은 앞에 나온 2년간 지역 문화 센터에서 2년 간 자원봉사 선생님으로 지역 문화를 위해 일해 온 것을 가리킨다.

7 ① 커다란 무대 한 가운데 서 있는 자신을 상상하며 스트레스를 줄일 수 있다고 해야 자연스러우므로 strengthen을 relieve로 바꿔 써야 한다.

8 By-ing는 '~함으로써'의 의미이다.

9 Wings and Motors에서는 매년 모형 비행기와 자동차 경주 대회를 개최하는 활동을 하는 반면 No Limits!에서는 학교 축제에 출품한 단편 영화를 매년 제작하고 있다.

10 어려운 사람들을 돕는 자원봉사를 하면서 약간의 시간과 노력을 기울이며 여러분의 인생에서 행복이 배가 될 거라고 말하며 자신들의 동아리를 홍보하고 있는 글이다.

11 자원봉사 동아리인 Little Helpers 출신의 몇몇 회원들이 졸업 후에도 봉사 활동을 계속 하고 있다고 했다.

12 〈예시 답안〉

How to Cook Shrimp Spaghetti

1. Boil water and put noodles in the pot.
2. Keep boiling for 10 minutes, then pour out the boiled water.
3. Add some oil and put in the tomato sauce, then fry it for 3 minutes.
4. Add the shrimp and keep frying for 3 minutes.

명령문은 보통 동사원형으로 문장을 시작한다.

UNIT 2 Living Life to the Fullest

교과서 핵심 정리 Check-Up

Words & Phrases

1. (1) to some extent (2) get the most out of (3) hang out (4) in terms of (5) at her best (6) on average

2. (1) accomplish (2) productive (3) reflective (4) seize (5) urgent

3. (1) checked the building in advance of the president's visit (2) struggled hard to meet the deadline (3) caught up with the work (4) prevent them from carrying weapons

1

(1) 나는 이 문제를 어느 정도 해결했다.
(2) 그는 직원들을 최대한 활용하려고 애썼다.
(3) 여기가 너희들이 항상 어울려 노는 곳이니?
(4) 그녀는 학생의 성적을 향상시키는 것에 관해 말하고 있었다.
(5) 그 가수는 발라드를 공연할 때 가장 최고였다.
(6) 가정에서는 일 년에 평균 700 달러어치의 음식을 버리고 있다.

2

(1) 달성하다: 성공적으로 성취하거나 끝내다; 완수하다
(2) 생산적인: 사용된 자원으로 많은 것을 생산해내거나 하는
(3) 사색적인: 자신이 한 어떤 일에 대해 깊이 생각하는
(4) 붙잡다: 뭔가를 재빨리, 단단히, 그리고 힘 있게 쥐다
(5) 긴급한: 빠른 조치나 주의를 요하는; 가능한 빨리 다룰 필요가 있는

Reading Comprehension(Focus on Structure)

1. (1) the plant that her grandma sent (2) robots that teach social skills

2. (1) speak/speaking (2) abandoned (3) boring

1

(1) 그녀는 할머니가 보내주신 화초를 식탁 위에 놓았다.
목적격 관계대명사 that (선행사인 the plant는 sent의 목적어이다)
(2) 그들은 아이들에게 사회적 기술을 가르쳐주는 로봇을 만들고 있다.
주격 관계대명사 that (선행사인 robots가 동사 teach의 주어이다)

2

(1) 너는 그가 인도식 영어 말투로 말하는 것을 들었니?
hear가 지각동사이고 목적어 him이 능동적으로 말하고 있는 상황이므로 목적격보어로 동사원형 또는 현재분사를 사용한다.
(2) 사람들은 길모퉁이에 그 차가 버려져 있는 것을 보았다.
see가 지각동사이고 목적어 the car가 수동적으로 버려진 상황이므로 목적격보어로 과거분사를 사용한다.
(3) 나는 그 기사가 아주 지루하다는 걸 알았다.
「find + 목적어 +목적격보어」의 구문에서 목적어 the article이 독자를 지루하게 만드는 것이므로 능동적 의미의 현재분사를 사용한다.

언어 기능별 집중 대비

Listen and Speak/ Into Real Life

1. ③ 2. ③ 3. ⑤ 4. (1) ⑤ (2) ②, ③

1

M: What time do you think is best to watch *The Lion King* this Saturday?
W: Can you make it at 3? I think we could watch the 3:30 show.
M: That sounds perfect.
W: Great. I'll mark it on my calendar.
M: I can't wait for the show!

같이 영화보기로 한 시간을 정하고 나서 영화에 대한 기대감을 표현하는 말이 오는 게 자연스럽다.

③ 그 영화(show) 정말 기대된다.(=보고 싶어 못 기다리겠어!)
① 천천히 해.
② 그게 나에게도 좋아. (= 나도 그게 좋아.)
④ 정말 즐거웠어.
⑤ 때까지는 안 될 것 같아.

2

W: Hey, I found a very interesting article.
M: What is it about?
W: It's about how many days or years we spend on certain activities in our whole life.
M: Sounds interesting. What do we spend most of our life on?
W: This might make you sad. The article says it is working. We spend 26 years working when we consider people live for 80 years on average.
M: Really? I'm surprised it's not sleep. What do we spend the least time on, then?
W: It says it's smiling. We only spend about 88 days doing this.
M: That is very disappointing. I think we'd better smile more, even when there is nothing to smile about.
W: I think so, too.
M: Can I get your advice on ways to stay more positive and smile more? I noticed you smile more than most people do.
W: I'm glad you think so. I'm happy to help you.

여자의 긍정적인 태도와 자주 웃는 것에 대해 어떻게 하면 자신도 그럴 수 있는 지에 조언을 구하고 있다.

① 건강한 삶을 사는 법
② 신문 기사를 비판적으로 읽는 법
③ 긍정적 태도와 많이 웃는 법
④ 하루의 스트레스를 효과적으로 해소하는 법
⑤ 수면 부족 문제를 해결하는 법

3

M: Hello?
W: Hi, Jinho. It's Jin. I'm so sorry, but I'm running a little late....
M: You're late again? How come you always come late?
W: I really tried not to be late, but my mom asked for help when I was about to leave.
M: Is everything okay?
W: Actually, she is very sick. She needed me to stay until my brother came back home.
M: Oh, no. Sorry to hear that. Well, now I'm worried.
W: Sorry I couldn't let you know earlier.
M: It's okay. I can wait. What time should I expect you? Can you make it at 4?
W: Yes, I think I can make it by then. I'll run.
M: Take your time.

여자는 약속 시간에 늦는 것에 대해 미안해하면서 사과하고 있다.

4

M: Everyone struggles to learn something new. However, if you know your personality type and the associated learning strategies, your learning will be assisted to a great extent. For example, if you are outgoing, having a discussion on the topic will help you investigate the topic further. Even teaching your friends will help you process the content better. If you are not so outgoing and rather shy, making mind maps could assist your learning. If you are reflective, ask yourself questions about the concept you are learning so that you can process it step by step. You might already have your own learning style that you developed, but I advise you not to stick to your own routine. It might not suit your personality type. What you are used to is not always the best! For further information, consult my blog. Good luck with your studies!

(1) 성격 유형에 맞는 학습 전략을 찾으라는 말을 하고 있다.
① 당신의 학습 스타일에 대해 돌이켜 생각해 보라.
② 수줍음 많은 사람들을 좀 더 외향적으로 되게 도와라.
③ 장기 기억 향상을 위해 마인드맵을 사용하라.
④ 나쁜 습관을 없애는 법에 대해 좀 더 찾아보라.
⑤ 성격 유형에 맞게 학습 방법을 맞춰라.

(2) 외향적 성격의 사람에게는 having a discussion과 teaching your friends의 학습 방법이 효과적이라고 말하고 있다.

Read and Think

1. ④ 2. ① 3. ③ 4. ① 5. ② 6. ④
7. ① 8. ③ 9. ②

1 통장에 매일 입금되는 돈이 비유하는 것이 하루에 주어지는 시간임을 말하는 부분에 위치하면 자연스러운 문장이다.

2 ⓐ의 앞 문장은 많은 시간이 매일 주어진다는 말이고, 뒤 문장은 그것이 소중하게 생각되지 않을 수도 있다는 말이므로 역접의 연결어인 however가 알맞다. ⓑ는 앞 문장들의 결론이므로 therefore가 알맞다.

3 ⓐ는 「find +목적어+현재분사/과거분사」의 구문으로 여기서는 목적어 yourself가 수동적으로 잡히는 것이므로, 과거분사 caught가 적절하다.
ⓑ는 「지각동사 see +목적어+동사원형/현재분사」의 구문으로 keeping이 적절하다.
ⓒ는 '한 시간이 얻어진다'는 뜻의 수동태이므로 과거분사 earned가 적절하다.

4 '어떤 일을 하기 전에 미리 계획을 짜면 일을 체계적으로 할 수 있다'는 내용이므로 Plan Ahead (앞서 계획하라)가 적절한 제목이다.

5 ②의 more를 less로 바꿔야 문맥이 자연스럽다.

6 ④에 들어갈 말은 앞에 나온 writing처럼 전치사 like의 목적어이므로 'solving'이라는 동명사 형태로 써야 한다.

7 요약문: 하루 중 당신이 가장 생산적일 수 있는 시간대를 파악하고 그것에 따라 할 일을 계획하라.
→ 하루 중 최상의 상태로 공부할 수 있는 시간대가 언제인지를 파악해서 그 시간에 공부하는 게 생산적이라는 내용이므로 ① the periods of the day가 요약문의 빈칸에 적절한 말이다.

8 이 글은 효과적인 시간 관리에 대한 글이다.
① 스트레스 관리
② 과제 연구
③ 효과적인 시간 관리
④ 학구적인 기술 향상
⑤ 학구적 논문 쓰는 법

9 우리에게 주어지는 시간은 제한적이고 돌이킬 수 없기 때문에 하루하루 충실해야 한다는 내용이므로 ②가 가장 관련이 깊은 속담이다.
① 늦더라도 하는 게 낫다.
② 세월(시간과 조류)은 사람을 기다려주지 않는다.
③ 일찍 일어나는 새가 먹이를 잡는다.
④ 모든 달걀을 한 바구니에 넣지 말라.(위험 요소가 있으면 분산시켜라.)
⑤ 최선을 기대하고, 최악을 대비하라.

Language Notes / Write It Right

1. (1) himself talking (2) them flying (3) (that) I am fond of (4) that/which drive (by) (5) (that/which) I recently read / I read recently
2. (1) Golf balls (represent the top responsibility).
(2) It means we should do unimportant things last only after finishing all the important ones.

1
(1) 「find + oneself + -ing」의 구문으로 '자신이 ~하고 있는 것을 알게 되다/발견하다'라는 뜻이다.
(2) 「지각동사+목적어+동사원형/현재분사」의 구문이다.
(3) 선행사 The cat을 수식하는 관계대명사절로서 이때 that은 전치사의 목적격으로 쓰여서 생략이 가능하다.
(4) 선행사 Cars를 수식하는 관계대명사절로서 이때 that/which는 주격 관계대명사이므로 생략할 수 없다. cars가 복수이므로 동사도 수 일치에 따라 drive를 쓴다.
(5) 선행사 books를 수식하는 관계대명사절로서 이때 that/which는 목적격 관계대명사이므로 생략할 수 있다.

2
(1) 골프공과 구슬, 모래, 그리고 물 중에서 가장 중요한 해야 할 일을 상징하는 것은 무엇인가?
(2) '마지막으로 병에 물을 붓다'라는 것은 무엇을 의미하는가?

수준별 단원평가 Basic

1. ④ 2. ③ 3. ② 4. ⑤ 5. ②
6. end up finishing none of them 7. ① 8. ③
9. ② 10. ⓐ 현재 ⓑ 선물 11. ⑤ 12. ⑤

1
M: I'm so lost in my science class. It's so hard to catch up with the new lessons.
W: Really? I'm actually quite enjoying it.
M: How do you do that? Can I get your advice on effective ways to study science?
W: Of course. I'd love to help you.
M: Thank you so much! It means a lot to me.
과학 공부 방법에 대해 조언해 달라는 부탁을 여자가 들어주겠다고 한 상황이므로 남자는 고마움을 표현하는 말을 하는 것이 자연스럽다.
① 나에게도 도움이 될 거야.
② 걱정 마. 천천히 해.
③ 괜찮아. 내가 할게.
④ 정말 고마워. 나에겐 정말 큰 의미야.
⑤ 전적으로 동감이야. 고마워.

2
(Phone rings.)
M: Hello?
W: Hi, Jinho. It's Jin. I'm so sorry, but I'm running a little late....
M: You're late again? How come you always come late?
W: I really tried not to be late, but my mom asked for help when I was about to leave.
M: Is everything okay?
W: Actually, she is very sick. She needed me to stay until my brother came back home.
M: Oh, no. Sorry to hear that. Well, now I'm worried.
W: Sorry I couldn't let you know earlier.
M: It's okay. I can wait. What time should I expect you? Can you make it at 4?
W: Yes, I think I can make it by then. I'll run.
M: Take your time.
대화에서 여자는 엄마가 아프셔서 늦는 것이라고 말하고 있다.

3 ② urgent: 긴박한

4 ⑤ get the most out of: ~를 최대한 활용하다

5 ③ finite: 유한한 ④ gigantic: 어마어마하게 큰

6 you may에 연결되는 동사구로서 「end up -ing」는 '결국 ~하게 되다'라는 뜻이다.

7 top responsibilities가 되는 것은 중요하고 긴급한 일들이므로 첫 번째 범주에 속하는 것이다.

8 ③에서 동사 heard는 지각동사이므로 「지각동사+목적어+동사원형 또는 분사」의 구문을 써야 한다. 따라서 to call은 call 또는 calling으로 고쳐야 맞다. 이 경우 목적어가 his name이면 Peter heard his name called.로 과거분사를 써야 한다.

9 ②의 주격 관계대명사 that은 생략할 수 없다.
① Mike가 추천한 호텔에 머물자.
② 나는 건조한 장소에서 잘 자라는 식물을 하나 샀다.
③ 네가 깬 그 거울은 비싼 거였어.
④ 우리 삼촌이 쓰신 책을 보여줄게.
⑤ 이것은 엄마가 나에게 사준 카메라이다.

10 ⓐ는 시간의 개념으로서 '현재'를 의미한다.
ⓑ는 우리에게 주어진 시간의 소중함을 말하는 개념으로서'선물'을 의미한다.

11 '그것은 정말 성공적이었다!'라는 말은 성공의 내용에 대해 세세히 말하기 바로 직전에 오는 것이 적절하다.

12 진우는 중요한 과제를 다 끝내고 나서 가족과 시간을 보냈으므로 ⑤는 내용과 일치하지 않는다.

수준별 단원평가 Advanced

1. ⑤ 2. ④ 3. ③ 4. ① 5. ②
6. ⓐ life/time ⓑ 86,400 seconds / 24 hours / a day ⓒ A day is gone. / 24 hours has passed. 등
7. ⓓ spend → spending 8. account
9. Those that fall under the first category
10. ① 11. Responsibilities in the Order of Importance
12. ② 13. the importance of each activity 14. ⑤
15. (1) found himself thinking (2) some tips that will help you manage your time more effectively 16. ⓐ golf balls ⓑ marbles ⓒ sand ⓓ water 17. 해설 참조

[1-2]

M: Everyone struggles to learn something new. However, if you know your personality type and the associated learning strategies, your learning will be assisted to a great extent. For example, if you are outgoing, having a discussion on the topic will help you investigate the topic further. Even teaching your friends will help you process the content better. If you are not so outgoing and rather shy, making mind maps could assist your learning. If you are reflective, ask yourself questions about the concept you are learning so that you can process it step by step. You might already have your own learning style that you developed, but I advise you not to stick to your own routine. It might not suit your personality type. What you are used to is not always the best! For further information, consult my blog. Good luck with your studies!

1 남자는 성격 유형에 맞는 학습 방법을 찾아서 개발하라고 말하고 있다.

2 사색적인(reflective) 학습자에게는 스스로에게 개념을 이해했는지에 대한 질문을 하는 방법을 추천하고 있다.

3

M: Wow, Kristin, it looks like you already finished your math project.
W: Hey, Tyler! Yes, I got it done yesterday.
M: How do you do that? I always finish everything at the last minute.
W: I used to be like that, too, but I'm trying to treat my time like money these days.
M: Can I get your advice on how to manage my time?
W: Well, it takes some time to fully explain it. Let's meet up some time and talk about it.
M: Why don't we do it tomorrow? Can you make it at 4 tomorrow to the school library after school?
W: I don't think I can make it by then. Can we push it back by 30 minutes?
M: Yes, that's fine too. Thanks a lot, Kristin!

Kristin은 수학 과제를 이미 끝냈고, Tyler는 늘 마감 일자 임박해서 과제를 끝내는 습관이 있으며, 이 둘은 4:30에 만나기로 하고 있다.

4 B의 응답으로 뒤에 It is working이 나오며 80년 동안 26년이나 일하면서 보낸다는 설명이 나오므로 ①의 질문이 가장 자연스럽다.

5 주간 계획을 짜서 생활하는 것의 장점을 말하고 있으므로 'in a timely fashion' 즉 '시기적절한 방식으로'라는 말이 가장 적절하다.

6 ⓐ 은행계좌는 우리에게 주어지는 시간 또는 삶을 의미한다.
ⓑ 86,400원은 하루 86,400초를 의미한다.
ⓒ 밤이 되면 그 모든 돈이 사라진다는 것은 하루의 시간이 다 지나가버리는 것을 의미한다.

7 ⓕ의 spend는 문장에서 주어의 역할을 해야 하므로 동명사 형태인 spending으로 써야 한다.

8 계좌 설명의 풀이에 해당하는 단어는 account이다.

9 those that ~은 '~한 것들'이라는 의미로 that은 형용사절을 이끄는 관계대명사이다.

10 ⓑ의 뒤에는 다음 주에 있을 시험을 예시로 들고 있으므로 for example 또는 for instance가 와야 한다.
ⓒ의 뒤에는 앞에 오는 문장과 역접 관계인 말이 오므로 but, however 등의 연결어가 적절하다.

11 할 일을 중요도 순으로 배치하라는 의미의 제목이다.

12 〈보기〉 그 회의는 꽤 격식이 없는 방식으로 진행되었다. (fashion은 '방식'이라는 의미로 쓰였다.)
① 그는 최신 유행하는 머리로 잘랐다.
② 그 부대는 잔인한 방식으로 행동했다.
③ 니스커트가 다시 유행하고 있다.
④ 보석과 의류의 유행은 계절에 따라 다양하다.
⑤ 그런 달라붙는 청바지는 오래 전에 유행이 지났다.

13 '그것을 바탕으로'에서 '그것'은 각 활동의 중요도를 말하고 있다.

14 바쁜 스케줄 안에서도 가족과의 소중한 시간을 갖는 것을 잊지 말라고 말하고 있으므로 ⑤ '가족과의 사간은 다른 중요한 일들만큼 똑같이 중요도가 높다'라는 말이 오는 게 적절하다.
① 바쁘더라도 쉴 필요가 있다
② 가족과의 시간은 해야 할 일 목록의 맨 첫 번째에 있어야 한다.
③ 가족과의 시간을 갖기 전에 모든 일을 끝내야 한다.
④ 소중한 시간을 친한 친구들과 함께 하라.

15 (1) 「find oneself -ing」의 구문을 활용하여 쓸 수 있다.
(2) 「선행사+관계대명사절」의 구문을 활용하여 쓸 수 있다.

16 병을 빈 공간 없이 가득 채우려면 부피가 큰 것부터 넣는 것이 좋으므로 ⓐ 골프공 ⓑ 구슬 ⓒ 모래 ⓓ 물의 순서로 넣는다.

17 〈예시 답안〉
I got the most out of the 10-minute break in school by solving five math problems during the break. However, I spent too much time in the afternoon using my cell phone and couldn't finish my history assignment. Tomorrow, I will try not to waste my time using my cell phone. I will assign more time to my history assignment which is due on Friday.

UNIT 3 Together We Make a Family

교과서 핵심 정리 Check-Up

Words & Phrases

1. (1) bridge the gap (2) suffer from (3) break out
(4) have any choice but (5) Watch your words
2. (1) slang (2) poverty (3) suffer
(4) endure (5) adopt
3. (1) tries to bridge the generation gap
(2) put up with your bad behavior any longer
(3) between the educated and uneducated
(4) satisfied with this situation

1
(1) 이 기금은 학생들의 (경제적) 필요와 그들의 소득 간의 간극을 메우기 위해 사용될 것이다.
(2) 우울증을 겪는 사람들은 무력하거나 짓눌리거나 화난 감정을 느낄 수 있다.
(3) 베트남 전쟁은 언제 발발했어?
(4) 나에겐 마음을 바꾸는 것 밖에는 다른 선택의 여지가 없는 것 같아요.
(5) 말조심하고 네가 무슨 말을 하고 있는 지 잘 생각해라.

2
(1) 특히 특정한 무리의 사람들이 주로 사용하는 매우 격식이 없는 언어
(2) 매우 가난한 상태
(3) 신체적 혹은 정신적 고통을 경험하다
(4) 뭔가 어렵거나 불쾌하거나 고통스러운 것을 견디어내다
(5) 다른 사람의 자녀를 자신의 가족으로 법적으로 받아들여 자신의 아이로 돌보다

Reading Comprehension(Focus on Structure)

1. (1) it difficult to study much at night
   (2) it impossible for me to get there
2. (1) had never been (2) had seen (3) had already started

1

(1) Emma는 하루 종일 일하고 난 후 밤에 많이 공부하는 것이 힘들다는 것을 알게 되었다. : find + it + 형용사 + to 부정사

(2) 엄마는 내가 그곳에 제 시간에 도착하는 게 불가능하다는 것을 알게 되었다.: to부정사의 의미상의 주어는 보통 「for +목적격」 형태로 쓴다.

2

(1) 일곱 살 생일이 되기 전까지 Linda는 한 번도 동물원에 가본 적이 없었다. : 일곱 살 생일이 '과거'시제이므로 그 전의 경험은 「had+p.p.」형태의 과거완료시제가 알맞다.

(2) Sam은 그 전 날 자신이 보았던 영화에 대해 말해주었다. : 영화를 본 것과 그 영화에 관해 말한 것 중 먼저 일어난 일을 과거완료로 나타낸다.

(3) 내가 거기 도착했을 때 사람들은 이미 찻잎을 따기 시작한 상태였다.: 내가 도착한 시점 이전에 사람들이 찻잎 따기를 시작했으므로 과거완료시제를 사용한다.

언어 기능별 집중 대비

Listen and Speak/ Into Real Life

1. ① 2. ⑤ 3. ⑤ 4. (1) ① (2) ④

1

M: Did you watch the movie *My Life* last night on TV? It was wonderful!
W: I did, but I couldn't focus on the movie.
M: Really? Why not?
W: It was because of my old TV. I'm not satisfied with my TV's bad speakers.

낡은 TV의 스피커가 상태가 좋지 않아 영화 시청 중 내용에 집중할 수 없었다고 말하고 있는 것으로 보아 기분이 좋지 않은 상태이다.

2

W: Welcome back. This is your DJ Jennifer on FM *Forever Teen*. Here is our second caller. Hello?
M: Hi, Jennifer. My name is Ted, and I'm calling from Seattle.
W: Hi, Ted. What can we help you with?
M: I'm having a hard time talking with my parents. I'm not satisfied with this situation.
W: I'm sorry to hear that. Can you tell me more about it?
M: When I talk to my parents, they keep asking me so many questions because they don't understand some of the words that I use.
W: Do you use Internet slang when you talk to them?
M: Yes, sometimes.
W: I know a lot of teens tend to use that kind of language, but we should watch our words.
M: But I like using those words because they are fun and cool.
W: Let's suppose your parents used words that you didn't understand. How would you feel?
M: Well... I guess I would feel pretty bad.
W: How about avoiding language like that when you talk with your parents?
M: I think it will take time to change my habit, but I'll try. Thanks for the tip.

How about avoiding language like that?이라고 충고하고 있으므로 속어 사용을 자제하라는 내용이 맞다.

3

M: Mina, we're going to visit your grandparents this weekend.
W: This weekend? Dad, I was planning to go to the library with Tyler.
M: Come on, it's been a while since you last saw them.
W: Well actually, when I talk to them, I get bored.
M: I think you should consider their age. It's natural to feel a generation gap.
W: Dad, I'd love to go, but I have nothing to do at their house.
M: Hmm... Why don't you try helping your grandfather this time?
W: Help? What do you mean?
M: Your grandfather told me that he wanted to learn how to send a photo with his cell phone. Can you help him?
W: Oh, I can do that. Also, I can show him how to write an email on his phone.
M: That's great. I'm sure your grandfather will be happy. What about your plans with Tyler, then?
W: I'll cancel plans with him.

send a photo with his cell phone과 write an email on his phone은 즉, 휴대전화로 사진 전송하는 것과 휴대전화로 이메일 쓰는 법을 알려드릴 예정이다.

4

W: Today we have a special guest, David Smith. He is on the stage now.
M: Thanks for inviting me to your show, Kelly. You look great today.
W: Thanks. We are so happy to have you as a guest again. I heard you recently wrote a new book about the digital divide. Can you explain it briefly?
M: Okay, as you know, these days it's hard to imagine our life without communication devices such as smartphones, computers, and the Internet. However, have you thought about some of the people living in the Amazon Rainforest? Their lives may be quite different from ours. Not everyone in the world has access to communication technology. To describe this difference, we use the term "digital divide."
W: So, when was this term created?
M: Since the late 1990s, the term has been used to describe the growing gap between those people who have Internet access and those who do not. This divide also exists between cities and rural areas.
W: Does the divide exist between generations?
M: That's a good question. The answer is yes. The gap between teens and older people is getting bigger. In my book, I cover some specific examples of the digital divide between generations and suggest how we can bridge the gap.

(1) 디지털 격차의 의미와 더불어 세대 간 디지털 격차에 관해 썼다고 얘기하고 있다.

(2) 디지털 격차는 1990년대 말부터 쓰이기 시작한 용어이다.

Read and Think

1. ③ 2. ④ 3. ⑤ 4. ③ 5. ③ 6. ③
7. ② 8. ① 9. ④

1 할아버지에게 비디오 파일을 보내드릴 수 없으니 직접 찾아뵐 수 있을 때까지 기다리는 수밖에 없다.

2 ④는 문맥상 세대 간 간극을 악화시킨다는 말이 적절하므로 'worsened'로 고쳐야 알맞다.

3 할아버지와의 gap은 스마트폰 사용을 좋아하는 나와 반대로 그것을 싫어하는 할아버지와 생긴 갈등이다.

4 가족 간의 유대감을 느낄 수 있는 사진을 설명하고 있으므로 첫 번째 사진 이야기 뒤에 위치하는 것이 적절하다.

5 보이지 않는 벽이란 스마트폰 사용에 집중하고 있는 자신들과 TV를 보고 계신 할아버지와의 사이에 의사소통 단절을 의미한다.

6 '할아버지에 대한 연민 – 할아버지에 대한 이해와 세대 간극 해소를 위한 방법 고민 – 가족 디지털 앨범을 만들자는 아버지의 제안 – 할아버지의 승낙'의 순서가 자연스럽다.

7 ②의 how did people suffer는 remembers의 목적어 역할을 하는 절이므로 간접의문문의 순서인 'how people suffered'로 써야 맞다.

8 음악에 대한 가족들의 애정을 기술하고 있으므로 ① '음악에 대한 애정이 우리 가족의 피에 흐르고 있다'라는 말이 적절하다.

9 ⓐ에서 interesting의 주체는 사람이 아닌 사물 it이고, ⓑ의 경우 「look + 형용사」의 구문이 맞다. ⓒ는 할머니가 좋아하는 노래를 이미 골랐다라는 현재완료 시제 구문이므로 has가 맞다.

Language Notes / Write It Right

1. (1) when World War I broke out (2) why she wants to become a soldier (3) the old man had given to me
   (4) to deepen my understanding toward other cultures
   (5) put up with the noise
2. (1) how much it cost to study in the U.K.
   (2) what kind of errors he made
   (3) whether(또는 if) Tony signed the contract (or not).
3. (1) the plane had already departed
   (2) we had owned for ten years (또는 since 2005) (3) had not [never] studied Thai
   (4) had repaired many cars

1
(1) 동사 know의 목적어로 쓰인 의문문이고 시제가 과거이므로 「when(의문사) + World War I (주어) + broke out (동사)」의 어순으로 쓴다.
(2) 동사 know의 목적어로 의문문이 삽입되는 구문이므로 「의문사 + 주어 + 동사」의 어순인 간접의문문으로 쓴다.
(3) '던진 것'이 과거 시제이므로 '노인이 준 것'은 그 이전에 일어난 과거완료 (had + p.p.)시제로 표현한다.
(4) 명사 opportunity를 뒤에서 수식하는 to부정사 구문이다.
(5) put up with는 '~을 견디다'라는 뜻이다.

2
(1) 그녀는 나에게 영국에서 공부하는 것이 비용이 얼마나 들었는지 물었다.
(2) 나는 그가 어떤 종류의 실수들을 했는지 궁금했다.
(3) Kate는 Tony가 계약서에 서명을 했는지 안했는지 알고 싶었다. (의문사가 없는 의문문을 간접의문문으로 바꿀 때는 whether 또는 if를 사용한다.)

3
(1) 내 오빠가 공항에 도착했을 때 비행기는 이미 (15분 전에) 이륙한 상태였다.
(2) 우리는 2005년부터 소유하고 있었던 집을 팔았다.
(3) 나는 태국으로 이사하기 전에는 태국어를 배워본 적이 없다.
(4) Sam은 기계공 면허를 받기 이전부터 많은 차를 수리했었다.

수준별 단원평가 Basic

1. ②	2. ⑤	3. ②	4. ②	5. ⑤	6. ①
7. ②	8. ③	9. ⓓ why he held on to			10. ③
11. ⑤	12. making a digital family album				
13. it difficult to stay awake					

1
W: Honey, what's wrong? Is it not working again?
M: It's working, but I'm not happy with this tablet. It's too complicated.
W: It's really easy. Let me show you how to use it.
M: Okay, thanks.

Let me show you how to ~라고 한 말 뒤에 이어지는 말이므로 감사의 표현이 적절하다.

2
W: Welcome back. This is your DJ Jennifer on FM *Forever Teen*. Here is our second caller. Hello?
M: Hi, Jennifer. My name is Ted, and I'm calling from Seattle.
W: Hi, Ted. What can we help you with?
M: I'm having a hard time talking with my parents. I'm not satisfied with this situation.
W: I'm sorry to hear that. Can you tell me more about it?
M: When I talk to my parents, they keep asking me so many questions because they don't understand some of the words that I use.
W: Do you use Internet slang when you talk to them?
M: Yes, sometimes.
W: I know a lot of teens tend to use that kind of language, but we should watch our words.
M: But I like using those words because they are fun and cool.
W: Let's suppose your parents used words that you didn't understand. How would you feel?
M: Well... I guess I would feel pretty bad.
W: How about avoiding language like that when you talk with your parents?
M: I think it will take time to change my habit, but I'll try. Thanks for the tip.

라디오 청취자 참여 전화 프로그램에서 자신의 고민을 상담하고 있다.

3 bridge the gap = narrow the gap: 간극을 좁히다

4 ① rural 시골의 – urban 도시의
② select 선택하다 – choose 선택하다
③ divide 나누다 – unify 통일하다
④ totally 전체적으로 – partially 부분적으로
⑤ darken 어둡게 하다 – brighten 밝히다

5 그녀는 인내심이 매우 강해서 모든 종류의 불편함을 참아냈다. (put up with: ~를 참아내다)

6 ① family bonds 가족의 유대감
② family conflicts 가족 간 갈등
③ generation gap 세대 간 간극
④ poor childhood: 가난한 어린 시절
⑤ high technologies 첨단 기술

7 ②He has not studied Italian before he moved to Italy.
→ He had not studied Italian before he moved to Italy. (이탈리아로 이사한 것이 과거 시제로 표현되었으므로, 그 이전에 경험한 것은 과거완료 시제로 나타내야 한다.)

8 ③ It doesn't matter how much money does he make.
→ It doesn't matter how much money he makes. 「의문사 + 주어 + 동사」의 형태인 간접의문문으로 나타내야 한다.

9 ⓓ why held he on to → why he held on to (간접의문문)

10 ③에서 말한 것처럼 글쓴이가 할아버지에게 디지털 격차에 대한 설명을 해드렸다는 언급은 없다.

11 디지털 가족 앨범의 제작으로 가족 간 연대를 돈독히 할 수 있을 것으로 보고 있으므로 strengthen the family bonds가 적절하다.

13 「find it + 형용사 + to 부정사」의 구문으로서 '~ 하는 것이 …하다는 것을 알게 되다'라는 의미이다.

수준별 단원평가 Advanced

1. ① 2. ③ 3. ② 4. ④
5. had no choice but to wait 6. ③ 7. digital 8. how I would handle certain situations 9. ③
10. ① interesting → interested 11. 해설 참조

1

M: Mina, we're going to visit your grandparents this weekend.
W: This weekend? Dad, I was planning to go to the library with Tyler.
M: Come on, it's been a while since you last saw them.
W: Well actually, when I talk to them, I get bored.
M: I think you should consider their age. It's natural to feel a generation gap.
W: Dad, I'd love to go, but I have nothing to do at their house.
M: Hmm... Why don't you try helping your grandfather this time?
W: Help? What do you mean?
M: Your grandfather told me that he wanted to learn how to send a photo with his cell phone. Can you help him?
W: Oh, I can do that. Also, I can show him how to write an email on his phone.
M: That's great. I'm sure your grandfather will be happy. What about your plans with Tyler, then?
W: I'll cancel plans with him.

미나는 할아버지 댁에 가면 할 게 없어서 지루하다고 불평하고 있다.

2

W: Andy, we're going to visit your grandparents this Sunday.
M: Sunday? Mom, I was planning to play soccer with Patrick.
W: Oh, come on. They really want to see you. You can play soccer next time.
M: Well, to be honest, when I visit them I get bored. Sometimes it's not easy for me to talk with them.
W: I know what you mean, but I think you should consider their age.
M: Mom, I want something exciting to do at their house.
W: Hmm... Why don't you try helping them this time?
M: What do you mean? How can I help them?
W: Your grandparents told me that they wanted to learn how to download music with their smartphone. Can you help them?
M: Sure. I could also show them how to download useful apps on their phone. I'll cancel my plans with Patrick.
W: That's great. I'm sure your grandparents will be happy.

Andy는 할아버지께 음악과 앱을 다운로드 받는 방법을 알려주려 하고 있다.

3

W: Welcome back. This is your DJ Jennifer on FM *Forever Teen*. Here is our second caller. Hello?
M: Hi, Jennifer. My name is Ted, and I'm calling from Seattle.
W: Hi, Ted. What can we help you with?
M: I'm having a hard time talking with my parents. I'm not satisfied with this situation.
W: I'm sorry to hear that. Can you tell me more about it?
M: When I talk to my parents, they keep asking me so many questions because they don't understand some of the words that I use.
W: Do you use Internet slang when you talk to them?
M: Yes, sometimes.
W: I know a lot of teens tend to use that kind of language, but we should watch our words.
M: But I like using those words because they are fun and cool.
W: Let's suppose your parents used words that you didn't understand. How would you feel?
M: Well... I guess I would feel pretty bad.
W: How about avoiding language like that when you talk with your parents?
M: I think it will take time to change my habit, but I'll try. Thanks for the tip.

속어를 쓰는 것은 Ted의 부모님이 아니라 Ted 자신이다.

4 디지털 격차는 인터넷 접근이 가능한 지역과 그렇지 못한 지역 사람들 사이에 발생하는 정보의 격차를 의미한다.

5 「have no choice but to + 동사원형」: ~하지 않을 수 없다

6 한국전쟁 발발 – 전쟁 이후 모두 힘들어했다는 이야기 – 할아버지가 돈을 벌러 서울로 상경한 이야기 – 사우디아라비아와 이란에 건축 업무를 위해 가서 고생했던 일 등의 순서가 가장 자연스럽다.

8 간접의문문의 순서 「의문사 + 주어 + 동사」의 구문으로 써야 한다.

10 it이 가목적어이므로 보어로는 interested가 아니라 interesting을 써야 한다

11 〈예시 답안〉
I can teach elderly how to use computers. / I can give a helpful guide on Internet Safety Tips for people.

1학기 중간고사 UNIT 1 – UNIT 3

01. ③ 02. ④ 03. ② 04. ② 05. ③ 06. ③
07. ④ 08. ⑤ 09. ⑤ 10. ① 11. ③ 12. ⑤
13. ⑤ 14. ② 15. ⑤ 16. ④ 17. ⑤ 18. ②
19. of yourself for making/producing (such) great short films (또는 that you made/produced such great short films)
20. baking 21. caught
22. keeping a calendar or making a daily to-do list
23. an invisible wall separating us from our grandfather
24. 해설 참조 25 해설 참조

1

M: Hi, Hwajin. How was your first week at school?
W: Well, everything is new to me. A week has passed so quickly. But I found my new homeroom teacher and classmates to be nice and friendly.
M: That's good. By the way, do you have any plans for this weekend?
W: Yeah, I teach Korean to Vietnamese children every Saturday.
M: Oh, is it part of a community service?
W: Yes, it is. I have worked as a volunteer teacher for two years at the community center. I think it's meaningful, and I am also really interested in teaching languages.
M: Of course. You can speak both Vietnamese and Korean. That's a perfect kind of volunteer work for you. Can I join you this weekend?
W: Sure, you can. What do you want to do for them?
M: I'm interested in mathematics, so I think I can teach them math.
W: Oh, that sounds good.

화진이의 친구도 지역 커뮤니티 센터에서 수학을 가르치는 자원봉사 활동을 하려고 하고 있다.

2

W: Welcome, freshmen! I am Jiwon, the head of the student council. What do you want to do in your free time? What are you most interested in? Our school clubs are looking forward to meeting all of you. Our school has 35 clubs.

and you're welcome to join any of them. The application period starts from this Wednesday and ends on Tuesday next week. You can get information about all our clubs on our school website. You can get the application form from your homeroom teacher and hand it in to each club room. When you choose a school club, you need to think about your hobbies and interests. You also need to consider your aptitude and dream job. Finding the right club is the key to a happy school life for the next three years. Think it through and then hurry to sign up!

지원서 양식(application form)은 담임 선생님에게서 받을 수 있다.

3

M: Everyone struggles to learn something new. However, if you know your personality type and the associated learning strategies, your learning will be assisted to a great extent. For example, if you are outgoing, having a discussion on the topic will help you investigate the topic further. Even teaching your friends will help you process the content better. If you are not so outgoing and rather shy, making mind maps could assist your learning. If you are reflective, ask yourself questions about the concept you are learning so that you can process it step by step. You might already have your own learning style that you developed, but I advise you not to stick to your own routine. It might not suit your personality type. What you are used to is not always the best! For further information, consult my blog. Good luck with your studies!

자신의 성격과 맞는 학습 전략을 찾아서 공부하라고 얘기하고 있다.

4

W: Welcome back. This is your DJ Jennifer on FM *Forever Teen*. Here is our second caller. Hello?

M: Hi, Jennifer. My name is Ted, and I'm calling from Seattle.

W: Hi, Ted. What can we help you with?

M: I'm having a hard time talking with my parents. I'm not satisfied with this situation.

W: I'm sorry to hear that. Can you tell me more about it?

M: When I talk to my parents, they keep asking me so many questions because they don't understand some of the words that I use.

W: Do you use Internet slang when you talk to them?

M: Yes, sometimes.

W: I know a lot of teens tend to use that kind of language, but we should watch our words.

M: But I like using those words because they are fun and cool.

W: Let's suppose your parents used words that you didn't understand. How would you feel?

M: Well... I guess I would feel pretty bad.

W: How about avoiding language like that when you talk with your parents?

M: I think it will take time to change my habit, but I'll try. Thanks for the tip.

여자의 충고에 관한 응답으로 속어를 쓰지 않으려고 하지만 습관이 되어버려서 다소 힘들 것이라고 말하고 있다.

5

W: Today we have a special guest, David Smith. He is on the stage now.

M: Thanks for inviting me to your show, Kelly. You look great today.

W: Thanks. We are so happy to have you as a guest again. I heard you recently wrote a new book about the digital divide. Can you explain it briefly?

M: Okay, as you know, these days it's hard to imagine our life without communication devices such as smartphones, computers, and the Internet. However, have you thought about some of the people living in the Amazon Rainforest? Their lives may be quite different from ours. Not everyone in the world has access to communication technology. To describe this difference, we use the term "digital divide."

W: So, when was this term created?

M: Since the late 1990s, the term has been used to describe the growing gap between those people who have Internet access and those who do not. This divide also exists between cities and rural areas.

W: Does the divide exist between generations?

M: That's a good question. The answer is yes. The gap between teens and older people is getting bigger. In my book, I cover some specific examples of the digital divide between generations and suggest how we can bridge the gap.

남자의 두 번째 말에 digital divide에 관한 설명이 있다.

6

W: Andy, we're going to visit your grandparents this Sunday.

M: Sunday? Mom, I was planning to play soccer with Patrick.

W: Oh, come on. They really want to see you. You can play soccer next time.

M: Well, to be honest, when I visit them I get bored. Sometimes it's not easy for me to talk with them.

W: I know what you mean, but I think you should consider their age.

M: Mom, I want something exciting to do at their house.

W: Hmm... Why don't you try helping them this time?

M: What do you mean? How can I help them?

W: Your grandparents told me that they wanted to learn how to download music with their smartphone. Can you help them?

M: Sure. I could also show them how to download useful apps on their phone. I'll cancel my plans with Patrick.

W: That's great. I'm sure your grandparents will be happy.

Andy가 조부모를 위해 유용한 앱을 내려 받는 법을 알려드리겠다고 하므로 조부모가 좋아하실 거라는 응답이 자연스럽다.

7 ④의 문장은 자동차와 비행기 모형을 조립하는 동아리 활동 홍보와 무관한 문장이다.

8 ⑤ be doubled → double (수동태가 아닌 능동태여야 맞다)

9 ⑤ 완벽한 공연을 위한 준비 사항에 대한 언급은 없다.

10 ① 86,400초가 매일 주어진다고 했을 때 그게 소중해 보이지 않을 수도 있다는 말이 이어서 나오는 게 적절하다.

11 ③ 초점을 잃지 않고 실제로 중요한 것을 해 내도록 도와준다는 말이 오는 것이 적절하다.

12 ⑤의 문장은 자투리 시간을 활용하는 것과 관련이 없는 문장이다.

13 (D) 해야 할 일들을 적어봄 → (C) 긴급하고 중요한 우선순위를 정함 → (B) 우선순위에 맞추어 과제를 수행함

14 ② 효과적인 시간 관리에 대한 글이다.

15 ⑤ hard: 어려운, 어렵게, 열심히 hardly: 거의 ~하지 않다

16 ④ 디지털 가족 앨범이 가족 간의 유대(bonds)를 강화할 수 있을 것으로 생각했다는 말이 적절하다.

17 진아의 할머니가 좋아하는 노래를 직접 불러서 녹음했다는 말은 나오지 않는다.

18 ② how suffered people → how people suffered (간접의문문)

19 '노력의 결과가 달콤하다'라는 의미는 수고해서 만든 영화에 관해 관객들의 박수갈채를 받을 때 '뿌듯해질 것'이라는 의미이다.

20 전치사 about의 목적어로 동명사 형태가 된다.

21 caught up with: ~에 사로잡힌

22 「지각동사 + 목적어 + 현재분사」의 구문을 사용하되 목적보어인 현재분사 2개가 or로 연결되어 있다.

23 an invisible wall을 수식하는 분사구(separating~)를 뒤에 쓴다.

24 디지털 기기를 사용하는 데서 오는 장점과 단점을 각각 생각해서 적는다.
〈예시 답안〉
① advantage: You can communicate with the people from all over the world through using digital devices. ② disadvantage: Cyber bullying can arise due to the use of social networking sites.

25 〈예시 답안〉
I wanted to develop my debating skills in English so I joined *Great Debaters Club*. We meet once a week with a different controversial topic and debate on the topic. I usually take the role of the keynote speaker, but sometimes I take the role of a moderator. Through this club activity, I learned how to think more logically and speak more persuasively.

UNIT 4 Let's Make Every Day Earth Day

교과서 핵심 정리 Check-Up

Words & Phrases

1. (1) root out (2) turn in (3) keep in mind
   (4) make up for (5) result in (6) At long last
2. (1) official (2) drought (3) shortage
   (4) alternative (5) leftover
3. (1) has resulted in the sinking
   (2) why we should use renewable energy
   (3) Make sure that you follow
   (4) transformed sea water into fresh water

1
(1) 그들은 경찰 부패를 뿌리 뽑기 위해 열심히 노력했다.
(2) 수업 후에 보고서 제출하는 것 잊지 마세요.
(3) 수리비용이 비싸다는 것을 명심해야 한다.
(4) 어떤 금액의 돈도 아이의 죽음을 보상해 줄 수 없다.
(5) 규칙적인 운동은 스트레스 수위를 낮춰줄 수 있다.
(6) 마침내 정부가 우리의 문제에 대해 귀를 기울이기 시작하고 있다.

2
(1) 권위를 가지고 공공연하게 발표된
(2) 비가 거의 내리지 않거나 전혀 내리지 않는 오랜 기간
(3) 뭔가가 충분하지 않은 상황
(4) 다른 것을 사용하고 싶지 않을 때 사용할 수 있는 것
(5) 사용되지 않거나 먹다가 남은 부분

Reading Comprehension(Focus on Structure)

1. (1) is being delivered by the drone
   (2) is being calculated by GPS
2. (1) inspired the researchers, who tried to solve the problem
   (2) My grandfather, who is 87 years old,
   (3) The film, which stars Tom Carter,

1
(1) 그 우편물은 드론에 의해 배송되고 있는 중이다. : 현재진행 수동태 – 「be동사의 현재형 + being + p.p.」
(2) 너의 목적지로 가는 그 경로는 GPS에 의해 계산되고 있는 중이다.

2
(1) 그것은 그 문제를 해결하기 위해 연구자들에게 영감을 주었고 그들은 애썼다.
(2) 우리 할아버지는 지금 87세이신데 매일 수영하러 다니신다.
(3) 그 영화는 Tom Cater가 주연을 맡았는데 금요일에 개봉된다.

언어 기능별 집중 대비

Listen and Speak / Into Real Life

1. ⑤ 2. ③ 3. ④ 4. (1) ② (2) ⑤

1
W: Ladies and gentlemen! May I have your attention, please? Please make sure that you turn your phones off before the forum begins. Today we have a special guest. She is the author of the book, *Seven Ways to Save Mother Earth*. Let's welcome Michelle Kim.
포럼이 시작되기 전에 청중들에게 휴대 전화를 꺼줄 것을 당부하고 있다.
① 포럼에 늦지 마세요.
② 사진을 찍으려면 허락을 구하세요.
③ 포럼에 휴대전화를 갖고 오지 마세요.
④ 특별 손님 사진을 찍지 마세요.

2
W: You know what? Our school is holding a poster contest to celebrate World Environment Day.
M: Oh, yeah? What kind of poster contest is it?
W: I took a picture of the notice on the board. Let me show it to you.
M: Sounds interesting. We're good at art. Can we make posters as a team?
W: Yeah, the rules say we can.
M: Are there any special rules about the design and size of posters?
W: It says posters should be 30cm × 45cm. Also, we can use any materials we want.
M: Should we write a slogan for the posters?
W: Good question. The rules say, "Make sure you don't copy any famous slogans. The school wants your creative ideas."
M: When do we have to turn the poster in?
W: By next Friday. And the rules say, "Don't forget to write your name on the back of your posters."
그림의 재료는 아무거나 원하는 대로 사용할 수 있다고 하고 있다.

3
W: Hi, Marco. What are you doing here?
M: I'm separating all the garbage produced in my classroom. It's my duty for this week.
W: Wait! You know what? The bottle caps do not belong with the glass.
M: Oh, you're right. I still get confused about which items go where.
W: I know what you mean, but I have a simple tip for you.
M Really? What's that?
W: When you're confused, you can just check if the items have a triangular symbol and numbers inside.
M: I can see a triangle and number 1 on this item.
W: Items marked "1" and "2" mean they can be recycled.
M: Got it. Thanks for the tip.
W: Make sure you don't mix up what is recyclable and what is not.

재활용 가능한 것과 쓰레기의 구별 방법을 알려주었으므로 이에 적절한 당부를 고른다.

① 물건에 적절하게 표시하도록 해라.
② 공공장소에서 쓰레기를 함부로 버리지 않도록 해라.
③ 분리수거하는 의무(일)를 반드시 해라.
④ 재활용 가능한 것과 가능하지 않은 것을 섞는 일이 없도록 해라.
⑤ 비윤리적 방법으로 생산된 제품은 구매하지 않도록 해라.

4

M: All across the world, people are facing serious environmental problems. It is May now, but it is already unusually hot. Today heat wave warnings were issued in Korea because the temperature was recorded at over 35 degrees Celsius. In India, the temperature reached 50 degrees Celsius for several days, and over a thousand people have died of heat-related illness so far. Beijing is covered with heavy yellow dust. Last Friday, schools were closed, and people were advised to avoid outdoor activities. Because of the heavy yellow dust, more than 300 flights were canceled at Beijing International Airport. Also, heavy rain and storms hit many cities in the United States. In Texas and Oklahoma, powerful storms killed at least nine people, and thirty people are still missing. On the other hand, California has been in a severe drought for the past five years. The water levels of lakes are getting lower and lower. To stop suffering from these problems, it's time for us to take action for our earth.

기후 변화로 인한 다양한 재난의 결과에 대해 말하고 있다.

① 대도시의 짙은 황사
② 기후 변화와 그것의 영향
③ 환경을 위한 에너지 절약법
④ 도시 지역의 심각한 가뭄의 증가
⑤ 인간 활동에 의한 자연 재해들

(2) 오염된 식수로 인한 전염병 발생은 언급되고 있지 않다.

Read and Think

1. ① have→ has	2. ④	3. ⑤	4. ②	5. ③
6. ①	7. ①	8. ①	9. ⑤	

1 ①「the number of + 복수명사」는 주어가 the number이므로 단수이다. 따라서 have를 has로 고쳐야 한다.
cf.「a number of +복수명사」: 주어가 a number 이므로 복수 취급한다.

2 폭풍으로 인한 사상자 수에 대해 보도하는 기사문이므로 '초강력 폭풍 백만 명 이상의 목숨을 앗아가다'라는 제목이 가장 적절하다.

3 지구온난화로 인한 기온의 상승이기 때문에 ⑤lower는 higher로 바꿔야 맞다.

4 물 부족 국가로서의 한국 – 획기적인 기술의 개발 – 해수의 담수화 가능 – 해양 생태계에 대한 악영향 없음, 식수 부족 해결 – 전 세계 깨끗한 물 부족으로 인한 질병 퇴치에도 도움

5 나무 심기를 언제부터 시작했는지에 대한 설명이므로 문맥상 (C)가 가장 적절하다.

6 오랫동안 지속해 온 어떤 노력에 대한 긍정적 결과를 표현하는 문장이므로 ① At long last (드디어)가 가장 적절한 접속 부사이다.

7 ① 은 '활력을 불어넣었다'가 맞는 말이다.

8 에너지 수요를 충족시키면서도 오염을 크게 야기하지 않는 특성을 말하고 있다.

9 (a) struggling 분투하고 있는 (b) hydrogen cars가 복수이므로 have를 사용한다. (c) 능동태의 분사구문이므로 -ing 형태로 쓴다.

Language Notes 

1. (1) are being trapped (2) are being developed
(3) which differs from drought
(4) which are powered (5) which made
2. (1) Carbon dioxide emissions (are). 또는 Greenhouse gases trapped within the earth's atmosphere (are).
(2) The sinking of the Maldives.

1

(1), (2)'~되고 있는 중이다'라는 의미이므로「be동사의 현재형 + being + p.p.」구문을 사용한다.
(3) 관계 대명사의 계속적 용법을 써서 주어진 우리말을 영어로 옮긴다.
(4) 선행사가 hydrogen cars로 복수 명사이므로 which are powered로 쓴다.
(5) 앞 문장 전체를 가리키는 관계대명사의 계속적 용법이다.

2

(1) 지구의 온도 상승에 있어서 주된 요인은 무엇인가?
(2) 해수면 상승의 결과로 무슨 일이 벌어졌는가?

수준별 단원평가 Basic

1. ③	2. ④	3. ②	4. ②	5. ⑤	6. ⑤
7. ④	8. are expected to breathe in the fresh air				
9. is being developed			10. which made my feet sore		
11. ④	12. ①	13. ①			

1

M: Oh, Seonmi. You didn't turn off the light again!
W: Sorry, Dad. I'll be returning to my room soon.
M: But you're watching TV in the living room now. Make sure you turn the light off when you're not using it.
W: Okay, sorry. I'll keep that in mind.

사용하지 않는 전기를 소등하라는 아빠의 말에 적절한 응답을 고른다.

2

W: You know what? Our school is holding a poster contest to celebrate World Environment Day.
M: Oh, yeah? What kind of poster contest is it?
W: I took a picture of the notice on the board. Let me show it to you.
M: Sounds interesting. We're good at art. Can we make posters as a team?
W: Yeah, the rules say we can.
M: Are there any special rules about the design and size of posters?
W: It says posters should be 30cm × 45cm. Also, we can use any materials we want.
M: Should we write a slogan for the posters?
W: Good question. The rules say, "Make sure you don't copy any famous slogans. The school wants your creative ideas."
M: When do we have to turn the poster in?
W: By next Friday. And the rules say, "Don't forget to write your name on the back of your posters."

표어는 모방하지 말고 창의적으로 만들어야 하지만 길이에 제한이 있지는 않다.

3 ② 분류하다 – 구분하다 이외에는 모두 반대의 의미를 갖는 말끼리 연결되어 있다.

4 emerge: 부상하다, 떠오르다 alter: 수정하다 substitute: 대체품

5 Make sure (that) ~구문은 '꼭 ~하시오'라는 뜻이므로 should check가 쓰인 ⑤의 표현이 〈보기〉의 문장에 가장 가까운 의미를 갖는다.

6 ⑤관계대명사의 계속적 용법에는 that이 쓰이지 않는다.

7 ④많은 회사들이 화석 연료의 부족을 벌충할 수 있는 좀 더 효과적인 에너지 원을 개발해 오고 있다.

8 be expected to: 기대되다
주말에는 '신선한 공기를 마실 수 있을 것으로 예상된다'라는 말이 들어간다.

11 상자 안의 문장에서 this new solution은 담수화 처리과정에서 발생한 고염도의 물을 재사용하는 방법을 말하므로 주어진 문장은 (D)에 위치하는 것이 적절하다.

12 ⓐ에는 앞 문장과의 반대 상황을 나타내는 접속 부사 However가 알맞고, ⓑ에는 '드디어'라는 의미를 갖는 접속 부사 In the end, 또는 Eventually가 적절하다.

13 깨끗한 식수의 부족으로 인해 생기는 질병을 근절하는 데 도움이 될 것으로 예상하고 있다.

수준별 단원평가 Advanced

1. ④ **2.** ③ **3.** ⑤ **4.** ⑤ **5.** ① **6.** ⑤
7. one-fifth of what it was **8.** ③
9. climate change 또는 global warming **10.** ④
11. 해설 참조

[1-2]
M: All across the world, people are facing serious environmental problems. It is May now, but it is already unusually hot. Today heat wave warnings were issued in Korea because the temperature was recorded at over 35 degrees Celsius. In India, the temperature reached 50 degrees Celsius for several days, and over a thousand people have died of heat-related illness so far. Beijing is covered with heavy yellow dust. Last Friday, schools were closed, and people were advised to avoid outdoor activities. Because of the heavy yellow dust, more than 300 flights were canceled at Beijing International Airport. Also, heavy rain and storms hit many cities in the United States. In Texas and Oklahoma, powerful storms killed at least nine people, and thirty people are still missing. On the other hand, California has been in a severe drought for the past five years. The water levels of lakes are getting lower and lower. To stop suffering from these problems, it's time for us to take action for our earth.

1 사람들에게 지구를 살리기 위한 실천의 필요성을 역설하고 있다.

2 desertification : 사막화

3
W: Hi, Marco. What are you doing here?
M: I'm separating all the garbage produced in my classroom. It's my duty for this week.
W: Wait! You know what? The bottle caps do not belong with the glass.
M: Oh, you're right. I still get confused about which items go where.
W: I know what you mean, but I have a simple tip for you.
M: Really? What's that?
W: When you're confused, you can just check if the items have a triangular symbol and numbers inside.
M: I can see a triangle and number 1 on this item.
W: Items marked "1" and "2" mean they can be recycled.
M: Got it. Thanks for the tip.
W: Make sure you don't mix up what is recyclable and what is not.
삼각형 안에 숫자 1이나 2가 있으면 재활용 가능한 쓰레기임을 알려 주었다.

4 root out : 뿌리 뽑다, 근절하다 (=eradicate, eliminate)

5 석유나 가스를 안 쓸 수는 없으므로 절약하자고 말하는 게 가장 적절하다.

6 ⑤의 decreased는 increased로 고쳐야 문맥상 알맞다.

7 예전의 5분의 1 면적이라는 표현이므로 「분수 + of + 이전 상태」의 순서로 나타낸다.

8 ⓔ는 3.6도 라는 뜻이므로 degree가 degrees로 바뀌어야 한다.

9 기후 변화(climate change) 또는 지구온난화 (global warming)에 대처하기 위한 forum이라고 볼 수 있다.

10 전기차 시장의 가속화 - 수소차의 등장 - 수소차의 효과 - 오염을 줄이고 에너지 위기 해결 기대

11 〈예시 답안〉
Renewable energy produces less air or water pollution and fewer carbon dioxide emissions than using fossil fuels. Renewable energy can meet energy demand without destroying our environment. `재생가능 에너지의 장점에 대한 문장을 기술한다.

UNIT 5 Bon Voyage

교과서 핵심 정리 Check-Up

Words & Phrases

1. (1) keep you posted (2) depending on (3) in person (4) a must (5) by himself (6) no wonder
2. (1) delicate (2) absorb (3) architecture (4) absolute (5) border
3. (1) considered to spoil the scenery of Paris (2) affected the entire landscape (3) to preserve natural habitats (4) deeply impressed by the view

1
(1) 내가 어떤 소식이라도 알게 되면 너에게 계속 알려줄게.
(2) 회원국들은 인구에 따라 자리가 할당된다.
(3) 그 배우는 화면에서 볼 때보다 실제로 보니 훨씬 더 키가 작아 보였다.
(4) 석사 학위가 필수인 직업이 셀 수 없이 많다.
(5) 그는 혼자 그것을 하고 있다. 그는 나나 내 남편의 어떤 도움도 필요하지 않다.
(6) 아이들은 지방질의 음식을 즐겨 먹는다. 그들이 점점 더 살찌고 건강이 나빠져 가는 것은 당연한 일이다.

2
(1) 섬세한: 재질이나 질이 정교한
(2) 흡수하다: (액체를) 빨아들이거나 마시다
(3) 건축: 건물의 특성이나 스타일
(4) 절대적인: 결점이 없거나 어떤 식으로든 제한이 없는; 완벽한, 완전한
(5) 경계, 국경: 정치적 분리나 지리적인 영역을 가르는 선

Reading Comprehension(Focus on Structure)

1. (1) is where you can take a museum tour
(2) is when workers are expected to return
2. (1) How smart do you think (2) he wants to keep
(3) When do you believe he will

1

(1) 그 마을은 네가 박물관 투어를 할 수 있는 곳이다. (선행사가 생략된 관계 부사절이 문장에서 보어 역할을 한다.)
(2) 그 연휴는 직장인들이 자신들의 고향 마을로 돌아가는 때이다.

2

(1) 너는 네가 얼마나 똑똑하다고 생각하니? (How smart가 의문사이다.)
(2) 너는 왜 그가 체중 감량을 유지하고 싶어 한다고 생각하니?
suppose도 think, believe와 같은 인식 동사이므로 「의문사 + do you suppose + 주어 +동사」의 구문을 쓴다.
(3) 너는 그가 언제 마을로 돌아올 거라고 믿니?

언어 기능별 집중 대비

Listen and Speak/ Into Real Life

1. ② 2. ③ 3. ① 4. (1) ③ (2) ⑤

1

M: Oh my gosh. We are finally flying in the sky. There are many clouds under our plane.
W: I know. I feel like we are flying on a huge bunch of cotton candy.
M: This is one of the most beautiful views I've ever seen.
W: You can say that again.
비행기 아래로 구름이 보인다는 표현이 있으므로 기내에서 이루어지는 대화임을 알 수 있다.

2

W: Mike. I've decided to go to New Zealand this summer.
M: Wow, that sounds awesome! Why New Zealand?
W: I'm a huge fan of the movie *The Hobbit: An Unexpected Journey*, so I've always wanted to visit the country that was the background for the movie. Here, this town on the North Island on this map is Hinuera, which has the Hobbiton movie set.
M: Oh, I remember this place. The Hobbiton movie set has one of the most memorable places from the movie.
W: Exactly. That town is where I want to go on the very first day of my trip.
M: Where else are you going to go to in New Zealand?
W: I'm going to go to Lake Wanaka on the South Island the next day. That place is very famous for skydiving.
M: But you don't even know how to skydive. Can you do it by yourself? That sounds really dangerous.
W: I don't need to do it by myself. They have professional instructors. They will take control as I enjoy an amazing view of New Zealand.
M: Lucky for you! How long are you going to stay in New Zealand?
W: I'll stay there for two weeks. I'm so excited!
M: I hope you have a great and safe trip.
all by herself는 '완전히 혼자서'라는 뜻이다. 여기서 여자는 스카이다이빙 조교와 같이 하는 것이므로 대화 내용과 일치하지 않는다.

3

(Phone rings.)
W: Lion Hotel. How can I help you?
M Excuse me. How do I get to your hotel? I made a reservation for today.
W: Where are you now? Tell me your location.
M: I'm near Woodlands subway station.
W: Woodlands station. Okay, you are not far from our hotel. Take line 5 toward the south, and get off at Newton station.
M: Line 5 toward the south and Newton station. I got it.
W: Then, you should go out of exit 6. After that, walk straight two blocks.
M: Exit 6, walk two blocks. Is that right?
W: You got it. After you walk two blocks, you can see the Jumbo restaurant on your right. That means you're almost here. It's just around the left corner. It's a very big hotel, so you can't miss it.
M: I really appreciate your help.
W: Oh, here is one more tip. If you have a cell phone, download the Singapore Subway Map app. It will make your trip easier.
M: I will Thanks
전철은 5호선 남쪽 방향이고, 내려야 할 역은 뉴튼 역이며 출구 번호는 6번이다.

4

W: Hi everyone. This is the Daehan High School Broadcasting System. As you know, we're going on a field trip next month to have some valuable learning experiences outside the school. To make your trip more interesting, Daehan High School will provide three field trip destinations for you to choose from.

1. Students who love beautiful nature are recommended to choose Ulleungdo and Dokdo. Ulleungdo is full of the beauty of nature including many unique rock formations and coastal cliffs. On the second day, you can actually visit Dokdo, a symbolic island in the hearts of Koreans. You can also do activities like sea fishing. We will take a bus and a ship to get there, and it takes about six hours in total.

2. If you love history and tradition, you can choose Andong. Andong Hahoe Folk Village is a UNESCO World Heritage site. You will stay in this village and experience the traditional ways of life in the past. You can also watch many traditional performances like a traditional wedding performance in the village. To get there, it's a three-hour train ride.

3. If you want some educational experiences from the trip, the Daejeon Citizen Observatory will be the perfect place for you. It's one of the largest space-themed parks in Korea. You can appreciate a beautiful night sky and the Milky Way on the mountain. In addition to this, you can take a tour of the Space Museum and do many space-related activities. We will take a bus to get there, and it only takes an hour and a half.
I hope you can choose the best place depending on your interests.

(1) 현장학습 장소 선정과 관련하여 각 코스의 장점 및 소요 시간을 설명해 주고 있다.
① 학생들에게 비교과 활동에 참여하라고 설득하려고
② 한국의 여행 명소에 대한 보고서를 쓸 수 있게 도와주려고
③ 학생들에게 현장 학습을 가게 될 장소를 선택하는 데 도움을 주려고
④ 학생들에게 체험 학습 갈 때 탈 교통편을 예약하라고 하려고
⑤ 학생들에게 온라인으로 예약하는 것의 장점을 알려주려고
(2) 대전 시민천문대 코스는 가는 데 걸리는 시간이 버스로 1시간 30분이다.

Read and Think

1. ①	2. ①	3. ④	4. ⑤	5. ②	6. ④
7. ②	8. ③	9. ⑤			

1 그라나다는 장소를 나타내는 말이므로 여기서는 관계부사 where가 와야 한다. 또한 관계부사 뒤에는 완벽한 절이 온다.

2 대명사 them이 가리키는 복수 명사(Iguazu Falls)가 앞 문장에 있어야 하고, 문맥상 '말로 표현하기에는 너무 아름다워서 네가 직접 봐야 할 정도다'라는 말이 가장 자연스럽게 이어지므로 (A)가 적절한 위치이다.

3 이어지는 응답이 가장 환상적인 명소에 관한 묘사이므로 '뭐가 가장 인상적이었니?'라는 질문이 오는 게 적절하다. ⑤ 거기서 가장 재미없는 활동은 뭐니?

4 궁전에 대한 묘사(depiction, description)가 주를 이루고 있고, 끝부분에서 꼭 한번 가보기를 권하는(recommendation) 말이 나오고 있다.
① 후회와 충고 ② 대조와 예측 ③ 비교와 설득 ④ 묘사와 격려

5 브라질 축구의 역사가 얼마나 오래 되었는지에 관한 말은 없다.

6 ④ '가이드가 우리의 다음 목적지는 수도 캔버라라고 말했다.'라는 문장은 호주의 원주민 벽화 예술에 대한 내용 중간에 들어가기에 적절하지 않다.

7 호주의 땅이 워낙 커서 가는 지역이 바뀜에 따라 4계절의 날씨를 골고루 체험하게 되었다는 표현이 적절하다. 나머지는 문장 자체로는 자연스러울 수 있으나 뒤에 이어지는 문장들과 문맥상 어울리지 않는다.
① 차로 그 나라를 횡단하는 데 일주일이 걸렸다.
③ 대중교통이 늘 가능한 건 아니었다.
④ 모든 관광 명소를 들러보는 것은 쉽지 않았다.
⑤ 우리가 이해할 수 없는 지역 사투리가 많았다.

8 주어진 문장에 있는 mirror라는 표현과 ③의 뒤에 이어지는 문장에서 see the sky and your reflection in the thin layer of water라는 표현이 서로 관련성이 깊다.

9 (a)는 전치사 in의 목적어이기 때문에 동명사 형태인 being이 맞고, (b)는 선행사 things가 있으므로 관계대명사 which가 맞으며, (c)에는 keep someone posted라는 표현을 써서 '~에게 계속 연락하며 알려주다'라는 뜻이므로 posted가 맞는 형태이다.

Language Notes / Write It Right

1. (1) a must for all lovers of detective stories (또는 a must for those who love detective stories) (2) When do you think we will be able to (3) most people make new resolutions (or most people make a new resolution) (4) keep us posted about (5) the most prestigious theaters are
2. (1) Who, you are (2) What, he wants for his birthday present (3) Where, happiness comes from
3. (1) is when there is a great danger for wildfires
(2) is where Eastern tradition and modern influences collide
(3) why my jeans do not fit any more
(4) how deaf and blind people learn how to communicate

1
(1) a must는 '필수적인 것'이라는 뜻이다. those who ~ 는 '~하는 사람들'이라는 뜻이다.
(2) 「의문사 + do you think + 주어 + 동사」
(3) 원래 문장에서 시간 부사구를 빼고 「관계부사 when + 주어 + 동사」의 명사절(보어)을 만든다.
(4) 「keep + 목적어 + p.p.」: ~를 계속 …된 상태로 유지하다
(5) 원래 문장에서의 장소 부사구를 빼고 「관계부사 where + 주어 + 동사」의 명사절(보어)을 만든다.

2
(1) 넌 네가 누구라고 생각하니?
(2) 너는 그가 생일 선물로 무엇을 받고 싶을 거라고 생각하니?
(3) 너는 행복이 어디서 온다고 믿니?

3 부사구에 있던 장소, 시간, 이유, 방법을 나타내는 말을 주어로 하고 「관계부사 + 주어 + 동사」의 보어를 만든다.
(1) 9월은 산불이 엄청 위험한 때이다.
(2) 상하이는 동양적 전통과 현대적 영향이 충돌하는 곳이다.
(3) 벨기에 초콜릿 때문에 내 바지가 더 이상 나에게 맞지 않는 것이다.
(4) 이것이 시청각 장애인들이 의사소통하는 법을 배우는 방법이다.

수준별 단원평가 Basic

1. ④ 2. ② 3. ① 4. ⑤ 5. ② 6. ③
7. ① 8. ① 9. ①
10. Why do you think they are famous? 11. ④
12. where East meets West
13. why I decided to go to Africa
14. How long do you think it took

1
M: Oh my gosh. We are finally flying in the sky. There are many clouds under our plane.
W: I know. I feel like we are flying on a huge bunch of cotton candy.
M: This is one of the most beautiful views I've ever seen.
W: <u>You can say that again.</u>

상대방의 말에 전적으로 동의하는 말이 이어지는 게 적절하다.

2
M: Look at this painting. This is one of the most impressive works I've ever seen.
W: This painting is called "The Dream."
M: It was a good decision to come to the Pablo Picasso Art Museum on this trip.
W: I totally agree. It's great to see his amazing works of art.

미술 작품에 대해 얘기하면서 이곳에 오기를 잘 했다고 말하고 있는 것으로 보아 미술관이 알맞다.

3 ① awesome은 '멋진'이라는 뜻이고 awful은 '끔찍한'이라는 뜻으로 반의어 관계이다.

4 ①~④: 동사-명사의 관계, ⑤ architect-architecture: '건축가 - 건축'

5 민주주의 사회에서 법은 필수적인 것이다.

6 ③은 간접의문문으로 'Where do you think the treasure box was buried?'로 써야 한다.

7 ①은 London is where most people want to work.로 써야 맞다.
② 벌레 때문에 난 농장에서 (식료품)주문하는 걸 두려워한다.
③ 3월은 비타민 D가 가장 낮은 수준이 되는 때다.
④ 그런 방식으로 그 매니저가 직원들을 대했다.
⑤ 극장은 연극 같은 라이브 공연을 보러 가는 곳이다.

8 글의 앞에서 궁전의 아름다움을 자세히 묘사했으므로 '궁전이 너무 아름다워서 차마 부술 수 없었다'고 하는 표현이 적절하다.

9 ①은 'They were why'로 바꾸어야 '내가 그것들 때문에 브라질에 가기로 한 것이다.'라는 문장이 된다.

10 '이구아수 폭포가 가장 크고 높은 폭포여서'라는 말이 이어지므로 '넌 왜 이구아수 폭포가 그렇게 유명하다고 생각하니?'라는 질문이 어울린다.

11 주어진 문장 뒤에는 (D)의 뒷 문장의 내용인 4만년이나 된 암석화가 지금까지 잘 보존되고 있는 것에 감명 받았다고 이어지는 게 가장 자연스럽다.

12~13 장소/이유는 「주어 + is + where/why + 주어 + 동사」의 구문으로 쓴다.
12. 터키는 동양과 서양이 만나는 곳이다.
13. 그 독특한 야생 때문에 내가 아프리카로 가기로 결심했다.

14 「의문사 + do you think + 주어 + 동사」의 구문을 사용한다.

수준별 단원평가 Advanced

1. ④ **2.** ③ **3.** ③ **4.** ⑤
5. ⑤ are expressed → is expressed **6.** ⑤ **7.** ⑤
8. ⑤ **9.** ③ **10.** ③ **11.** in Korea's being the tenth nation to build **12.** ⑤ various kind of → various kinds of
13. ③ **14.** ⑤ **15.** 해설 참조

1

W: Hi, Cheolsu. How was your trip to India? You were really worried about your first overseas trip with your family.
M: Well, my family was really impressed by the cultures of India.
W: That sounds interesting! What was so impressive about the country?
M: First of all, the food. We had a lot of local food like Indian curries and liked everything we ate very much.
W: That's good to hear. Oh, did you see any traditional performances?
M: Yes! We arrived there on the last day of the Hemis Festival. Luckily, we got to see the last performance.
W: You were very lucky. Where else did you go?
M: We also visited lots of UNESCO World Heritage sites, like the Taj Mahal.
W: You did? I heard that the architecture is really amazing.
M: It was one of the most beautiful buildings I have ever seen. Actually, it was so wonderful that it looked unreal.
W: Wow. Now that I have heard your story, I want to fly to India!

철수의 가족은 Hemis 축제의 마지막 공연만 볼 수 있었다.

2

W: Mike, I've decided to go to New Zealand this summer.
M: Wow, that sounds awesome! Why New Zealand?
W: I'm a huge fan of the movie *The Hobbit: An Unexpected Journey*, so I've always wanted to visit the country that was the background for the movie. Here, this town on the North Island on this map is Hinuera, which has the Hobbiton movie set.
M: Oh, I remember this place. The Hobbiton movie set has one of the most memorable places from the movie.
W: Exactly. That town is where I want to go on the very first day of my trip.
M: Where else are you going to go to in New Zealand?
W: I'm going to go to Lake Wanaka on the South Island the next day. That place is very famous for skydiving.
M: But you don't even know how to skydive. Can you do it by yourself? That sounds really dangerous.
W: I don't need to do it by myself. They have professional instructors. They will take control as I enjoy an amazing view of New Zealand.
M: Lucky for you! How long are you going to stay in New Zealand?
W: I'll stay there for two weeks. I'm so excited!
M: I hope you have a great and safe trip.

호빗 영화 촬영 세트 방문과 스카이다이빙이 주요한 활동이다.

3

W: Hi everyone. This is the Daehan High School Broadcasting System. As you know, we're going on a field trip next month to have some valuable learning experiences outside the school. To make your trip more interesting, Daehan High School will provide three field trip destinations for you to choose from.

1. Students who love beautiful nature are recommended to choose Ulleungdo and Dokdo. Ulleungdo is full of the beauty of nature including many unique rock formations and coastal cliffs. On the second day, you can actually visit Dokdo, a symbolic island in the hearts of Koreans. You can also do activities like sea fishing. We will take a bus and a ship to get there, and it takes about six hours in total.
2. If you love history and tradition, you can choose Andong. Andong Hahoe Folk Village is a UNESCO World Heritage site. You will stay in this village and experience the traditional ways of life in the past. You can also watch many traditional performances like a traditional wedding performance in the village. To get there, it's a three-hour train ride.
3. If you want some educational experiences from the trip, the Daejeon Citizen Observatory will be the perfect place for you. It's one of the largest space-themed parks in Korea. You can appreciate a beautiful night sky and the Milky Way on the mountain. In addition to this, you can take a tour of the Space Museum and do many space-related activities. We will take a bus to get there, and it only takes an hour and a half.
I hope you can choose the best place depending on your interests.

안동에서 어떤 한국 전통 음식을 먹을지는 언급되지 않았다.

4 '그를 직접 볼 수 있다면 정말 멋질 텐데'라는 표현이다. (in person:직접) ⑤face to face:직접 대면해 본다

5 Their emphasis on water는 단수이므로 be동사를 is로 써야한다.

6 물에 맑게 비치는 것들에 관해 말하는 문장이므로 호수가 거울 같다는 표현 뒤에 오는 것이 자연스럽다.

7 수상 크루즈 여행 –
(C)여행에서 본 야생 동물들 – (B)이틀 째 날 활동 중 암석화 체험 – (A)원주민 암석화 미술이 잘 보존되고 있는 것에 대한 감동의 순서로 이어지는 게 자연스럽다.

8 궁전이 아름답다는 묘사 다음에 세부적으로 궁전 안의 방들이 어떤 모양인지 묘사하는 말이 따라오는 게 자연스럽다.

9 부사구 뒤에 「동사 + 주어」로 되었으므로 The Nasrid Palaces를 받는 were가 되어야 한다.

10 요약문: 궁전 안의 많은 분수와 연못과 수로들은 물이 생명과 부(wealth)를 가져다준다는 아랍 사람들의 믿음을 반영(reflect)한다.

11 「take pride in + (소유격) + 동명사」 : ~가 …인 것을 자랑스럽게 여기다

13 영훈은 자신과 자신의 동료들이 남극에서 하고 있는 일이 미래 세대에 유용하기를 바라고 있다.

15 〈예시 답안〉
I'd like to travel to the U.K. during the winter vacation. It'll take about 12 hours from Incheon to London by plane. As the country has so many famous and beautiful tourist attractions, I think I have to stay there for at least ten days to see them all. London Eye, the British Museum, Oxford University, Stonehenge are some of the places I really want to visit.

1학기 기말고사 UNIT ❹ – UNIT ❺

01. ⑤ **02.** ④ **03.** ③ **04.** ④ **05.** ③ **06.** ②
07. ⑤ **08.** ② **09.** ③ **10.** ② **11.** ④ **12.** ④
13. ③ **14.** ⑤ **15.** ① **16.** ① **17.** ④ **18.** ②
19. ④ **20.** ④
21. ⓐ the largest part ⓑ the second smallest
22. (1) What do you think is the most valuable thing in life?
(2) Please wait a minute while your application is being processed
23. (1) why she chose the college
(2) where the old meets the new
24. rising sea level has resulted in the sinking
25. 해설 참조

1

M: Have you heard about the earthquakes in Oklahoma?
W: No, I haven't. Why do you ask?
M: I heard that they were disasters caused by human activities.
W: Really? How so?
M: Some scientists found out the earthquakes were caused by the oil and gas business.
W: Are you sure? I thought they could cause environmental pollution.
M: Well, it seems the process can actually cause earthquakes.
W: That's terrible. Then should we stop using gas?
M: It's not easy to stop using gas.
W: Then what should we do?
M: We have to make sure we don't waste our energy from now on.

에너지 사용을 안 할 수는 없지만 에너지를 절약할 필요가 있음을 말하는 것이 적절한 응답이다.

2

W: You know what? Our school is holding a poster contest to celebrate World Environment Day.
M: Oh, yeah? What kind of poster contest is it?
W: I took a picture of the notice on the board. Let me show it to you.
M: Sounds interesting. We're good at art. Can we make posters as a team?
W: Yeah, the rules say we can.
M: Are there any special rules about the design and size of posters?
W: It says posters should be 30cm × 45cm. Also, we can use any materials we want.
M: Should we write a slogan for the posters?
W: Good question. The rules say, "Make sure you don't copy any famous slogans. The school wants your creative ideas."
M: When do we have to turn the poster in?
W: By next Friday. And the rules say, "Don't forget to write your name on the back of your posters."

그리기 재료는 아무런 제한이 없다.

3

W: Hi, Marco. What are you doing here?
M: I'm separating all the garbage produced in my classroom. It's my duty for this week.
W: Wait! You know what? The bottle caps do not belong with the glass.
M: Oh, you're right. I still get confused about which items go where.
W: I know what you mean, but I have a simple tip for you.
M: Really? What's that?
W: When you're confused, you can just check if the items have a triangular symbol and numbers inside.
M: I can see a triangle and number 1 on this item.
W: Items marked "1" and "2" mean they can be recycled.
M: Got it. Thanks for the tip.
W: Make sure you don't mix up what is recyclable and what is not.

삼각형 모양 안에 숫자 1 또는 2가 적혀 있는 경우는 재활용 가능한 플라스틱이다.

4

W: Mike, I've decided to go to New Zealand this summer.
M: Wow, that sounds awesome! Why New Zealand?
W: I'm a huge fan of the movie *The Hobbit: An Unexpected Journey*, so I've always wanted to visit the country that was the background for the movie. Here, this town on the North Island on this map is Hinuera, which has the Hobbiton movie set.
M: Oh, I remember this place. The Hobbiton movie set has one of the most memorable places from the movie.
W: Exactly. That town is where I want to go on the very first day of my trip.
M: Where else are you going to go to in New Zealand?
W: I'm going to go to Lake Wanaka on the South Island the next day. That place is very famous for skydiving.
M: But you don't even know how to skydive. Can you do it by yourself? That sounds really dangerous.
W: I don't need to do it by myself. They have professional instructors. They will take control as I enjoy an amazing view of New Zealand.
M: Lucky for you! How long are you going to stay in New Zealand?
W: I'll stay there for two weeks. I'm so excited!
M: I hope you have a great and safe trip.

스카이다이빙은 조교(instructor)가 도와주기 때문에 혼자 하는 게 아니라고 말한다.

[5~6]

W: Hi everyone. This is the Daehan High School Broadcasting System. As you know, we're going on a field trip next month to have some valuable learning experiences outside the school. To make your trip more interesting, Daehan High School will provide three field trip destinations for you to choose from.

1. Students who love beautiful nature are recommended to choose Ulleungdo and Dokdo. Ulleungdo is full of the beauty of nature including many unique rock formations and coastal cliffs. On the second day, you can actually visit Dokdo, a symbolic island in the hearts of Koreans. You can also do activities like sea fishing. We will take a bus and a ship to get there, and it takes about six hours in total.
2. If you love history and tradition, you can choose Andong. Andong Hahoe Folk Village is a UNESCO World Heritage site. You will stay in this village and experience the traditional ways of life in the past. You can also watch many traditional performances like a traditional wedding performance in the village. To get there, it's a three-hour train ride.
3. If you want some educational experiences from the trip, the Daejeon Citizen Observatory will be the perfect place for you. It's one of the largest space-themed parks in Korea. You can appreciate a beautiful night sky and the Milky Way on the mountain. In addition to this, you can take a tour of the Space Museum and do many space-related activities. We will take a bus to get there, and it only takes an hour and a half.

I hope you can choose the best place depending on your interests.

5 대전을 가는 경우는 천문대와 과학박물관을 방문하는 것으로 일정이 되어 있다.

6 안동에서는 민속촌에 들러 전통 생활 방식을 체험할 예정이다.

7 ⑤ have → has (주어가 a rise이므로 3인칭 단수에 맞는 동사형태가 와야 한다.)

8 ② to dealing → to deal (다루기 위한)

9 drought: 가뭄 flood: 홍수 enhance: 증진시키다 reduce: 줄이다 contaminate: 오염시키다 eliminate: 제거하다

10 ② 3도의 기온 변화가 왜 중요한지에 대해 의구심을 가질 수 있다는 말이므로 그 의구심을 풀어주는 설명 앞에 위치하는 것이 적절하다.

11 ④ 재생 가능한 대체 에너지원을 지속적으로 개발해 내고 있다는 내용이다.

12 ④ 환경 자동차의 기능에 대한 설명은 친환경 자동차 시장의 경쟁을 묘사하는 전체 문맥과 어울리지 않는다.

14 (A) 수동태 구문이므로 과거분사형태인 expressed가 알맞다.
(B) 주어가 Nasrid Palaces로서 복수이므로 be동사는 were가 알맞다.
(C) 앞에 있는 must는 조동사가 아닌 명사이므로 명사를 수식할 수 있는 to 부정사의 형용사적 용법이 쓰인다.

15 ① where do you think should I go → where do you think I should go

16 ① Grace의 응답이 the Devil's Throat의 경치에 대한 묘사이므로 '어디가 가장 인상적인 곳이었니?'라는 질문이 가장 적절하다.

17 ④ 축구 박물관이 있는데 심지어(even) 그 안에는 브라질 축구 역사에 관한 전용 방도 있다고 말하는 게 자연스러운 연결이다.

18 ② 큰 축구 경기가 있을 때 상파울로는 마치 모든 사람들이 휴가 나온 듯 한 분위기라고 묘사하고 있다. (실제로 휴가를 가는 것은 아니다.)

19 (A) 야생 악어를 본 것이 과거 시제로 쓰였으므로 그 이전의 경험을 표현하는 말은 과거완료「had + p.p.」 시제를 사용한다.
(B) 수식하는 단어가 record로서 사람이 아닌 사물이므로 현재분사 형태의 형용사가 알맞다.
(C) 「keep + 사람 + posted」: 계속적으로 소식을 전하다

20 ④ 왜 호주 원주민들이 바위에 동물들을 그렸는지는 설명되지 않았다.

21 ⓑ Hydro가 the smallest part라면 Renewables는 두 번째로 작은 (the second smallest) 부분을 차지하고 있다.

22 (1) 「의문사 + do you think + (주어) + 동사 ~?」
(2) 현재진행형 수동태: 「be 동사 + being + p.p.」

23 「주어(*A*) + be동사 + why/where/when/how + 주어(*B*) + 동사」: B가 ~한 것은 A 때문이다 / A에서이다 / A 때이다 / A를 통해서이다.

24 해수면의 상승이 몰디브가 물에 잠기는 것을 초래하고 있는데, 그곳은 유명한 관광지다.

25 환경을 위해 할 수 있는 다양한 방안을 기술한다.
〈예시 답안〉
First, we need to recycle, reuse, and reduce waste. Second, we should develop more innovative renewable energy resources. Finally, we can help the environment and reduce greenhouse gases by taking stairs instead of elevators.

UNIT 6 Fuel Your Creativity

교과서 핵심 정리 Check-Up

Words & Phrases

1. (1) get in shape (2) pump up (3) except for (4) on a daily basis (5) upside down
2. (1) portrait (2) daydream (3) scholar (4) insight (5) infinite
3. (1) because I tend to gain weight easily
(2) will go beyond what you imagine
(3) fence off the land to protect the wetland
(4) people who can think outside the box

1
(1) 건강한 몸매를 갖고 싶으면 조깅이나 스피드 워킹을 해 보세요.
(2) 그 나라는 수출과 경제 전반을 증강하려고 노력 중이다.
(3) 그 장학금은 수업료를 제외한 모든 비용을 커버해 줄 것이다.
(4) 소량의 음주도 매일 하는 거면 간 손상을 일으킬 수 있다.
(5) 아기는 책을 거꾸로 들고 있었다.

2
(1) 대개 사람의 머리와 어깨 정도를 포함하는 그림이나 사진
(2) 깨어 있는 상태에서 삶이나 미래에 관한 즐거운 생각을 하다
(3) 한 주제를 오랜 시간 공부해서 그것에 관해 아는 게 많은 사람
(4) 사람이나 상황에 관해 아주 명확한 방식으로 이해할 수 있는 능력
(5) 한계가 없거나 엄청 크거나 매우 엄청난

Reading Comprehension(Focus on Structure)

1. (1) seems to be jealous of her younger sister
(2) seemed that Miriam was aware of the situation
2. (1) Deeply concerned about her safety (2) Barking loudly

1
(1) Emma는 여동생을 질투하는 것 같다. : seems와 that 절의 동사 is가 시제가 같기 때문에 단순 to 부정사를 사용한다.
(2) Miriam은 상황을 알고 있는 것 같았다. : It seemed that 절로 바뀔 때는 to 부정사의 동사를 적절한 인칭과 시제에 맞추어 써야 한다.

2
(1) 자신의 안전에 많은 염려가 되어 Kate는 집에 남아있기를 원했다.: 접속사와 주어를 생략하고 동사를 분사로 바꾸어 표현하 것이 분사구문이다.
(2) 시끄럽게 짖으면서, 그 개는 우리를 겁먹게 했다.

언어 기능별 집중 대비

Listen and Speak / Into Real Life

1. ③ 2. ⑤ 3. ③ 4. (1) ⑤ (2) ④

1
DIALOGUE
M: Hey, Grace. Did you watch that documentary about Jeong Yakyong last night?
W: You mean the late Joseon dynasty scholar? — the one who wrote *Mokminsimseo*?
M: That's right. He also built the Hwaseong Fortress in Suwon with his creative invention.

W: I haven't seen the documentary, but I did read a book about him. His creativity was incredible. I was particularly impressed reading about the system he invented to handle heavy building materials. What was it called... *Geojunggi*?

M: That's the one. And I agree — I think *geojunggi* is his greatest invention. What a brilliant idea it is, right?

W: You can say that again. Do you know how to operate it? I was surprised to see it lifting huge stones.

M: Yes, actually, I saw one once at a folk village and tried it out.

W: That sounds pretty cool. I'm interested in engineering. If you have a moment, can you tell me more about it?

M: Sure. Let's talk about it during lunch time.

W: Thanks. See you soon.

Grace는 공학(engineering)에 관심이 많아 거중기의 작동 방식을 알고 싶어 한다.

2

MONOLOGUE

M:Do you know how to get in good shape? Perhaps you're thinking about a workout. But when was the last time you thought about a brain workout? Training your brain is just as important as maintaining a healthy body. Studies show that with one hour of brain training a week, you not only improve the thinking skills you use every day but also prevent memory disorders. With regular brain training, you will notice that you have better memory and greater creativity in your daily life. Train your brain by doing different types of brain questions on a daily basis or by approaching daily problems in a way you're not used to. Just make a conscious effort to think of different ways of doing things.

뇌를 훈련시키는 방법으로 남자가 제안하고 있는 것은 새로운 방식으로 어떤 일을 하는 것을 시도해 보라는 것이다.

① 몸매를 위해 규칙적으로 운동하라.
② 비판적 읽기 기술을 향상시키기 위해 노력하라.
③ 창의적 질문을 물음으로써 기억 장애를 예방하라.
④ 매일 가능한 많은 수학 문제를 풀어라.

3

M:Ugh, I hate food stains on clothes. Do you know how to remove food stains?

W: Yes, you can use a spoonful of salt.

M: A spoon of salt? Can you explain how it works?

W: Sure. All you have to do is mix it with warm water and wash your clothes.

M: Wow, what a brilliant idea!

stain on clothes라는 표현과 더불어 따뜻한 소금물로 제거할 수 있다는 표현이 나온다.

4

W: Ladies and gentlemen, welcome to the *Creativity Talk Show*. Have you ever heard of the Six Thinking Hats strategy? Well, let me introduce a psychologist, Dr. de Bono, who can help everyone think more creatively.

Dr. de Bono: Thank you for inviting me. One day, I was trying to solve a problem. I found myself thinking about many things at the same time and got confused with no solutions. So, I tried to think about one thing at a time and each time, in a different way. That helped me a lot, and I was able to come up with the Six Thinking Hats strategy. Let's suppose you wear six hats, each with a different color: white, red, blue, green, yellow, and black, and the way you think changes with each hat. Wouldn't it be fun?

W: Indeed. So each hat would make a person think in a different way. Is that right?

Dr. de Bono: Yes. Let's start with the white hat. It remembers all information you need and deals with facts. The red hat, on the other hand, loves feelings and emotions.

W: What about the green one?

Dr. de Bono: The most important hat you wear is the green one. It focuses on new ideas and creativity. With this hat on, any thought is welcome!

W: What a brilliant idea!

Dr. de Bono: Also, you get to think positively and explore the bright side of things with the yellow hat on. The black hat gives warnings and makes you think critically about things. Above all, there is a hat that manages and balances the whole process — a blue hat. It is the boss of all hats.

W: How interesting! How can we apply this strategy in real life? Please give us an example.

(1) 색다른 방식으로 생각하고 창의력을 기르라는 말이 주된 내용이다.
(2) 노란색 모자는 긍정적으로 생각하는 두뇌를 상징한다.

Read and Think

1. ④	**2.** ⑤	**3.** ②	**4.** ②	**5.** ②	**6.** ④
7. ⑤	**8.** ④	**9.** ①			

1 어려운 문제 해결에 도움이 되지 않을 수 있다는 의미의 문장이므로 전통적인 해결 방식에 대한 말 다음에 오는 게 알맞다.

2 (C) 문제의 조건 - (D) 문제 상황 - (B) 약간의 힌트 - (A) 문제에 대한 해결 방안의 순서로 글이 이어진다.

3 익숙하지 않은 방식으로 문제에 접근하는 것이 창의적 사고이다.

4 ②는 분사구문이 올 자리이므로 using이 알맞다. (~를 사용하여서)

5 그 반대 방식으로 하지 않았다는 말은 그들은 울타리 안에 있는 것에만 주목하고 밖에 있는 것에 집중하지 않았다는 의미이다.

6 콜럼버스가 이 실험에서 보여주고자 했던 것은 신대륙의 발견 그 자체가 위대한 것이라기보다 처음 그 발상을 했던 것이 위대한 것이라는 것이다.

7 익숙하지 않은 방식으로 문제에 접근해야 하는데 단지 왕의 초상화를 뚫어져라 쳐다보거나 노란 배경을 바라보는 기존의 방식(comfort zone)으로는 문제를 해결할 수 없다는 내용이다.

8 ⓑ 다른 말로 하자면 ⓒ 그러나, 하지만

9 think outside the box가 창의적인 사고를 하라는 의미이다.

Language Notes / Write It Right

1. (1) listen to the teacher, not the other way around
(2) until you step out of your comfort zone
(3) write down ideas that come to your mind
(4) wasn't wearing anything except for his/her diaper
(5) fence off the children's play area

2. (1) to be upset about the decision
(2) to be plenty to eat in the kitchen
(3) Paul had been ill for quite a long time

3. (1) Having curiosity about daydreaming
(2) Eaten by mosquitoes (3) Frightened by the loud fireworks
(4) Mike had to leave the field

1

(1) 교사가 학생의 말을 듣는 것은 the other way around에 해당한다.
(2) not until의 구문을 이용하여 '~할 때 까지는 …하지 않다'라는 의미를 표현

할 수 있다.
(3) ideas를 수식하는 관계대명사절을 사용한다.
(4) except for는 '~를 제외하고'라는 뜻이다.
(5) fence off는 '울타리를 치다'라는 뜻이다.

2
(1) Jasmin은 그 결정에 대해 화가 난 것 같다.
(2) 부엌에는 먹을 것이 많은 것처럼 보였다.
(3) Paul은 꽤 오랫동안 아팠던 것 같이 보였다. (seemed가 과거형이면 아팠던 것은 그 전에 있었던 일이므로 과거완료 형태로 써야 한다.)

3
(1) 몽상에 대한 호기심을 가지고 있어서 그는 몽상에 대해 연구했다.
(2) 모기에게 물어 뜯겨서 우리는 호텔 예약을 했었더라면 좋았을 걸 하는 생각이 들었다.
(3) 시끄러운 불꽃놀이에 놀라서 그 개는 의자 밑에 숨었다.
(4) 축구 시합 도중 부상을 입어, Mike는 운동장을 떠나야 했다.

수준별 대비 단원평가 Basic

1. ⑤ 2. ① 3. ⑤ 4. ② 5. ⑤ 6. ⑤
7. ① require → requires 8. ① 9. ⓐ stand ⓑ shown
10. to think beyond what you are used to 11. ② 12. ④
13. seemed to be a pleasant and comfortable place
14. Printed in haste

1
W: We're lost. I don't know which way to go. To the west? Or to the east?
M: Let's look at our location on the map.
W: Oh, yes! What a great idea! Do you know how to read signs and symbols on a map?
길을 잃고서 지도를 봐야 하는데 여자가 남자에게 지도 볼 줄 아느냐고 묻는 말에 대한 적절한 응답은 ⑤이다.

2
M: Ugh, I hate food stains on clothes. Do you know how to remove food stains?
W: Yes, you can use a spoonful of salt.
M: A spoon of salt? Can you explain how it works?
W: Sure. All you have to do is mix it with warm water and wash your clothes.
M: Wow, what a brilliant idea!
소금물에 옷을 빨면 옷에 있는 음식 얼룩을 지울 수 있다.

3 ①~④는 반의어 관계이다.
① 유한한 – 무한한 ② 나누다 – 결합하다 ③ 훌륭한 – 어리석은
④ 포함하다 – 불포함하다 ⑤ 대각선의 – 원형의

4 ②는 형용사 – 명사의 관계인데 비해 나머지는 모두 동사 – 명사의 관계이다.

5 think outside the box는 '창의적으로 생각하다' 또는 '새로운 방식으로 생각하다'라는 의미이다.

6 그 팝 가수는 연장된 홍보 투어를 통해 앨범 판매를 증진하려고 노력하고 있다.

7 동명사구인 Solving challenging problems가 주어이므로 단수로 취급된다. 그러므로 동사에 -s/es를 붙인 형태의 현재형이 와야 한다. ① require → requires

8 여기서 전통적인 방식이라는 것은 늘 하던 '익숙한 방식'을 얘기한다.

9 ⓐ make 다음에는 목적보어로 동사원형이 온다.
ⓑ 주어가 사물이며 '보여지는'것이므로 show는 shown이 와야 한다.

10 어려운 것은 처음으로 새롭게 생각하는 것이다.

11 「It seems (that) + 주어 + 동사」의 형태가 되어야 하므로 ②는 It seems my mother knows what is bothering me.라고 해야 맞다.

12 ④는 Receiving the phone call, Miriam began to cry.라고 해야 맞다. (전화를 받은 것은 수동태가 아닌 능동태임)

13 「주어 + seem/seems/seemed + to부정사」의 구문을 활용한다.

14 As the book was printed in haste, it contains many errors.에서 접속사가 있는 부분을 분사구문으로 고친 것이다.

수준별 단원평가 Advanced

1. ① 2. ③ 3. ④ 4. ⑤
5. he can hit diagonally 또는 swinging two times for 11 yards in a diagonal direction 6. 정확히 200야드를 치려면 50야드씩 4번 쳐야 한다고 일반적으로 생각할 것이기 때문에 7. ①
8. ③ 9. ① 10. ② 11. blow 12. 해설 참조

1
M: Hey, Grace. Did you watch that documentary about Jeong Yakyong last night?
W: You mean the late Joseon dynasty scholar? — the one who wrote *Mokminsimseo*?
M: That's right. He also built the Hwaseong Fortress in Suwon with his creative invention.
W: I haven't seen the documentary, but I did read a book about him. His creativity was incredible. I was particularly impressed reading about the system he invented to handle heavy building materials. What was it called... *Geojunggi*?
M: That's the one. And I agree — I think *geojunggi* is his greatest invention. What a brilliant idea it is, right?
W: You can say that again. Do you know how to operate it? I was surprised to see it lifting huge stones.
M: Yes, actually, I saw one once at a folk village and tried it out.
W: That sounds pretty cool. I'm interested in engineering. If you have a moment, can you tell me more about it?
M: Sure. Let's talk about it during lunch time.
W: Thanks. See you soon.
Grace는 정약용이 발명한 거중기의 작동 방법에 대해 공학적인 측면에서 관심을 가지고 있다.

2 남자가 민속촌에서 거중기를 작동시켰던 것에 대해 얘기해 주겠다고 했다.

3
M: Do you know how to get in good shape? Perhaps you're thinking about a workout. But when was the last time you thought about a brain workout? Training your brain is just as important as maintaining a healthy body. Studies show that with one hour of brain training a week, you not only improve the thinking skills you use every day but also prevent memory disorders. With regular brain training, you will notice that you have better memory and greater creativity in your daily life. Train your brain by doing different types of brain questions on a daily basis or by approaching daily problems in a way you're not used to. Just make a conscious effort to think of different ways of doing things.
창의적으로 생각하는 법을 연습하라는 것이 주제이다.

4 전통적이고 익숙한 방식으로는 창의적 문제 해결이 가능하지 않다. 따라서 ⑤는 문맥상 적절하지 않다.

5 익숙하지 않은 방식으로 생각하는 것의 예는 골프공을 사선 방향으로 칠 수 있다는 것이다.

6 익숙한 방식의 계산법은 50야드를 칠 수 있으니까 200야드면 4번을 치면 되지 않을까 하는 계산이다. 이것도 가능하지만 가장 적은 타수는 아닌 것이다.

7 가장 적은은 the smallest이다.

8 수학자가 가장 적은 양의 철사로 가장 넓은 면적을 울타리 친 사람이어서 우승자가 된 것이다.

9 자신이 서 있는 땅 밖은 다 울타리를 친 것이라는 의미이다.

10 (A)는 빈 상자를 받은 고객의 불평(complaint).
(B)는 상자 스캐너를 구입(purchase)하는 회사.
(C)는 비누로 가득한 상자는 무거워서(heavy) 바람에 날아가지 않을 것임

11 조립 라인 구석에 놓인 선풍기가 빈 비누상자를 날려 보내는(blow away) 해결 방식이다.

12 〈예시 답안〉
I think one of the best inventions in history is the wheel. Without it, things would be really different. We rely on wheels for transportation and carrying things. Wheels are ubiquitous in our everyday life, facilitating our transportation and commerce.

UNIT 7 The Name of the Game in Creative Industries

교과서 핵심 정리 Check-Up

Words & Phrases

1. (1) give life to (2) make use of (3) accounts for (4) a great number of (5) take part in
2. (1) icon (2) glamor (또는 glamour) (3) release (4) revive (5) phenomenon
3. (1) a wide range of opinions
(2) Contrary to our expectation
(3) billions of dollars in the project
(4) accounts for about a third of

1
(1) 그 축제는 지역에 활기를 불어넣어 줄 것이다.
(2) 우리는 좀 더 효율적인 방식으로 자원을 활용할 수 있을 것이다.
(3) 중국 시장이 회사 수입의 35%를 차지하고 있다.
(4) 그 회사는 도시 지역에 상당히 많은 일자리를 창출하고 있다.
(5) 많은 유명인들이 루게릭병을 앓고 있는 사람들을 돕기 위한 아이스버킷 챌린지 행사에 참여한다.

2
(1) 널리 알려진 상징(물)
(2) 아주 흥미롭고 매력적인 자질
(3) 어떤 것을 사람들에게 획득가능하게 하다
(4) 어떤 것이나 사람을 강하고 건강하게 또는 다시 활기차게 만들다
(5) 관찰되고 연구될 수 있으며 보통 흔하지 않거나 완전히 이해하기 어려운 사실이나 사건

Reading Comprehension(Focus on Structure)

1. (1) to have written for newspapers
(2) has sent (또는 sent) messages via Facebook to his girlfriend
2. (1) knew the formula for the volume of a sphere, could solve the math problem
(2) it were not raining, go golfing

1
(1) 그녀가 10년 이상 신문에 글을 썼었다는 것이 알려져 있다.: 알려진 것은 현재시제이고 신문사에 글을 기고한 것은 과거시제이므로 완료부정사 (to + have + p.p.)를 써야 한다.
(2) 그 스파이는 페이스북을 통해 자신의 여자 친구에게 메시지를 보내왔다고 믿어진다. : 완료부정사를 절로 바꿀 때에는 앞에 있는 be동사의 시제보다 한 단계 이전인 시제를 쓴다.

2
(1) 그는 구의 부피를 구하는 공식을 모른다. 그는 그 수학 문제를 풀 수 없다. → 그가 만약 구의 부피를 구하는 공식을 안다면 그 수학문제를 풀 수 있을 텐데. (가정법 과거)
(2) 비가 오고 있다. 나는 골프 치러 갈 수 없다. → 비가 오고 있지 않다면 골프 치러 갈 텐데. (가정법 과거): 현재 사실의 반대 상황을 가정하는 가정법 과거는 동사의 과거형을 쓴다.

언어 기능별 집중 대비

Listen and Speak/ Into Real Life

1. ② 2. ⑤ 3. ④ 4. (1) ② (2) ①

1
W: I'm really into musicals. What is popular these days?
M: Let me search the Internet. This website has a chart of this month's top five musicals.
W: This chart indicates that *Hero* is ranked first!
M: Do you want to go see it together?
W: Sounds great.
웹 사이트에서 인기 뮤지컬 순위를 보며 대화하고 있다.

2
W: You look quite excited today. What's up?
M: My favorite band YBB is going to the Edinburgh Festival Fringe!
W: Congratulations! But what is the Fringe?
M: Oh, the Edinburgh Festival Fringe is a huge arts festival held in Edinburgh, Scotland every August.
W: Cool! Nothing compares to attending an arts festival. So is it for bands only?
M: No. This festival includes plays, comedy, dance, and concerts.
W: So it's a festival for all the performing arts?
M: Exactly. Several Korean performers have taken part so far. A few years ago, *Nanta* performed there and was invited to *Broadway afterwards*.
W: This must be a great opportunity for your favorite band then!
M: Yes, it is. Oh, I really want to fly to Edinburgh!
W: Where can you buy tickets?
M: You can buy them from the website or from street musicians there.
표는 축제가 열리는 지역 길거리 음악가들에게서도 구입할 수 있다.

3
M: Hello, Suji. Thank you for taking the time to talk to us. How was your world tour?
W: It was great. I was amazed that so many fans from abroad came to my concert.
M: Actually, I brought a newspaper article about your concert in Indonesia. The graph in the article indicates that your concert sold the most tickets this month in the country. Congratulations!
W: Thank you. I feel grateful to all my international fans.
M: Singing your songs in front of many international fans must feel very different.

W: Actually, they aren't so different from Korean fans. They even knew some words in my songs and sang along with me.
M: They must have learned the Korean language from Korean dramas and movies. Speaking of the Korean language, you also visited a Korean language center in Vietnam.
W: Yes, I did. It was a very meaningful experience to meet students learning Korean.
M: You must have been very proud of the Korean Wave and its influence in various areas.
W: Of course. Some of my European fans greeted me in *hanbok* at the airport.
M: How wonderful!
W: I think people are appreciating Korean culture more and more internationally. And I feel honored to be part of this great Korean Wave.

베트남에 있는 한국어 학당 방문이 의미 있는 경험이었다고 말하고 있다.

4

W: Okay, Jihun. Let's get started on our newspaper article about movies. Look at this pie chart.
M: Is this the one about students' favorite movies?
W: Yes. The graph reveals that 40% of students chose history movies as their favorite.
M: Interesting. It also says here that sci-fi movies account for 35%.
W: And the most popular movie was *The Admiral*. It seems like nothing compares to the dynamics of movies about Korean history.
M: I can't believe *The Admiral* beat *Interstellar*.
W: *Interstellar* came in second by only five votes.
M: What about the remaining 25%?
W: They chose action movies, animations, or others.
M: This will be a great article for the school newspaper.

(1) 좋아하는 영화의 종류에 대한 설문 조사였다.
(2) 역사적 내용을 소재로 한 영화가 가장 인기 있는 장르라고 설문 결과가 나왔으므로 이 내용을 실을 예정이다.

Read and Think

1. ③	2. ③	3. ⑤	4. ①	5. (A) making
(B) had (C) have gained			6. ⑤	7. ③	8. ③
9. ④				

1 프로도 효과를 예시로 들면서 창조적 경제에 대한 개념을 정의하고 있다.

2 빈칸 뒤에 이어지는 문장에서 상상력이 풍부한 문학 작품의 예시들이 나오고 있으므로 영국의 창조적 경제의 바탕은 문학적 상상력임을 알 수 있다.

3 ⑤ Combining → Combined : 분사구문에서 수동적 의미(결합되어서)를 나타내고 있으므로 Being이 생략된 과거분사를 사용한다.

4 주어진 문장은 미국 문화 산업의 특징을 두괄식으로 말하고 있으므로 할리우드나 브로드웨이에 관한 예시문 앞에 위치하는 게 알맞다.

5 (A) 능동적 의미의 분사구문이므로 현재분사형태가 알맞다.
(B) 가정법 과거의 문장이므로 동사의 과거형이 알맞다.
(C) 추정되는 게 현재인데 반해 벌어들인 것은 과거의 일이므로 완료부정사(「to have +p.p.」)가 알맞다.

6 전체적인 요지는 한류와 최첨단 기술의 결합으로 인해 더 큰 성공이 이루어지고 있다는 것이다.

7 본문에서 '이 방법'이란 만화영화 시리즈를 TV에서 보여주고 나서 해당 캐릭터 상품을 다양한 방법으로 디자인하여 구매하도록 하는 전략을 의미한다.

8 외국의 한류 팬들에 대한 마케팅 전략에 대해 얘기하고 있고, 방송에서 한국 연예인들이 사용하는 아이템에 대한 간접적 홍보 효과가 이루어짐을 얘기하고 있다.

9 기존과 달리 상상력이 풍부한 공상가 또는 창의적 작가가 다음 세대의 주요 CEO가 될 수도 있음을 시사하고 있다.

Language Notes Write It Right

1. (1) A great number of reporters gathered
   (2) can make use of this auditorium/hall
   (3) were estimated to have gained weight
   (4) to have suffered from heart attack
   (5) were given one more chance to speak
2. (1) seems to have quit the job
   (2) is believed to have gone on for ten days
   (3) the caterpillar has a sting equivalent to a mild electrical shock
   (4) the U.K. economy had grown by 2.6%
3. (1) had not eaten a lot, I would not have felt sick
   (2) pass the exam if she studied hard
   (3) were not always late for work, he could be promoted

1

(1) 「a great number of + 복수명사」 *cf.* the number of: ~의 수
(2) not everyone: 부분부정 (모두가 ~하는 것은 아니다)
(3) 체중이 늘어난 것은 추정되고 있는 것보다 이전에 일어난 일이므로 완료부정사 「to have + p.p.」를 사용한다.
(5) '만약 ~한다면'이라는 의미는 가정법 과거의 구문으로 나타낸다. 따라서 「if + 주어 + 동사의 과거형, 주어 + would/could/should/might + 동사원형」의 형태로 쓰면 된다.

2

(1) 「It seems (that) 주어 + 과거동사」 → 「주어 seem(s) + to have p.p.」
(2) It is believed (that) 주어 + 과거동사」 → 「주어 is/are believed + to have p.p.」 : ~했다고 믿어진다
(3) 주절의 시제와 that 절의 시제가 같으므로 단순부정사를 사용한다.
(4) 과거 시제(was estimated)보다 하나 앞선 시제는 과거완료「had + p.p.」 시제이다.

3

(1) 너무 많이 먹어서 탈이 났다. (직설법-과거) → 너무 많이 먹지 않았더라면 탈이 나지 않았을 텐데. (가정법 과거완료: 「if + 주어 + had + p.p. -, 주어 + would/should/could/might + have + p.p.」)
(2) 열심히 공부하지 않아서 시험에 합격할 수 없다. (직설법) → 열심히 공부한다면 합격할 수 있을 텐데. (가정법 과거)
(3) 직장에 항상 지각해서 승진을 못하고 있다.(직설법) → 직장에 항상 지각하지 않는다면 승진할 수 있을 텐데.(가정법 과거)

수준별 단원평가 Basic

1. ④	2. ①	3. ①	4. ②	5. ①	6. ③
7. ③	8. ②	9. ④	10. ④	11. ①	12. ⑤

13. had a sewing machine, I could make clothes for myself
14. to have been using at least five fake names

1

W: You look quite excited today. What's up?
M: My favorite band YBB is going to the Edinburgh Festival Fringe!
W: Congratulations! But what is the Fringe?
M: Oh, the Edinburgh Festival Fringe is a huge arts festival held in Edinburgh, Scotland every August.
W: Cool! Nothing compares to attending an arts festival. So is it

for bands only?
M: No. This festival includes plays, comedy, dance, and concerts.
W: So it's a festival for all the performing arts?
M: Exactly. Several Korean performers have taken part so far. A few years ago, *Nanta* performed there and was invited to Broadway afterwards.
W: This must be a great opportunity for your favorite band then!
M: Yes, it is. Oh, I really want to fly to Edinburgh!
W: Where can you buy tickets?
M: You can buy them from the website or from street musicians there.

한국 공연 팀이 축제에 참가하기는 하지만 그 팀 수가 정확하게 언급되지는 않았다.

2

W: What are you reading?
M: I'm reading *The Hunger Games*. Have you ever read it?
W: No, I haven't. But I've seen the movie.
M: Me, too. But I prefer the books because nothing compares to the original.

남자는 'The Hunger Games' 영화와 책 중에 책으로 읽는 게 더 좋았다고 말하고 있다.

3 ①에서 the number of lions는 '사자들의 수'라는 뜻으로 단수이다. 따라서 동사의 3인칭 단수형 is를 써야 한다.

4 ②mice가 복수이고, mouse가 단수형이다. 나머지는 앞의 단어가 단수형이고 뒤에 오는 단어가 복수형이다.

5 ①의 terrific (훌륭한, 멋진)과 terrible(끔찍한)은 반의어 관계이고 나머지는 모두 유의어 관계다.

6 그 회사는 어느 정도 수익을 내고 있으나 내야 할 만큼의 수익을 내고 있지는 못하다.

7 ③ to withhold (억제하는, 보류하는) → to support (지지하는, 후원하는)

8 여기에서 쓰인 Who knows?의 의미는 뒤에 언급된 일이 지금은 가능성이 없어 보이지만 미래에는 충분히 일어날 수 있는 일임을 암시하고 있다.

9 미국 문화 산업의 두 개의 큰 중심축은 할리우드 영화와 브로드웨이 뮤지컬이라고 말하고 있다.

10 브로드웨이 뮤지컬 역시 미국 문화 산업의 특징인 화려함을 보여준다.

11 한류의 마케팅 전략에 대한 예시들이 나오므로 ①이 적절하다.

13 내 옷을 직접 만들어 입고 싶은데 재봉틀이 없다. (직설법-현재) → 재봉틀이 있다면 내 옷을 직접 만들어 입을 텐데. (가정법 과거)

14 알려져 있는 것이 현재시제(is known)인 반면, 그가 가짜 이름을 사용했던(used)것은 과거시제이므로 「주어 + is known + to have used」의 형태로 문장을 구성한다.

수준별 단원평가 Advanced

1. ①	**2.** ⑤	**3.** ①	**4.** economic, profitable	
5. ①	**6.** ②	**7.** ②	**8.** ③	**9.** ②
10. 해설 참조				

[1~2]
M: Hello, Suji. Thank you for taking the time to talk to us. How was your world tour?
W: It was great. I was amazed that so many fans from abroad came to my concert.
M: Actually, I brought a newspaper article about your concert in Indonesia. The graph in the article indicates that your concert sold the most tickets this month in the country. Congratulations!
W: Thank you. I feel grateful to all my international fans.
M: Singing your songs in front of many international fans must feel very different.
W: Actually, they aren't so different from Korean fans. They even knew some words in my songs and sang along with me.
M: They must have learned the Korean language from Korean dramas and movies. Speaking of the Korean language, you also visited a Korean language center in Vietnam.
W: Yes, I did. It was a very meaningful experience to meet students learning Korean.
M: You must have been very proud of the Korean Wave and its influence in various areas.
W: Of course. Some of my European fans greeted me in *hanbok* at the airport.
M: How wonderful!
W: I think people are appreciating Korean culture more and more internationally. And I feel honored to be part of this great Korean Wave.

1 인도네시아에서 수지의 인기가 얼마나 높은지 실제 신문 기사를 인용하여 말하려고 신문을 가져왔다.

2 유럽의 팬들 중 일부는 한복을 입고 공항에 마중 나왔다.

3

M: Hello, Daehan High School students. Today in our weekly school news, we'd like to show you the results of the school survey "What is your favorite genre of the performing arts?" Our club members asked more than 200 students in the school to participate in this survey. Please take a look at this pie chart. This chart indicates that 50% of students chose concerts while 35% chose musicals. The remaining 15% chose dance, plays, and others. It was good to see that Daehan High School students have a variety of tastes in the performing arts. Next week, we will bring you more interesting news about our school. See you then!

통계 자료를 보면서 분석적인(analytical) 어조로 말하고 있다.

4 문화적 내용과 상상력을 사용하는 것과 관련된 경제 활동인 창조적 산업은 많은 수익을 창출한다.

5 glamor가 미국 문화 산업의 공통적 특징이라고 말하고 있다.

6 한국의 창조적 산업이 지난 10여 년간 세계적으로 성공적이었다는 주제문이 오고 이어지는 문장들은 그 사례들이다.

7 홀로그램 콘서트는 실제로 무대에서 가수들을 만나는 게 아니라 as if the singer were actually on stage (가수가 마치 무대에 진짜 있는 것처럼 느끼게 하는) 기술을 사용한 것이다.

8 This story ~는 *Uncle Tom's Cabin*을 가리킨다. 그러므로 ③에 들어가는 것이 적절하다.

9 ⓑ to change → to have changed (미국의 역사를 바꾼 것은 이전에 일어난 일임)

10 〈예시 답안〉
Welcome to the new center of the Korean Wave. I'd like to introduce you to K-drama, which refers to Korean soap operas. Soap operas are one of the most popular types of TV shows in the world. Now, Korea is shining in the soap opera light, having a strong fan base from around the world. Korean soap operas have shown remarkable development thanks to creative writers and producers. From "Goblin" to "Descendents of the Sun", Korean dramas are attracting more watchers around the world.

UNIT 8 What Makes a Good Citizen?

교과서 핵심 정리 Check-Up

Words & Phrases

1. (1) pushed aside (2) was ashamed of (3) watch out for
   (4) are willing to (5) are faced with
2. (1) frown (2) jaywalk (3) misbehavior
   (4) regulation (5) extinguish
3. (1) to keep accidents from occurring
   (2) I felt so ashamed of myself for making
   (3) neglect but help their neighbors in need
   (4) were faced with unexpected challenges

1
(1) 그는 수위를 밀치고 그 문을 열었다.
(2) 그녀는 아버지가 알코올 중독이라는 것이 부끄러워 아무에게도 그 말을 하지 않았다.
(3) 당신은 길에서 놀고 있는 아이들을 조심해야 한다.
(4) 만약 야간 비행을 기꺼이 하시겠다면 훨씬 더 싼 표를 살 수 있어요.
(5) 우리는 젊은 세대와 나이든 세대의 필요를 조율할 임무에 직면해 있다.

2
(1) 찌푸리다: 승인하지 않는 표정으로 보거나 화난 표정을 짓다
(2) 무단 횡단하다: 정식 횡단보도가 아닌 곳으로 길을 건너다
(3) 잘못된 행동: 맞지 않거나 적절하지 않거나 나쁜 행동
(4) 법규: 법, 규칙, 또는 직권으로 규정된 그 외의 명령
(5) 끄다: (불이나 전기를) 끄다

Reading Comprehension(Focus on Structure)

1. (1) she had been a beauty queen (2) had neglected his duty
2. (1) had been trapped (2) had been adopted (3) I could go

1
(1) Emma는 미인대회 최고 미인이었다는 것에 대해 말하지 않았다.: 말하지 않은 것이 과거시제이면 최고 미인이었다는 과거 이전 사실은 과거완료시제로 표현한다.
(2) Ted는 자신의 의무를 게을리 한 것에 대해 비난받았다. : 비난 받은 것이 과거시제이면 의무를 게을리 했다는 과거 이전 사실은 과거완료로 표현한다.

2
(1) 그 팀은 안에 갇혀 있었던 일가족을 구조했다.: 주절의 동사가 rescued로 과거형이므로 안에 갇혀 있었던 것은 과거완료 시제가 알맞다.
(2) 나는 아이일 때 유럽으로 입양되었었던 두 명의 여성을 인터뷰했다. : 두 명의 여성은 입양되었던 것이므로 수동태로 표현한다.
(3) 나는 연주회에 같이 갈 수 있으면 좋겠어.: 「I wish + 주어 + 과거동사」 형태의 가정법과거로 표현한다.

언어 기능별 집중 대비

Listen and Speak/ Into Real Life

1. ④ 2. ② 3. ④ 4. (1) ① (2) ②

1
M: Mom, do you really have to drive so slowly?
W: I'm just trying to be safe!
M: But we are late!
W: Trust me. It's always better to be safe than sorry.

"Better safe than late."는 "늦더라도 안전하게 가는 게 낫다."라는 뜻으로 ④의 '안전한 게 제 시간에 늦지 않고 가는 것보다 더 중요하다'라는 의미와 같다.

2
W: Taylor, will you borrow some books from the library for me?
M: Why can't you do that yourself?
W: Last time, I returned some books past the due date. So I can't borrow books for the next ten days.
M: What a shame!

여자가 책을 빌릴 수 없는 상황이 되었으므로 ②와 같은 유감의 표현이 적절하다. ⑤는 '이런 우연의 일치가 있나!'라는 의미이다.

3
W: Jinu, you have to wait for the green light.
M: Do I really have to do that? I'm late!
W: Didn't you hear the news about Mingming?
M: What happened to her?
W: Last Friday, she got hit by a car while jaywalking and broke her arm.
M: That's terrible news!
W: No kidding. I also recently saw on the news that out of all the causes of teenage traffic accidents, jaywalking ranked first.
M: What a shame!
W: It seems like a little thing to just wait for the light, but if you don't, you could face serious problems.
M: You're right. And I hope Mingming gets better soon.
W: I'm going to visit her this weekend. Will you join me?
M: Absolutely!
W: Oh, let's go. The light's green.

Mingming은 무단 횡단하다가 난 교통사고에서 다리가 아니라 팔을 다쳤다.

4
W: How was your first week in Singapore as an exchange student, Ed?
M: Great. I noticed that the country is so clean.
W: Throwing trash on the street is illegal here.
M: Many other countries have that law, too. But I feel like it's much better kept in Singapore.
W: Maybe it's because of the penalty. When you are caught three times, you have to clean the city once a week wearing certain clothes.
M: That must be embarrassing. (pause) Will you hold my stuff while I drink some water?
W: You mean, you want to drink it here on the subway? If I were you, I'd wait until we get off the subway.
M: Do I really have to do that? I'm thirsty.
W: Drinking and eating on the subway are illegal in Singapore.
M: Really? I didn't know that. Is there anything else I should know?
W: Let me tell you one more thing. Bringing smelly fruit on the subway is illegal, too.
M: You mean like strong-smelling fruit? Thanks for telling me.

(1) 지하철에서 물을 마시는 것이 허용되지 않는다고 말하고 있다.
(2) 특정한 옷을 입는 것은 법규에 어긋나지 않는다.

Read and Think

1. ③ 2. ④ 3. ① 4. ④ 5. ③ 6. ①
7. ④ 8. ② 9. ④ 10. ③

1 밑줄 친 부분 앞에 제시된 예시들은 모두 공공질서에 반하는 행동들이다.

2 ④의 fortunately는 앞에 be동사의 보어인 형용사 형태 fortunate로 바

꾸어야 한다.

3 소방차 운전자는 긴급 차량이 신속히 현장에 접근하는 것을 방해하는 운전자들에 대해 불평을 하고 있다.

4 ⓐ는 앞 뒤 문장이 서로 반대의 상황이므로 However가 적절하다.
ⓑ는 앞 문장의 경우보다 더 심한 경우를 이야기하고 있으므로 '게다가' 또는 '더군다나'의 의미를 갖는 furthermore가 적절하다.

5 응급 전화 – (B) 통화 내용과 소방차 출동 – (C) 소방관이 오기 전에 화재 진화를 돕고 있던 이웃들 모습 – (A) 진화 후 소방 활동에 대한 인터뷰의 순서가 가장 적절하다.

6 이어지는 문장에 이웃 주민들이 소방차가 들어올 길을 마련해 놓았다는 표현이 나오므로 '주차 문제'에 직면하지 않았다는 말이 온다.

7 주제문에서 제시된 책임 있는 시민행동의 순서가 '법규 준수'-'좋은 행동 규범'-'공공한 이웃돕기'의 순서이므로 주어진 문장은 마지막 예시로 나오는 것이 적절하다.

8 열정적인 응원과 함께 시민들이 질서를 지키고 거리를 깨끗이 청소했다는 내용이 나오므로 ②의 '사람들의 바른 행동 양식'이 적절하다.

9 타이타닉 호가 그 당시 뉴스 잡지에 의해 강력하고 안전하다고 칭송을 받아와서 승객들은 구명보트로 하선 명령을 받았을 때, 배를 떠나야 할 필요성을 느끼지 못했다. 그러므로 주어진 문장은 문맥상 (D)에 들어가는 것이 알맞다.

10 지문에서 가장 주요하게 언급하고 있는 것은 타이타닉이 가라앉지 않을 거라는 사람들의 지나친 확신이다. ① 사건이 일어난 날 밤은 달빛도 거의 없고 어두웠다. ② 위험을 경계하는 업무를 맡은 사람이 자신의 안경을 끼고 있지 않았다. ③ 타이타닉호가 가라앉지 않을 거라 생각했던 승객들은 배를 떠나 구명정으로 옮겨 타지 않았다. ④ 모든 승객을 위한 구명정이 충분하지 않았다. ⑤ 승객들은 배가 조금 더 오래 물 위에 떠 있는 상태로 있을 거라는 잘못된 희망을 가지고 있었다.

Language Notes / Write It Right

1. (1) for not having done your responsibility
   (2) having taken care of them
   (3) had been lost
   (4) that / which had been kept
   (5) that / which had been washed
2. (1) She fell down the stairs.
   (2) Looking at the smartphone while walking down the stairs.

1
(1) 「be ashamed of + (not) having + p.p.」: ~했던 것(하지 않았던 것)에 대해 부끄러움을 느끼다
(2) 감사했다(thanked)는 것과 두 수녀가 그들을 돌봐준 것은 시제 상에 차이가 있으므로 전치사의 목적어로 완료동명사 형태를 쓰는 게 적절하다.
(3) 알아차린 것(realized)은 과거시제이고, 소화기가 이전에 분실되었던 것은 과거완료시제이며, 여기서는 수동태로 써야 하므로 「had been + p.p.」 형태가 온다.

수준별 단원평가 Basic

1. ⑤ 2. ④ 3. ③ 4. ② 5. ② 6. ①
7. ④ 8. make way
9. who crossed the street at a red light blocked the way
10. ④
11. ⓐ had been hurt ⓑ had been taken
12. a better place is not difficult
13. Their help kept the fire from turning into a bigger disaster.

1
W: Let's get going!
M: Before we start, you should wear this helmet.
W: Dad, do I really have to wear this funny-looking helmet when I ride my bike?
M: Absolutely. It will keep you safe.
여자 아이는 웃기게 생긴 헬멧을 쓰고 싶어 하지 않는다.

2
W: Taylor, will you borrow some books from the library for me?
M: Why can't you do that yourself?
W: Last time, I returned some books past the due date. So I can't borrow books for the next ten days.
M: What a shame!
여자는 반납 기한을 지나 반납한 책이 있어서 지금 책을 대출할 수 없다.

3 A: Sam이 아파서 연주회에 못 갔어.
B: 이런, 안됐네!

4 ② extinguish: (불을) 끄다

5 ① 탐지하다 – 숨기다 ② 심한 – 심한 ③ 가짜인 – 진짜인 ④ 공공의 – 사적인 ⑤ 무시하다 – 고려하다

6 ① put out the fire: 불을 끄다 (= extinguish the fire)

7 ④는 '차선을 빨리 바꾸지 않아 응급 차량의 도착을 지연시킨 차량 운전자들'이므로 'responsible citizens(책임감 있는 시민들)'의 사례에 속하지 않는다.

8 응급 차량의 원활한 운행을 방해한 운전자들에 대한 불만이므로 make way (길을 양보해주다)라는 표현이 와야 한다.

9 보행자들(pedestrians)이라는 선행사를 수식하는 관계대명사절이 먼저 오고 나서 동사가 따라온다.

10 ④ The song that she had composed received mixed review. : 그녀가 작곡했던 그 노래는 복합적인 평가를 받았다. (능동태)

12 주어가 동명사 Making이므로 be동사를 3인칭 단수형 is로 쓴다.

13 「주어 + keep + 목적어 + from + -ing」: ~를 …하지 못하도록 막다

수준별 단원평가 Advanced

1. ② 2. ① 3. ③ 4. ⑤ 5. ③
6. ⓐ empty ⓑ drowned 7. ④ 8. ③ 9. ④
10. Some people pushed one another (and hurt others).
11. responsible citizens 12. 해설 참조

[1~2]
W: Last Saturday, a high school student was walking down the stairs looking at her smartphone. As a result, she fell down the stairs and broke her leg. Fortunately, Mr. Park, a janitor who was in the building discovered her. After checking her leg, he called 119. The emergency rescue team arrived at the building shortly afterwards and gave the girl emergency treatment. After she was transferred to the hospital, a doctor operated on the girl successfully. The girl said, "I thank everyone. I thank the janitor for staying with me until the ambulance came. Thanks to the rescue team, I received emergency treatment. Thanks to the doctor, my leg is recovering."

1 넘어져서 다친 소녀에게 응급처치를 해 준 것은 수위 아저씨의 전화를 받고 온 응급 구조팀이다.

2 사고를 당했을 때 자신을 도와 준 사람들에 대한 감사의 표현을 하고 있다.

3

M: Look at this picture! Isn't this wonderful?
W: You call this wonderful? I think it looks dangerous!
M: I'd go for the challenge if I could get a picture as beautiful as this.
W: Please tell me you are not serious.
M: I think the man in the picture is really brave.
W: He risked his life for this one picture. How silly!
M: (laughing) Take it easy. It's a joke.
W: What do you mean it's a joke?
M: Look at this other picture. People took fake pictures here, so it looks like they are actually hanging on a real cliff.
W: Thank goodness! It's a fake cliff that's only a little above the ground!

사진에서 남자가 매달려 있는 절벽은 실제 절벽이 아니다.

4 A의 말에 just wait for the light라는 표현이 나오므로 '무단 횡단'이 알맞은 원인이 된다.

5 타이타닉 사고의 여러 가지 안 좋았던 정황을 기술한 후에 이보다 더 나쁜(worse) 상황을 기술하려고 하고 있으므로, 사고에 대한 경각심 없이 배에 남아 있었던 사람들의 행동 바로 직전에 위치하는 게 적절하다.

6 구명보트로 옮겨 타지 않은 사람들 때문에 텅 빈(empty) 구명보트가 많이 남게 되었고, 따라서 침몰 후 많은 사람들이 익사한(drowned)것이다.

7 ④ helping → to help : 「be willing + to부정사」

8 소방차가 화재 현장에 도착해서 주차하는 데 아무런 문제가 없었다는 문장 뒤에 그 이유에 관한 주어진 문장이 오는 게 적절하다.

9 이웃 주민들이 그 건물의 진화 및 인명 구조에 여러 가지 도움을 주었다고 말하고 있다.

10 축제 장소에서 발생한 사고는 사람들이 서로를 떠미는 과정에서 생겼다.

11 다른 사람들을 고려하고 배려하는 사람들이란 시민의식이 있는 시민들(responsible citizens)을 의미한다고 할 수 있다.

12 〈예시 답안〉
- Don't panic. Remain calm and proceed towards the nearest exits.
- Stay low. (The gases and smoke are more dangerous than the actual flames.)
- Never use an elevator during a fire.

그 밖의 가능한 답안
- Once outside the building, move away from the building.
- Do not re-enter the building until you are told to do so by the fire department.

2학기 중간고사 UNIT ❻ – UNIT ❽

01. ① **02.** ① **03.** ④ **04.** ③ **05.** ⑤ **06.** ③
07. ③ **08.** ② **09.** ③ **10.** ⑤ **11.** ④ **12.** ⑤
13. ⑤ **14.** ④ **15.** ④ **16.** ④ **17.** ① **18.** ④
19. ① **20.** ② **21.** it is not limited only to seeing images
22. where members contribute to one another's happiness
23. (1) You should be ashamed of yourself for violating traffic laws.
(2) If I had more time, I could/would stay longer in this city.
24. (1) to be an honest accountant
(2) Loving his wife so much
(3) to have had been exposed to the disease while traveling
25. 해설 참조

1

M: Ugh, I hate food stains on clothes. Do you know how to remove food stains?
W: Yes, you can use a spoonful of salt.
M: A spoon of salt? Can you explain how it works?
W: Sure. All you have to do is mix it with warm water and wash your clothes.
M: Wow, what a brilliant idea!

놀라운 해결책에 대한 감탄의 응답이 적절하다.

2

M: Do you know how to get in good shape? Perhaps you're thinking about a workout. But when was the last time you thought about a brain workout? Training your brain is just as important as maintaining a healthy body. Studies show that with one hour of brain training a week, you not only improve the thinking skills you use every day but also prevent memory disorders. With regular brain training, you will notice that you have better memory and greater creativity in your daily life. Train your brain by doing different types of brain questions on a daily basis or by approaching daily problems in a way you're not used to. Just make a conscious effort to think of different ways of doing things.

두뇌 훈련의 효과와 방법에 관한 이야기이다.

3

W: Okay, Jihun. Let's get started on our newspaper article about movies. Look at this pie chart.
M: Is this the one about students' favorite movies?
W: Yes. The graph reveals that 40% of students chose history movies as their favorite.
M: Interesting. It also says here that sci-fi movies account for 35%.
W: And the most popular movie was *The Admiral*. It seems like nothing compares to the dynamics of movies about Korean history.
M: I can't believe *The Admiral* beat *Interstellar*.
W: *Interstellar* came in second by only five votes.
M: What about the remaining 25%?
W: They chose action movies, animations, or others.
M: This will be a great article for the school newspaper.

Interstellar는 The General보다 5표가 덜 나왔다.

4

M: Hello, Daehan High School students. Today in our weekly school news, we'd like to show you the results of the school survey "What is your favorite genre of the performing arts?"

Our club members asked more than 200 students in the school to participate in this survey. Please take a look at this pie chart. This chart indicates that 50% of students chose concerts while 35% chose musicals. The remaining 15% chose dance, plays, and others. It was good to see that Daehan High School students have a variety of tastes in the performing arts. Next week, we will bring you more interesting news about our school. See you then!

연주회와 뮤지컬 이외의 공연예술에 대한 선호도는 15%이다.

5

W: How was your first week in Singapore as an exchange student, Ed?
M: Great. I noticed that the country is so clean.
W: Throwing trash on the street is illegal here.
M: Many other countries have that law, too. But I feel like it's much better kept in Singapore.
W: Maybe it's because of the penalty. When you are caught three times, you have to clean the city once a week wearing certain clothes.
M: That must be embarrassing. (pause) Will you hold my stuff while I drink some water?
W: You mean, you want to drink it here on the subway? If I were you, I'd wait until we get off the subway.
M: Do I really have to do that? I'm thirsty.
W: Drinking and eating on the subway are illegal in Singapore.
M: Really? I didn't know that. Is there anything else I should know?
W: Let me tell you one more thing. Bringing smelly fruit on the subway is illegal, too.
M: You mean like strong-smelling fruit? Thanks for telling me.

강한 냄새가 나는 과일 반입을 금한다는 규칙을 말해 준 것에 관해 내용을 확인한 후 말해 줘서 고맙다는 응답을 하는 것이 적절하다.

6

(Siren sounds.)
M: Ladies and gentlemen, your attention, please. We have detected signs of a fire on the fifth floor of the building. Please leave the auditorium immediately through the doors on the right. Use the exit stairs to the ground level. Please follow the safety instructions and do not panic. Make sure you do not use the elevators. Stay close to the floor, and if possible, cover your mouth and nose with wet tissues. Your attention, please. We would like to inform you again that we have detected signs of a fire ....
승강기가 아닌 비상계단(emergency stairs)을 통해 1층으로 내려오도록 안내하고 있다.

7 ③ 창의성의 개념을 '이전에 생각해보지 않았던 방식으로 생각하는 것'이라고 정의하고 있다.

8 ② 도전적인 질문에 대한 답을 찾으려면 평소의 사고방식에서 벗어나 창의적인 접근을 해야 한다는 메시지이다.

9 ③ shows → is shown (수동태)

10 ①~④의 it이 공통적으로 가리키는 것은 daydreaming이고, ⑤의 it은 the brain을 가리킨다.

11 (A) 관계부사 where (이어지는 문장이 완전한 문장이다.)
(B) 주어가 the industries로서 복수 형태이므로 be동사 are가 맞다.
(C) be related to ~에서 to는 전치사이므로 동명사 형태의 using이 맞는 형태이다.

12 (A) 소유격 관계대명사 whose (바로 뒤에 명사인 cultural attractions가 온다.)
(B) lie: 놓여 있다 lay: 놓다
(C) 분사 구문이 쓰인다. (making use of -: ~를 활용하면서)

13 ⑤ Attracting → Attracted (~에 매료되어서) (=As they are attracted)

14 ④ paying → pay (주어 Korean Wave fans abroad에 맞게 동사가 올 위치이다.)

15 ④의 예는 문화 창조적 산업이 아닌 단순한 축제에 대한 이야기이다.

16 ④ 구급차 운전자는 다른 차량들이 응급 차량에게 길을 양보해 주지 않는 것에 대해 화가 나서 불평하고 있다.

17 (A) 사람들의 잘못된 행동 – misbehavior
(B) 이어지는 문장에 있는 연결사 however는 두 문장을 역접의 관계로 잇는다. 즉, 법규를 지키는 사람이 있지만 어기는 사람도 있다는 연결이 된다.
(C) furthermore 더군다나 nonetheless 그럼에도 불구하고

18 (C) 소방차와 응급차가 도착했을 때 소방차가 댈 자리를 미리 내어주기 위해 차를 미리 다른 곳으로 이동주차한 시민들 → (D) 응급팀이 건물 안으로 들어갔을 때 미리 소화기로 불을 꺼서 응급환자 구조를 도왔던 시민들 → (B) 시민들의 협조에 대한 감사의 표현

19 ① parking problem이 없었다는 것은 소방차가 진입할 자리를 내어주기 위해 미리 주차했던 차량을 이동시켜 놓았다는 의미이다.

20 ② 간단한 법규를 지키고 남을 위해 자원봉사를 하는 것들은 모두 책임감 있는 시민이 되기 위한 손쉬운 방법들이다.

21 상상력이란 볼 수 있는 이미지에 국한한 것이 아니라 오감을 모두 사용하여 느낄 수 있는 것을 포함한다.

22 community를 수식하는 관계부사절이 따라온다. 「관계부사 where + 주어 + 동사」

23
(1) be ashamed of ~ for -ing: ~한 것에 대해 부끄러워하다
(2) 가정법 과거 구문: 「if + 주어 + 과거동사 ... 주어 + could/should/would/might + 동사원형」

24
(1) 「it seems that 주어 + 동사」 = 「주어 seem/seems + to 부정사」
(2) 「접속사 + 주어 + 동사 ~ 주어 + 동사」
접속사가 있는 종속절의 동사를 현재분사 형태(-ing)로 바꾸어 분사구문을 만든다.
(3) 「It is known that 주어 + 과거동사」 = 「주어 + is/are known + to have p.p.」 ~였다고/했다고 알려져 있다.

25 〈예시 답안〉
Last year, I did volunteer service of delivering free lunch to some elderly people living alone in my neighborhood. Doing this volunteer work, I realized that our social welfare system, though it is getting better, cannot solve all the problems of the poor elderly people who have almost no economic support from the family. Also, I realized how much elderly people need someone to talk to and tried my best to listen to their life stories even for five or ten minutes.

UNIT 9 Maps Used to the Max

교과서 핵심 정리 Check-Up

Words & Phrases

1. (1) based on (2) composed of (3) as well as (4) look it up (5) rely on
2. (1) rely (2) spatial (3) represent (4) navigation (5) augment
3. (1) drawn and illustrated by hand
   (2) into the augmented reality map
   (3) the shortest route to our destination
   (4) brought about a great leap in map-making skills

1
(1) 그 영화는 토마스 만의 단편 소설에 바탕을 두고 있다.
(2) 청중은 가난하고 나이든 사람들로 구성되어 있었다.
(3) 우리 담임 선생님은 똑똑할 뿐 아니라 재치가 있다.
(4) 그 단어가 무엇을 의미하는지 모르면 사전에서 그걸 찾아봐라.
(5) 선거 기간 동안 그들이 돈과 인력에 의존하는 것은 자연스럽다.

2
(1) 의존하다: 확신 있게 기대다
(2) 공간적인: 위치나 지역 그리고 사물의 크기와 관련이 된
(3) 나타내다: 사물이나 사람을 보여주거나 묘사하다: 무엇인가의 상징이 되다
(4) 운항: 배나 항공기 등을 한 장소에서 다른 장소로 이끌어가는 행동
(5) 증강시키다: 어떤 것에 뭔가를 추가함으로써 크기나 가치를 증진시키다

Reading Comprehension(Focus on Structure)

1. (1) that she struggles with anxiety (2) against the belief that
2. (1) than anybody(anyone) else / strongest (man)
   (2) intelligent than any other person in our class / intelligent person in our class

1
(1) 그녀는 자기가 불안감에 시달리고 있다는 것을 숨겼다.: the fact는 that 절 이하와 동격이다.
(2) 그는 예방접종이 자폐증을 야기했다는 믿음에 대항하여 주장하였다.: the belief는 that 절 이하와 동격이다.

2
(1) Hercules만큼 강한 사람은 없었다. = Hercules는 가장 강한 사람이었다. : 「부정주어 + 원급 비교」는 최상급의 의미를 갖는다.
(2) 우리 반에서 Monica만큼 똑똑한 애는 없다. = 우리 반에서 Monica가 가장 똑똑하다.

언어 기능별 집중 대비

Listen and Speak/ Into Real Life

1. ① 2. ③ 3. ② 4. (1) ④ (2) ⑤

W: Let's go to the *Hanbat Library* in Daejeon this weekend.
M: Okay. I'll look up how to get there on the Internet.
W: Why don't you use a map application? It will give you the fastest route and the best transportation service.
M: That's a great idea! Can you tell me more about the application? I'd be interested to know how it works.

남자가 마지막에 I'd be interested to know how it works.라고 하고 있으므로 it이 가리키는 map application을 어떻게 쓰는 건지 알고 싶어 하는 것으로 볼 수 있다.

2
W: Hey, how was your trip?
M: It was great except that my friends and I constantly argued over directions.
W: Oh, no. Didn't you have a map with you?
M: Of course we did. We just had different opinions about which was the fastest way.
W: That happens quite frequently when you are traveling with a lot of people.
M: I guess so. But arguing about the shortest route made us spend more time getting to places.
W: That's too bad. The journey to a place should be a fun part of traveling.
M: I totally agree with you. I'd be interested to know how people traveled thousands of years ago.
W: I'm sure traveling was more difficult then. By the way, did you know that maps existed even in the 6th century B.C.?
M: Really? That's quite a long time ago.
W: Yes. I'm surprised that they had the means to develop maps at that time.
M: Me, too.

남자가 친구들과 여행하면서 최단 경로에 대해 의견이 분분하여 오히려 목적지에 가는 데 더 오랜 시간이 걸렸다고 불평하고 있다.

3
M: Hello, and welcome to *All About Eating Out*. Today, we're going to explore good Korean restaurants in the neighborhood. Our first choice is *Seoulite*. This restaurant offers over 70 different kinds of Korean food in 10 different categories. The menu includes popular dishes like *bulgogi* and *bibimbap* as well as some lesser known but equally good ones. This restaurant can comfortably accommodate 200 guests. And it's always full! Let me talk to one of the customers waiting here.
M: Hello. What's your name?
W: I'm Sarah.
M: Sarah, I'm surprised that this huge restaurant can be so full of people! Are you a regular customer here?
W: Yes. I've been coming here regularly since the restaurant opened three years ago.
M: I'd be interested to know why you like this place so much.
W: I can always enjoy a great variety of delicious Korean food at reasonable prices.

Seoulite는 70여 가지의 다양한 한국 음식을 제공하고 있으므로 ②의 'only a few popular Korean dishes'를 제공한다는 말은 일치하지 않는다.

4
W: Good morning, everyone. For next week's geography class, we are going to examine the old maps of our city. We will also compare them with the city's latest maps. You'll be very surprised to see how much the city's features have changed in the past few decades. But before we investigate maps next week, today we are going to look at some old photos of our city. First, find some pictures of the city from the past on the Internet. Then, write down some similarities and differences between the city's past and present. Lastly, I want you to share what you found with the rest of the class. I'd be interested to know what kind of things you can learn just by looking at the photos.

(1) 다음 주 수업에서는 학생들이 사는 도시의 옛날 지도(old maps)를 조사할 것이라고 예고하고 있다.
(2) today we are going to look at some old photos of our city라고 교사가 말하고 있으므로 옛날 사진을 찾아보고 현재의 도시 모습과 비교해 보는 활동을 할 것임을 알 수 있다.

Read and Think

1. ③ 2. ④ 3. ③ 4. ② 5. (D) 6. ④
7. (D)-(C)-(B)-(A) 8. ⑤ 9. ⓐ in ⓑ as 10. ③

1 주인공의 하루 생활에서 얼마나 다양하게 지도가 사용되고 있는지에 대해 얘기하고 있다. ① 지도 읽는 법 ② 제한된 지도의 형태들 ③ 일상에서의 지도의 사용 ④ 길안내 하는 법 ⑤ 지도 서비스의 질

2 인구 밀집 지역 파악을 위한 지도 사용의 예시는 글에 나와 있지 않다.

3 ③ were made → made : 문장의 동사가 were heavily influenced이기 때문에 ③의 위치에는 which / that were made에서 관계대명사와 be동사가 생략된 made가 오는 게 맞다.

4 지도가 한 국가의 군사적 또는 경제적 목적을 위한 엄청난 가치를 지닌 것이라고 믿었기 때문에 이를 국가적 그리고 상업적 비밀로 취급했다(treated them as national and commercial secrets)라고 하는 것이 자연스럽다.

5 주어진 문장에서 주어 This technology는 항공사진(air photo)의 사용과 지도제작 기술의 획기적인 도약을 가리키므로 이 내용이 바로 다음에 위치하는 게 자연스럽다.

6 (A) lead to: ~(결과로) 이끌다
(B) 뒤에 원급 비교에 쓰이는 as가 있기 때문에 이와 맞추어 as를 사용한다.
(C) consist of는 수동태로 쓰이지 않는다.
(D) 「make it possible to + 동사원형」: 가목적어 it과 진목적어인 to 부정사 형태가 쓰인 문장이다.

7 지도의 일반적 용도와 지도 제작의 발전 → 최신 지도들의 사용 목적 예시 →미래 지도 제작에 대한 전망 → 증강 현실 지도의 개발에 대한 예측

8 옛날 지도에서 얻어지는 아이디어들을 활용하여 우리 삶의 방식을 변혁할 수 있으리라는 예상에 관한 문장이다.

9 ⓐ in full scale: 본격적으로 ⓑ as a part of:~의 부분으로써

10 신증동국여지승람의 제작 동기는 언급되어 있지 않다.
① 1530년 ② 55권 ④ 팔도총도 ⑤ 독도와 울릉도 포함

Language Notes / Write It Right

1. (1) No other movie is as romantic
(2) that companies(corporations) should take(do) their social responsibilities
(3) was as brave as him(he)
(4) as effective as soaking in salt water 또는 more effective than soaking in salt water
(5) that smoking is harmful
2. (1) Coast lines, islands, rivers, and harbors were included.
(2) It's because people at the time believed that maps had great value for military and economic purposes.

1
(1), (3)부정 주어 「no other + 명사」를 원급 비교의 표현을 써서 문장을 완성한다.
(2) the opinion과 동격인 절을 that으로 시작하여 쓴다.
(4) 부정주어 nothing과 비교급 비교 표현이 같이 쓰여 최상급의 의미를 나타낸다.
(5) the fact와 동격인 절은 접속사 that으로 시작하여 쓴다.

2
(1) 15, 16세기 지도에 어떤 지리적 특징들이 포함(첨가)되어 있는가?
(2) 16세기에 왜 지도가 국가적 그리고 상업적 비밀로 취급되어 왔는가?

수준별 단원평가 Basic

1. ① 2. ⑤ 3. ④ 4. ② 5. ④
6. no other geography book was as comprehensive
7. ③ 8. ① 9. ① 10. ② 11. ②
12. the belief that the earth is the center
13. can accommodate as many cars as this one

1
W: Let's go to the *Hanbat Library* in Daejeon this weekend.
M: Okay. I'll look up how to get there on the Internet.
W: Why don't you use a map application? It will give you the fastest route and the best transportation service.
M: That's a great idea! Can you tell me more about the application? I'd be interested to know how it works.
여자가 남자에게 map application을 사용하여 도서관 가는 길을 찾아보라고 권하고 있다.

2
M: Excuse me.
W: Good morning. How can I help you?
M: I'd be interested to know about tourist spots in Seoul.
W: There are many beautiful places you can visit in Seoul. The nearest one is *Gyeongbokgung*. It's a famous palace.
M: Great! I've always wanted to visit a palace in Korea. Can you tell me how to get there?
W: Turn right at the next corner and walk straight to the end of the block.
M: Okay. Let me write that down.
W: Then turn left and go straight for about 10 meters. You'll see the palace on your right.
M: Great! Thank you for your help.
W: You're welcome. Enjoy your tour!
서울의 유명한 관광지에 대한 정보를 제공해 주고 있으므로 여행자 정보 센터(tourist information center)가 가장 적절하다.

3 서면역에서 내린 다음 지도에서 쇼핑센터를 찾아가면 된다고 하는 게 자연스러우므로 ④의 After getting on(승차한 후)을 After getting off(하차로 바꾸어야 한다.

4 augment 강화하다

5 ④ similarity 유사점 – difference 차이점

6 「부정주어 + 원급 비교」 표현으로 완성할 수 있다.

7 be composed of: ~로 구성되다
① 새로운 단어를 만나면 사전에서 그 단어를 찾아보아라.
② 그 밴드의 공연은 불꽃(이 터지는 것)과 같은 시간에 이루어지도록 계획되었다.
③ 물은 수소와 산소로 구성되었다.
④ 다이어트는 뼈의 문제뿐 아니라 우울증을 치료하는 큰 역할도 한다.
⑤ 이 프로젝트의 성공은 모든 사람이 노력을 하는 것에 달려 있다.

8 쉽게 움직일 수 있고 항상 북극을 가리키는 바늘을 가진 방향 찾는 도구:
①나침반 ②드론 ③계산기 ④휴대전화 ⑤온도계

9 기원전 6세기에 고대 바빌로니아에 세계 지도가 있었으므로 ①은 내용과 일치하지 않는다.

10 ②의 that은 관계대명사 that이고 나머지는 모두 동격절을 이끄는 접속사 that이다. ① 그녀는 아이가 있다는 사실을 숨겼다. ② 이것들은 여성들이 직장에서 직면하는 편견의 예시들이다. ③ 이 책은 사람들은 이기적이라는 내 생각을 바꿔 주었다. ④ 이 연구는 동물들이 우울해질 수 있다는 생각을 지지한다. ⑤ 나는 모든 학생들이 매일 체육 수업을 받아야 한다는 의견에 동의한다.

11 〈보기〉: 다른 어떤 과목도 지리보다 흥미롭지는 않다.
① 지리는 흥미롭지 않은 과목이다.

② 지리는 가장 흥미로운 과목이다.
③ 지리는 흥미롭지만 과목이 아니다.
④ 지리는 다른 과목들만큼 흥미롭지 않다.
⑤ 지리만큼 흥미롭지 않은 과목은 없다.

12 믿음(the belief)과 동격인 that절을 사용한다.

13 「no other + 명사」로 시작하는 부정어를 주어로 사용하고 원급 비교 또는 비교급 비교 표현을 써서 최상의 의미를 나타낼 수 있다.

수준별 단원평가 Advanced

1. ④ 2. ② 3. ① 4. ①
5. The world was described as a flat thing(circle).
6. ④ had little value → had great value
7. Maps are a big part of our daily lives.
8. the development of the geographic information system (GIS)
9. ④ 10. future maps 11. 해설 참조

[1~2]
M: Hi, Suji. Have you heard about the new construction project in our town?
W: Yes. I heard that a new community center will be built. But I don't know when it starts.
M: It starts tomorrow. Which path have you been taking to get home from school?
W: I have been taking the one through the park. A lot of people take that route to get to the town hall from the big road.
M: Oh, you can't go that way anymore. The park is near the construction site.
W: Oh. Then, which way should I go to get home?
M: You need to go around the parking lot to get home.
W: Did you find out how long the construction will take?
M: It will take about two months.
W: Okay. Thank you for telling me. I wonder why there is no construction notice.

1 공사는 모레(the day after tomorrow)가 아닌 내일(tomorrow) 시작된다고 말하고 있다.

2 construction notice(공사에 대한 공지 사항)가 없어서 공사 일정을 모르고 있었다.

3
M: Why are you looking at a map? Are you planning to go on a trip?
W: No. This is not a regular map. It's a map of famous restaurants in Korea.
M: That sounds awesome! I'd be interested to know about good restaurants in Korea.
W: Then, this map will be very useful to you.
M: Can I take a look at it?
W: Sure. Go ahead.
M: This is great! I'm surprised that it even has information about the restaurants in my neighborhood.
W: Yes. It also has tips on prices, quality of service, and parking.
M: Do you know who made it?
W: An expert food critic made the map. So, I think it's quite reliable.
M: With this map, I won't have trouble finding a good place to eat. Thanks a lot!
W: No problem!

음식 비평 전문가(an expert food critic)가 만든 지도여서 꽤 신뢰할 만 하다고 말하고 있다.

4 식당 찾기와 같은 단순한 것에서부터 학문적 목적에 이르기까지 다양한 용도로 지도가 사용되는 것에 대한 글이므로 ① '지도의 역할'이 가장 적절한 제목이다.

5 기원전 6세기 고대 바빌로니아 지도와 서양 중세 시대에 그려진 지도의 공통점은 모두 지구를 flat(평평한)하게 묘사했다는 점이다.

6 지도를 굉장히 중요한 비밀 요소로 취급했다는 것은 지도의 가치를 높이 평가했다는 의미이므로 ④의 had little value (가치가 거의 없었다)를 had great value(엄청난 가치가 있었다)로 바꾸는 게 알맞다.

7 지도가 우리 생활의 큰 일부라는 게 글의 주제이다.

8 검색을 하고, 공간적 정보를 분석하고, 지도 정보를 우리 스스로 편집하는 것은 지리정보시스템(GIS)의 개발을 통해 가능해졌다.

9 주어진 문장에 indoor areas(내부 공간들)를 포함하여 모든 물리적 공간 정보를 다 포함한 지도라고 되어 있으므로 이에 적절한 예시가 바로 뒤에 이어질 수 있도록 (D)에 위치하는 것이 알맞다.

10 본문 모두가 최신 지도 제작의 기술과 더불어 미래 지도의 양상을 설명하고 있으므로 '미래의 지도가 어떨지 알게 되면 놀랄 것이다.'라는 의미로 문장을 완성하는 것이 적절하다. 그러므로 미래의 지도가 빈칸에 알맞다.

11 〈예시 답안〉
Daehan High School is a new school located in Sejong City. It has a great view of the Geum River and beautiful mountains. Also, the city hall and lots of governmental offices are near the school. The school itself is not quite big, but it has a lot of facilities equipped with highly technological devices. Most students walk or bike to school and it takes them 10 to 15 minutes to commute from home to school.

UNIT 10 What Matters Most in Life

교과서 핵심 정리 Check-Up

Words & Phrases

1. (1) take action (2) helped, out (3) lost herself in
(4) have mercy on (5) get back at (6) took, away
2. (1) hermit (2) declare (3) possess
(4) property (5) grant
3. (1) digging a hole to hide its bone in
(2) badly wounded (or wounded badly) in the explosion
(3) to make peace with his son before he died
(4) made up my mind yet about where to go

1
(1) 우리는 그의 결정이 나오자마자 행동을 취할 것이다.
(2) Paul은 골목길에 있는 눈을 치움으로써 그의 나이 든 이웃을 도왔다.
(3) 나의 엄마는 음악에 몰입되어서 내가 부르는 소리를 못 들었다.
(4) 그녀는 자신의 남편을 선처해 달라고 판사에게 호소했다.
(5) 나는 그녀가 회의에서 말한 것 때문에 그가 복수하려는 거라고 생각한다.
(6) 나는 직원이 와서 내 여권을 가져갔을 때 조금 걱정이 되었다.

2
(1) 은자: 사회에서 동떨어져서 특히 종교적인 목적으로 혼자 사는 사람
(2) 공표하다: 뭔가를 명확히, 단호히, 공개적 또는 공식적으로 알리다
(3) 소유하다: 뭔가를 가지거나 소유하다, 또는 어떤 자질을 가지다
(4) 재산, 부동산: 어떤 사람에게 속한 물건
(5) 부여하다, 수여하다: 공식적인 방식으로 누군가에게 뭔가를 주거나 허락하다

Reading Comprehension(Focus on Structure)

1. (1) to begin(start) with (2) To be honest
2. (1) had not helped me with the project, I could not have finished it
   (2) If I had had some money with me, I could have bought
   (3) had been smart (enough), he could have solved the problem

1
(1) to begin(start) with 무엇보다 (우선)
(2) be disappointed with −에 실망하다

2
(1) Sarah가 그 프로젝트 하는 것을 도와주지 않았더라면 나는 그것을 끝내지 못했을 것이다.
(2) 나는 수중에 가진 돈이 없어서 그에게 생일 선물을 사주지 못했다.
(3) 만약 Jason이 똑똑했더라면 그 문제를 풀 수 있었을 것이다.

언어 기능별 집중 대비

Listen and Speak/ Into Real Life

1. ① 2. ⑤ 3. ④ 4. (1) ⑤ (2) ④

1
W: Can I ask you a favor?
M: Of course. How can I help you?
W: I have to move some stuff this weekend, but I need a helper. Some of my stuff is way too heavy.
M: It sounds like you need more than just one helper. Let's get Jinu, too.

무거운 짐이 있어서 옮기는 걸 도와달라고 부탁하고 있다.

② 자기에게 좋은 것을 사달라고
③ 더 힘 센 조력자를 구해달라고
④ 그의 친구들과 잘 지내라고
⑤ 그 이웃집 사람이 물건 옮기는 것을 도와주라고

2
M: Hi, Leah. Can I ask you a favor?
W: Sure, how can I help you?
M: I know you like reading books. Can you recommend a good book?
W: No problem. What kind of books do you like to read?
M: I like to read novels.
W: What about this novel written by a French author?
M: Can you tell me more about it?
W: Hector, the main character, travels to find the answer to the question of when the most important time in a person's life is. Have you ever thought about this question before?
M: Well... I think the past is the most important given the fact that we learn a lot from experience in the past.
W: Of course. History is important, but the past is the past.
M: What about the future? The future is full of excitement and possibilities.
W: The future is also important, but it hasn't come yet.
M: Oh, I see. You mean that the most important time is now because in the present we can take action.
W: Yes, you got it. That's what this book is about.

여자는 과거도 미래도 아닌 현재의 중요성에 대해 말하고 있다.

3
W: Edward, may I ask you a favor?
M: I'd be glad to help out. What is it?
W: I argued with my mom this morning. And I don't know what to do.
M: Oh, I was wondering why you had such a long face. What happened exactly?
W: I went to bed late last night because I was playing online games until late, which my mom really hates. Then I got up late this morning. My mom was really mad at me as if I were a little girl.
M: Your mom was really mad at you because she worries about you.
W: I know, but I also know that I kept being rude. This made her even angrier.
M: You should always remember that the most important person is the one closest to you.
W: I know. But it's easier said than done.
M: You'd better go and say sorry to her as soon as possible.
W: Okay, I will. Thank you for your advice.

잘못된 행동을 하고도 사과하지 않고 무례하게 굴어서 엄마가 더 화가 났다고 말하고 있다.

4
M: Good morning, students. Today we are going to read a great play that was adapted from a story written by Leo Tolstoy. So we need to learn about its author. As you may know, Leo Tolstoy was a Russian novelist, regarded as one of the greatest novelists of all time. He is best known for War and Peace and Anna Karenina.
W: I've heard of those. They sound like great novels.
M: Yes, he first achieved literary fame in his twenties.
W: May I ask a question?
M: Sure. What is it?
W: Did he write any plays or short stories?
M: That's a good question. He wrote plays and several philosophical short stories. Until his death from a serious disease at the age of 82, Tolstoy consistently attempted to find the truth through his works and in his real life.

(1) 작가 Tolstoy 및 그의 대표적인 작품을 소개하고 있다.
(2) 노년에 쓴 작품들에 대해서는 언급하지 않았다.

Read and Think

1. ② 2. ③ 3. ⑤ 4. ③ 5. ④ 6. ②
7. ① 8. ② 9. ⑤

1 help+목적어+동사원형(또는 to 부정사): -가 ...하는 것을 돕다

2 ① 왕은 중요하지 않은 일을 하면서 시간을 낭비하고 싶어 하지 않았다. (세상에서 가장 중요한 일이 무엇인지 알고 싶어 하므로 이는 추론 가능하다.) ② 왕은 중요한 일을 달성하는 데 자신을 도울 사람이 필요하다고 생각했다. (지문에 언급됨) ③ 왕은 많은 실패의 경험들 때문에 어떤 일을 하기 두려워했다. (이 부분은 내용과 다름) ④ 왕은 그 나라의 사람들이 가지고 온 답에 만족하지 않았다. (그래서 은자를 찾아간 것임) ⑤ 왕은 그 질문들에 대해 답하는 사람은 큰 보상을 받을 가치가 있다고 생각했다. (답을 갖고 오는 사람에게 크게 포상한다고 했으므로 추론가능하다.)

3 왕의 질문에 은자는 아무런 답변도 하지 않고 마치 무관심한 듯이 행동하고 있음을 볼 수 있다.

4 ③의 doing을 done으로 바꾸어야 한다. : get something done
get someone to do something : -로 하여금 뭔가를 하게 하다
= get something (to be) done

5 왕은 은자에게 답을 재촉하면서 답을 줄 수 없다면 얼른 궁으로 돌아가겠다고 말하고 있으므로 다소 조급한(impatient) 심정임을 알 수 있다.

① 외로움
② 곤혹스러운, 이해하지 못하고 있는
③ 당혹한, 복잡한
⑤ 우울한

6 크게 불러도 의식을 차리지 못해서 혹시 살아있는 건지 확인하려고 손을 남자의 목에다 대어본 것이다.

7 크게 부상을 입은 상태라는 게 뒤에 나오므로 휘청거리며 걸어온다는 지문이 적절하다

8 (A) forgive someone for something : -가 ...한 것을 용서하다
(B) When/As I knew → Knowing (분사구문) : 알고서, 알았을 때
(C) if you had not saved → 가정법 과거완료 : 구하지 않았더라면

9 ① 수염 난 남자는 왕에게 용서를 구하고 있다.
② 수염 난 남자의 형은 왕에 의해 죽임을 당했다.
③ 수염 난 남자는 왕에게 복수하려고 애썼다.
④ 수염 난 남자는 왕 덕분에 목숨을 구할 수 있었다.
⑤ 수염 난 남자는 한때 왕의 충성스러운 신하였다. (본문 내용과 다름)

Language Notes / Write It Right

1. (1) To begin(start) with (2) To be honest
(3) If I had studied physics (4) If she had been wise
(5) I would have majored in philosophy
2. (1) When is the most important time? / Who is the most important or necessary person? / What is the most important thing to do?
(2) The most important time is now. / The most important or necessary person is the one who you are with. / The most important thing to do is to do good to that person.

1
(1) 독립 부정사를 의미에 맞게 써 준다. 위치는 문장의 앞, 중간, 뒤 등 다양하게 쓰인다.
(3) '물리학을 공부했었더라면'은 가정법 과거완료 구문(if +주어+had p.p.... 주어 + should/could/might/should + have p.p.)으로 영작할 수 있다.
(4) "지혜로웠다면"은 과거 지혜롭지 못했던 상황을 반대로 가정한 것이므로 가정법 과거완료 구문을 사용한다.

2
(1) 본문 안에 질문 세 개가 들어 있다.
(2) 각 질문에 대한 대답 역시 본문 안에 모두 들어있다.

수준별 단원평가 Basic

1. ⑤ 2. ② 3. ③ 4. ② 5. ⑤
6. (a) knew all the answers (b) he would not fail 7. ⑤
8. ③ 9. ② did not dig → had not dug
10. ① 11. ③
12. cared for me, I should have died
13. To be honest, I never thought 14. present

1
W: May I ask a favor of you?
M: Of course. What do you need?
W: My computer keeps giving me the "blue screen of death."
M: Let me check and find out what the problem is.

컴퓨터에 왜 블루 스크린이 뜨는 지에 대해 도움을 요청한 것이므로 '살펴보고 문제가 뭔지 알아볼게.'라는 응답이 적절하다.

2
W: Chris! You're late again.
M: Sorry, I'm late.
W: What happened this time?
M: I met Edward on my way here and stopped to talk with him for a second. I didn't know that I would be late for this meeting.
W: Oh, Chris. It sounds like you don't know when to do what with whom.
M: You're right, Seonmi. I often get confused when deciding what I need to do first, and then I make mistakes.
W: You'd better stick with the plan you made in the first place. Otherwise, you'll get behind your schedule.
M: Thanks, Seonmi. I'll keep that in mind.
W So let's start working on this team project. If we don't, we're not going to be able to meet the due date.
M: Okay. Let's get started. And thank you for your advice.

stick to the plan이라는 표현이 나오므로, 중간에 계획을 바꾸지 말고 세운 계획대로 행동하라는 조언을 하고 있음을 알 수 있다.

3 B: 물론이지. (내가 너를) 도와 줄 수 있으면 좋지. 라고 대답했기 때문에 ③의 '도와줄까?'가 적절한 답이다.
⑤ Would you mind ~의 답변은 Of course not. 으로 해야 한다

4 〈보기〉 그는 자기 친구들에게 못되게 굴었다. (비열하게 굴었다.)
① 일부러 너를 화나게 하려던 건 아니야. : 의도하다
② 그가 그녀를 초대하지 않은 것은 비열한 행동이었다. : 비열한
③ 이 주의 GDP는 평균 이하이다. : 평균
④ Miriam이라는 이름이 너에게 무슨 의미가 있는 거니? : 의미를 지니다
⑤ 아이들에게 '안 돼'라고 할 거면 진심으로 안 된다고 해야 한다. : 진심으로 하다

5 ① 수여하다 – 제공하다 ② 무기 – 무기 ③ 다치게 하다 – 상처를 입히다
④ 공표하다 – 알리다 ⑤ 자비로운 – 잔인한

6 간접화법에서 가정법은 시제가 바뀌지 않는다. (가정법 과거: 「if + 주어 + 과거형 동사 …, 주어 + could/should/would/might + 동사원형」).

7 ⑤ to make matters worse는 '설상가상으로'라는 의미이므로 더 안 좋은 일을 말할 때 쓰는 부사구이다.

8 그녀는 자신에게 굴욕을 준 것에 대해 그에게 복수하려고 했다. (get back at ~에게 앙심을 품다, 보복하다)

9 ②는 가정법 과거완료(~했더라면 …했었을 텐데) 구문이 와야 하므로 had not dug가 문법적으로 맞다.

10 ① 가장 필요한 사람은 '지금 당신과 함께 있는 그 사람'이고, 가장 중요한 일은 '그 사람을 위해 좋은 일을 하는 것'이다.

11 〈보기〉 만약 우리가 택시를 탔더라면 비행기를 놓치지 않았을 것이다.(가정법 과거완료) → ③ 택시를 타지 않았기 때문에 비행기를 놓쳤다. (직설법-과거)

12 가정법 과거완료의 가정절에는 「had + p.p.」를 쓴다.

13 to be honest : 솔직히 말하자면 (= to be frank = frankly speaking)

14 now에 해당하는 단어는 '현재'라는 의미의 the present이다.

수준별 단원평가 Advanced

1. ⑤ 2. ⑤ 3. ① 4. ④ 5. ① 6. ④
7. ③ 8. Yes, you have something to forgive me for.
9. who sought to get back at you 10. 해설 참조

1
W: Chris, are you going to give your presentation next week?

M: Yes. It is my turn to present for the project work.
W: Are you ready for your presentation?
M: Well... I'm working on it.
W: I know you've got a really tight schedule.
M: No problem. I'm going to complete the project on time. By the way, may I ask you a favor?
W: Sure. What is it?
M: I decided to change my presentation topic to tsunamis.
W: That sounds great! That's a really interesting topic.
M: I searched on the Internet for more information, but actually, I couldn't find much information on tsunamis.
W: It sounds like you need some help. Don't worry. I think I can help you with your new topic.
M: Thank you, Ms. Smith.

자료 수집에서 어려움을 느껴 새로운 주제인 쓰나미에 대한 정보나 자료 찾는 걸 도와달라고 하고 있다.

2

M: Good morning, students. Today we are going to read a great play that was adapted from a story written by Leo Tolstoy. So we need to learn about its author. As you may know, Leo Tolstoy was a Russian novelist, regarded as one of the greatest novelists of all time. He is best known for *War and Peace and Anna Karenina*.
W: I've heard of those. They sound like great novels.
M: Yes, he first achieved literary fame in his twenties.
W: May I ask a question?
M: Sure. What is it?
W: Did he write any plays or short stories?
M: That's a good question. He wrote plays and several philosophical short stories. Until his death from a serious disease at the age of 82, Tolstoy consistently attempted to find the truth through his works and in his real life.

Tolstoy의 인생철학이 가장 잘 드러난 작품에 대해서는 구체적으로 언급되지 않았다.

3

W: Edward, may I ask you a favor?
M: I'd be glad to help out. What is it?
W: I argued with my mom this morning. And I don't know what to do.
M: Oh, I was wondering why you had such a long face. What happened exactly?
W: I went to bed late last night because I was playing online games until late, which my mom really hates. Then I got up late this morning. My mom was really mad at me as if I were a little girl.
M: Your mom was really mad at you because she worries about you.
W: I know, but I also know that I kept being rude. This made her even angrier.
M: You should always remember that the most important person is the one closest to you.
W: I know. But it's easier said than done.
M: You'd better go and say sorry to her as soon as possible.
W: Okay, I will. Thank you for your advice.

가장 가까이 있는 가족이 가장 소중한 사람일 수 있으므로 못되게 굴지 말고 잘 대해 주라는 충고를 하고 있다.

4 ④ 연극의 3대 요소인 극본/희곡(script), 인물/배우(characters), 청중/관객(audience)에 대한 설명이다.

5 왕이 왜 포상을 하면서까지 그 질문에 대한 답을 얻고 싶어 하는지에 대한 이유가 설명된 문장이다.

6 ⓐ 부상의 정도를 보고 판단하건데, ⓑ 살아날 수 있다(해내다)

7 ③ 왕은 수염 난 자의 상처가 심각하다고 생각하지 않는 것 같다. (글의 내용과 일치하지 않음)

8 여기서 Yes는 왕이 말한 앞 문장(부정문)을 부정하는 단어로서, '아니오, 용서를 구할 것이 있습니다.'라는 의미이다. 따라서 Yes, you have something to forgive me for. 또는 Yes, I have something to ask you for forgiveness for.를 의미한다.

9 ⓑ는 선행사인 enemy of yours를 수식하는 관계대명사절이다.

10 〈예시 답안〉
Title : The Alchemist
The story is about a shepherd boy named Santiago who travels from Spain to Egypt in search of hidden treasure. He learns life lessons along the way. More importantly, he realizes that his dreams are not just his but part of the soul of the universe. The story shows that what is important is not the result of a journey but the journey itself. This book made me think about my own dream and where I can/should find my true treasure.

2학기 기말고사 UNIT 9 – UNIT 10

01. ① **02.** ④ **03.** ② **04.** ③ **05.** ① **06.** ②
07. ④ **08.** ④ **09.** ③ **10.** ② **11.** ④ **12.** ⑤
13. (D) – (B) – (C) **14.** ① **15.** ⑤ **16.** ④ **17.** ⑤
18. ⑤ **19.** ②
20. ⓐ when you were attending to him ⓑ the one who(m) you are with **21.** The (the) most important
22. is impossible to know (tell)
23. the most creative architect
24. Whole-world maps that resemble those of today's maps began to appear in the early 16th century.
25. 해설 참조

1

W: Hey, how was your trip?
M: It was great except that my friends and I constantly argued over directions.
W: Oh, no. Didn't you have a map with you?
M: Of course we did. We just had different opinions about which was the fastest way.
W: That happens quite frequently when you are traveling with a lot of people.
M: I guess so. But arguing about the shortest route made us spend more time getting to places.
W: That's too bad. The journey to a place should be a fun part of traveling.
M: I totally agree with you. I'd be interested to know how people traveled thousands of years ago.
W: I'm sure traveling was more difficult then. By the way, did you know that maps existed even in the 6th century B.C.?
M: Really? That's quite a long time ago.
W: Yes. I'm surprised that they had the means to develop maps at that time.
M: Me, too.

the quickest way to the destination에 관해 친구들과 논란이 있었다고 말하고 있다.

[2~3]
M: Hi, Suji. Have you heard about the new construction project in our town?

W: Yes. I heard that a new community center will be built. But I don't know when it starts.
M: It starts tomorrow. Which path have you been taking to get home from school?
W: I have been taking the one through the park. A lot of people take that route to get to the town hall from the big road.
M: Oh, you can't go that way anymore. The park is near the construction site.
W: Oh. Then, which way should I go to get home?
M: You need to go around the parking lot to get home.
W: Did you find out how long the construction will take?
M: It will take about two months.
W: Okay. Thank you for telling me. I wonder why there is no construction notice.

2 지역 community center 공사에 대한 공지를 하는 표시판이 없음을 아쉬워하고 있다.

3 parking lot을 돌아가야 한다고 조언하고 있다.

4

M: Why are you looking at a map? Are you planning to go on a trip?
W: No. This is not a regular map. It's a map of famous restaurants in Korea.
M: That sounds awesome! I'd be interested to know about good restaurants in Korea.
W: Then, this map will be very useful to you.
M: Can I take a look at it?
W: Sure. Go ahead.
M: This is great! I'm surprised that it even has information about the restaurants in my neighborhood.
W: Yes. It also has tips on prices, quality of service, and parking.
M: Do you know who made it?
W: An expert food critic made the map. So, I think it's quite reliable.
M: With this map, I won't have trouble finding a good place to eat. Thanks a lot!
W: No problem!

인근지역(neighborhood)의 식당 정보까지 다 나와 있다는 사실에 놀랐다고 말한다.

5

W: Chris! You're late again.
M: Sorry, I'm late.
W: What happened this time?
M: I met Edward on my way here and stopped to talk with him for a second. I didn't know that I would be late for this meeting.
W: Oh, Chris. It sounds like you don't know when to do what with whom.
M: You're right, Seonmi. I often get confused when deciding what I need to do first, and then I make mistakes.
W: You'd better stick with the plan you made in the first place. Otherwise, you'll get behind your schedule.
M: Thanks, Seonmi. I'll keep that in mind.
W So let's start working on this team project. If we don't, we're not going to be able to meet the due date.
M: Okay. Let's get started. And thank you for your advice.

우선순위로 정한 것을 다른 것 때문에 미루거나 늦게 하거나 하는 태도에 대해 조언을 해 주고 있다.

6

M: Good morning, students. Today we are going to read a great play that was adapted from a story written by Leo Tolstoy. So we need to learn about its author. As you may know, Leo Tolstoy was a Russian novelist, regarded as one of the greatest novelists of all time. He is best known for *War and Peace* and *Anna Karenina*.
W: I've heard of those. They sound like great novels.
M: Yes, he first achieved literary fame in his twenties.
W: May I ask a question?
M: Sure. What is it?
W: Did he write any plays or short stories?
M: That's a good question. He wrote plays and several philosophical short stories. Until his death from a serious disease at the age of 82, Tolstoy consistently attempted to find the truth through his works and in his real life.

Tolstoy의 단편 소설들은 철학적(philosophical)이라고 말하고 있으므로 철학적 질문을 담고 있다는 것으로 볼 수 있다.

7 ④다양한 형태의 지도가 다양한 목적으로 일상생활에서 쓰인다는 내용이다.

8 ④의 their는 people을 가리키는 대명사이고, 나머지는 모두 maps를 가리킨다.

9 ③인쇄기가 발명되기 이전의 모든 지도는 손으로 그린 것이므로 주어진 문장은 the invention of printing 바로 앞에 위치하는 것이 적절하다.

10 application: 응용, 앱 appliance: 가전제품, 전자기기
adoption: 채택 geological: 지질학적인
geographical: 지리적인 geography: 지리

11 GIS가 지도 제작에 끼친 영향을 말하고 있으므로 ④의 내용(만약 GIS 관련 직업을 생각하고 있다면 프로그래밍, 리모트 센싱, 그리고 웹 개발 분야를 공부해야 한다.)은 무관한 문장으로 볼 수 있다.

12 ⓔdeliver → delivered
「have + 목적어(사물) + p.p.」

14 ① 지도가 완전하고 정확해야만 유용하다는 오래된 생각은 폐기되었다. (윗글에서 언급되지 않았다.)

15 ⑤ 의미상 왕이 평민들처럼 소박한 옷을 입은 채 은자를 방문했다고 했기 때문에 현재분사가 와야 한다.
to wear → wearing

16 ④왕은 질문에 대한 답을 얻기 위해 필사적(desperate)인 태도를 보이고 있고, 이에 반해 은자는 무관심한(indifferent) 태도를 취하는 듯이 보인다.

17 ⑤의 대사는 의사에게 하는 말이라기보다 자신에게 하는 말로서 그 사람의 정체가 뭔지 생각할 겨를이 없다는 내용의 말이다.

18 ⑤ did not save → had not saved (가정법 과거완료 구문이다.)

19 ② 왕은 나중에 왕궁으로 돌아가면 은자를 궁에 초대하고 싶어 한다. (내용과 일치하지 않는다.)

20 ⓐ 가장 중요했던 때는 왕이 그 부상당한 남자를 돌본 그 시간이었다.
ⓑ 가장 중요한 사람은 당신과 지금 같이 있는 사람이다.

22 There is no telling ~ : ~아는 것은 불가능하다. (= It is impossible to know/tell)

23 「No other + 명사 + is + as + 형용사(원급) + as + 비교대상」: 최상급의 의미

24 대명사 that(= 「the + 단수명사)」/ those (= 「the + 복수명사」)

25 〈예시 답안〉
I gave up learning to play the violin last year and I regret it. If I had not quit the violin lesson, I could have learned to play the violin beautifully. If I had practiced harder, I could have mastered several songs and might be playing the violin in front of the people.